First World War
and Army of Occupation
War Diary
France, Belgium and Germany

32 DIVISION
Divisional Troops
168 Brigade Royal Field Artillery
3 January 1915 - 31 October 1919

WO95/2381/1

The Naval & Military Press Ltd
www.nmarchive.com
Published in association with The National Archives

Published by

The Naval & Military Press Ltd

Unit 10 Ridgewood Industrial Park,

Uckfield, East Sussex,

TN22 5QE England

Tel: +44 (0) 1825 749494

www.naval-military-press.com

www.nmarchive.com

This diary has been reprinted in facsimile from the original. Any imperfections are inevitably reproduced and the quality may fall short of modern type and cartographic standards.

© Crown Copyright
Images reproduced by permission of The National Archives, London, England, 2015.

Contents

Document type	Place/Title	Date From	Date To
Heading	WO95/2381/1		
Heading	32nd Division Divl Artillery 168th Bde R.F.A. Jan 1916-1919 Oct		
Heading	32nd Divisional Artillery. Arrived Havre 29.12.15. 168th Brigade R.F.A. January 1916 Dec 1918		
War Diary	Fovant	27/12/1915	27/12/1915
War Diary	Southampton	28/12/1915	28/12/1915
War Diary	Havre	29/12/1915	29/12/1915
War Diary	St. Sauveur	30/12/1915	30/12/1915
War Diary		03/01/1915	03/01/1915
War Diary	LA. Neuville	04/01/1915	04/01/1915
War Diary	Meaulte	04/01/1916	19/01/1916
War Diary	Warloy	24/01/1916	29/01/1916
Heading	32nd Divisional Artillery. 168th Brigade R.F.A. February 1916		
War Diary	Henencourt	12/02/1916	12/02/1916
War Diary	Albert	26/02/1916	27/02/1916
Heading	32nd Divisional Artillery. 168th Brigade R.F.A. March 1916		
War Diary	Albert	01/03/1916	03/03/1916
War Diary	Albert-Meaulte	04/03/1916	04/03/1916
War Diary	Meaulte	04/03/1916	31/03/1916
Heading	32nd Divisional Artillery. 168th Brigade R.F.A. April 1916		
War Diary	Meaulte	02/04/1916	07/04/1916
War Diary	Bouzincourt	19/04/1916	30/04/1916
Heading	32nd Divisional Artillery. 168th Brigade R.F.A. May 1916		
War Diary	Bouzincourt.	01/05/1916	31/05/1916
War Diary		26/05/1916	31/05/1916
Heading	32nd. Div. Arty. Headquarters 168th Brigade R.F.A. June 1916		
War Diary	Bouzincourt.	01/06/1916	30/06/1916
Heading	Headquarters. 168th Brigade. R.F.A. (32nd Division) July 1916		
War Diary	Authville	01/07/1916	09/07/1916
War Diary	Warloy	11/07/1916	19/07/1916
War Diary	Boot Des Pres	20/07/1916	20/07/1916
War Diary	Aubrometz	21/07/1916	21/07/1916
War Diary	Anvin	22/07/1916	22/07/1916
War Diary	Lespesses	28/07/1916	28/07/1916
War Diary	Lapugnoy	29/07/1916	29/07/1916
Heading	32nd Divisional Artillery. 168th Brigade R.F.A. August 1916		
War Diary	Lapugnoy	04/08/1916	05/08/1916
War Diary	Annequin North	06/08/1916	28/08/1916
Heading	32nd Divisional Artillery. 168th Brigade R.F.A. September 1916		
War Diary	Annequin North	07/09/1916	30/09/1916

Type	Description	From	To
Heading	32nd Divisional Artillery 168th Brigade R.F.A. October 1916		
War Diary	Annequin North	01/10/1916	20/10/1916
War Diary	Mailly-Maillet	21/10/1916	31/10/1916
Heading	32nd Divisional Artillery. 168th Brigade R.F.A. November 1916		
War Diary	Mailly-Maillet	01/11/1916	30/11/1916
Map	Approximate Line Held by at End of November 1916		
Map			
Miscellaneous	Headquarters Staff-168th. Brigade R.F.A. Appendix "B"		
Miscellaneous	'A' Battery-168th Bde., R.F.A.		
Miscellaneous	'B' Battery.-168th. Brigade R.F.A.		
Miscellaneous	'C' Battery-168th Brigade, R.F.A.		
Miscellaneous	'D' Battery-168th Brigade, R.F.A.		
Miscellaneous	Nominal Roll of all ranks who have joined the 168th. Bde. R.F.A. during the month of November 1916	21/11/1916	21/11/1916
Heading	32nd Divisional Artillery. 168th Brigade R.F.A. December 1916 Nominal Roll all ranks attached.		
War Diary	Mailly-Maillet.	01/12/1916	31/12/1916
Miscellaneous	'A' Battery-168th. Bde. R.F.A. Nominal Roll of all Ranks 31/12/1916	31/12/1916	31/12/1916
Miscellaneous	'B' Battery-168th. Bde. R.F.A. Nominal Roll of all Ranks 31/12/1916	31/12/1916	31/12/1916
Miscellaneous	'C' Battery-168th. Bde. R.F.A. Nominal Roll of all ranks. 31/12/1916	31/12/1916	31/12/1916
Miscellaneous	'D' Battery-168th. Bde. R.F.A. Nominal Roll of all Ranks. 31/12/1916	31/12/1916	31/12/1916
Miscellaneous	168th. Brigade. R.F.A.	00/12/1916	00/12/1916
Heading	Confidential. War Diary of 168th. Brigade R.F.A. from January 1st 1917 to January 31st. 1917. (Volume XIII)		
War Diary	St Ouen.	02/01/1917	02/01/1917
War Diary	Amplier	03/01/1917	03/01/1917
War Diary	Louvencourt	04/01/1917	04/01/1917
War Diary	Mailly-Maillet	05/01/1917	31/01/1917
Operation(al) Order(s)	168th. Brigade. R.F.A. Operation Order No. 8. Appendix A	03/01/1917	03/01/1917
Operation(al) Order(s)	Operation Order No 10. Appendix 'B'	07/01/1917	07/01/1917
Miscellaneous	Programme Of Fire. "X" & "Y" Days. "X" Day		
Miscellaneous	'Y' Day.		
Operation(al) Order(s)	168th. Brigade. R.F.A. Operation Order No. 9-7/1/17 Appendix C	07/01/1917	07/01/1917
Miscellaneous	Barrage Table For 18-Pounders		
Miscellaneous	Barrage Table for 4.5" Howitzers.		
Miscellaneous	168th Brigade R.F.A. Appendix D	18/01/1917	18/01/1917
Operation(al) Order(s)	168th Brigade R.F.A. Operation Order No. 11 Appendix E	21/01/1917	21/01/1917
Miscellaneous	Table "A" Battery Zones		
Miscellaneous	Table "B" Liaison Officers & Night O.P.		
Miscellaneous	Night Lines.		
Operation(al) Order(s)	168th. Brigade. R.F.A. Operation Order No. 12 Appendix "F"	30/01/1917	30/01/1917
Diagram etc			
Miscellaneous	Headquarters Staff-168th Brigade R.F.A. Nominal Roll of all ranks. Appendix 'G'		

Type	Description	Date From	Date To
Miscellaneous	A Battery-168th Bde. R.F.A. Nominal Roll of all ranks 31/1/17	31/01/1917	31/01/1917
Miscellaneous	B Battery-168th Bde. R.F.A. Nominal Roll of all Ranks 31/1/17	31/01/1917	31/01/1917
Miscellaneous	C Battery-168th Bde. R.F.A. Nominal Roll of all ranks 31/1/17	31/01/1917	31/01/1917
Miscellaneous	D Battery-168th Bde. R.F.A. Nominal Roll of all ranks 31/1/17	31/01/1917	31/01/1917
Miscellaneous	168th Brigade R.F.A.	00/01/1917	00/01/1917
Heading	War Diary of 168th. Brigade. R.F.A. from 1st. February 1917 to 28th. February 1917. (Volume 14.)		
War Diary	Courcelles	01/02/1917	19/02/1917
War Diary	Wargnies.	20/02/1917	21/02/1917
War Diary	Argoeuves.	22/02/1917	22/02/1917
War Diary	Domart	23/02/1917	28/02/1917
Operation(al) Order(s)	Left Group Operation Order No. 17	26/02/1917	26/02/1917
Miscellaneous	Headquarters Staff-168th Bde. R.F.A. Nominal Roll of all ranks 28/2/17	28/02/1917	28/02/1917
Miscellaneous	'A' Battery-168th Bde R.F.A. Nominal Roll of all ranks 28-2-17	28/02/1917	28/02/1917
Miscellaneous	'B' Battery-168th Bde. R.F.A. Nominal Roll of all ranks 28-2-17	28/02/1917	28/02/1917
Miscellaneous	'C' Battery-168th Bde. R.F.A. Nominal Roll of all ranks 27/2/17	27/02/1917	27/02/1917
Miscellaneous	'D' Battery-168th Bde. R.F.A. Nominal Roll of all ranks 28-2-17	28/02/1917	28/02/1917
Heading	War Diary of the 168th. Brigade R.F.A. From 1st. March 1917 to 31st March 1917. (Volume XV)		
War Diary	Warvillers.	01/03/1917	31/03/1917
Miscellaneous	Left Group-32nd Divnl. Artillery.	12/03/1917	12/03/1917
Miscellaneous	Headquarters Staff-168th. Bde. R.F.A. Nominal Roll of all Ranks 31/3/1917	31/03/1917	31/03/1917
Miscellaneous	A Battery-168th. Bde. R.F.A. Nominal Roll of all Ranks-31/3/17	31/03/1917	31/03/1917
Miscellaneous	B Battery-168th. Bde. R.F.A. Nominal Roll of all Ranks-31/3/1917	31/03/1917	31/03/1917
Miscellaneous	C Battery-168th. Bde. R.F.A. Nominal Roll of all Ranks-31/3/1917	31/03/1917	31/03/1917
Miscellaneous	D Battery-168th. Bde. R.F.A.	31/03/1917	31/03/1917
Operation(al) Order(s)	Left Group-32nd Divl. Art'y Operation Order No. 21	09/03/1917	09/03/1917
Heading	War Diary of the 168th. Brigade. R.F.A. from 1st. April 1917 to 30th April 1917		
War Diary		01/04/1917	30/04/1917
Miscellaneous	O.C./168th. Bde. R.F.A. Appendix 'A'	03/04/1917	03/04/1917
Miscellaneous	32nd Divisional Artillery Instructions	03/04/1917	03/04/1917
Operation(al) Order(s)	168th. Brigade. R.F.A. Operation Order No. 25	06/04/1917	06/04/1917
Operation(al) Order(s)	168th. Brigade. R.F.A. Operation Order No. 26	10/04/1917	10/04/1917
Miscellaneous	O.C. /168th Bde. R.F.A.	12/04/1917	12/04/1917
Miscellaneous	A Form. Messages And Signals.		
Heading	M36 E.Q. Quiant St. Quentin Rd. 70 H.E 30 Shrop		
Diagram etc	18 Pdr Creeping Barrage.		
Diagram etc	4.5 How Tasks.		
Miscellaneous	Officer Commanding /168th Bde. R.F.A.	24/04/1917	24/04/1917
Miscellaneous	Headquarters Staff-168th Brigade R.F.A. Nominal Roll of all ranks 30/4/17	30/04/1917	30/04/1917

Miscellaneous	'A' Battery-168th Brigade R.F.A. Nominal Roll of all ranks 30/4/17	30/04/1917	30/04/1917
Miscellaneous	'B' Battery-168th Brigade R.F.A. Nominal Roll of all ranks 30/4/17	30/04/1917	30/04/1917
Miscellaneous	'C' Battery-168th Brigade R.F.A. Nominal Roll of all ranks 30/4/17	30/04/1917	30/04/1917
Miscellaneous	'D' Battery-168th Bde. R.F.A.	01/05/1917	01/05/1917
Heading	War Diary of the 168th. Brigade, R.F.A. from 1st. May 1917 to 31st. May 1917 Vol 16		
War Diary		01/05/1917	31/05/1917
Miscellaneous	Headquarters Staff-168th Brigade R.F.A. Nominal Roll of all ranks 31/5/17	31/05/1917	31/05/1917
Miscellaneous	'A' Battery 168th Brigade R.F.A.	31/05/1917	31/05/1917
Miscellaneous	'B' Battery.-168th Brigade R.F.A.	31/05/1917	31/05/1917
Miscellaneous	'C' Battery.-168th Brigade R.F.A.	31/05/1917	31/05/1917
Miscellaneous	'D' Battery.-168th Brigade R.F.A.	31/05/1917	31/05/1917
Operation(al) Order(s)	168th Brigade R.F.A. Operation Order No. 30	07/05/1917	07/05/1917
Miscellaneous	Table "A"		
Heading	War Diary of 168th Brigade R.F.A. from 1st. June 1917 to 30th. June 1917		
War Diary		01/06/1917	30/06/1917
Operation(al) Order(s)	'F' Group-36th Divisional Artillery. Operation Order No. 37. Appendix "A"	05/06/1917	05/06/1917
Miscellaneous Diagram etc	O.C. /168th Bde. R.F.A. Appendix "B"	06/06/1917	06/06/1917
Operation(al) Order(s)	168th Brigade R.F.A. Operation Order No. 39-18/6/17. Appendix 'C'	18/06/1917	18/06/1917
Miscellaneous	A.B.C./168. 144 Infantry Brigade	28/06/1917	28/06/1917
Miscellaneous	Headquarters Staff-168th Brigade R.F.A. Nominal Roll of all ranks 30/6/17	30/06/1917	30/06/1917
Miscellaneous	'A' Battery Nominal Roll of all ranks 30/6/17	30/06/1917	30/06/1917
Miscellaneous	'B' Battery. Nominal roll of all ranks.	30/06/1917	30/06/1917
Miscellaneous	'C' Battery. Nominal Roll of all Officers and other Ranks.	30/06/1917	30/06/1917
Miscellaneous	'D' Battery. Nominal Roll of all Ranks. 30/6/17	30/06/1917	30/06/1917
Miscellaneous	'A' Battery-168th Brigade R.F.A.		
Miscellaneous	'A' Battery-168th Bde. R.F.A.		
Miscellaneous	B Battery-168th Bde. R.F.A.		
Miscellaneous	C Battery-168th Bde. R.F.A.		
Miscellaneous	D Battery-168th Bde. R.F.A.		
Heading	War Diary of the 168th. Brigade R.F.A. From 1st. July 1917 to 31st. July 1917		
War Diary		01/07/1917	31/07/1917
Miscellaneous	O.C. /168th Brigade R.F.A.	30/06/1917	30/06/1917
Operation(al) Order(s)	A Group R.F.A. Operation Order No. 42	25/07/1917	25/07/1917
Miscellaneous	O.C. /168th. Bde. R.F.A.	28/07/1917	28/07/1917
Operation(al) Order(s)	A Group R.F.A. Operation Order No. 44	27/07/1917	27/07/1917
Miscellaneous	Headquarters Staff 168 Bde. R.F.A.	01/07/1917	01/07/1917
Miscellaneous	A Battery-168th Bde. R.F.A.	01/07/1917	01/07/1917
Miscellaneous	A Battery : 168th. Bde. R.F.A.		
Miscellaneous	B Battery-168 Bde. R.F.A.	01/07/1917	01/07/1917
Miscellaneous	B Battery : 168 Bde. R.F.A.		
Miscellaneous	C Battery-168th Bde. R.F.A.	01/08/1917	01/08/1917
Miscellaneous	C Battery : 168th. Bde. R.F.A.		
Miscellaneous	D Battery-168th. Bde. R.F.A.	01/07/1917	01/07/1917
Miscellaneous	D Battery-168th. Bde. R.F.A.		

Heading	War Diary of the 168th. Brigade R.F.A. from 1-8-17 to 31-8-1917		
War Diary		01/08/1917	31/08/1917
Miscellaneous	Headquarters Staff.-168th Brigade R.F.A. Nominal Roll of Ranks	01/09/1917	01/09/1917
Miscellaneous	'A' Battery.-168th Brigade R.F.A. Nominal Roll Of All Ranks	01/09/1917	01/09/1917
Miscellaneous	'B' Battery.-168th Brigade R.F.A. Nominal Roll Of All Ranks	01/09/1917	01/09/1917
Miscellaneous	'C' Battery.-168th Brigade R.F.A. Nominal Roll Of All Ranks	01/09/1917	01/09/1917
Miscellaneous	Nominal Roll of All Ranks Posted To 'B' Battery. During Month. August 1917	00/08/1917	00/08/1917
Miscellaneous	'D' Battery Nominal Roll of All Ranks Evacuated During Month		
Miscellaneous	'D' Battery.-168th Brigade R.F.A. Nominal Roll Of All Ranks 1/9/17	01/09/1917	01/09/1917
Miscellaneous	Nominal Roll Of All Ranks Posted To 'C' Battery During Month August 1917	00/08/1917	00/08/1917
Miscellaneous	Nominal Roll Of All Ranks Posted To 'A' Battery During August 1917	00/08/1917	00/08/1917
Miscellaneous	Nominal Roll Of All Ranks Posted To 'D' Battery During Month. August 1917	00/08/1917	00/08/1917
Miscellaneous	Artillery Programme for Feint Raid. to be carried out in conjunction with 'B' Group. Appendix A	06/08/1917	06/08/1917
Operation(al) Order(s) Miscellaneous	'A' Group R.F.A. Operation Order No. 49 Appendix B Table 'A'	08/08/1917	08/08/1917
Operation(al) Order(s) Miscellaneous	168th Brigade R.F.A. Operation Order No. 51 Table 'A'	24/08/1917	24/08/1917
Miscellaneous	H.Q. 33rd Divisional Artillery. H.Q. 32nd Divisional Artillery.	25/08/1917	25/08/1917
Miscellaneous	O.C. A.B. & C. 168th Brigade R.F.A. Appendix D	26/08/1917	26/08/1917
Heading	War Diary of the 168th. Brigade R.F.A. from 1st. Sept. 1917 to 30th Sept. 1917. Vol 20		
War Diary		01/09/1917	30/09/1917
Miscellaneous	Headquarters Staff.-168th Brigade R.F.A. Nominal Roll of All Ranks For Month Of September 1917	00/09/1917	00/09/1917
Miscellaneous	'A' Battery-168th Brigade R.F.A. Nominal Roll Of All Ranks. 1/10/17	01/10/1917	01/10/1917
Miscellaneous	'B' Battery.-168th Brigade R.F.A. Nominal Roll Of All Ranks September 1917	00/09/1917	00/09/1917
Miscellaneous	'C' Battery. 168th Brigade R.F.A.		
Miscellaneous	'D' Battery-168th Brigade R.F.A.	01/10/1917	01/10/1917
Heading	War Diary of the 168th. Brigade, R.F.A. from 1st. October 1917 to 31st Octr 1917. (Volume 22)		
War Diary		01/10/1917	31/10/1917
Miscellaneous	Headquarters Staff.-168th Brigade R.F.A.	00/10/1917	00/10/1917
Miscellaneous	'A' Battery-168th Brigade R.F.A. Nominal Roll of All Ranks 1/11/17	01/11/1917	01/11/1917
Miscellaneous	Nominal Roll Of All Ranks 1/11/17	01/11/1917	01/11/1917
Heading	War Diary of 168th. Bde. RFA. from 1st November 1917 to 30th November 1917. (Volume 24)		
War Diary		01/11/1917	30/11/1917
Miscellaneous	Nominal Roll Of All Ranks. 1/12/17	01/12/1917	01/12/1917
Heading	War Diary of the 168th. Bde. R.F.A. from 1st December 1917 to 31st Dec. 1917		

War Diary		01/12/1917	30/12/1917
Heading	A/168 R.F.A. Diary G. R. Army Book 136. From Records of 168th Bde R.F.A.		
War Diary		01/01/1917	04/08/1918
Heading	War Diary of the 168th Brigade R.F.A. From 1st January 1918 to 31st January 1918. (Volume XXV)		
War Diary		01/01/1918	31/01/1918
Heading	War Diary of the 168th Brigade R.F.A. From 1st February 1918 to 28th February 1918. Volume XXVI		
War Diary		01/02/1918	28/02/1918
Heading	32nd Divisional Arty. 168th Brigade Royal Field Artillery March 1918		
Heading	War Diary of the 168th Brigade RFA. From 1st March 1918 to 31 March 1918. Volume XXVIII		
War Diary		01/03/1918	31/03/1918
Miscellaneous	32nd Division VI. Corps. War Diary. Headquarters. 168th Brigade. R.F.A. April 1918		
Heading	War Diary of the 168th Brigade R.F.A. From 1st April 1918 to 30th April 1918. Volume XXVIII		
War Diary		01/04/1918	30/04/1918
Heading	War Diary of The 168th Brigade R.F.A. From 1st May 1918 to 31st May 1918 Volume XXIX		
War Diary		01/05/1918	31/05/1918
Heading	War Diary Of The 168th Brigade R.F.A. From 1st June 1918 to 30th June 1918. Volumne XXX		
War Diary		01/06/1918	30/06/1918
Heading	War Diary of the 168th Brigade R.F.A. From 1st July 1918 to 31st July 1918 Volume XXXI		
War Diary		01/07/1918	31/07/1918
Heading	War Diary of the 168th Brigade R.F.A. From 1st Aug 1918 to 1st Sept 1918 Volume XXXIII Vol 31		
War Diary		01/08/1918	31/08/1918
War Diary		01/09/1918	30/09/1918
Heading	Cover for Documents. Nature of Enclosures. 168th Brigade R.F.A. (32nd D.A.) War Diary for the month of October 1918. Vol 33		
War Diary		01/10/1918	31/10/1918
Heading	168th Brigade R.F.A. War Diary November 1918. Vol 34		
War Diary		01/11/1918	30/11/1918
Heading	War Diary. 168th Brigade R.F.A. December 1918		
War Diary	168th Brigade Royal Field Artillery.	01/12/1918	31/12/1918
Heading	Lancashire Division (Late 32nd Divn) 168th Bde R.F.A. Jan-Oct 1919		
Heading	War Diary 168 Brigade R.F.A. January 1st-31st 1919 Vol 36		
War Diary	168 Bde. Royal Field Artillery	01/01/1919	31/01/1919
War Diary	Germany	01/03/1919	31/03/1919
War Diary	S.E. Bonn Germany	01/04/1919	01/05/1919
War Diary		14/04/1919	14/04/1919
War Diary	S.E. Born Germany	05/05/1919	31/08/1919
War Diary	Ramersdorf Germany	01/10/1919	31/10/1919

WO95/2381/1

32ND DIVISION
DIVL ARTILLERY

168TH BDE R.F.A.
   JAN 1916 - ~~DEC 1919~~ 1919 OCT
1-2ND ~~WELCH BDE R.F.A.~~
1-4TH ~~WELCH BDE R.F.A.~~ NOV 1915

32ND DIVISION
DIVL ARTILLERY

32nd Divisional Artillery.

Arrived Havre 29.12.15.

168th BRIGADE R. F. A.

JANUARY 1 9 1 6

Dec 1915

Army Form C. 2118

WAR DIARY
or
INTELLIGENCE SUMMARY
(Erase heading not required.)

168 Brigade R.F.A.
Commanded by Lieut. Col. J.T. Oldham

Place	Date	Hour	Summary of Events and Information	Remarks and references to Appendices
FOVANT	27/12/15		The Brigade entrained for service overseas, Headquarters leaving during the early afternoon and arriving at SOUTHAMPTON the same evening. The Batteries entraining (following) in succession with part of the Brigade Headquarters on H.T. INVENTOR	
SOUTHAMPTON	28/12/15		INVENTOR sailed in evening for HAVRE	
HAVRE	29/12/15		Headquarters with part of Brigade disembarked at HAVRE and entrained in the evening.	
ST. SAUVEUR	30/12/15		Headquarters followed by rest of brigade detrained just west of AMIENS and marched to St SAUVEUR where they were billeted.	
	3/1/16		Brigade proceeded to LA NEUVILLE and went into billets. B.A.C. remained at St SAUVEUR.	
LA NEUVILLE	4/1/16		Brigade proceeded to MEAULTE and Batteries came into action in alternative positions of 84th Brigade N. Division. B.A.C. still at ST SAUVEUR. Headquarters at MEAULTE.	

Army Form C. 2118

161st Brigade R.F.A.

WAR DIARY
or
INTELLIGENCE SUMMARY
(Erase heading not required.)

Instructions regarding War Diaries and Intelligence Summaries are contained in F.S. Regs., Part II. and the Staff Manual respectively. Title Pages will be prepared in manuscript.

Place	Date	Hour	Summary of Events and Information	Remarks and references to Appendices
MEAULTE	4/1/16 to 18/1/16		Batteries in action under administration of O.C. 84th Brigade R.F.A.	
	19/1/16		Batteries came out of action. Headquarters moved to WARLOY	
WARLOY	24/1/16		"A" Battery came into action near ALBERT "C" " " " " AVELUY "D" " " " " MARTINSART (partially) but still not under 161 Brigade control.	
	29/1/16		Headquarters moved to HENENCOURT.	

V. Noble
2/Lieut. Adjutant
for

32nd Divisional Artillery.

168th BRIGADE R. F. A.

FEBRUARY 1 9 1 6

Army Form C. 2118

168th Brigade R.F.A.

WAR DIARY
or
INTELLIGENCE SUMMARY
(Erase heading not required.)

Instructions regarding War Diaries and Intelligence Summaries are contained in F. S. Regs., Part II. and the Staff Manual respectively. Title Pages will be prepared in manuscript.

Place	Date	Hour	Summary of Events and Information	Remarks and references to Appendices
HENENCOURT	19/2/16		Headquarters moved to BEAUCOURT-SUR-L'HALLUE	
ALBERT	26/2/16		Headquarters moved to ALBERT to take over F & F ii subsectors group commanded by Lieut-Colonel A.S. COTTON, 161 Brigade R.F.A. A & D batteries moved to ALBERT (Corps Wing) –	
	27/2/16		Right group taken over by Lieut-Colonel Q.T. OLDHAM. A.C. & D Batteries in action throughout February but nothing of interest occurred.	

V.C. Noble
Lieut adjutant
for

32nd Divisional Artillery.

168th
168th BRIGADE R. F. A.

MARCH 1916

WAR DIARY or INTELLIGENCE SUMMARY

(Erase heading not required.)

Army Form C. 2118

168 Brigade R.F.A.

Commanded by Lieut. Col. F.T. OLDHAM.

Place	Date	Hour	Summary of Events and Information	Remarks and references to Appendices
ALBERT	1/3/16		Groups reorganised. LIEUT. COLONEL F.T. OLDHAM is ordered to take over Centre Group.	
	3/3/16		Group arrangements cancelled again. LIEUT. COLONEL F.T. OLDHAM is ordered to take over new Right Group from 18th Division carrying of E i & E ii Subsectors, stretching approximately from X 26 d 83.62 to X 13 d 20.0.5. Supporting the 97th Infantry Brigade. The 32nd Division will now have a 3 Brigade Front. Right Group - LIEUT. COLONEL F.T. OLDHAM 168th Brigade R.F.A. "Centre Group - " " P. BUNBURY 155 Brigade R.F.A. "Left Group - " " A.S. COTTON 161 Brigade R.F.A.	Reference OVILLERS TRENCH MAP. 57 D.S.E. 4 1/10,000.
			4.5 Howitzer Batteries are to attach to each group as follows :- A/164 to Right Group: B/164 to Centre Group: C/164 to Left Group.	
ALBERT - MEAULTE	7/3/16		Headquarters established at MEAULTE, taking over from 84th Brigade R.F.A. 18th Division command by Lieut. Colonel BLOIS. Batteries take over positions today, as follows. B/168 from B/84 at E5c 7.2 C/168 " D/82 " E4d 4.6 D/168 " C/83 " W 29 d 5.6 A/164 " D/85 " E 12 a 1.6 Guns were exchanged, and registration and ammunition taken over.	OVILLERS TRENCH MAP. 57 D.S.E. 4 & MEAULTE TRENCH MAP 62 D N.E. 2. 1/10,000.

WAR DIARY or INTELLIGENCE SUMMARY

Army Form C. 2118

168 Brigade R.F.A.

Commanded by Lieut. Col. F.T. SLOHAM.

Place	Date	Hour	Summary of Events and Information	Remarks and references to Appendices
MEAULTE	5/3/16	6 p.m.	F. & E.: Subsections taken over from 18th Division. A/155 Bde R.F.A. were the Group for a few days, to when they will be relieved by A/168. D Battery were then moved to DERNAN COURT. B - - - Just South of ALBERT A & C Batteries - still at ALBERT.	
	6/3/16	2 p.m.	Relief of A/155 at W.29.c.4.5 by A/168 complete. Gun exchange.	
	7/3/16		A & C Batteries Wagon lines moved to LAVIEVILLE. Batteries have been busy checking their registers takes over and registering their points.	
	8/3/16		A/164 Bde R.F.A. (4.5" How.) fired 100 rounds H.E. on a trench in vicinity of X.27.a.20.90 with object of damaging parapets & trenches after the rain. Some very accurate shooting was done.	
	9/3/16		5/168 carried out wire-cutting Cab. They ran the gun up to W.30.6.18.37 and cut wire at X.20.d.70.25, covered by fire from A/168 and A/164 a diversion & trenches. 100 rounds were 18 P.R. shrapnel was expended by the wire cutting gun and a lane 20 yds wide and 15 yds deep was cut. The Infantry were quite satisfied.	

WAR DIARY or INTELLIGENCE SUMMARY

Army Form C. 2118

168 Brigade R.F.A.

Commanded by Lieut. Col. F. T. OLDHAM.

Place	Date	Hour	Summary of Events and Information	Remarks and references to Appendices
MEAULTE	16/3/16		A/168 cut wire, moving a gun up to W30.c.10.37, and battery wire at X26.a.25.85. The wire was not very strong at trick and did not present a good target. Results not so satisfactory. D/168 covered. 76 I.B.B.R. shrapnel used.	
			B/168 ran a gun up to cut wire at Y26.C.81.21 – 50 18 PR shrapnel and 14 18 PR HE were used. The wire was in 3 rows and was badly damaged for a width of 20 yds but a lane was not cut right through wire there now. C/168 covered.	
	17/3/16		Divisional shoot was held at 11 a.m. in R.31.C.6.C. – Danzig Alley and on ALBERT which the shells hit within the second day. The German retaliate probably small. We lost a considerable number of casualties.	
	18/3/16		B/168 wakes gap in enemy wire at X26.6.91.24. A raid is anticipated on the German line and then gap is the line are cut with out object.	
			The Germans have been more active this week.	

WAR DIARY or INTELLIGENCE SUMMARY

168 Brigade R.F.A. Army Form C. 2118

Commanded by Lieut. Col. F.T. Oldham.

Place	Date	Hour	Summary of Events and Information	Remarks and references to Appendices
MEAULTE	29/3/16		Enemy has been quieter the last few days - Nothing has occurred beyond the ordinary routine work. Our infantry seem pleased with artillery work and whenever towards or prophitise of Retaliation a Verual Matter.	
	30/3/16		Ammunition very restricted. There has been a minimum of shooting.	
	31/3/16	12.45 a.m.	Raid attempted after springing a mine at LA BOISSELLE "Y" Sap. X.10.c.50.55. All our artillery opened fire as soon as the mine was sprung and the shooting was very good. The centre group controlled the shoot, and our D Battery took part. About 100 bombs were fired in all. The German reply was vigorous, and plastered the front trenches - E.ii. with Grand Mortars, killing Lt. Lowing, 18. The raiding party found the trench at the point raided full of Germans, and no prisoners were taken. The "Y" sap was flattened and 4 German sentry shot. The Dorsets carried out the raid. They lost a few casualties including an Officer who was left wounded in the German line. Everything was very quiet after 3 a.m. The enterprise was not a great success but much valuable experience & information was gained.	

WAR DIARY or INTELLIGENCE SUMMARY

168 Brigade R.F.A. Army Form C. 2118

Commanded by Lieut. Col. J.T. OLDHAM.

Place	Date	Hour	Summary of Events and Information	Remarks and references to Appendices
MEAULTE	31/3/16		Bo & Bettur widened gaps in wire at X 26 c 81.21 and X 20 d 70.25	
	31/3/16		Enemy has been very quiet for the last 10 days. It appears to be acting purely on the defensive and to be making no attempts to develop a attack or further improvements at this point. He is doing an immense amount of work to his line and trenches. It seems futile is how his line is strongly held at this point.	

J.B. Oldham
Lieut. Colonel, R.F.A.
Commanding 163th Brigade R.F.A.

32nd Divisional Artillery.

168th BRIGADE R. F. A.

APRIL 1 9 1 6

Vol IV Sheet 1

XXXII / 168 RFA

Army Form C. 2118

WAR DIARY
or
INTELLIGENCE SUMMARY

(Erase heading not required.) of 168 Brigade R.F.A. Commanded by Lieut. Col. F.T. OLDHAM.

Place	Date	Hour	Summary of Events and Information	Remarks and references to Appendices
MEAULTE	2/4/16	NIGHT	Raid to be attempted at X 26 d. 70.25 - Abandoned owing to the night being too light.	Appx. "A" 57 D.S.G.
	3/4/16	"	1 Section of B. Battery relieved by Section of battery from 21st Division and relieved 1 Section of 3" West Riding Battery, 49th Division at W 36 3.4. "B" Battery comes under Group control of O.C. 161 Brigade R.F.A. as soon as occupation of new position commences.	
	5/4/16	-	Relief of a & b B/168 completed.	
	6/4/16	"	1 Section of A, C, & D Batteries relieved by 1 Sect of 36th, 32nd & 33rd Batteries of 8th Division.	
	7/4/16	"	Above reliefs completed. "D" Battery goes into action in a orchard to open just North of "B" Battery, and come under O.C 161 Bde R.F.A. Major Lines as follows :- A & C Batteries and Ammunition Column to WARLOY. B & D - - to SENLIS.	
		7p.m	Headquarters relinquish command of the R.F.A. 8th Division. Headquarters R.F.A. 8th Division.	
		8.30 pm	Relief complete. Headquarters transferred to BOUZINCOURT to take charge of work of digging telephone cable, & O.P.'s for what will eventually be the Left Group in the event of a push being made here.	

Army Form C. 2118

WAR DIARY
or
INTELLIGENCE SUMMARY
(Erase heading not required.)

Vol IV Sheet 2

Instructions regarding War Diaries and Intelligence Summaries are contained in F. S. Regs., Part II. and the Staff Manual respectively. Title Pages will be prepared in manuscript.

Place	Date	Hour	Summary of Events and Information	Remarks and references to Appendices
BOUZINCOURT	19/4/16	Night	"A" Battery moved into action at W 12 c 9.0	Map ref. Henencourt 57 D S.E. 2 & 4.
	20/4/16	—	"C" Battery moved into action at W 10 a 5.5	
	23/4/16	9.35 p.m. to 10.45 p.m.	All Batteries except "C" took part in a short bombardment raiding party composed of 3 Officers & about 100 of 17th H.L.I. Each battery fired between 400 & 500 rounds at a quick rate. A Battery has one gun out of action through a jam but still managed to keep up the required rate of fire. The shooting was very accurate and the raid a complete success. 13 prisoners being taken without the loss of a single life in the raiding party.	
	30/4/16		Nothing of interest to report. All batteries are in the line headquarters are simply superintending the work of preparation presumably for an attack. Raids have become very frequent and are seen to have developed recently a most marked Artillery superiority over the enemy.	

N. Wooley
Captain
168 Brigade R.F.A.
Adjutant

1875 Wt. W593/826 1,000,000 4/15 J.B.C. & A. A.D.S.S./Forms/C. 2118.

32nd Divisional Artillery.

168th BRIGADE R. F. A.

MAY 1916

WAR DIARY or INTELLIGENCE SUMMARY

Army Form C. 2118

168th. Brigade R.F.A.

Commanded by Lieut-Col. F. T. Oldham.

Place	Date	Hour	Summary of Events and Information	Remarks and references to Appendices
BOUZIN-COURT.	1/5/16		Batteries in action in same position still under 32nd. Divnl. Artillery Group. Uneventful trench warfare continued. Headquarters continued to prepare for active offensive operations, digging O.P's and burying telephone cables 6 feet.	
	5/6/5/16		96th. Infantry Brigade made successful night raid on enemy trenches bringing back 16 prisoners of which 5 had to be shot as they attempted to escape. All batteries partook in Artillery Bombardment which the Infantry afterwards declared to be excellent.	
	26/5/16		Divisional Artillery re-organised. 'D' Bty. transferred entire to 164th. Bde. R.F.A. and Six Trench Mortar Batteries, A/32, B/32, W/32, X/32, Y/32, Z/32 come under the Brigade for administration.	
	31/5/16		The month has been uneventful. The most noticeable points are (1) that the initiative rests now with us. (ii) Our marked aerial superiority. A German aeroplane is hardly ever seen now behind our lines.	

[signature]
Adjutant 168 Brigade R.F.A.

32nd Div. Arty.

Headquarters

168th BRIGADE R. F. A.

J U N E

1 9 1 6

Army Form C. 2118

WAR DIARY
or
INTELLIGENCE SUMMARY
(Erase heading not required.)

168th Brigade R.F.A.

Commanded by Lt-Col. F. T. Oldham.

Place	Date	Hour	Summary of Events and Information	Remarks and references to Appendices
BOUZIN-COURT.	June 1st.		Orders received to hasten preparation for offensive operations. The O.P's and Forward Telephone Exchange are nearly complete but the buried cables rather behindhand. Trench warfare continued on ordinary lines. Marked aerial activity on the part of the Royal Flying Corps.	Ref. Map 57D. S.E. 1/20,000 Trench
	15/6/16.		C/168 move into their forward position at W.6.d.7.7 in AUTHUILLE WOOD. A/168 exchange positions with C/161 moving into position at W.18.a.1.5. Batteries are all now in their Battle Positions.	
	17/6/16.		Definite orders received regarding offensive operations. Their will be 5 days' Bombardment named U, V, W, X, & Y days with the attack on Z day. 'U' Day will be reserved for 18 Pdr. wire-cutting. Lieut-Colonel F. T. Oldham will assume Command of the Group on the night of T/U. Date of T Day will be notified later.	
	23/6/16.		T Day. Lieut-Colonel F. T. Oldham assumes Command of the Left Group, 32nd. Divnl. Artillery with Lieut-Col. H. Sheppard D.S.O. as 2nd. in Command. Headquarters remain at BOUZINCOURT for the time being, and Lieut. R.B.Burwell, Adjutant 155th. Bde. R.F.A. goes to "Adjutant's Post" the forward Telephone exchange at Q.35.a.2.8. The Group is composed as follows:—	

WAR DIARY / INTELLIGENCE SUMMARY

Army Form C. 2118

168th Brigade R. F. A. Commanded by Lieut-Colonel F. T. Oldham.

(Erase heading not required.)

No. of Position.	Battery.	Map Square.	O.P.	Nature of Bty.
2	A/168.	W.18.a.1.5	Q.35.A.38.80	18-Pdr.
7	D/164	W.9.d.8.5	Q.29.a.3.3.	4.5" How.
9	Spare	W.10.a.5.5		
11	B/168.	W.3.b.4.5.	Q.35.a.36.80	18-Pdr.
12	C/164.	Q.33.d.4.0	Q.29.a.10.42	18-Pdr.
14.	B/155.	Q.35.d.4.8	Q.29.a.3.3.	18-Pdr.
15.	C/155.	Q.35.b.5.1	Q.35.a.27.95	18-Pdr.
16.	A/155	Q.35.d.4.7	Q.35.a.26.98.	18-Pdr.
18.	C/168.	W.6.d.7.7.	Q.29.a.25.04	18-Pdr.
22	D/164.	W.17.a.2.9	Q.29.a.12.39	4.5" How.

Place	Date	Hour	Summary of Events and Information	Remarks and references to Appendices
	June 24th		The zone covered is the 96th. Infantry Bde. Front; Northern Boundary a line running through points R.25.b.23.63 - along Northern edge of THIEPVAL CEMETERY inclusive - R.26.a.45.95 - R.20.c.85.15: Southern Boundary a line running through points R.31.a.50.45 - R.26.a.5.1 - R.27.c.25.75. 'U' Day. A/155, B/155, & C/155 cut wire all day on Support and Reserve trenches with A/168, B/168, C/164, D/155, & D/164 covering them. During the night A/168 B/168, and C/164 fired on gaps made by in wire and roads behind Front Line System. A/168 and C/168 cut wire during the day for the Right Group.	
	June 25th		'V' Day. Wire-cutting batteries continued. Trench Mortar Batteries started cutting wire on Front Line. Night Firing as before.	

Army Form C. 2118

WAR DIARY
or
INTELLIGENCE SUMMARY

(Erase heading not required.)

168 Bde. R. F. A.

Commanded by Lieut-Colonel F.T.O'dham.

Place	Date	Hour	Summary of Events and Information	Remarks and references to Appendices
	June 26th.	2.30 p.m.	'W' Day. Wire-cutting batteries as before. Night Firing as before. Discharge of Gas and Smoke as a blind whilst 36th. Division on our left carried out a successful raid. Headquarters moved to THE BLUFF. Q.36.c.7.7. the Adjutant moving to ADJUTANT'S POST.	
	June 27th.		'X' DAY. Wire-cutting continued and night firing as before. During night 17th. H.L.I. supported by Artillery of Right Group carried out unsuccessful raid, enemy barrage being too strong. Infantry Bde. Hdqrs. moved to THE BLUFF. More gas discharged in afternoon.	
	June 28th.		'Y' Day. Wire-cutting on Front Line where Trench Mortars had not been successful. Night Firing as before. Zero time for attack to-morrow fixed at 7.30 a.m. Attack postponed 48 hours owing to rain.	
	June 29th.		Y.1 Day. Wire cutting on Front Line continued. All wire on support & Reserve line flat now. Night Firing as before.	
	June 30th.		Y.2. Day. Same as Y.1 Day. Attack fixed for 7.30 a.m. 1st. July 1916.	

Wade Lieut. R.G.A.
Adjutant 168 Brigade R.G.A.

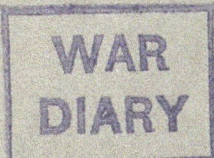

Headquarters,

168th BRIGADE, R.F.A.

(32nd Division)

J U L Y

1 9 1 6

Army Form C.2118

WAR DIARY
or
INTELLIGENCE SUMMARY

168th. Brigade R. F. A.

Commanded by Lieut. Colonel F. T. Oldham.

(Erase heading not required.)

Instructions regarding War Diaries and Intelligence Summaries are contained in F.S. Regs., Part II. and the Staff Manual respectively. Title Page R. F. A. will be prepared in manuscript.

Place	Date	Hour	Summary of Events and Information	Remarks and references to Appendices
AUTHUILE	July 1st.	a.m. 6.25	Preliminary Bombardment commenced for big attack.	
		7.20	Intense fire concentrated on Front line trenches.	
		7.30	Fire lifted onto Support lines. Infantry attack commences in intense smoke barrage.	
		8.10	Order received to keep barrage on intermediate line (MOUQUET SWITCH), Infantry having reported that some of their men have gone through into THIEPVAL but front line trench apparently still held by enemy. 36th. Division on our left are apparently through. Right Infantry Brigade, 32nd. Division held up at HINDENBURG REDOUBT.	
		10.15 to 10.30.	Concentrated fire on WUNDWERK.	
		10.30 onwards.	Slow barrage on intermediate line.	
		3.45 pm. to 4 pm.	Very intense fire on THIEPVAL (Front Line trenches) which was to cease at 4 p.m. punctually. Infantry apparently not ready & so attack failed. Roads and Communication trenches barraged all night.	
	July 2nd.		Steady fire on normal day and night tasks.	
	3rd. July.	2 a.m.	Preliminary Bombardment commenced for second attack.	
		2.45	Attack postponed to 6.15 a.m. Bombardment ceased.	
		5.30	Bombardment renewed.	
		6.15	Attack commenced - Front Line held for some time but battalion was compelled to withdraw owing to supports not coming up. Casualties apparently not very great. Steady fire on roads & Communication trenches during day and night.	

WAR DIARY

INTELLIGENCE SUMMARY

168th. Brigade R.F.A.
Commanded by Lt-Col F. T. Oldham.

(Erase heading not required.)

Instructions regarding War Diaries and Intelligence Summaries are contained in F.S. Regs, Part II. R.F. and the Staff Manual respectively. Title Page will be prepared in manuscript.

Place	Date	Hour	Summary of Events and Information	Remarks and references to Appendices
	4th. July.	12 noon.	Very Heavy Thunder Storm. Both dugouts at Adjutant's Post flooded to the roof. Communications temporarily stopped but makeshift arranged within a few minutes by tapping in at Test boxes. Exchange fitted up again in the open & kept so all night. Fortunately no shelling.	
	4th. to 9th. July.		Steady fire kept up day and night on communications. Enfilade batteries sniping at Germans in trenches.	
	9th. July.		Group taken over by O.C., 164th. Brigade R.F.A. Hdqrs. 168th. Bde R.F.A. to WARLOY.	
WARLOY	11th July.		'A' Bty and 'C' Bty. exchanged positions (personnel only.)	
	12th July.		'A' Battery moved to No 7 Position.	
	18th July.		Batteries withdrawn to Wagon Lines preparatory to marching.	
	19th July.		Brigade moved marched to BOUT DES PRES.	
BOUT DES PRES	20th July.		Brigade marched to AUBROMETZ.	
AUBROMETZ	21st.	"	" " " ANVIN.	
ANVIN	22nd.	"	" " " LESPESSES.	
LESPESSES	28th.	"	Brigade Horse Show - Turnout very good after weeks cleaning up.	
LAPUGNOY	29th.	"	Brigade marched to LAPUGNOY.	

1875 Wt. W593/826 1,000,000 4/15 J.B.C. & A. A.D.S.S./Forms/C.2118.

32nd Divisional Artillery.

168th BRIGADE R. F. A.

AUGUST 1 9 1 6

WAR DIARY
or
INTELLIGENCE SUMMARY

(Erase heading not required.)

168th Brigade R.F.A. Commanded by Lt-Colonel F.T.Oldham.

Instructions regarding War Diaries and Intelligence Summaries are contained in F.S. Regs., Part II. and the Staff Manual respectively. Title Pages will be prepared in manuscript.

Place	Date	Hour	Summary of Events and Information	Remarks and references to Appendices
LAPUGNOY	4/8/16.		Brigade marched to Wagon Lines just East of BETHUNE about E 18 b.8.2. 1 Section of each Battery proceeded into action after dark. Battery Positions as follows :- A/168 F 30 c 97.95 B/168 A 14 d 60.13 C/168 F 24 c 60.93	(A)
	5/8/16.		Remaining Section of each battery proceeded into action. Headquarters removed to ANNEQUIN NORTH F 23 b 3.4	(A)
ANNEQUIN NORTH.	6/8/16.	6 a.m.	Lt-Col.F.T. Oldham assumes Command of Right Group 32nd Divisional Artillery, covering CAMBRIN SECTOR. Group consists of following batteries:- A/168.. F 30 c 97.95 Capt. WAKELING B/168.. A 14 d 60.13 Capt. FITZGIBBON C/168.. F 24 c 60.93 Capt. POLLOCK. B/161.. L 6 a 55.33 Major WEATHERBE C/161.. A 25 b 90.44 Capt. CHISHOLM. D/161. F 30 c 54.03 Capt. PEASE WATKINS.	(A)
	10/8/16.		Headquarters moved to F 23 d 9.7	(A)
	11/8/16.		Lt-Col. R. FITZMAURICE assumes Command of the Brigade, Lt-Col. F. T. OLDHAM having been posted to Command of 258th. Brigade R.F.A., 51st. Division.	(A)
		4.10 p.m.	Combined shoot with Trench Mortars on Front and Support lines A 28 a 6.5 to A 28 d 0.2 Excellent results reported both by Infantry & R.F.C.	
	17/8/16.	3.15 to 3.18	Concentrated fire on Front & Support lines A 27 b 80.45 to A 27 b 7.8	
		3.38 to 3.41	Repeated. Trench Mortars fired in conjunction and enemy trenches were considerably damaged.	

WAR DIARY
INTELLIGENCE SUMMARY
(Erase heading not required.)

168th Brigade R.F.A.
Commanded by Lt-Col. R. Fitzmaurice.

Instructions regarding War Diaries and Intelligence Summaries are contained in F.S. Regs., Part II. and the Staff Manual respectively. Title Pages will be prepared in manuscript.

Place	Date	Hour	Summary of Events and Information	Remarks and references to Appendices
			References Maps :- 36° N.W. 1/20.CCC. & LA BASSEE Trench Map, 1/10.CCC.	
	18/8/16.	6.30 p.m.	Enemy sprung small mine about A 27 b 6.5; No damage done or material advantage gained by the enemy.	
	19/8/16.	11 p.m.	Concentrated fire on Front & Support lines A 28 o 9.1 to A 28 o 65.50.	
	20/8/16.	4.30 a.m. 5.30 p.m.	Repeated. Repeated.	
	21/8/16.		C/168 moved a single gun up in the evening to wire-cutting position about A 26 o 15.45.	
	22/8/16.		C/168 cut wire at about A 27 b 95.18. The shoot was very satisfactory, a lane about 20 to 25 yards being completely cleared. About 200 shrapnel were used. A/168 and B/161 provided covering fire. The wirecutting gun was quite in the open but never found, the enemy shelling a dummy position about 300 yards in front.	
	24/8/16.	11.40 p.m.	Special Bombardment commenced of Hostile Trenches in conjunction with the 8th. Division on our Right. The object of the Bombardment was to feint a raid whilst the 8th Divn. made the real raid at H 7 d 1.2 to H 13 a 2.8. The bombardment commenced as follows:- 4 18-pdr frontal batteries on A 28 a 40.75 to A 28 a 0.2. 2 " " guns enfilade A 28 a 5.0 to A 28 a 10.33. 2 " " guns barrage A 28 o 4.8 to A 28 a 50.23. 2 " " guns " A 28 a 0.2 to A 28 a 45.35. 1 4.5 How.Bty. " on A 28 a 50.05 - A 28 a 70.42 - A 28 a 3.8 - A 28 a 10.42. 1 60-pdr gun enfilades A 28 a 05.75 to A 28 a 8.9. 1 " " " A 28 a 46.25 to A 28 b 00.47 1 " " " A 28 o 8.7 to A 28 b 18.26 1 6" How. fires on trenches about A 28 a 20.15.	
	25/8/16.	12.0 a.m.	Frontal batteries lift to support line.	
		12.5 to 12.6.	" " back on to front line.	
		12.6 to 1.15 a.m.	" " lift to Support line and all keep up a steady rate of fire.	

WAR DIARY or INTELLIGENCE SUMMARY

(Erase heading not required.)

168th Brigade R.F.A.

Commanded by Lt-Col. R. Fitzmaurice.

Place	Date	Hour	Summary of Events and Information	Remarks and references to Appendices
ANNEQUIN NORTH		9 pm.	The bombardment was carried out with success and enemy retaliation was poor. When our guns ceased firing at 1.15 there was not a sound from the enemy. About 4,500 rds. 18-Pdr., 200 rds 4.5"How., 200 rds 60-pdr., and 30 rds. 6" How. were expended. C/168 moved one section to new position at PHILOSOPHE, this battery coming under the 8th Divnl. Artillery for a few days pending the arrival of the 3rd Divnl. Artillery. B/168 moved the section not in action into C/168 old position.	
	26/8/16.	9 pm.	C/168 moved remaining section into new position and B/168 moved 1 gun from their original enfilading position so that they now have here at A 14 d 6.1 to C/168 old position so that they now have 3 guns in action at C/168 old position (A 25 b 9.5) and one gun in enfilading position (A 14 d 6.1.)	
	28/8/16.	4 p.m. 5 p.m.	Heavy Artillery (9.2" and 6" Howrs) commence Special Bombardment of hostile trenches round RAILWAY POINT (A 28 c 2.8). C/161, B/161, A/168 and D/161 commenced bombardment of front line trench in same area; about 300 rds per 18-pdr. battery and 200 rds 4.5"How. were expended. 2" Trench Mortars fired in conjunction with Field Artillery. A lot of damage was done by batteries of each calibre & Trench Mortars. The enemy retaliated heavily with Trench Mortars round A 27 b 2.5 (Boyau 16.) and damaged HIGH STREET a good deal. Our shooting seemed very good, the weather conditions being exceptionally good for observation.	

OAM Ramsmm Lt.Col.
Commanding 168 Brigade R.F.A.

32nd Divisional Artillery.

168th BRIGADE   R. F. A.

SEPTEMBER 1 9 1 6

Army Form C. 2118

WAR DIARY
or
INTELLIGENCE SUMMARY

168th Brigade, R.F.A.

(Erase heading not required.) Commanded by Lieut. Colonel. R. FITZMAURICE.

Place	Date	Hour	Summary of Events and Information	Remarks and references to Appendices
ANNEQUIN NORTH.			Reference Sheet 36 b N.E. and 36c N.W. 1/20,000	
	7/9/16.	1 a.m.	B/168 and D/161 co-operated with Left Group in supporting raid by 14th Brigade. At 1.15 a.m. batteries were ordered to cease firing and raid was cancelled, Infantry not being in position at Zero hour.	
	8/9/16.	1:40 a.m.	All batteries of the Group assisted by Left Group and Left Group 8th Divisional Arty. supported raid by 16th Lancashire Fusiliers on enemy trenches about A 28 c 10.95. Raiding party found wire uncut and withdrew without loss.	
	9/9/16.	2.20 a.m.	C/161 and D/161 assisted the 8th Division Left Group in covering raid by 2nd West Lancs Regt. It is understood that no identifications were obtained.	
	11/9/16.	2.30 a.m.	Raid attempted on 8/9/16 at 1.40 a.m. was repeated successfully. 3 prisoners were obtained and one dead German was brought back. The infantry advanced very close under our barrage which was reported to be most satisfactory. Casualties in raiding party were 7 men slightly wounded.	
	14/9/16.		B/168 moved wagon lines to E 18 b 5.3.	
	15/9/16.		Reorganization into 6 gun batteries commenced.	
	15/16th. Night.		A/168 withdrew one section from action at F 30 c 97.95 to B/168 Wagon Lines to complete B/168 to a 6 gun battery. Relieved by one section of C/164 which was taken on strength of Brigade. C/168 withdrew one section to C/161 wagon line. This section is struck off the strength of the Brigade. B/168 moved one gun from F 24 c 60.93 to A 14 d 60.13 being relieved by 1 section of A/161.	
	16/17th. Night.		B/168 withdrew 1 section to wagon lines. C/168 withdrew one section from action and moved into action again alongside B/164 at F 24 a 30.85. B/164 are taken on the strength of the Brigade and with C/168 section form the new C/168. C/164 withdraws one section to its wagon lines at F 8 b 9.3 and is taken on strength of Brigade, forming new A/168 with one section of old A/168.	

WAR DIARY or INTELLIGENCE SUMMARY

Army Form C. 2118

168th Brigade R.F.A.

Commanded by Lieut-Colonel. R. FITZMAURICE

Place	Date	Hour	Summary of Events and Information	Remarks and references to Appendices
				Reference Sheet 36b N.E. and 36c N.W. 1/20,000
	17/9/16.	12 noon.	D/164 How. Battery is taken on strength of Brigade. Re-organization is complete as under :- A/168 — old C/164 and ½ A/168 commanded by Major C.E.Lawder. B/168 — old B/168 and ½ A/168 commanded by Major F. FitzGibbon. C/168 — old B/164 and ½ C/168 commanded by Capt. H. Cottee. D/168 — old D/164. commanded by Major D.K. Tweedie. D.S.O. Lt-Colonel R. Fitzmaurice remains in Command of the Right Group which remains the same in gun power, only 4 guns of each battery being in action. Positions are occupied as follows :- A/161 — F.24 c 60.93 commanded by Capt. R. Ellis. B/161 — L.6 a 55.33 " " Major W. Weatherbe. C/161 — A.19 b 90.44 " " Capt. E. Chisholm. D/161 — F.30 c 54.03 " " Capt. W. Pease Watkin. A/168 — F.30 c 97.95 " " Major C. E. Lawder. B/168. — A.14 d 60.13 (1 Section only) commanded by Major F. FitzGibbon.	
	17/18th. night.		1 Section of A/168, B/161, C/161, and D/161 withdraw to their wagon lines. 1 Section of B/168 moves into action at F 24 c 60.93. 1 Section of A/168 moves into action alongside the two sections already in action at F 30 c 97.95. 1 Section of B/155 in action at G 7 b 9.1 and D/155 in action at F 30 c 1.4 come under the orders of Lt-Col. R. Fitzmaurice commanding Right Group.	
	18/19th. night.		1 Section of A/161, B/161, C/161, and D/161 withdraw to their wagon lines. 1 Section of B/168 move into action at F 24 c 60.93 Right Group now consists of :- A/168 — (6 guns) at F 30 c 97.95 B/168 — (4 guns) at F 24 c 60.93 — (2 guns) at A 14 d 60.13 B/155 — (2 guns) at G 7 b 9.1 D/155 — (4 Hows) at F 30 c 1.4.	

Army Form C. 2118

WAR DIARY
INTELLIGENCE SUMMARY

(Erase heading not required.)

168th Brigade R.F.A.
Commanded by Lieut-Colonel R. FITZMAURICE

Place	Date	Hour	Summary of Events and Information	Remarks and references to Appendices
			Map Reference:- Sheet 36 B., N.E. and 36 C., N.W. 1/20,000	
	21/9/16	8 a.m.	Lt.Col. R. Fitzmaurice proceeds on leave, and Major D.K.Tweedie D.S.O. takes command of the Brigade and the Right Group.	
	29/9/16	12.45 a.m.	Raid on enemy trenches at A 28 c 68.43 attempted by party from 2nd Btn. Manchester Regt. B/168, B/155, and D/155 open fire at 12.45 a.m. enfilading communication trenches and the Support Line. The Raid was not successful owing to the Bangalore Torpedo not cutting the wire properly. Batteries kept up their fire until 1.45 to cover withdrawal of the raiding party. Machine guns caused rather heavy casualties.	
	30/9/16.		The enemy during the month has been very quiet and only fires in retaliation. Even then his fire has all been from light Trench Mortars and Heavy Minenwerfer. During the past week he has used these fairly freely and has done a considerable amount of damage to our trenches. Strong retaliation with howitzers has however got him well in hand again during the last few days. Hostile Artillery Fire has been practically nil, and even when a raid is attempted no barrage is put up.	

September 30th. 1916.

Fitzmaurice
Lieut-Colonel.
Commanding 168th. Brigade, R.F.A.

32nd Divisional Artillery

168th BRIGADE R.F.A.

OCTOBER 1916

Army Form C. 2118

WAR DIARY
or
INTELLIGENCE SUMMARY
(Erase heading not required.)

168th. Brigade R.F.A.
Commanded by Lt-Col. R. Fitzmaurice R.F.A.

Instructions regarding War Diaries and Intelligence Summaries are contained in F.S. Regs., Part II. and the Staff Manual respectively. Title Pages will be prepared in manuscript.

Place	Date	Hour	Summary of Events and Information	Remarks and references to Appendices
ANNEQUIN NORTH.	1/10/16.		Reference Sheet 36b N.E. and 36 o N.W.	
	1/10/16 to 10/X/16.		Lt.Col. R. Fitzmaurice returned from leave and resumed Command of the Brigade. Ordinary Trench warfare. Nothing of interest to report.	
	11/X/16.		ml section C/168 in action at F 18 c 3.1 is transferred to 5th Composite Divnl Artillery, two sections transferred to Right Group, the remaining 1 section D/168 in action at A 20 c 4.5 is transferred to Right Group – the remaining section being transferred to 5th Composite Divnl Artillery. The Right Group 32nd Divisional Artillery now consists of:–	
			A/168 – 6 guns at F 30 c 97.95	
			B/168 – 5 " " F 24 c 60.93	
			" – 1 " " A 14 d 60.13	
			C/168. – 2 guns " F 18 c 3.1	
			D/155 – 4 Hows " F 30 c 1.4	
			D/168 – 2 Hows " A 20 c 4.5	
			The Front covered by the Right Group is extended North to A 21 d 9.8 (Boyau 27.) Three Battalions in the line.	
	12/X/16.		C/155 moves into action at F 30 c 6.1 and is attached to D 155 for instruction.	
	15/X/16. Night.		Front covered by Right Group is taken over by 8th Divisional Artillery, Lt-Col. R. Fitzmaurice R.F.A. retaining Command – 2 sections A/168, 2 sections B/168, 1 section D/168, withdrawn to wagon lines. D/155 relieved by 53rd Battery R.F.A. C/155 withdrawn to wagon line, 1 section C/168, 1 Howitzer D/168 relieved by 5th Composite Divnl Artillery	
	16/X/16. 6 a.m.		Remaining section A/168, B/168, withdrawn to wagon line.	
	10 a.m.		Command of Right Group taken over by Major Sir T. Larcom Bart. Commanding 'Z' Bty. R.H.A.	

WAR DIARY or INTELLIGENCE SUMMARY

(Erase heading not required.)

168th Brigade R.F.A.
Commanded by Lt-Col. R. Fitzmaurice R.F.A.

Army Form C. 2118

Instructions regarding War Diaries and Intelligence Summaries are contained in F.S. Regs, Part II and the Staff Manual respectively. Title Pages will be prepared in manuscript.

Place	Date	Hour	Summary of Events and Information	Remarks and references to Appendices
	16/X/16.	4 p.m.	168th Bde R.F.A. less 1 section of C/168 and 1 How. D/168 marches to LAPUGNOY.	
		Night.	1 section C/168 and 1 How. D/168 relieved by 5th Composite Divisional Artillery and march to LAPUGNOY.	
	17/X/16.	9.45 a.m.	Reference LENS Sheet 11. 1/100.000. Brigade marches to MAGNICOURT-EN-COMTE.	168
	18/X/16.	9 a.m.	Brigade marches to ROZIERES.	168
	19/X/16.	8 a.m.	Brigade marches to AMPLIER.	168
	20/X/16.	10 a.m.	Brigade marches to wagon lines at LOUVENCOURT. Brigade comes under orders of 51st Divisional Artillery.	
			Reference Sheet 57d S.E. 1/20.000 BEAUMONT Trench Map 1/10.000.	
		After dusk.	Batteries move into action in the open in front of MAILLY-MAILLET as under :- 'A' Battery at Q. 14 a. 3.4. 'B' " " Q. 8 c. 3.3. 'C' " " Q. 7 b. 6.2. 'D' " " Q. 7 b. 45.05.	
			Headquarters established at in MAILLY-MAILLET. The Brigade comes under the orders of Lt-Col. F. T. Oldham R.F.A. Commanding No. 3 Group 51st Divisional Artillery.	H.P.
MAILLY-MAILLET	21/X/16.		Batteries register new front, Q. 10 d 66.88 to Q. 14 d 91.31. Zones allotted as follows :- 'A' Battery, Q. 10 d 66.88 to 10 b 75.42 'B' " Q. 10 b 75.42 " Q. 10 b 80.95 'C' " Q. 10 b 80.95 " 4 d 91.31. 'D' " Q. 10 b 80.70 " 4 d 91.31.	H.P.
	22/X/16.	11.5 p.m.	Registration continued during the day. 3 minute burst of fire by all batteries to cover wire-cutting by Bangalore Torpedoes. 1 round per gun per minute all H.E. on trenches in Battery Zones, 300 yards behind front line.	168

WAR DIARY or INTELLIGENCE SUMMARY

Army Form C. 2118

168th. Brigade R.F.A.

Commanded by Lt-Col. R. Fitzmaurice R.F.A.

(Erase heading not required.)

Place	Date	Hour	Summary of Events and Information	Remarks and references to Appendices
MAILLY-MAILLET	23/X/16.	12.35 a.m.	3 minute burst of fire repeated.	
		6 - 6.15 a.m.	Special Bombardment. 1 round per gun per minute all H.E. on trenches in Battery Zones.	
		7.15 a.m. onwards.	Wire-cutting; about 1100 rounds per 18-Pdr. Battery mostly H.E.; 600 rounds per 4.5" Howitzer Battery.	
		7 to 10.30 p.m.	Intermittent burst of fire of 12 rounds every 6 minutes to cover "tanks" coming up, by 'A' and 'C' Batteries. 200 rounds AX each.	VCR
	24/X/16.	6 - 6.15 a.m.	Special Bombardment as on 23/X/16.	
		7 - 10.30 p.m.	'A' & 'C' Batteries fire as on previous night.	
		11.5 p.m.	3 minute burst of fire as on 22/X/16.	VCR
	25/X/16.	12.35 a.m.	3 minute burst of fire repeated.	
		6.10 - 6.15 a.m.	Special Bombardment as on previous days. 'B' Battery supports raid by 51st Division Infantry on enemy trenches in Q.10 b.	
		7 to 7.25 p.m.	'C' Battery fire 40 rds. H.E. 2 rds. per gun per minute on Support Line. during the night on communication trenches behind Reserve Line.	VCR
	26/X/16.	6 - 6.15 a.m.	Special Bombardment as on previous days. Wire cutting continued by 'A' 'B' & 'D' Batteries.	
		7 - 10.30 p.m.	'A' & 'C' Batteries fire as on 23/X/16 but only 100 rds. H.E. each.	VCR
	27/X/16. to 30/X/16.	6 - 6.10 a.m.	Special Bombardment as on previous days. Wire cutting continued by 'A', 'B' & 'D' Batteries.	VCR

WAR DIARY
or
INTELLIGENCE SUMMARY

168th. Brigade R.F.A. Commanded by Lt-Col. E. Fitzmaurice, R.F.A.

(Erase heading not required.)

Place	Date	Hour	Summary of Events and Information	Remarks and references to Appendices
	31/X/16	6/6 to 6.15 a.m.	Special Bombardment as on previous days. 'C' & 'D' Batteries bombard trench Q.11 a 95.78 to Q.5 a 9.1 expending about 80 - 4.5" How. H.E. and 100 18-Pdr. H.E.	
			No.L.29412 Corpl. T. Brown, C/168, has been awarded the MILITARY MEDAL for meritorious service when his battery was in action in the front edge of AUTHUILLE WOOD during the preliminary bombardment and operations in the early part of July 1916.	

Fitzmaurice.
Lieut-Colonel.
Commanding 168th. Brigade, R.F.A.

31st October 1916.

32nd Divisional Artillery.

168th BRIGADE R. F.A.

NOVEMBER 1 9 1 6

Vol. XII sheet 1

Army Form C. 2118

WAR DIARY
or
INTELLIGENCE SUMMARY
(Erase heading not required.)

168th. Brigade, R. F. A.
Commanded by Lieut.-Col. R. FITZMAURICE.

Instructions regarding War Diaries and Intelligence Summaries are contained in F. S. Regs., Part II. and the Staff Manual respectively. Title Pages will be prepared in manuscript.

Place	Date	Hour	Summary of Events and Information	Remarks and references to Appendices
MAILLY-MAILLET.	1/11/16.	6.10 pm to 6.15 pm.	Reference :- BEAUMONT TRENCH MAP 1/10,000 HEBUTERNE " 1/20,000. Sheet 57 D - S.E. Special Bombardment. All Batteries fired 3 rounds per gun per minute on the barrage lines allotted for 'Z' Day as far as time allowed. Barrage lines for the Brigade lift along the lane between the lines Q.10 b 77.27 to Q.6 d 95.45 and Q.4 d 85.05 to Q.6 b 0.0.	APP. 'A'
	3/11/16.	6.40 to 6.45 a.m.	Special Bombardment repeated as on 1/11/16.	
	4/11/16.	4.30 to 4.35 p.m.	" " " "	
	5/11/16.	8.50 to 8.55 a.m.	" " " "	
	6/11/16.	1.10 to 1.15 p.m.	" " " "	
	7/11/16.	5.45 to 5.50 p.m.	" " " "	
			All Batteries fired in support of raid by 154th Infantry Brigade at Q.4 d 87.02 Raid unsuccessful owing to mud but Artillery support reported excellent.	
	10/11/16.	5.45 to 6.0 a.m.	Special Bombardment - All batteries fired 1 rd. per gun per minute on Communication Trenches, Approaches, and Trench Junctions in their zones.	
			Wire-cutting continued daily.	
	11/11/16.	'X' Day. 5.45 to 6.0 a.m. 6.0 to 7.0 a.m. 7 a.m. onwards	Special Bombardment repeated as on 10/11/16 Pause. Enemy wire, trenches, machine-gun emplacements and defences bombarded. Batteries fired 200 rds per gun.	
	12/11/16.	'Y' Day. 5.45 to 6.0 a.m. 6.0 to 7.0 a.m. 7 a.m. onwards.	Special Bombardment repeated as on 10/11/16. Pause. 18-Pdr. batteries fired about 1200 rounds each on wire. Wire reported well cut. 'D' Battery fired 800 rounds on M. G. Emplacements.	
	13/11/16.	'Z' Day. 5.45 a.m.	Infantry attacked from opposite SERRE across the ANCRE to STUFF REDOUBT.	

Vol. XII Sheet 2.

WAR DIARY
or
INTELLIGENCE SUMMARY
(Erase heading not required.)

Army Form C. 2118

168th Brigade R.F.A.

Commanded by Lt-Col R. FITZMAURICE.

Place	Date	Hour	Summary of Events and Information	Remarks and references to Appendices
(Continued)	13/11/16.		Batteries of 168th Bde. R.F.A. covered part of the advance of 51st Division barraging along the lane between the lines Q 10 b 77.27 to Q 6 d 95.45 and Q 4 d 85.05 to Q 6 b 0.0. Batteries all along opened well together at a rapid rate of fire. The morning was very misty and dark, which assisted the Infantry at first but prevented aeroplane reconnaissance all day. Barrages lifted at an average rate of 100 yards every 4 minutes with a 40 minute pause in the middle of the bombardment, until FRANKFORT TRENCH Q 6 c 95.35 to Q 6 c Central) was reached when they ceased firing. Infantry afterwards reported wire well out and the barrage excellent. The attack was successful, BEAUMONT HAMEL being captured with many prisoners. The final objective was not reached but the Green line East of BEAUMONT HAMEL was consolidated (see attached map). Batteries fired on FRANKFORT TRENCH during the night.	APP. 'A'
	14/11/16.	5.50 a.m.	Infantry advanced against FRANKFORT TRENCH. The Brigade covered the same area but extended its right to the line Q 6 c 40.95 to Q 6 c 80.05 to Q 6 c 90.05. Infantry captured MUNICH TRENCH running from Q 6 c 60.35 to Q 6 c 6.9.	
		2.50 p.m.	6 minute burst of fire 100 yards beyond FRANKFORT TRENCH to cover attack. Infantry captured FRANKFORT TRENCH but was driven out. During the night Infantry dug new trench 150 yds. behind MUNICH TRENCH which was too much damaged to hold. Batteries kept up intermittent fire 150 yards beyond FRANKFORT TRENCH and on back approaches, being especially active just before dawn.	
	15/11/16.		New trench named NEW MUNICH TRENCH. Situation unchanged. Batteries fired on aeroplane targets and kept up slow rate at intervals on barrage lines 50 yards EAST of FRANKFORT TRENCH. Firing during the night as on previous night.	
	16/11/16.		Batteries fired very little, only testing barrage and engaging aeroplane targets.	

Vol XII Sheet 3.

Army Form C. 2118

WAR DIARY
or
INTELLIGENCE SUMMARY
(Erase heading not required.)

168th Brigade R.F.A.
Commanded by Lt-Col. R. FITZMAURICE.

Instructions regarding War Diaries and Intelligence Summaries are contained in F.S. Regs., Part II. and the Staff Manual respectively. Title Pages will be prepared in manuscript.

Place	Date	Hour	Summary of Events and Information	Remarks and references to Appendices
	16/11/16.	4.15 to 4.25 p.m.	'B' Bty. fired 3 rds. per minute on barrage line. Suspected counter-attack. 'D' Battery fired on communication trenches during the day. Night firing as on previous night.	
	17/11/16.	Night. Night.	No shooting during the day. Batteries advanced to new positions as follows :- 'A' Battery - Q 3 d 15.30 'B' " Q 3 d 95.30 'C' " Q 4 a 10.20 'D' " Q 4 c 40.00 Only 4 guns taken into action, the 3 odd sections being put into 'C' Battery's old position.	
	18/11/16.	Dawn.	32nd Division Infantry attacked MUNICH TRENCH without success. Light too bad to register. No firing at all. A good deal of shelling near battery positions	
	19/11/16.	Night.	All batteries registered zero line on PENDANT COPSE L 31 a 5.6. 'B' & 'C' Batteries each had a gun slightly damaged by shell fire.	
	20/11/16.		All batteries registered MUNICH TRENCH Q 6 a and c. Enemy quieter during the day.	
	23/11/16.	3.30 to 4.15 p.m. 4.15 to 9 p.m.	An attempt was made to rescue a party reported to be marooned in FRANKFORT TRENCH in dug-outs in Q. 6 b 95.70. The Brigade supported the attempt, barraging MUNICH TRENCH from Q. 6 c 7.8 to Q. 6 c 55.05, lifting due East over FRANKFORT TRENCH. The rescuing party entered MUNICH TRENCH and captured 18 prisoners who had to be killed as it was found they were being used as a decoy whilst others bombed our men from behind. FRANKFORT TRENCH was entered also and apparently neither was strongly held. The mud was the worst obstacle. In support of a small scheme by 37th Division, Brigade fired on trench from Q. 6 d 65.05 to C. 6 b 5.3 and GLORY LANE C. 6 c 7.8 to Q. 6 b 9.3. Operations rather obscure but apparently progress was made in neighbourhood of MUCK TRENCH.	

Vol. XII Sheet 4

Army Form C. 2118

Instructions regarding War Diaries and Intelligence Summaries are contained in F. S. Regs., Part II. and the Staff Manual respectively. Title Pages will be prepared in manuscript.

WAR DIARY or INTELLIGENCE SUMMARY

(Erase heading not required.)

168th Brigade R.F.A.

Commanded by Lt-Col. R. FITZMAURICE.

Place	Date	Hour	Summary of Events and Information	Remarks and references to Appendices
	24/11/16.	7.35 p.m. to 8.30 p.m.	The Brigade fired in support of a minor operation as follows :- MUNICH TRENCH C.6.c.7.8 to C.6.a.55.20 GLORY LANE Q.6.c.7.9 to Q.6.b.9.3.	
	25/11/16.		'B' Battery moved 1 section to new position at Q.3.a.8.7.	
	26/11/16.	12 noon.	The Brigade comes under the orders of Col. ROUSE C.B., D.S.O. Commanding RIGHT GROUP, 2nd Divisional Artillery. Zones :- 'A' Bty. Q.6.c.7.8 to Q.6.a.55.10 'B' Bty. Q.6.a.55.10 to Q.6.a.6.4 'C' Bty. Q.6.a.6.4 to Q.6.a.4.7 'D' Bty. Q.6.c.7.8 to Q.6.a.4.7.	
		Night.	Brigade fired 500 rounds 18-pounder and 70 rds. 4.5" Howitzer on back approaches and communication trenches between 4.30 p.m. and 7.30 a.m. Brigade covering 91st Infantry Brigade. Lt-Col. R. FITZMAURICE in Command of the Group whilst Col ROUSE is living with the Infantry Brigadier. 'C' Battery brings all six guns into action. 'B' moved one section to new position C.3.a.8.7.	
	27/11/16.	2.30 p.m. to 2.38.	Feint barrage on MUNICH TRENCH. Batteries fire on their zones. 2.30 to 2.34 Front line. 2.34 to 2.36 Lift 150 yards. 2.36 to 2.38 Front line. 18-pdrs. 3 rds. per gun per minute. 4.5"Hows. 2 rds. " " " " Night firing as before.	
	28/11/16.	8.30 a.m. to 8.38.	Feint Barrage of previous day repeated. Foggy day - observation poor. Night firing as before.	

Vol XVI Sheet 5

Army Form C. 2118

Instructions regarding War Diaries and Intelligence Summaries are contained in F.S. Regs, Part II. and the Staff Manual respectively. Title Pages will be prepared in manuscript.

WAR DIARY
or
INTELLIGENCE SUMMARY
(Erase heading not required.)

168th. Brigade R.F.A.

Commanded by Lt-Col. R. FITZMAURICE.

Place	Date	Hour	Summary of Events and Information	Remarks and references to Appendices
	29/11/16.		Foggy again — Observation poor. Enemy shewed unusual artillery activity especially on NEW BEAUMONT ROAD and the valley beside it. All batteries were shelled a good deal, chiefly 'A' Battery who lost two 3 men wounded. MAILLY-MAILLET shelled with 3 quick bursts of fire during the morning. Night firing as usual. 'B' Battery moved one section to Q.3.a.8.7.	
	30/11/16.		Observation still poor but light improved. MAILLY-MAILLET shelled again in the afternoon. Batteries have now been in action practically since 20th. October. There has been considerable discomfort but casualties have not been heavy and the shooting has been good. In their present positions they are apparently overlooked from MUNICH TRENCH but there has not yet been deliberate fire on the batteries. The importance of capturing MUNICH TRENCH cannot be exaggerated as it overlooks NEW BEAUMONT ROAD along which all supplies and troops move, and all the valley on either side of it. 1/5.000 Map shewing recent operations as far as this Brigade is concerned is attached; also Nominal Roll of the Brigade.	

RFitzmaurice
Lieut-Colonel.
Commanding 168th. Brigade, R.F.A.

30/11/1916.

REDAN

EDITION 2, CANCELLING ALL PREVIOUS ISSUES

1:5,000

Scale - 1:5,000

Contours from Captured German Map.
TRENCHES CORRECTED TO 12-10-16

APPENDIX A

APPENDIX "A"

APPX A

APPENDIX "B"

Headquarters Staff — 168th. Brigade R.F.A.

Nominal Roll of all Ranks.

Officers :— Lt-Col. R.Fitzmaurice.
Lieut. J.C.Poole.
2/Lieut. A.Lumb.
Capt. D.Ferguson R.A.M.C. (Attached)
Capt. A.V.Reid A.V.C. (Attached)

Other ranks:—

31508	a/R.S.M.	Smith W.
L.25839	Corpl.	Lee G.
L.28154	"	Thackra J.T.
29811	Bdr.	Anderton A.
L.29801	"	Normanton A.
12245	a/Bdr.	Wright H. (R H.A)
L.29430	"	Eyre F.
L.25881	"	Gibson H.
L.28042	"	Sugden E.
L.26206	Gnr.	Ackroyd H.
L.25810	"	Bothomley C.
59668	"	Clark B.J.
L.29404	"	Greenwood C.
55188	"	Heard H.
L.25480	"	Lucas E.
L.29394	"	Rangeley P.S.
L.25399	"	Ramsden A.
L.25626	"	Slater H.
L.28179	"	Sykes C.A.
L.29296	"	Windle A.T.
L.25422	Dvr.	Armytage J.R.
L.32440	"	Baker G.
L.29304	"	Bamforth S.
L.32540	"	Blake F.
L.28026	"	Cowham S.
L.32488	"	Dutton J.W.
L.29287	"	Fisher S.
37566	"	Hirons E.
L.32511	"	Iredale A.
L.25825	"	Iredale E.
L.28189	"	Mellor A.
L.29351	"	Newsome A.E.
79511	"	McIntyre A.
L.29424	"	Parker J.
L.29423	"	Pollard W.
L.25853	"	Radley T.
L.29357	"	Reddington M.
L.29389	"	Stansfield P.
L.27531	Gnr.	Postlethwaite P.
6267	S/S.	Pereira A.T. (Attached)
A.O.C.625	S/Sgt.	Barker H. (Attached)

'A' Battery   -   168th Bde., R.F.A.

NOMINAL ROLL of all Ranks.

Officers:-   Major R. Emmett.
                Capt. W. R. Brown.
                Lieut.H. W. E. Ainley.
                2/Lt. G. O. d'Ivry.
                2/Lt. W. A. Ebbels.
                2/Lt. J. G. Bell.

Other Ranks:-

28514	B.S.M.	Patchett W.J.	L.25783	Cpl.S/S Town E.
43312	Sgt.	McGowan A.H.	L.28173	S/S Taylor J.E.
L.25719	"	Ainley W.	L.25568	" Sykes J.H.
L.25406	"	Royston P.B.	L.29282	" Nuttall G.T.
L.25426	"	Field J.P.	L.28175	" Waterhouse L.
L.25679	"	Roberts J.F.	L.25690	" Kaye J.T.
L.28064	"	Brearley H.	L.32485	Sdlr Jackson W.T.
L.25425	"	Firth A.	62728	" Oliver J.E.
43323	Far.Sgt.	Spillett H.	147472	Ftr. Hellewell A.
L.25697	Cpl.	Rhodes L.	L.25709	Gnr. Hanson J.W.
L.25776	"	Lewis R.J.	L.25790	" Allott C.V.
L.25561	"	Povey J.	~~107780~~ L.32529	Gnr Booth L.
L.25619	"	France W.	L.25593	Gnr. Billington T.
L.25711	"	Kirkham T.	L.28014	" Bray E.H.
L.25693	"	Littlewood N.	L.28127	" Bower E.
L.29407	"	Taylor F.	L.25396	" Beasley G.
L.26416	"	Collins C.	100556	" Beamish R.
L.25505	Bdr.	Tee G.	100774	" Baird S.
L.29300	"	Wood F.	L.28180	" Bolton H.
L.28100	"	Pitchforth A.	L.28104	" Barker N.
L.29313	"	Armitage W.B.	L.29579	" Beaumont L.
L.25708	"	Crawshaw J.I.	134769	" Campey H.
L.25574	"	Whiteley C.H.	~~L.25658~~	
L.28035	"	Barnes H.	L.32471	" Calvert F.
L.25414	"	Wood B.	L.25444	" Crimlisk M.J.
L.32479	"	Bentley J.	L.29307	" Catley H.
L.25731	"	Rhodes J.	5556	" Chappell A.
L.32553	"	Taylor W.J.	L.28178	" Dawson W.
L.28188	"	Padgett S.	L.25823	" Hynes W.A.
L.28174	a/Bdr.	Tetlow H.	L.28068	" Harwood E.
L.32539	"	Fenton E.	L.25610	" Hopwood H.
L.28072	"	Bentley C.	L.25528	" Hey J.I.
L.25768	"	Brooksbank S.	L.28159	" Hewitt R.
L.25792	"	Thompson P.S.	L.28151	" Hopson T.C.
L.25669	"	Oates H.	L.29427	" Kettle J.L.
L.20310	"	Adams E.H.	L.29411	" Knockton J.
L.32581	"	Williams W.J.	L.32512	" Lumb W.
L.25464	"	Richardson G.H.	L.28177	" Leatham F.
L.28172	"	Iredale W.H.	L.28184	" Lockwood H.
L.32457	Supy.		L.25842	" Marshall H.
	a/Bdr.	Womersley C.	L.28129	" Marshall L.
L.28060	"	Kennedy H.	L.28221	" Merriman H.A.

L.25536	Gnr.	Mansfield W.G.	L.25472	Dvr.	Green N.
L.25592	"	Milnes H.	L.25579	"	Griffiths T.C.
L.29297	"	Noble G.	L.25677	"	Holroyd A.
L.25443	"	Nuttall P.	L.28153	"	Harrison J.F.
L.28186	"	Perkins J.C.	L.28201	"	Horsfall E.
L.25736	"	Pearson H.	L.28073	"	Hirst J.
L.28057	"	Pearson W.	L.25849	"	Holmes E.
L.29306	"	Pearson F.	L.29347	"	Hardcastle C.W.
L.29272	"	Parker W.	L.29417	"	Hinchliffe H.
L.28185	"	Proctor E.C.	L.32467	"	Hirst J.A.
L.25513	"	Peace A.	L.25519	"	Holding J.
L.25582	"	Quarmby W.A.	L.29235	"	Jessop E.S.
L.25653	"	Rushworth A.	L.32541	"	Kershaw C.
L.32491	"	Roberts J.	L.25419	"	Kerton E.
L.28006	"	Singleton H.W.	L.28163	"	Lodge A.
38151	"	Slack A.W.	L.25384	"	Livesey T.C.
125107	"	Starinsky J.A.	L.28022	"	Marsden J.A.
L.25781	"	Sykes J.	L.28021	"	Mallinson J.
52972	"	Stocker G.	L.25639	"	Millard H.
L.25566	"	Shaw J.C.	L.25641	"	Murphy H.
81446	"	Slack H.	L.32474	"	Malone W.
126074	"	Spence R.	L.32464	"	Pogson S.
L.25738	"	Spencer H.	L.28135	"	Priest G.W.
L.25771	"	Thornton J.	147682	"	Orriss H.
L.29340	"	Taylor J.	35664	"	Quinn D.
L.29359	"	Townend P.	L.28074	"	Robertshaw G.
L.25535	"	Thomber W.H.	18878	"	Ridsdale L.
L.25539	"	Thompson J.W.	L.28075	"	Roe J.
L.29355	"	Townend J.	94119	"	Radford H.
L.25764	"	Wilkinson B.	L.28103	"	Sykes W.
L.28038	"	Wilkinson T.	99859	"	Spencer P.C.
L.25575	"	Walker W.T.	L.25633	"	Shaw E.
L.32441	"	Walker A.	L.28008	"	Shaw J.
L.32469	"	Wilson J.	L.25505	"	Shaw H.
L.26468	"	Woollen F.	L.28136	"	Shaw N.
L.29318	"	Wood E.C.	L.28224	"	Shaw C.A.
L.25844	"	Weldrake E.	L.25450	"	Smith J.C.
L.25649	"	Wood C.E.	L.25797	"	Singleton V.
L.25485	"	Williams G.L.	L.28101	"	Taylor S.H.
			L.25460	"	Twigg J.
107780	Dvr.	Archer W.	L.25483	"	Varley L.
L.25524	"	Bamforth H.	L.28214	"	Wood W.N.
L.28054	"	Beevers M.	L.25660	"	Wood A.
119393	"	Blake W.	L.29331	"	Woodcock A.
L.25525	"	Bray H.	L.25718	"	Wilson J.
L.25456	"	Brearley A.	L.28037	"	Walters H.
L.25587	"	Brown H.	L.25394	"	Wortley T.
L.25660	"	Brook L.	L.25541	"	Woodhead E.
L.25395	"	Brooke G.L.	L.25571	"	Wilson I.
L.25658	"	Chapman B.	L.25819	"	Whitehead J.A.
L.29323	"	Cartwright P.			
L.25678	"	Collins R.			
L.25592	"	Crowther J.C.			
L.25843	"	Digman W.J.			
L.29409	"	Dyson W.		Attached.	
L.28079	"	Green F.			
L.25820	"	Ganley J.	S.E.1514	A.V.C.Sgt.	Jolly A.J.
L.29316	"	Gledhill J.R.			

'B' Battery. - 168th. Brigade R.F.A.

NOMINAL ROLL of all Ranks.

Officers :-
        Major P. FitzGibbon.
        Lieut. H. Stead
        2/Lt. W. P. Robinson.
        2/Lt. H. Fisher.
        2/Lt. L. M. Hastings.
        2/Lt. W.L. Chamberlain.

Other Ranks :-

58472	B.S.M.	Stenning T.	L.29390	Gnr.	Ashwell A.
L.32437	BQ.M.S.	Lane A.J.	L.25362	"	Ainley W.H.
L.32514	Far.Sgt.	Sutcliffe R.	L.25423	"	Barker H.
L.25548	Sergt.	Beaumont F.	L.25418	"	Battye T.
L.29324	"	Chambers W.	L.25655	"	Bentley H.V.
L.25599	"	Crooks H.	L.32549	"	Berry A.
L.25420	"	Deakin T.	L.25616	"	Billington T.
L.29344	"	Guthorie A.	L.32483	"	Binns A.O.
L.25786	"	Naylor S.	L.32521	"	Bottoms H.
L.25606	"	Palframan F.	L.25873	"	Broadbent T.
L.25862	Corpl.	Hartley J.A.	L.29265	"	Broadley J.T.
L.32504	"	Jenkins R.	L.29301	"	Brooke E.
L.29357	"	Reeve A.	L.25756	"	Broomhead H.
L.25390	"	Taylor H.	L.32496	"	Burton G.
L.25571	"	Walker S.	L.25609	"	Clark S.
L.25481	Cpl.S/S	Sykes A.	L.25671	"	Cocker F.
L.25446	Bdr.	Bottomley T.	L.29363	"	Crosland E.
L.25716	"	Fisher W.W.	L.28218	"	Dyson A.
L.25863	"	Holmes L.	79093	"	Drewitt W.C.
L.29241	"	Martin F.	L.29392	"	Eccles J.L.
L.25416	"	Pullan H.	L.29263	"	Fowler B.
L.25874	"	Shaw L.	11578	"	Gouldsmith S.C.
L.25451	"	Spendlove T.	L.29244	"	Greenwood A.A.
L.25484	"	Willans C.	L.29262	"	Greenwood L.A.
L.32480	a/Bdr.	Bancroft L.	L.29380	"	Hanson E.
L.28138	"	Bramley B.M.	L.25746	"	Hargreaves A.
L.25756	"	Broomhead W.H.	L.32454	"	Hargreaves D.
L.28045	"	Burch H.	111819	"	Harris G.
L.28208	"	Croft L.H.	L.25554	"	Harrison W.
L.28210	"	Greenwood M.R.	L.25664	"	Hartley A.
L.25547	"	Ibbotson M.	L.29399	"	Hollas J.W.
24990	"	Mayers A.	L.29242	"	Hoyle G.
L.29326	"	Temperton H.K.	L.28046	"	Houldsworth A.
L.29360	"	Thornton J.	34627	"	Hylands C.
L.25545	"	Turner J.F.	128006	"	Isles H.
5035	S/S	Boswell H.	L.25689	"	Kenyon C.W.B.
L.29273	"	Driver W.	L.25458	"	Kiddle F.
L.25552	"	Hoyle G.	L.32510	"	Knight S.
L.25510	"	Readyhough G.W.	L.25562	"	Lawford F.
L.25452	"	Sidebottom	L.28220	"	Laycock A.
L.25747	Saddler	Brocksbank G.	L.25623	"	Lee F.
L.25607	"	Stansfield F.	L.25622	"	Littlewood A.
L.25596	Whlr.	Yates F.	L.28126	"	Mallinson F.
L.32456	Fitter.	Hill W.	L.29400	"	Mitchell D.
			L.32444	"	Mitchell R.
			L.28076	"	Merry A.
			L.29402	"	Merry B.

L.29395	Gnr. Noble F.	L.29270	Dvr. Ledgard E.
L.25632	" Onion A.	L.32519	" Markham C.
L.25836	" Owen W.	L.28132	" Martin J.
L.25827	" Riddlesden A.	L.28077	" Martin L.
L.29782	" Riley A.	L.25744	" McVeagh T.
L.25723	" Scott E.	L.28066	" Medley O.
L.25463	" Scott N.	L.28127	" Mellor H.
L.25645	" Senior P.	L.29401	" Moody A.
L.25491	" Sherwood J.T.	L.25870	" Murray A.
L.32473	" Stafford H.	L.25675	" Nicholson J.
L.32557	" Sykes G.B.	L.28194	" North M.
L.29272	" Tidswell H.	L.25880	" Pearson W.
114525	" Thomas O.	L.28071	" Robinson F.
L.25683	" Thompson J.T.	L.25861	" Robinson T.
L.25598	" Townsend W.	L.29416	" Robinson W.
L.25725	" Toothill E.	L.25512	" Robinson W.J.
L.25629	" Turner H.	L.25730	" Rushworth E.
L.25727	" Wintringham E.	L.25625	" Scott J.J.
L.29431	" Wood G.H.	L.28041	" Schofield G.
L.25704	" Youngman A.	L.25464	" Senior G.
		L.32579	" Shepherd N.
L.29381	Dvr. Barraclough H.	L.25644	" Singleton L.M.
L.25381	" Barraclough T.E.	L.25454	" Snell A.
L.28213	" Beaumont H.	L.29397	" Southwell J.
L.28199	" Berry A.	L.28090	" Stanton A.
L.29245	" Berry Arthur	L.28109	" Sugden C.
L.25837	" Berry S.	L.25569	" Turner J.
L.32576	" Bentley T.	L.25866	" Townsend H.
L.32528	" Borrissow F.	L.25499	" Tallis G.
L.32566	" Braithwaite J.P.	L.25793	" Tyas J.M.
L.25470	" Brook J.W.	L.28142	" Walker J.
L.25471	" Buckley T.	D.32567	" Walker M.
L.25878	" Clear A.	L.25631	" Wheelwright G.
L.32443	" Crossley A.	L.32478	" Widdop T.
L.28112	" Crossley F.	L.32515	" Wilkinson L.
L.28113	" Crossley J.	L.29257	" Wilkinson F.
L.32518	" Crowther J.	L.32552	" Wilson J.W.
L.25466	" Davies J.W.	L.29269	" Wood H.
L.25837	" Dickinson E.	L.28089	" Wright F.
L.29383	" Dewar W.		
L.25742	" Dyson F.		
L.25442	" Eastwood G.		
L.25603	" Ellis M.		
L.25752	" Firth H.		
L.32538	" Gray D.		attached :-
L.29367	" Greenwood J.W.		
L.25728	" Greenwood C.	S.E.8949	A.V.C.Sgt. White F.A.
L.25831	" Hall H.		
L.28204	" Harrison F.		
L.25479	" Hattersley F.		
L.32524	" Hawthornthwaite T.W.		
L.25822	" Hinchcliffe A.		
L.25558	" Hobson A.		
L.32506	" Holmes S.		
L.25403	" Horrocks H.		
L.32447	" Jackson F.		
L.28070	" Jowett J.H.		

'C' Battery   -   168th Brigade, R.F.A.

NOMINAL ROLL of all ranks.

Officers :-   Captain Cottee H.
                 Lieut. Firth L. G.
                 Lieut. Groves B. T.
                 2/Lt.   Lockwood H.
                 2/Lt.   James H. L.

Other Ranks.:-

53473	B.S.M.	Malone M.J.	4770	Gnr.	Anderson G.H.
L/2568	B.Q.M.S.	Tomlinson S.	147564	"	Balls H.N.
L.27727	Sergt.	Ward E.	L.11994	"	Barr J.
L.11952	"	Oates R.T.	L.11996	"	Bridgeland J.W.
L.11931	"	Townsend W.	L.12026	"	Beach J.
L.19483	"	Booth P.P.	L.11929	"	Brady B.
L.12004	"	Turgoose W.	L.19485	"	Briggs B.J.
L.28115	"	Andrews R.	L.25575	"	Booth H.
L.25389	"	Kettlewell E.	L.27987	"	Broadhead F.
L.11975	Corpl.	Booth J.	L.29303	"	Bottomley G.J.
L.27732	"	Widdowson A.	L.28200	"	Brook J.
53087	"	Keefe H.	L.11981	"	Cockill G.
L.11923	"	Imms E.	L.28147	"	Chapman T.
22239	"	Fitzgerald W.	60219	"	Davison J.
L.29412	"	Brown T.	L.25702	"	Denton F.
L.19481	Bdr.	Ward J.S.	129947	"	Deveaney F.
L.19479	"	Wardle L.M.	L.11921	"	Drabble H.
L.19478	"	Todd J.A.	L.29414	"	Elliott C H.
L.27730	"	Walton H.	147114	"	Creeper H.
L.19482	"	Earey F.P.	107906	"	Copping H.E.
L.12050	"	Sanderson G.	L.25411	"	Ellis W.
L.19494	"	Marshall H.	L.29286	"	Fearns P.
L.12016	"	Maguire T.P.J.	L.12017	"	Farmery J.W.
L.19484	"	Bailey B.C.	L.12019	"	Froggett E.
L.28121	"	Palmer R.	L.12092	"	Garfoot C.W.
L.28191	"	Garside I.	L.19489	"	Gregory H.S.
L.12028	a/Bdr.	Craven W.A.	L.11975	"	Howarth H.
L.11930	"	Theobald E.J.	L.11992	"	Halton R.
L.11993	"	Holroyde T.	L.12034	"	Harrison G.W.
L.11959	"	Ellis W.R.	L.11989	"	Howarth R.
L.19487	"	Carr W.G.	L.88771	"	Hall N.
L.19519	"	Milnthorpe G.	L.19490	"	Homer C.
105077	"	Carruthers T.	34446	"	Hutt R.
L.25812	"	Terry L.	394444	"	Holden F.
L.25473	"	Earnshaw S.	L.25751	"	Higgins H.
L.29308	"	Sanderson H.	110744	"	Huggett T.
57207	"	Smith P.W.	L.28102	"	Hirst N.
30751	Farr. Staff Sergt.	Bishop G.	L.11938	"	Issatt H.
L.11991	Cpl.S/S	Halton G.	L.12020	"	Inman H.
L.11926	S/S.	Fletcher F.	63915	"	Irving W.A.
L.27751	"	Bailey H.	120111	"	Jolly W.
L.25594	"	Chappell E.	122010	"	Kenny S.
L.11934	Gnr.(cold shoer)	Ismay T.H.	L.25575	"	Lee H.
L.19518	Dvr.(cold shoer)	Thompson J.	L.19514	"	Lyons J.
L.29360	Cpl.Ftr.	Hinchcliffe J.	L.12047	"	Martin T.
L.14862	Wheeler	Pringle E.	L.11968	"	Mosley O.
L.11918	Saddler	Iveson J.	L.11932	"	Mulheir J.W.
L.11937	"	Hall J.	L.12002	"	Nowell E.M.

L.11939	Gnr.	Prince W.J.	L.11949	Dvr.	Pickard H.
L.11971	"	Parkin W.	25445	"	Pipe E.
134691	"	Robinson A.E.	L.27691	"	Pointon G.W.
8864	"	Richardson T.J.	L.19516	"	Priestley B.
L.19496	"	Saburton H.	2869	"	Price W.
L.27999	"	Spittle T.A.	L.28031	"	Parkin H.
95017	"	Smith C.A.	L.25850	"	Pogson H.
L.13907	"	Swinn J.	L.12011	"	Roberts H.W.
33802	"	Thompson F.	L.11965	"	Ross C.A.
L.25715	"	Taylor J.T.	L.28134	"	Roberts W.
L.19502	"	Wallfes W.	L.12037	"	Garfitt T.G.
L.19500	"	Walstow L.	L.19497	"	Schofield W.
L.12003	"	Waldron T.	L.12033	"	Senior E.K.
L.19503	"	Watson G.	L.20413	"	Shipman H.
L.19616	"	Waller A.E.	L.29293	"	Sutcliffe W.
L.12007	"	Wilkinson P.	L.28164	"	Spivey P.
L.11962	"	Wilcock G.	L.28149	"	Scott J.R.
L.34602	"	Wright H.	L.28010	"	Steele J.W.
L.19717	"	Wardle G.H.	L.25448	"	Singleton N.
L.12022	Dvr.	Ainsworth H.	L.29809	"	Simpson G.A.
L.11969	"	Backhouse G.H.	L.27993	"	Senior J.W.
L.19504	"	Blackburn J.	L.11920	"	Thompson R.
L.11942	"	Bolton T.	L.27747	"	Toothill A.C.
L.12000	"	Brook J.	32459	"	Turner H.
L.11935	"	Brooks G.	L.27986	"	Taylor E.
L.11980	"	Burnley W.S.	L.28095	"	Turner A.B.
L.28116	"	Broadbent J.	L.12035	"	Watley A.
L.29280	"	Bradley H.	L.12008	"	Wales A.
L.11982	"	Clark E.W.	L.12021	"	Walshaw E.
L.28197	"	Crawshaw H.	L.12006	"	Wrigglesworth F.
57926	"	Coles J.	L.11940	"	Woollen H.
L.25612	"	Clark R.W.	L.11978	"	Williams H.
L.28232	"	Chapman H.	L.28169	"	Williams J.
50755	"	Chapman W.	L.28124	"	Walton R.
L.11960	"	Eubenk T.A.	L.29322	"	White L.
L.28107	"	Ellis H.	6074	"	Overload H.
L.12055	"	Farmery T.			
L.19505	"	Firth G.			
L.19506	"	Fretwell H.			
L.25474	"	Earnshaw E.			
L.19520	"	Garfoot E.			
L.11922	"	Hulley A.W.			
L.11964	"	Hunter J.			
L.11941	"	Hart W.			
L.11967	"	Hancock H.N.			
L.19510	"	Horsfall E.			
L.19569	"	Hudson J.			
L.28054	"	Ingham H.			
L.12041	"	Kershaw H.			
L.12040	"	Kaye A.			
L.11929	"	Kemp R.			
L.19492	"	Lapish J.			
L.19513	"	Lamb M.			
L.20285	"	Lord J.			
L.28051	"	Lawton H.			
L.85728	"	Maddocks J.			
L.14919	"	Marshall S.			
L.18909	"	Mitchell W.			
77571	"	O'Keeffe J.A.			

Attached :-

2461 A.V.C. Sgt. Harding W.

'D' Battery — 168th. Brigade R.F.A.

NOMINAL ROLL of all Ranks.

Officers :-

    Major D. K. Tweedie D.S.O.
    Lieut. R. Dunbar
    2/Lt. G. C. Wood.
    2/Lt. A. A. Steward.
    2/Lt. J. J. Caterer.

Other Ranks :-

13705	B.S.M.	Perigo W.	12271	Gnr.	Fall W.
100360	Farr.Sgt.	Greenwood J.	26676	"	Gregory G.
11948	Sergt.	Allen A.J.	19848	"	Hellewell G.W.
35383	"	Hartley B.W.	97625	"	Howlett S.
19894	"	Lambley J.T.	35415	"	Hadley J.
19826	"	Needham H.L.	148368	"	Keane T.C.
L.29329	"	Rowley W.	27510	"	Marshall H.
72512	Cpl.S/S	Emms H.	21259	"	McLellan
19893	" "	Lomas S.	25317	"	Langford W.G.
26450	Cpl.Sdlr	Lawson J.J.	27532	"	Newton L.
27618	Cpl.Ftr.	Thresh E.	19796	"	Parkinson G.H.
27518	Corpl.	Holmes G.	28069	"	Ramsden R.
35406	"	Sykes H.M.	124923	"	Richardson H.
19914	"	Moffitt F.E.	25490	"	Sykes
27756	Bdr.	Bonner S.	19934	"	Shaw J.
35409	"	Dinsdale J.	73072	"	Spink J.
12257	"	Husband A.	27520	"	Stacey I.
19965	"	Hawkes T.G.H.	97676	"	Starkey E.
19840	"	Hempsall J.	26449	"	Shaw F.
19919	"	Scholey E.	129128	"	Smith W.E.
26400	"	Smith W.	26463	"	Townsend A.V.
27590	a/Bdr.	Bradford J.	20010	"	Thompson J.
35389	"	Dobson E.	35391	"	Trimley J.
19930	"	Flannigan P.	12044	"	Ward E.
35381	"	Guest W.	35404	"	Williams J.
27757	"	Hetherington J.	35402	"	Hepworth G.H.
47570	"	McComiskey J.	27627	Dvr	Ackroyd T.
27523	S/S	Hellewell A.	27601	"	Archer S.T.
27497	"	Innocent R.	19783	"	Armitage G.
19984	"	Methley J.	35402	"	Bainbridge J.G.
27759	"	Popplewell J.	27757	"	Battin W.
27612	"	Smith J.	26401	"	Bell A.
26447	"	Varney J.	26452	"	Bellamy J.W.
78446	Sdlr	Batley J.	35392	"	Beckett E.
113012	"	Molyneux D.	12107	"	Bond P.
26676	"	Schofield J.	27615	"	Bowers F.
146171	Ftr.	Collar P.A.	28059	"	Barker W.
12100	Gnr.	Ashcroft J.	20007	"	Bradley J.
123068	"	Allen C.	20008	"	Croft J.
26385	"	Boler H.E.	27621	"	Denby F.
27580	"	Briddock J.A.	27622	"	Dixon L.
25688	"	Cain J.E.	27606	"	Fisher A.
19947	"	Dalby E.	19799	"	Fisher G.
27596	"	Dixon H.A.	19944	"	Flint F.
27537	"	Ebsom G.H.	19841	"	Gilman B.T.S.
27628	"	France P.	19947	"	Green J.
19837	"	Foster E.	19803	"	Greenwood J.
27275	"	Fowler A.S.	35395	"	Hamilton T.H.Z
19950	"	Flannigan J.			

20002	Dvr.	Hanson C.B.
1986	"	Hempsall T.
26422	"	Havenhand H.
19953	"	Howson W.
19749	"	Hughes H.
27610	"	Jewitt W.
35411	"	Jackson F.
31126	"	Johnson P.H.
35376	"	Lowe G.
35380	"	Lumb G.
1094	"	Lewellynm T.
35379	"	Middleton W.
35414	"	Padgett J.H.
19789	"	Peacock J.E.
25560	"	Parmer J.
27598	"	Pollard J.
19939	"	Porter E.
26410	"	Roper W.
27595	"	Roebuck L.
27624	"	Roebuck M.
40494	"	Seabrooke J.H.
26406	"	Savage W.
27609	"	Smith J.
29405	"	Stewart A.
26568	"	Spencer C.
27505	"	Shone W.
27600	"	Sykes J.
19736	"	Thompson A.D.
71721	"	Thompson J.G.H.
24085	"	Tilston R.
27566	"	Trafford I.
12031	"	Wilkinson J.W.
27758	"	Wood J.
27498	"	Wright B.
19794	"	Wheelan J.
154969	"	Whitaker W.

Attached :-

8078 A.V.C. Sgt. Moore W.

Nominal Roll of all ranks who have joined the 168th. Bde.
R.F.A. during the month of November 1916.

Headquarters.

    79511 Driver Mc.Intyre A.   21/11/16.

'A' Battery.

No.	Rank	Name	From	Date
5556	Dvr.	Chappell A.	from D.A.C.	21/11/16.
107780	"	Archer W.	" "	-do-
147682	"	Orriss E.	" "	-do-
10586	"	Westgate F.	" "	27/11/16.
16989	Gnr.	Halliday R.	" "	-do-
45354	Dvr.	Taylor J.	" "	-do-
		Major R. Emmett		28/11/16.

'B' Battery.

125511	a/Bdr.	Christie H.	from D.A.C.	21/11/16.
	"	Cawthorne R.J.C.	" "	27/11/16.

'C' Battery.

147564	Gnr.	Balls H.F.	from D.A.C.	21/11/16.
147114	"	Creeper A.	" "	21/11/16.
107905	"	Copping E.E.	" "	21/11/16.
50755	Dvr.	Chapman W.	" "	21/11/16.
57926	"	Coles J.	" "	21/11/16.
6074	"	Overload E.	" "	21/11/16.
78830	Gnr.	Frazer J.	" "	27/11/16.
63727	"	Goddard W.E.	" "	27/11/16.

'D' Battery.

12271	Gnr.	Pinn.	from D.A.C.	6/11/16.
148368	"	Keene F.G.	" "	6/11/16.
25490	"	Sykes	" "	-do-
129128	"	Smith W.E.	" "	-do-
154969	Dvr.	Whitaker W.	" "	-do-
25405	"	Steward A.	" "	-do-
1094	"	Lewellyn J.	" "	-do-
L.25560	"	Palmer J.	" "	-do-
40484	Gnr.	Goodman J.	" "	27/11/16.
39240	Dvr.	Vidorsky L.	" "	-do-
21259	Gnr.	McLellan W.	" "	-do-
25517	"	Langford G.	" "	-do-

Nominal Roll of all ranks of 168th Bde R.F.A.
evacuated during month of November, 1916.

Headquarters,
      31508   a/R.S.M.Smith W.   due to rejoin from leave on
                                                19/11/16 not rejoined -30/12/16.
      L.29311 Bdr. Haigh W.   evacuated 24/11/16.

'A' Battery.
      L.28209 BQ.M.S.Greenwood G. to England on Cadet Course
                                                      9/11/16.
      Major G. H. Lawder.   evacuated to England - 18/11/16.
      Lieut F.W.D.Ainley to England on Gunnery Course 30/11/16

'B' Battery.
      L.25457 Gnr. Smith G.   Evacuated   21/11/16.
      L.23655 S/S Allchurch W.   "   -do-
      L.25645 Gnr. Senior F.   "   30/11/16.

'C' Battery.
      L.12040 Dr. Kaye H.   to Base (under age) 11/11/16.
      L.11936 Cpl. Dacre H.   Evacuated   12/11/16.
      L.12010 Dr. Race A.   to Base (under age) 13/11/16.
      L.12043   "   Cutts J.   Evacuated   1/11/16.
      L.12003 Gr. Twigger W.   -do-   -do-

'D' Battery.
      L.19871 Gnr. Milner H.   Evacuated   2/11/16.
      L.26411 Dvr. Speight A.   do   -do-
      19904   Gnr. Pearson F.   -do-   -do-
      19963   BQ.M.S. Howarth H. to England Cadet Course 23/11/16
      L.25490 Gnr. Sykes H.   Evacuated   30/11/16.
      12100   "   Ashcroft J.   -do-   -do-

32nd Divisional Artillery.

168th BRIGADE R. F. A.

DECEMBER 1 9 1 6

Nominal Roll all ranks attached.

Army Form C. 2118

WAR DIARY
or
INTELLIGENCE SUMMARY
(Erase heading not required.)

168th. Brigade R.F.A.
Commanded by Lt-Col. R.FITZMAURICE.

Instructions regarding War Diaries and Intelligence Summaries are contained in F.S. Regs., Part II. and the Staff Manual respectively. Title Pages will be prepared in manuscript.

Place	Date	Hour	Summary of Events and Information	Remarks and references to Appendices
MAILLY-MAILLET.			Reference 57d. S.E. 1/20.000 LENS SHEET 11.	
	1/12/16.		Apparently in reply to Bombardment by 11th. Division on our right, the enemy fired intermittently during the morning on the front covered by the Brigade and in the valley in C.3 & 4. One man in 'D' Battery was wounded. 'A','B', and 'C' Batteries fired during the day on back approaches chiefly in L.31.c. and R.1.b., also retaliated for ½ hour at rapid rate on MUNICH TRENCH. During the night 'A', 'B', & 'C' batteries fired 20 rds. per battery between 7 and 9 p.m. and 5 and 6 a.m. and at a normal rate during rest of night-on back approaches and communication trenches. 'D' Battery fired 90 rds. during the night on back areas. Night firing was rather in excess of normal owing to suspected relief. Weather foggy.	
	2/12/16.		Between 11.45 and 12.45 enemy shelled MAILLY-MAILLET 3 times with high velocity gun, probably 15 cm. Naval H.E. shell shewn in page 30c in "Amendments to notes on German Shells". Gun appeared to fire from direction of PUISIEUX and sent over about 12 shell each time at intervals of about 2 minutes. A considerable amount of damage was done and several casualties inflicted in the village.	
		12.15 a.m.	BEAUMONT-HAMEL shelled fairly heavily.	
			Our 18-pdrs. fired intermittently during the day on back approaches.	
			Night firing the same as previous night. Weather foggy.	
	3/12/16.		Enemy activity normal. Our batteries hardly fired at all, being busy removing ammunition preparatory to withdrawal	

Army Form C. 2118

WAR DIARY
or
INTELLIGENCE SUMMARY
(Erase heading not required.)

168th. Brigade R. F. A.

Commanded by Lieut-Colonel .B.FITZMAURICE.

Instructions regarding War Diaries and Intelligence Summaries are contained in F. S. Regs., Part II. and the Staff Manual respectively. Title Pages will be prepared in manuscript.

Place	Date	Hour	Summary of Events and Information	Remarks and references to Appendices
	4/12/1916.	4 p.m.	Headquarters and Batteries withdrew to Wagon lines at LOUVENCOURT.	
	5/12/1916.		Brigade marched to AMPLIER.	
	6/12/1916.		" " " ST OUEN.	
	7/12/16 to 31/12/16.		Brigade training at ST OUEN.	

31st. December 1916.

OBMaurice
Lieut-Colonel.
Commanding 168th. Brigade, R. F. A.

'A' Battery -:- 168th. Bde. R.F.A.

Nominal Roll of all Ranks 31/12/1916.

-:-:-:-:-:-:-:-:-:-:-:-:-

Officers :-   Major R. EMMET.
              Capt. W. R. BROWN.
              Lieut. H. W. E. AINLEY.
              2/Lt. O. d'IVEY.
              2/Lt. W. A. EBBELS.
              2/Lt. J. G. BELL.
              2/Lt. A. C. MILLER (Attached)

Other Ranks :-

28514	B.S.M. Patchett W.J.	L.25790	Gnr. Allott G.V.
L.28064	B.Q.M.S. Brearley H.	L.32529	" Booth L.
L.25426	Sgt. Field P.J.	L.25595	" Billington T.
43312	" McGowan A.E.	L.28014	" Bray E.H.
L.25679	" Roberts J.F.	L.28217	" Bower E.
L.2545	" Firth A.	L.25396	" Beasley G.
L.25697	Cpl. Rhodes L.	100556	" Beamish R.
L.25561	" Povey J.	100774	" Baird S.
L.25619	" France W.	L.28180	" Bolton H.
L.25776	" Lewis E.J.	L.28104	" Barker N.
L.25711	" Kirkham T.	L.29579	" Beaumont L.
L.25693	" Littlewood K.	~~L.24109~~	" ~~Banpey L.~~
L.29407	" Taylor F.	32471	" Calvert F.
L.25505	Bdr. Tee G.	L.25444	" Crimlish M.J.
L.28100	" Pitchforth A.	L.29307	" Catley H.
L.32479	" Bentley J.	5556	" Chappell H.
L.29313	" Armitage W.B.	L.28178	" Dawson W.
L.25708	" Crowthew J.S.	169899	" Halliday R.
L.25574	" Whiteley C.H.	L.25823	" Hynes W.H.
L.28035	" Barnes H.	L.28088	" Harwood E.
L.25751	" Rhodes J.	L.25610	" Hopwood H.
L.25414	" Wood B.	L.25528	" Hey J.T.
L.28188	" Padgett S.	L.28159	" Hewitt R.
L.32533	" Taylor W.J.	L.28151	" Hopson T.C.
L.25464	a/Br Richardson C.H.	L.29427	" Kettle J.L.
L.32581	" Williams W.J.	L.29411	" Knookton J.
20310	" Adams E.C.	L.32512	" Lumb W.
L.28172	" Iredale W.H.	L.28177	" Leathem F.
L.28174	" Tetlaw H.	L.28184	" Lockwood H.
L.28072	" Bentley C.	L.25842	" Marshall H.
L.32539	" Fenton H.	L.28129	" Marshall J.
L.25768	" Brocksbank S.	L.28221	" Merryman H.A.
L.25792	" Thompson P.S.	L.25536	" Mansfield W.G.
L.25669	" Oates H.	L.25392	" Milnes H.
L.32479	S/L/Br Womersley G.	L.29297	" Noble G.
L.28060	" Kennedy F.	L.25443	" Nuttall T.
15325	Far.Sgt Spillett H.	L.28186	" Perkins J.C.
L.25785	Cpl.S/S Town B.	L.25736	" Pearson H.
L.28173	S/S Taylor J.E.	L.29306	" Pearson F.
L.25568	" Sykes J.H.	L.28185	" Proctor R.C.
L.29282	" Nuttall G.W.	L.25513	" Pease A.
L.28175	" Waterhouse L.	L.25584	" Quarmby W.H.
L.25690	" Kaye J.T.	L.25653	" Rushworth A.
L.32485	Sdlr Jackson W.T.	L.32491	" Roberts J.
62728	" Oliver J.E.	L.28006	" Singleton H.
147472	Ftr. Hellawell A.	38151	" Slack A.W.
121451	Whlr Weaver R.	125107	" Stapinsky E.

L.25781	Gnr.	Sykes J.		18878	Dvr.	Ridsdale L.
L.25566	"	Shaw J.		L.28075	"	Roe F.
52972	"	Stocket G.		94119	"	Radford H.
81446	"	Slack H.		L.28103	"	Sykes W.
126074	"	Spence R.		99859	"	Spencer G.
L.25778	"	Spencer H.		L.25633	"	Shaw E.
86310	"	Squire A.E.		L.28008	"	Shaw J.
L.25771	"	Thornton J.		L.28136	"	Shaw N.
L.29359	"	Townend P.		L.25503	"	Shaw H.
L.25559	"	Thompson J.W.		L.28224	"	Shaw C.A.
L.32516	"	Thornber W.H.		L.25450	"	Smith J.R.
L.29355	"	Townend J.		L.25797	"	Singleton M.
L.25764	"	Wilkinson B.		L.29340	"	Taylor B.
L.28036	"	Wilkinson T.		L.28101	"	Taylor T.H.
L.25775	"	Walker W.T.		L.25460	"	Twigg J.
L.32441	"	Walker A.		L.25483	"	Varley L.
L.32469	"	Wilson J.		L.28214	"	Wood W.N.
L.29318	"	Wood R.		L.25650	"	Wood A.
L.25844	"	Weldrake E.		L.29331	"	Woodcock W.
L.25649	"	Wood C.E.		L.28087	"	Walters H.
L.25485	"	Williams G.		L.25394	"	Wortley T.
L.29300	"	Wood F.		L.25541	"	Woodhead E.
				L.25571	"	Wilson J.
				L.25819	"	Whitehead J.
107780	Dvr.	Archer W.		105865	"	Westgate F.
L.25524	"	Bamforth H.				
L.28034	"	Beavers M.				
119393	"	Blake W.				
L.25525	"	Bray H.		Attached :-		
L.25587	"	Brown N.				
L.25436	"	Brearley H.		S.E.1514 A.V.C. Sgt. Jolly A.J.		
L.25660	"	Brook L.				
L.25395	"	Brook J.L.				
L.25658	"	Chapman B.				
L.29323	"	Cartwright P.				
L.25678	"	Collins P.				
L.25592	"	Crowther J.G.				
L.25843	"	Digman W.J.				
L.29409	"	Dyson W.				
L.28079	"	Green F.				
L.25820	"	Ganley J.				
L.29366	"	Gledhill J.R.				
L.25472	"	Green N.				
L.25579	"	Griffiths T.C.				
L.25677	"	Holroyd H.				
L.28153	"	Hanson F.				
L.28201	"	Horsfall E.				
L.28073	"	Hirst J.H.				
L.25849	"	Holmes E.				
L.29347	"	Hardcastle C.W.				
L.29417	"	Hinchcliffe H.				
L.32467	"	Hirst F.A.				
L.25519	"	Holding J.				
L.29235	"	Jessop E.L.O.				
L.32541	"	Kershaw G.				
L.25419	"	Kerton E.				
L.28163	"	Lodge A.				
L.25384	"	Livesey A.C.				
L.28022	"	Marsden J.A.				
L.28021	"	Mallinson J.				
L.25639	"	Millard H.				
L.25641	"	Murphy H.				
L.32474	"	Malone W.				
L.32464	"	Pogson S.				
L.28135	"	Priest G.W.				
147682	"	Orriss H.				
L.25864	"	Quinn D.				
L.28074	"	Robertshaw G.				

'B' Battery -:- 168th. Bde. R.F.A.

NOMINAL ROLL of all Ranks 31/12/1916.

-:-:-:-:-:-:-:-:-:-:-:-:-

Officers :-

Major FITZGIBBON F.
Capt. STEAD H.
2/Lieut. FISHER H.
" ROBINSON W. P.
" HASTINGS L. M.
" CHAMBERLAIN W. L.

Other Ranks :-

58482	B.S.M.	Stenning T.	L.29390	Gnr. Ashworth A.
L.32437	B.S.S.M.	Lane A.W.	L.25382	" Ainley W.H.
L.32514	Far.Sgt.	Sutcliffe R.	L.25418	" Batye T.
L.25448	Sergt.	Beaumont F.	L.25655	" Bentley H.V.
L.29324	"	Chambers W.	L.32549	" Berry A.
L.25599	"	Crooks H.	L.25616	" Billington T.
L.25420	"	Deakin T.	L.32483	" Binns L.
L.29344	"	Gutherie A.	L.32521	" Bottoms F.
L.25606	"	Palframan F.	L.25873	" Broadbent T.
L.25862	Cpl.	Hartley J.A.	L.29265	" Broadley J.T.
L.29337	"	Reeve A.	L.29301	" Brook E.
L125481	" S/S	Sykes A.	L.25756	" Broomhead H.
L.25390	Cpl.	Taylor H.	L.32496	" Burton G.
L.25781	"	Walker S.	L.25671	" Cocker F.
L.25446	Bdr.	Bottomley T.	L.29363	" Crosland E.
L.25763	Cpl.	Fisher W.W.	L.28218	" Dyson A.
L.25863	Bdr.	Holmes L.	79093	" Drewitt W.H.
L.29241	"	Martin F.	L.29392	" Eccles J.L.
L.25864	Cpl.	Mason R.C.	L.29263	" Fowler B.
L.25416	Bdr.	Pullan H.	11578	" Gouldsmith S.C.
L.25874	"	Shaw L.	L.29244	" Greenwood A.A.
L.25451	"	Spendlove T.	L.29262	" Greenwood L.A.
L.32480	"		L.29380	" Hanson E.
L.28138	"	Bramley S.M.	L.25746	" Hargreaves A.
L.28210	"	Greenwood M.E.	L.32454	" Hargreaves D.
L.29326	"	Temperton H.K.	111819	" Harris G.
L.29360	"	Thornton J.	L.25554	" Harrison W.
L.25545	"	Turner J.F.	L.25664	" Hartley A.
L.32480	a/Br	Bancroft L.	L.29399	" Hallos J.H.
L.25756	"	Broomhead W.H.	L.29242	" Hoyle G.G.
L.28043m	"	Burch H.	L.28046	" Holdsworth A.
125511	"	Christie H.	L.25639	" Kenyon J.E.
L.28208	"	Croft L.H.	L.25458	" Kiddle F.
16381	"	Cawthorne J.	L.32510	" Knight S.
L.25549	"	Ibbotson M.	L.25562	" Lawford F.
24990	"	Mayers A.	L.28220	" Laycock A.
L.28218	"	Dyson A.	L.25623	" Lee F.
5015	S/S	Boswell H.	L.25622	" Littlewood A.
L.29273	"	Driver W.	L.28126	" Mallinson F.
L.25552	"	Hoyle C.	L.29400	" Mitchell D.
L.25510	"	Readyhough C.W.	L.32544	" Mitchell R.
L.25452	"	Sidebottom J.	L.28076	" Murray A.
L.25747	Sdlr	Brooksbank G.	L.29402	" Murray E.
L.25607	"	Stansfield F.	L.29395	" Noble F.
L.25596	Whlr	Yates F.	L.25632	" Onyon A.
L.32456	Ftr.	Hill W.	L.25836	" Owen W.

(Continued)

L.25827	Gnr. Riddlesden A.		L.25750	Dvr. Rushworth E.
L.29382	" Riley A.		L.25625	" Scott J.J.
L.25723	" Scott E.		L.28041	" Scholefield A.
L.25463	" Scott N.		L.25464	" Senior G.
L.25491	" Shirwood J.T.		L.32579	" Shepherd N.
53092	" Stubbs E.		L.25644	" Singleton L.M.
L.32475	" Stafford H.		L.25454	" Snell A.
L.29372	" Tidswell E.T.		L.29397	" Southwell J.
11625	" Thomas O.		L.29090	" Stanton A.
L.25683	" Thompson J.T.		L.28109	" Sugden G.
L.25598	" Townsend W.		L.25569	" Turner J.
L.25725	" Toothill E.		L.25866	" Townsend H.
L.25629	" Turner H.		L.25499	" Tallis G.
L.25727	" Wintringham E.		L.25795	" Tyas J.M.
L.29431	" Wood G.H.		L.28142	" Walker J.
L.25704	" Youngman A.		L.32567	" Walker M.
			L.25631	" Wheelwright G.
			L.32478	" Widdop T.
L.29381	Dvr Barraclough H.		L.26301	" Wilkins R.C.J.
L.29258	" Barraclough T.E.		L.32515	" Wilkinson L.
L.28213	" Beaumont H.		L.29257	" Wilkinson F.
L.28199	" Berry A.		L.32552	2 Wilson J.W.
L.29245	" Berry A.		L.29269	" Wood H.
L.25837	" Berry S.		L.28089	" Wright F.
L.32576	" Bentley T.			
L.32528	" Borrisaw E.			
L.32566	" Braithwaite J.S.		Attached :-	
L.25470	" Brook J.W.			
L.25471	" Buckley F.		8949 A.V.C. Sgt. White F.A.	
L.25878	" Clear A.			
L.32443	" Crossley A.			
L.28112	" Crossley F.			
L.28113	" Crossley J.			
L.32518	" Crowther J.			
L.25446	" Davies J.W.			
L.29383	" Dewar W.			
L.25742	" Dyson F.			
L.25442	" Eastwood G.			
L.25608	" Ellis N.			
L.25732	" Firth H.			
L.32538	" Gray D.			
L.29367	" Greenwood J.W.			
L.25728	" Greenwood C.			
L.25831	" Hall H.			
L.28204	" Harrison F.			
L.25479	" Hattersley F.			
L.32524	" Hawthornethwaite T.W.			
L.25822	" Hinchcliffe A.			
L.25523	" Hobson A.			
L.32506	" Holmes W.			
L.29271	" Holmes S.			
L.29403	" Horrocks H.			
L.32447	" Jackson P.			
L.28070	" Jowett J.H.			
L.29270	" Ledgard E.			
L.28132	" Hanson J.			
L.28077	" Martin J.			
L.25774	" McVeagh T.			
L.28066	" Medley O.			
L.28127	" Mellor F.			
L.29401	" Moody A.			
L.25870	" Murray R.			
L.25675	" Nicholson J.			
L.28194	" Nash N.			
L.25882	" Pearson W.			
L.28071	" Robinson F.			
L.25861	" Robinson T.			
L.29416	" Robinson W.			
L.25512	" Robinson W.J.			

'C' Battery.   -;-   168th. Bde. R.F.A.

NOMINAL ROLL of all ranks. 31/12/1916.

- - - - - -;-:-:- - - - -

Officers :-

    Major H. COTTEE.
    Capt. L. G. FIRTH.
    Lieut. B. T. GROVES.
    2/Lt. H. LOCKWOOD.
    2/Lt. H. L. JAMES.
    2/Lt. W. L. SCOTT.

Other Ranks:-

53473	B.M.S.	Malone M.J.	
L.2568	B.Q.M.S.	Tomlinson S.	
L.27727	Sergt.	Ward A.	
L.11952	"	Oates R.T.	
L.11931	"	Townsend W.	
L.19483	"	Booth P.P.	
L.12044	"	Turgoose W.	
L.28115	"	Andrews R.	
L.25389	"	Kettlewell E.	
L.11973	Corpl.	Booth J.	
53807	"	Keefe J.	
L.11923	"	Imms E.	
D.22239	"	Fitzgerald W.	
L.29412	"	Brown T.	
6086	"	Broderick W.	
L.19494	"	Marshall H.	
L.19481	Bdr.	Ward J.S.	
L.19479	"	Wardle L.M.	
L.19478	"	Todd J.H.	
L.19482	"	Earey H.	
L.12050	"	Sanderson G.	
L.27730	"	Walton H.	
L.12016	"	Moguire T.F.J.	
L.19484	"	Bailey B.F.E.	
L.28121	"	Palmer R.	
L.28195	"	Garside I.	
L.12028	"	Craven W.A.	
L.11930	a/Br.	Theobald E.J.	
L.11993	"	Holroyd I.	
L.11959	"	Ellis W.R.	
L.19487	"	Carr W.C.	
L.19519	"	Milnthorpe G.	
105077	"	Carruthers T.	
L.25812	"	Terry L.	
L.25473	"	Earnshaw S.	
L.29308	"	Sanderson H.	
L.37207	"	Smith W.W.	
30751	Far.Sf.Sgt.	Bishop G.	
L.11991	Cpl.S/S	Halton G.	
L.11926	S/S.	Fletcher F.	
L.27751	"	Bailey H.	
L.25954	"	Chappell E.	
L.11934	Gnr.Cold Shoer	Ismay T.H.	
L.19518	Dvr. " "	Thompson J.	
L.29360	Cpl.Ftr.	Hinchcliffe J.	
L.14862	Whlr.	Pringle E.	
L.11918	Sdlr.	Iveson J.	
L.11937	"	Hall J.	
4770	Gnr.	Anderson G.H.	
L.147564	Gnr.	Balls H.R.	
L.11994	Gnr.	Barr J.	
L.11996	"	Bridgeland J.W.	
L.12026	"	Beach J.	
L.11929	"	Brady B.	
L.19485	"	Briggs E.J.	
L.25575	"	Booth H.	
L.27987	"	Broadhead F.	
L.29303	"	Bottomley G.J.	
L.28200	"	Brock J.	
L.11981	"	Cockell G.	
L.28147	"	Chapman I.	
60219	"	Davison J.	
L.25702	"	Denton F.	
L.129947	"	Deveaney F.	
L.11921	"	Drabble H.	
L.147114	"	Creeper H.	
L.167905	"	Copping H.E.	
L.29414	"	Elliott C.H.	
L.25411	"	Ellis W.	
L.78830	"	Fraser J.	
L.29286	"	Fearns F.	
L.12017	"	Farmery J.W.	
L.12019	"	Froggett E.	
L.163727	"	Goggard W.E.	
L.12092	"	Garfoot G.W.	
L.19489	"	Gregory H.S.	
L.11975	"	Howarth H.	
L.11992	"	Houlton R.	
L.12034	"	Harrison G.W.	
L.11989	"	Haworth R.	
88771	"	Hall N.	
L.19490	"	Horner C.	
34446	"	Hutt R.	
394444	"	Holden F.	
L.25751	"	Higgins H.	
L.10744	"	Huggett T.	
L.28102	"	Hirst N.	
L.11938	"	Issatt H.	
L.12020	"	Hindman H.	
63915	"	Irving W.A.	
L.120711	"	Jolley W.	
L.19809	"	James T.	
122010	"	Kenny S.	
L.25575	"	Lee H.	
L.19514	"	Lynes J.	
L.12047	"	Martin T.	

L.11968	Gnr.	Mosley O.	85728	"	Maddox J.
L.11932	"	Mulheir J.W.	14919	Dvr.	Marshall S.
L.12022	"	Rowell E.N.	L.18909	"	Mitchell W.
L.11939	"	Prince W.J.	6074	"	Overland H.
L.11971	"	Parkin W.	97571	"	O'Keefe J.A.
L.134691	"	Robinson A.E.	L.11949	"	Pickard H.
8864	"	Richardson J.	75445	"	Pipe E.
L.19496	"	Saberton F.	L.27691	"	Poynton G.W.
L.27999	"	Spittle J.A.	L.19516	"	Priestley D.
95007	"	Smith C.A.	L.2869	"	Price W.
L.19907	"	Swinn J.	L.28031	"	Parkin H.
33802	"	Thompson F.	L.25850	"	Pogson H.
L.25715	"	Taylor J.T.	L.12011	"	Roberts E.W.
L.19502	"	Wales W.	L.11965	"	Ross C.A.
L.19500	"	Walston L.	L.28134	"	Roberts W.
L.12003	"	Waldron T.	L.19497	"	Shofield W.
L.19503	"	Watson G.	L.28164	"	Spivey P.
L.19616	"	Waller A.E.	L.28149	"	Scott J.R.
L.12007	"	Wilkinson P.	L.28010	"	Steele J.W.
L.11962	"	Wilkock G.	L.25448	"	Singleton N.
34602	"	Wright E.	L.29309	"	Simpson G.H.
L.19717	"	Wardle G.H.	L.27993	"	Senior J.W.
			L.11920	"	Thompson R.
			L.27747	"	Toothill A.C.
			L.32459	"	Turner H.
			L.27986	"	Taylor E.
L.12022	Dvr.	Ainsworth H.	L.28095	"	Turner A.B.
L.11969	"	Backhouse G.H.	L.12015	"	Wathey A.
L.19504	"	Blackburn J.	L.12008	"	Wales A.
L.11942	"	Boulton T.	L.12021	"	Walshaw E.
L.12000	"	Brook J.	L.12006	"	Wrigglesworth F.
L.1195	"	Brookes G.	L.11940	"	Woollen H.
L.11980	"	Burnley W.S.	L.11973	"	Williams H.
L.28116	"	Broadbent J.	L.28169	"	Williams J.
L.29280	"	Bradley H.	L.28124	"	Walton R.
L.11982	"	Clark E.W.	L.29322	"	White L.
57926	"	Coles J.	L.13444	"	Young T.
L.28197	"	Crawshaw H.			
L.25612	"	Clark R.W.			
L.28232	"	Chapman J.			
50755	"	Chapman W.			
L.11960	"	Eubank J.A.			
L.28107	"	Ellis H.			
L.12055	"	Farmery T.			
L.19505	"	Firth G.			
L.19506	"	Fretwell H.			
L.25474	"	Earnshaw B.			
L.12037	"	Garfitt J.T.			
L.19520	"	Garfoot E.			
L.11922	"	Hartley A.W.			
L.11964	"	Hunter J.			
L.11941	"	Hart W.			
L.11967	"	Hancock N.			
L.19510	"	Horsfall E.			
L.19509	"	Hudson J.			
L.12041	"	Kershaw H.			
L.11979	"	Kemp E.			
L.19492	"	Lapish J.			
L.28054	"	Ingham J.			
L.19513	"	Lamb N.			
L.29285	"	Lord J.			
L.28051	"	Lawton H.			

Attached :-

2849 A.V.C.Sgt. Harding W.

'D' Battery — : — 168th. Bde. R.F.A.

NOMINAL ROLL OF ALL RANKS 31/12/1916.

Officers :—

Major D. K. TWEEDIE D.S.O.
Lieut. R. DUNBAR.
2/Lt. G. C. WOOD.
2/Lt. A. A. STEWARD.
2/Lt. J. J. CATERER.

Other Ranks :—

13705	B.S.M.	Fergio W.	27596	Gnr	Dixon H.A.
100360	Fr.Sgt.	Greenwood J.	27537	"	Elsom G.H.
19948	Sgt.	Allen A.J.	27197	"	Fowler A.S.
35383	"	Hartley B.W.	19950	"	Flannigan J.
19894	"	Lambley J.T.	12271	"	Fall W.
L29329	"	Rowley W.	40424	"	Goodman A.
78512	Cpl S/S	Emms H.	19848	"	Hellewell G.W.
19893	" "	Lomas S.	97625	"	Howlett S.
26450	Cpl.Sdlr.	Clawson J.	35402	"	Hepworth G.H.
27618	Cpl.Ftr.	Thresh E.	35413	"	Hadley J.
27518	Corpl.	Holmes G.	148368	"	Keen T.C.
35406	"	Sykes H.M.	27510	"	Marshall H.
19914	"	Wooffitt F.E.	21259	"	McLellan.
27756	Bdr.	Bonner S.	25317	"	Langford W.G.
35409	Corpl.	Dinsdale J.	27532	"	Newton L.
19965	"	Hawkes T.G.H.	19796	"	Parkinson G.H.
12257	Bdr.	Husband A.	28069	"	Ramsden R.
19846	"	Hempsall J.	124923	"	Richardson W.H.
19919	"	Scholey E.	73072	"	Spink A.
26400	"	Smith W.	26125	"	Simmons A.G.
27590	"	Bradford J.	27520	"	Stacey I.
35389	"	Dobson J.E.	97676	"	Starkey E.
19930	"	Flannigan P.	26449	"	Shaw F.
27757	"	Hetherington J.	129128	"	Smith W.E.
35381	a/Br.	Guest W.	26463	"	Townsend A.V.
47570	"	Macomesky J.	20010	"	Thompson J.
27628	"	France F.	35391	"	Trumby J.
19887	"	Foster C.	12044	"	Ward E.
26462	"	Bellamy J.W.	35404	"	Williams J.
35395	"	Hamilton T.H.			
19984	S/S	Methley J.			
27759	"	Popplewell G.			
27612	"	Smith J.	27627	Dvr.	Ackroyd T.
26447	"	Varney J.	27601	"	Archer S.T.
27523	"	Hellawell A.	19783	"	Armitage G.
27497	"	Innocent R.	35402	"	Bainbridge J.G.
78446	Sdlr.	Batley J.	27757	"	Battin W.
113012	"	Molyneux D?	26401	"	Bell A.
26676	"	Schofield J.	26524	"	Bellamy F.
146171	Ftr.	Colar P.A.	35392	"	Beckett E.
128066	Gnr.	Allen J.	12107	"	Bond P.
26385	"	Boler H.B.	27615	"	Bowers F.
27580	"	Briddock J.A.	28059	"	Barker W.
25688	"	Cain J.E.	20007	"	Bradley J.
19947	"	Dolby E.	20008	"	Croft J.

27621	Dvr.	Denby F.
27622	"	Dixon L.
27606	"	Fisher A.
19799	"	Fisher G.
19944	"	Flint F.
19841	"	Gillman B.T.S.
19943	"	Green J.
19803	"	Greenwood J.
20002	"	Hanson C.B.
1986	"	Hempsall T.
26422	"	Havenhand H.
19953	"	Howson W.
19749	"	Hughes H.
27610	"	Jewitt W.
35411	"	Jackson F.
31126	"	Johnson P.H.
35376	"	Lowe G.
35380	"	Lunn G.
1094	"	Lewellyn T.
35379	"	Middleton W.
35414	"	Padget J.
19789	"	Peacock J.E.
25560	"	Palmer J.
27598	"	Pollard J.
27222	"	Phillips F.
19939	"	Porter E.
26410	"	Roper W.
27595	"	Roebuck L.
27624	"	Roebuck V.
40494	"	Seabrook J.H.
26406	"	Savage W.
27609	"	Smith J.
29405	"	Stewart A.
26568	"	Spencer C.
27505	"	Shone W.
27600	"	Sykes J.
34341	"	Turner A.
19736	"	Thompson A.D.
71271	"	Thompson J.C.H.
24085	"	Tilston R.
27566	"	Trafford I.
39240	"	Vidofsky L.
12031	"	Wilkinson J.W.
27758	"	Wood J.
27498	"	Wright D.
19794	"	Whelan J.
154969	"	Whitaker W.
25718	"	Wilson J.

Attached :-

8018 A.V.C.Sgt. Moore W.

168th. Brigade, R.F.A.

Nominal Roll of all ranks who have joined the
Brigade during December 1916.

'A' Battery.

```
10586 Dvr.Westgate F.        Posted from 32nd.D.A.C.      27/11/16.
16989 Gnr.Halliday R.                Do.                     Do.
45354 Dvr.Taylor B.                  Do.                     Do.
86310 Gnr.Squire A.E.                Do.                  11/12/16.
121451 Whlr.Weaver J.        Posted from 153rd Bde R.F.A. 14/12/16.

      2/Lt. A.C.MILLER       Posted from T.M.Bty. 32 Divn.29/12/16.
```

'B' Battery.

```
16381 a/Br Cawthorne R.J.C. Posted from 32nd D.A.C.     27/11/16.
L.26301 Dvr. Wilkinso R.C.J.     "      "    "             do.
53092 Gnr. Stubbs H.Z            "      "    "          11/12/16.
```

'C' Battery.

```
78830 Gnr.Frazer J.         Posted from 32nd D.A.C.     27/11/16.
105727  "  Goddard W.E.          "      "    "             do.
      2/Lieut. W.L.SCOTT       From 32nd Div.Arty.       8/12/16.
19809 Gnr.James L.          Posted from 32nd D.A.C.      8/12/16.
6086  Cpl.Broderick W.           "      "    "          16/12/16.
```

'D' Battery.

```
40484 Gnr.Goodman J.        Posted from 32nd D.A.C.     27/11/16.
39240 Dvr.Vidofsky L.            "      "    "             do.
54341 Dvr.Turner A.              "      "    "          11/12/16.
27222  "  Phillips F.            "      "    "             do.
26125 Gnr.Simmons A.J.           "      "    "             do.
      Capt.SYMONS.             Attached from 32 D.A.    20/12/16.
```

168th Brigade, R.F.A.

Nominal Roll of all ranks who have left the Brigade during December 1916.

'A' Battery.

L.25719 Sgt.Ainley W.	Evacuated 'Sick'	16/12/16.
L.29272 Gnr.Parker W.	" "	15/12/16.
L.26468 " Woollin F.	To Base.(Medically unfit)	25/12/16.

'B' Battery.

L.32557 Gnr.Sykes J.C.	Evacuated 'Sick' to England.	1/12/16.
L.25428 " Barker H.	Evacuated 'Sick'	12/12/16.
L.25609 " Clark S.	" "	do.
34627 " ~~Clark~~ Hylands C.	" "	do.
L.25787 Dvr.Dickerson E.	" "	do.
128006 a/Br Isles H.	Posted to 2nd Field Survey Co.	16/12/16.
L.32504 Cpl.Jenkins R.	To Base (Medically unfit)	25/12/16.
L.25786 Sgt.Naylor S.	To England (Candidate for Commission.	31/12/16.

'C' Battery.

~~78830~~ ~~Gnr.Fraser J.~~		
L.27752 Cpl.Widdowson A.	Evacuated 'Sick'	16/12/16.

'D' Battery.

26676 Gnr.Gregory C.	Evacuated 'Sick'	27/11/16.
19826 Sgt.Needham H.L.	" "	10/12/16.
39240 Dvr.Vidofsky L.	" "	16/12/16.

CONFIDENTIAL.

WAR DIARY

of

168th. Brigade R.F.A.

from January 1st 1917 to January 31st. 1917.

(Volume XIII)

Vol 12

Volume XIII Sheet 1

Army Form C. 2118.

WAR DIARY
or
INTELLIGENCE SUMMARY.
(Erase heading not required.)

168th. Brigade, R.F.A.
Commanded by Lt.Col.B. FITZMAURICE.

Instructions regarding War Diaries and Intelligence Summaries are contained in F.S. Regs., Part II. and the Staff Manual respectively. Title pages will be prepared in manuscript.

Place	Date	Hour	Summary of Events and Information	Remarks and references to Appendices
	1917.		Reference Map Sheet 57d.S.W. 1/20,000 HEBUTERNE	
ST OUEN.	2nd Jan:		Brigade marched from ST OUEN to AMPLIER.	
AMPLIER	3rd.	"	Brigade Headquarters marched to LOUVENCOURT. 1 Section per battery moved into action as under :-	
			Battery Position. S.O.S.Lines etc.	
			A/168. Q.3.a.8.3.	
			B/168. Q.3.c.7.8.	See Appendix "A".
			C/168. Q.3.c.5.8.	
			D/168. Q.9.c.1.9.	
			The Brigade comes under the orders of the 7th Divisional Artillery.	
LOUVENCOURT	4th Jan.		Batteries moved remaining sections into action. Headquarters moved to CAMP JOUBDAIN, MAILLY-MAILLET. Batteries registered.	
MAILLY-MAILLET 5th. to 8th Jan:			Batteries registered.	
	9th Jan:		"X" Day. Batteries carried out systematic bombardment behind enemy lines, according to orders. Zone allotted to the Brigade for this bombardment is the line between the line Q.6.a.6.5. to L.21.d.2.central and the line Q.6.a.3.9. to L.21.central. This zone was allotted to Batteries as under :-	
			"B" Battery - the Northern half.	
			"A" " - " Southern " .	
			"C" " - thickening over the whole.	
			"D" " - the whole.	
			Programme of shooting is shewn on attached Appendix "B".	

Volume XIII Sheet 2

Army Form C. 2118.

WAR DIARY
or
INTELLIGENCE SUMMARY.
(Erase heading not required.)

168th Brigade R.F.A. Commanded by Lt-Col. R. FITZMAURICE.

Instructions regarding War Diaries and Intelligence Summaries are contained in F.S. Regs., Part II. and the Staff Manual respectively. Title pages will be prepared in manuscript.

Reference Sheet 57dNW Trench map BEAUMONT & HEBUTERNE

Place	Date	Hour	Summary of Events and Information	Remarks and references to Appendices
	10th Jan:		"Y" DAY. 7th Division Infantry attacked and captured MUNICH TRENCH at 2 a.m. This Brigade took no part. Systematic bombardment continued as shown on attached appendix "a".	
	11th Jan:		"Z" DAY. At 6.40 a.m. the 7th Division attacked MUNICH TRENCH. This Brigade supported the attack as detailed in attached appendix "b". Batteries fired on Defensive barrage all day, reducing rate to 24 rounds per hour at 12.30 p.m. and eventually to 18 rounds per battery per hour, Howitzers 12 rounds. The following new S.O.S. lines are allotted:—	
			"A" battery. — Q.6.b.1.5. to Q.6.c.95.95. "B" " — Q.6.c.95.95. to K.36.c.6.5. "C" " — K.36.c.6.5. to K.36.c.0.48. "D" " — K.36.d.2.5. — K.36.c.4.4. — Q.6.b.1.5. — Q.6.b.65.80.	
			Batteries fired all night on their S.O.S. lines – 18 rds per battery per hour.	
		8.0 p.m.	Lt-Col. R. FITZMAURICE proceeded on leave. Brigade commanded temporarily by Major D.K. TWEEDIE D.S.O.	
	12th Jan: 9 a.m.		Rate reduced to 8 rounds per battery per hour. Fire continued on S.O.S.lines. Reconnaissance carried out by 2/Lieuts. EBERLS and WOOD seemed to establish that infantry had taken MUNICH TRENCH. No observation possible from it but barrages just beyond MUNICH TRENCH were checked by 1 salvo per battery fired at previously arranged times.	
		12 noon.	Enemy put up a heavy barrage on REDAN RIDGE – BEAUMONT HAMEL.	
		4.0 p.m.	Above bombardment repeated. No counter attack followed.	

Volume XIII Part 3

Army Form C. 2118.

WAR DIARY
or
INTELLIGENCE SUMMARY.
(Erase heading not required)

168th Brigade R.F.A.
Commanded by Lt-Col. R. FITZMAURICE.

Instructions regarding War Diaries and Intelligence Summaries are contained in F.S. Regs., Part II. and the Staff Manual respectively. Title pages will be prepared in manuscript.

Place	Date	Hour	Summary of Events and Information	Remarks and references to Appendices
(Reference Sheet 1/20000 French Map) BEAUMONT & HEBUTERNE	15th Jan;		Fire on S.O.S. lines at 8 rounds per battery per hour continued. Reconnaissance by Major F. FITZGIBBON proved that we did not actually occupy MUNICH TRENCH in Q.6.4. between WALKER AVENUE and CRATER LANE owing to the bad state of the trench. Posts were established in rear. – K.36.c.1.5 is occupied by us.	
		10 a.m.	Rate of Fire reduced to 4 rds. per battery per hour.	
		11 p.m.	Targets for Day & Night firing changed to the following :-	
			18-Pounders. New German line in process of being dug. K.36.a.2.6. to Q.6.b.o.8. Dugouts – Q.6.b.0.8.	
			+.5"Hows.	
			Rate of Fire – 15 rds per group per hour.	
	15th Jan;	6 a.m.	18-Pdr. batteries, especially "A" Battery heavily shelled with 15 cm and 7.7c.m. Brigade ordered to prepare to relieve the 40th Brigade R.F.A. 3rd Divisional Artillery. Reconnaissance carried out by Brigade Commander and Battery Commanders.	
	16th Jan;	3.30 p.m.	1 section per battery withdraw and relieve one section of batteries of 40th Bde R.F.A.	
			Positions as follows :-	
			"A" Battery. – K.27.c.2.7.	
			"B" " – K.25.b.95.45.	
			"C" " – K.26.a.0.6.	
			"D" " – K.27.d.00.55.	
	17th Jan;	3 p.m.	Remaining section move to new positions. Headquarters move to COIGNEUX.	
	18th Jan;		Headquarters move to OUR WELLS. O.C. 168th Brigade R.F.A. takes over from O.C. 40th Brigade R.F.A. the 2nd Divisional Artillery covers its own Infantry for the first time since leaving AMEQUIN last October. 168th Brigade R.F.A. covers the Battalion of the 96th Infantry Brigade holding C.3 Subsector. S.O.S. lines being laid out from K.29.d.25. to K.23.d.70.15. see appendix "D".	

A5834 Wt. W4973/M687 750,000 8/16 D.D. & L. Ltd. Forms/C.2118/13

VOLUME XIII Part 4

Army Form C. 2118.

WAR DIARY
or
INTELLIGENCE SUMMARY.

(Erase heading not required.)

168th. Brigade R. F. A.
Commanded by Lt-Col.R.FITZMAURICE.

Instructions regarding War Diaries and Intelligence Summaries are contained in F. S. Regs., Part II. and the Staff Manual respectively. Title pages will be prepared in manuscript.

Place	Date	Hour	Summary of Events and Information	Remarks and references to Appendices
	19th Jan:		Batteries registered as far as possible, but visibility only fair.	
	20th Jan:		"D" Battery shelled in the morning from 11.20 a.m. to 12.15 p.m. by 5.9"How. Bombardier PRANCE killed. Heavies retaliated vigorously with counter battery work. Visibility NIL. 1 Section of B/155 is posted to D/168, forming the latter into a 6 gun battery.	
	21st Jan:		Visibility slightly better. A little registration was done. One 4.5 Howitzer of D/168 completely blown up by premature in bore. 2 Howitzers of new section brought into action and one of the old guns withdrawn for overhaul.	
	22nd Jan:	10 a.m.	Owing to re-adjustment of 32nd Division front, the front covered by 168th Bde R.F.A. is extended South as far as K.5.c.7.5. Brigade reinforced by 12th Battery R.F.A. (7th Divl.Artillery) and the whole called "D" GROUP. Particulars of disposition of Infantry, S.O.S. lines, Zones, etc., will be found in attached appendix "B".	
	23rd Jan:		Very cold brilliant day but too much haze for good visibility.	
	24th Jan:		At about 6.15 a.m. enemy opened lively artillery fire on Right Subsector and then on Left Subsector. We replied vigorously with all batteries. A raid was expected but apparently nothing materialised. Cold weather continues. Lieut-Col. R. FITZMAURICE returns from leave and resumes Command of Brigade.	
	25th Jan:		Enemy very quiet. Batteries registered with aeroplane observation. 20 degrees of frost.	
	29th Jan:		Lieut-Col. R. FITZMAURICE assumes temporary Command of 32nd Divisional Artillery in place of Brig.Gen. J. A. TYLER, C.M.G., who is in temporary Command of 32nd Division. 168th. Brigade R.F.A. commanded by Major F. FITZ GIBBON.	

Volume XIII Part 6

Army Form C. 2118.

WAR DIARY
or
INTELLIGENCE SUMMARY.

(Erase heading not required.)

168th Brigade, R.F.A.
Commanded by Lt.-Col. R. FITZMAURICE.

Instructions regarding War Diaries and Intelligence Summaries are contained in F. S. Regs., Part II. and the Staff Manual respectively. Title pages will be prepared in manuscript.

Place	Date	Hour	Summary of Events and Information	Remarks and references to Appendices
			Reference Sheet 1/20,000 Beamont Hamel & Hebuterne	
	31st Jan:	5.15 to 5.45 a.m.	Left battalion from K.29.a. & c. heavily shelled. All batteries retaliated. A raid was suspected but the only result was that 2 Germans fell into our hands.	
		9 a.m.	12th Battery R.F.A. reverts to command of 75th Brigade R.F.A.	
			C/151 comes under orders of O.C., 168th Brigade R.F.A., See Appendix "E".	
			C/16 positions K.27.c.2.7. heavily shelled all day. 1 man killed and 1 wounded and considerable damage done to dug-outs. Fire apparently directed by Aeroplane. About 200 shell, 10.5 cm. and 15 cm. fell in the position, and others in the vicinity.	
			Cold weather shows no sign of lifting.	
			The following casualties have occurred during the month:-	
			"A" Battery - Nil.	
			"B" Battery - L.29901 (Gnr Brooke H., L.2725 Gnr Scott H., L.2575 Gnr Toothill A. L.2645 (Gnr Bentley E.V. (Wounded by shell on 7/1/17)	
			"C" Battery - Nil.	
			"D" Battery - E.802 (Gnr Hepworth J.E. (Wounded on 13/7/17) L.27628 a/Cr France P. (Villes - 20/1/17) 7202/2 Gnr Spink J. (Wounded by Premature.)	
	1st. February 1917.			

J. Fitzmaurice
Major.
Commanding 168th. Brigade R.F.A.

S E C R E T.

Appendix A

168th. Brigade, R.F.A.

OPERATION ORDER No.8.

1. Each Battery will place one Section in action to-night, and the remainder to-morrow.
   Batteries will not clear MAILLY – MAILLET before 3.40 p.m.

2. A dump of 200 rds per gun and 150 per howitzer will be maintained.
   Only 1 wagon per gun will be taken in by batteries
   Arrangements are being made to deliver ammunition by rail to certain points near batteries. Batteries will arrange for G.S.Wagons to take it to positions.

3. Front of 168th Bde. R.F.A. :-

   Q.5.b.9.7. to Q.6.a.5.3.

   S.O.S Lines :-

   Q.6.a.3.9. to Q.6.a.7.3.

   'A' Battery – 1/3rd of front on right.
   'B'   "   –   "   "   "   in centre.
   'C'   "   –   "   "   "   on left
   'D'   "   – will select 4 points in rear of S.O.S. lines.

4. 168th Bde. R.F.A. will be known as "B" Group.

5. In order to avoid any apparent increase in fire on the front of 7th Division, 18-pdrs. will arrange among themselves hours of registration and inform O.C. 25th Battery R.F.A. who will inform O.C. 35th Bde. R.F.A.

6. Batteries will report guns in action, also points registered daily.
   They may use O.P's of 7th Division, but must eventually report site of their own O.P's when selected.

7. H.Q., 'B' Group will be at 87a, MAILLY-MAILLET till the 6th. inst., after that at 67a.

                                              Lieut.
                                    Adjt. 168th Brigade, R. F. A.

3/1/1917.

Appendix "B"

168th. Brigade, R.F.A.

OPERATION ORDER No 10.

Reference 7th Divisional Group, Instructions for forthcoming Operations No.1 dated 7th January 1917.

1. It will be assumed that "X" Day will be 9th. January.

2. Wire will be cut in front of MUNICH TRENCH by "A", "B", Batteries on "X" and "Y" Days, as under :-

   'A' Battery   Q.6.a.6.5. to Q.6.a.3.9.
   'B'   "   Q.6.a.3.9. to K.36.c.67.17.

   Expenditure. 200 rds. per battery per day.

   One section only will be used at a time, and the ordinary bombardment shewn on the attached tables will be carried out as well.

3. With reference to paras.7 and 11, programmes of fire for 'X' and 'Y' Days are attached.
   'C' Battery will not fire at night.
   The zone for 'B' Group for the bombardment will be the lane between the line Q.6.a.6.5 to L.31.a Central and the line Q.6.a.3.9 to L.31 Central.
   'B' Battery's zone will be the Northern half of this line.
   'C' Battery's zone will be the Southern half of this line.
   'A' Battery will thicken over the whole group zone.
   'D' Battery will cover the whole group zone.

4. Ammunition. A minimum of 300 rds per gun for 18-Pdrs. and 200 rds per howitzer will be maintained. These amounts must be at gun positions at Zero hour on "Z" Day.
   During the barrage on "Z" Day one section will fire Ax only if available and the two other sections A.
   A truck-load of Ax will be sent up to-morrow night.

5. S.O.S.Barrage. para.8. Batteries of 'B' Group will fire in these tests only for an attack on 7th Division. the officer detailed to report on this barrage is Major H. COTTEE.
   Rate of Fire will be that at present in force for S.O.S. Calls.
   All H.E. will be used if available.

6. Reference to para.9. the report on H.E. Barrage will be forwarded to this office as soon after the S.O.S. Test as possible.

7. On "Z" Day 2/Lt. W. A. EBBELS will go forward as F.O.O.
   A line will be laid to the REDAN and as soon as MUNICH TRENCH is consolidated he will select a forward O.P., and extend the line to it. He will be armed and have an armed orderly with him.

8th Jany: 1917.   Adjt. "B" GROUP.
                                                 Lieut.

PROGRAMME OF FIRE. "X" & "Y" DAYS.

"X" DAY

Time.	TASK.	RATE OF FIRE.	Rounds 18-Pdrs.	4.5"Hows.
8 a.m. to 11.26 a.m.	18-Pdrs shell all communications in zones. 4.5"Hows.shell communication trenches & Trench junctions in zone.	16 rds per battery per hour.	159	53
10.30 a.m. to 10.40 a.m. and 10.50 a.m.to 11 a.m.	S.O.S. Test.	3 rds gun fire then Section fire 15 secs. 1 rd.gun fire then Section fire 30 secs.	414	44 44
11.20 a.m. to 11.50 a.m. 11.50 a.m. to 1.20 p.m.	PAUSE. 18-pdrs shell all communications in zones. 4.5"Hows shell Communication Trenches and Trench Junctions in zone	16 rds per battery per hour.	72	24
1.20 p.m. to 1.24 p.m.	18-Pdrs. fire on Barrage A in zones allotted in Operation Order No.9.	2 rds. per gun per minute.	144	—
1.24 p.m. to 1.27 p.m.	18-pdrs.will search quickly forward by lifts of 100 yards onto Barrage B.	2 rds per gun per minute.	108	
1.27 p.m. to 1.30 p.m.	18-pdrs.will fire on Barrage A.	3 rds per gun per minute.	162	
1.20 p.m. to 1.30 p.m.	4.5"Hows will fire on Q.6.b.5.2.28, Q.6.b.9.3. Q.5.b.0.15. Q.6.a.78.42	2 rds per How per minute. 16 rds per bty. per hour.	143	80 48
1.30 p.m. to 4.30 p.m.	As from 8 a.m. to 11.20 a.m.			
4.30 p.m. to 4.45 p.m.	PAUSE.			
4.45 p.m. to 4.50 p.m.	As from 8 a.m. to 11.20 a.m.			
4.50 p.m. to 4.57 p.m.	18-pdrs fire on Barrage A " " fire on Barrage B search by lifts of 100 yards to Barrage B	2 rds per battery.	6	2
4.57 p.m. to 5.0 p.m.	" " Hows as for 1.20 p.m. to 1.30 p.m.	2 rds per gun per minute. 3 rds per gun per minute. 2 rds per How per minute.	52 162	1 80
4.50 p.m. to 5.0 p.m.	'A' & 'B' Btys shell all communications in zones.			
5.0 p.m. to 5.0 p.m.		24 rds per bty per hour. 16 rds per bty. per hour.	32	10
5.40 pm.to 9.40 p.m.	4.5"Hows as from 8 a.m. to 11.20 a.m.			
5.40 p.m to 9.40 p.m.	PAUSE.			
9.40 pm to 8 am.('Y' Day.)	As from 8 a.m. to 11.20 a.m.	'A' & 'B' Btys.24 rds per bty per Hour 'D' Bty. 16 rds per bty per hour.	496	170
			555	555

'Y' DAY.

Time.	TASK.	RATE OF FIRE.	Rounds 18-pdrs.	Rounds 4.5"Hows.
8 a.m. to 8.7 a.m.	18-Pdrs fire on Barrage 'A'.	2 rds per gun per minute.	144	-
8.7 a.m. to 8.7 a.m.	18-pdrs will search quickly forward by lifts of 100 y.rds onto Barrage 'B'.			
8.7 a.m. to 8.10 a.m.	18-Pdrs will fire on Barrage 'A'.	2 rds per gun per minute.	108	-
8 a.m. to 8.10 a.m.	4.5"Hows. 8.6.0 52.8 — 8.6.b.9.3. 8.6.b.15. — 8.6.a.78.42	3 rds per gun per minute	162	-
8.10 a.m. to 1 p.m.	18-pdrs shell all communications in zones.	2 rds per How per minute.	-	80
	4.5"Hows shell communication Trenches and Trench Junctions in zone	16 rds per Bty. per hour.	240	80
1 p.m. to 1.20 p.m.	PAUSE.			
1.20 p.m. to 5.0 p.m.	As from 8.10 a.m. to 1.0 p.m.	16 rds per bty per hour.	176	58
5.0 p.m. to 5.20 p.m.	PAUSE. as from 8.10 a.m. to 1.0 p.m.	3 rds. per bty.	...	3
5.20 p.m. to 5.30 p.m.	18-Pdrs fire on Barrage 'B'		...	9
5.30 p.m. to 5.37 p.m.	" search quickly by 100 yards lifts to Barrage 'B'	2 rds per gun per minute.	252	-
5.37 p.m. to 5.30 p.m.	18-Pdrs fire on Barrage 'A'	3 rds per gun per minute.	162	-
5.30 p.m. to 5.40 p.m.	4.5"Hows. as from 8 a.m. to 8.10 a.m.	2 rds per How per minute	-	80
5.40 p.m. to 9.40 p.m.	PAUSE.		...	...
9.40 p.m. to 7 ('Z' Day) (or as ordered)	'A' and 'B' Batteries shell all communications in zones. 'D' Battery shells all Communication Trenches and Trench Junctions in zone.	24 rds per bty per hour. 16 rds per bty. per hour.	432	144
			1685	455

SECRET.

169th. Brigade R.F.A.
Operation Order No.9 - 7/1/17.

Appendix C.

1. With reference to Appendix to 7th. Divisional Operation Order No. 82 dated 6th. January 1917, barrages will be allotted to 18-pounder Batteries as follows :-

    'A' Battery will barrage along the lane between the line
       Q.6 a 60.15 to Q.6 b 1.5 and the line Q.6 a 6.5
       to Q.6 b c5.75.

    'C' Battery will barrage along the lane between the line
       Q.6 a 6.5 to Q.6 b c5.75 and the line Q.6 a 4c.65
       to Q.6 a 95.95.

    'B' Battery will barrage along the lane between the line
       Q.6 a 4c.65 to Q.6 a 95.95 and the line
       Q.6 a 1.9 to K 36 c 95.25.

    The Final Defensive Barrage will be divided up as follows :-
       'A' Battery.   K.36 c 9.0   to K.36.c 812
       'C' Battery.   K.36 c 8.2   to K.36 c 6.40.
       'B' Battery.   K.36 c 6.40 to K.36 c 6.8.

2. Barrage Table for 18-pounders and 4.5" Howitzers is attached.

7th Jany. 1917.   Lieut.
                      Adjutant - 'B' Group.

Appendix.

BARRAGE TABLE FOR 18-POUNDERS

Time.	Barrage.	Rate of Fire.
- 3 mins. to + 0.8	Barrage "A".	2 rounds per gun per minute.
+ 0.8 to + 0.10	Lift 25 yards.	" " " " " "
+ 0.10 to + 0.12	" " "	" " " " " "
+ 0.12 to + 0.14	" " "	" " " " " "
+ 0.14 to + 0.15	" " "	" " " " " "
+ 0.15 to + 0.18	" " "	3 rounds per gun per minute.
+ 0.18 to + 0.20	Lift onto Barrage "B".	" " " " " "
+ 0.20 to + 0.26	Barrage "B".	" " " " " "
+ 0.26 to + 0.30	Lift onto Barrage "C".	2 rds. per gun per minute.
+ 0.30 to + 0.60	Barrage "C".	2 rounds per gun per minute.
+ 0.60 to + 2 hrs.	" "	1 round " " " "
		½ " " " " "

When firing on Barrage "C" from + 0.26 onwards alternate guns of each battery will search forward at frequent intervals for 400 yards, approximately to line R.1.a.6.0 to L.31.c.6.5.

BARRAGE TABLE for 4.5" HOWITZERS.

Time.	Target.	Rate of Fire.
- 5 mins. to zero.	S.6 & 6.5 C.6 & 1.5	2 rds. per How. per minute.
zero.	Lift to Q.6 & 9.4 C.6 & 1.5	
zero to +0.20'	"	2 rds. per How. per minute.
+0.20' to +0.60'	"	1 rd. " " " "
+0.60' to +2 hrs.	"	½ rd. " " " "

Appendix D

168th Brigade R.F.A.

Provisional Instructions for Artillery covering C3 sector.

1. C3 sector will be covered by batteries of 168th. Brigade R.F.A. as under :-

			Battery Position.	Zones.
'A' Bty.	6	18-Pdrs.	K.27.c.2.7.	K.29.d.2.5 to K.29.b.15.10.
'B' "	6	18-Pdrs.	K.25.b.95.45	K.29.b.15.10 to K.29.b.50.65.
'C' "	6	18-Pdrs.	K.26.a.6.6.	K.29.b.50.65 to K.23.d.70.15.
'D' "	4	4.5 Hows.	K.27.a.00.55.	K.29.d.2.5 to K.23.d.70.15.

   For nightlines 18-Pdr. batteries will form a barrage on the enemy's front line to cover the whole of their zones. 'D' Battery will select Trench Junctions in the support and reserve line and will report points selected to this Office.

2. **S.O.S.**

   The rocket signal will be one white rocket, 1 red rocket, 1 white rocket, fired in quick succession until the artillery opens fire.

   Fire will be opened as soon as 1 white and 1 red rocket are seen at the following rates:-

   For 5 minutes — 3 rounds per gun per minute.
   " 10 " — 2 " " " " "

   After that, 1 round per gun per minute until situation is cleared up. 18-Pounders will direct their fire on the enemy's wire.

   S.O.S. messages by wire will be sent in the following form:- S.O.S. followed by name of Battalion subsector (e.g., C3).

   In response to S.O.S. Call fire will be opened on the whole Battalion front.

   S.O.S. signals received will always be repeated to Brigade Headquarters as soon as fire has been opened.

3.   TEST S.O.S.
   In the case of a Test S.O.S. being sent, the Battery called upon will only fire 1 round unless otherwise ordered.

   Careful note must always be made of the time of receipt of the message and the hour the round was fired.

   The time between handing in the message and firing the shot should not exceed one minute.

   Code call will be TEST followed by name of sub-sector (e.g., C_3).

4.   RETALIATION SCHEMES.
   Retaliation Schemes A, B, C, D, E, F, G, H & K taken over from 3rd Divisional Artillery will remain in force. If batteries have not taken them over on relief this office must be notified at once.

   The following Retaliation Scheme is added:-
CODE WORD   " RETALIATE DUMP "

	Target
'A' Battery	
'B' ")	Enemy Dump L.25.b.4.2.
'D' ")	

   Rate of Fire
2 minute bombardment – 18-pdrs. 3 rds. per gun per minute.
                       4.5"Hows. 2 rds. per How per minute.
15 minute pause – then repeat.

   This scheme is for retaliation for heavy fire on EUSTON DUMP which will be reported by C/161, batteries being notified by this office.

5.   AMMUNITION.   Dumps at Gun positions will be established and maintained as follows :-

   18-Pounder batteries – 400 rounds per gun.
   4.5"How. Battery   – 300 rounds per How.

   Echelons will be kept full.

   Except in the case of hostile attack the proportionate expenditure for 18-pdr batteries will not exceed 25%. In the event of a hostile attack no restriction is put on expenditure.

(Continued)

6. **LIAISON.**

One Liaison Officer is required at Battalion Headquarters night and day. He will be provided by batteries in rotation, 24 hour reliefs.

'C' Battery's O.P. will be manned each night under the same arrangements as for Liaison Officers. For the next few days these officers will be provided as under :-

	Liaison Officer.	Night O.P.
18th Jan.	'A' Battery.	'D' Battery.
19th "	'C' "	'B' "
20th "	'D' "	'A' "
21st "	'B' "	'C' "

A further list will follow.

7. **TRENCH BOARDS.**

The following Trench Boards are in position :-

E	Junction of	HINDU & DUNDEE	K.28.d.6.3.
F	"	" ROB ROY & CENTRAL	K.29.a.50.55
G	"	" ROB ROY & NORTHERN	K.29.a.6.8.
H	"	" MAY & NORTHERN	K.28.b.70.85

8. **ALTERNATIVE POSITIONS.**

Batteries are responsible for the up-keep of the following positions :-

A8.	K.27.a.2.2.	'A' Battery.
A7.	K.27.c.1.9.	'B' "
A12	K.27.b.9.5.	'C' "
B2.	K.27.b.6.6.	'D' "

Lettered Boards are posted at each position.

9. Pending further instructions in regard to shooting Batteries will continue registration and will engage any targets which present themselves. Any retaliation for hostile fire will be vigorous and must always be well in excess of hostile fire. Particulars as to ammunition allotment are not yet to hand but ammunition must not be spared in the event of hostile Artillery proving aggressive. Registration reports will be rendered to this office as usual.

10. **ACKNOWLEDGE.**

Lieut.

18/1/1917.   Adjt. 168th. Brigade, R. F. A.

SECRET.

Appendix E

168th Brigade R.F.A.
OPERATION ORDER No.11.

21st January 1917.

Reference 1/10,000 BEAUMONT & HEBUTERNE.

1. The front of the 32nd Division is being readjusted so as to hold the line on a front of three Brigades permanently in the line.

2. The readjustment will be carried out as under :-

   (a) Night of Jan. 22/23rd. The 14th Infantry Brigade will relieve the 96th Infantry Brigade in that portion of the front from its Southern Boundary (i.e. the Southern Boundary of the present C.1 Subsector) to DELAUNEY AVENUE (exclusive)

   (b) Night. Jan. 23/24th. The 14th Infantry Brigade will extend its right and relieve the 97th Infantry Brigade as far South as Wagon Road (Wagon Road and Post 15 and No.1 exclusive to 14th. Infantry Brigade).

3. The 168th Brigade R.F.A. reinforced by the 12th Battery R.F.A. will form "B" Group, 32nd Divisional Artillery and will cover the 96th Brigade in the line.
   The Group will be composed as under :-

A/168 Bde.R.F.A.	6	18-pdr. Guns.
B/168 " "	6	" "
C/168 " "	6	" "
12th Bty. R.F.A.	6	" "
D/168 Bde.R.F.A.	4	4.5" Howrs. (6 in a few days)

4. The disposition of the 96th Infantry Brigade in the line will be as follows :-

   Right Subsector held by one Battalion (less two Companies) extends from K.35.a.35.60 to K.29.c.80.15.
      Battn. Headquarters at LEGEND TRENCH K.34.b.3.8.

   Left Subsector held by one Battalion extends from K.29.c.80.15 to K.23.d.15.15. Battn. Hqrs. at K.28.b.50.15.

5. The Right Subsector will be covered by C/168 and one Section 12th Battery R.F.A.
   The Left Subsector will be covered by 'A' & 'B'/168 and two sections 12th Battery R.F.A.
   D/168 will cover the whole front.
   Zones, O.P's, etc., are shown on attached Table "A".

6. LIAISON ARRANGEMENTS. Liaison officers will be found as under, commencing night of 22/23rd January :-
   Right Battalion - "C" & "D"/168 alternately.
   Left   "   - "A" & "B"/168   "
   Further details are shown on attached Table "B".

7. These orders will come into force at 10 a.m. the 22nd January 1917.

8. A C K N O W L E D G E.

21st Jany. 1917.   Lieut.
                            Adjt. 168th. Brigade, R. F. A.

TABLE "B".

BATTERY POWER.

Covering Right Subsector.

Battery.	Position.	No. of Guns.	Zone.	O.P.
C/168.	K.27.c.2.7.	6	K.35.d.7.6. to K.29.d.10.30.	K.33.b.7.5.
12th. Bty. R.F.A.	Q.15.b.5.2.	2	"	"

Covering Left Subsector.

A/168.	K.25.b.95.45	6	K.29.d.10.30 to K.29.b.5.35	K.21.d.3.2.
B/168.	K.26.a.0.6	6	K.29.b.35 to K.23.d.7.3.	K.27.b.30.75
12th. Bty R.F.A.	Q.15.b.5.2.	4	K.29.d.10.30 to K.23.d.7.3.	K.33.b.7.5.

Covering both subsectors.

| D/168. | K.27.a.00.55 | 6 -4.5"ows. | K.35.a.7.6. to K.23.d.7.3. | R.2.c.9.0. |

TABLE "B"

LIAISON OFFICERS & NIGHT O.P.

	Right. Btn.	Left Btn.	Night O.P.
22nd Jan.	D	B	A
23rd "	"	"	C
24th "	C	A	D
25th "	"	"	B
26th "	D	B	A
27th "	"	"	C
28th "	C	A	B
29th "	"	"	D
30th "	D	B	A
31st "	"	"	C

NIGHT LINES.

Night Lines for 'A', 'B', & 'C' Batteries on the German front line trench in their zones.

12th Battery R.F.A. enfilade the front line of the Group Zone, placing guns on points where communication trenches join front line.

<u>D/166</u>.   1 Howitzer on each of the following points :-

~~K.35.b.50.55~~   K.35.b.22.95
K.29.d.40.45 -   K.29.b.70.05 -
K.29.b.55.45 -   K.30.a.1.9. -
K.29.d.63.15

:o:

F.F.G.

SECRET.   Copy No. 9

Appendix "F"

168th. BRIGADE, R.F.A.
OPERATION ORDER No 12.

1. From 9 a.m. on January 31st. until further orders, the 18-pdr. batteries of the 22nd. Brigade R.F.A., and "T" Battery, R.H.A. of the 14th. Brigade, R.H.A. will be under the orders of 63rd. Divisional Artillery.

2. The following alterations in the grouping of 32nd. Divisional Artillery and attached Brigades will be made :-

   (a) The 12th. Battery R.F.A. will revert to the control of O.C., 35th Brigade R.F.A. Group from 9 a.m. on 31st. instant.

   (b) O.C., "A" Group will place C/161 under the orders of O.C., "B" Group from 9 a.m. on 31st instant until further orders.

3. The Left Infantry Brigade Sector will therefore be covered from 9 a.m. 31st instant as under :-

                                        Zone.
   C/168. 6 18-pdrs.   K.35.b.15.70 to K.29.d.10.35
   C/161. 6 18-pdrs.   K.29.d.10.35 to K.29.b.1.0.
   B/168. 6 18-pdrs.   K.29.b.1.0   to K.29.b.35.60
   A/168. 6 18-pdrs.   K.29.b.35.60 to K.23.d.7.3.
   D/168. 6 4.5" Hows. K.35.b.15.70 to K.23.d.7.3.

   For Night Lines each 18-pdr. battery will cover its whole zone, barraging the old German front line, except C/168 which will barrage the old support line.

   D/168 will fire on the following points :-
       K.29.d.40.45   K.30.a.1.9.   K.29.b.55.45
       K.30.c.14.42   K.29.b.70.65 K.29.d.55.80.

(Continued)

4. Night & Day firing will be carried out as at present - a tracing shewing amended zones is attached.

5. **LIAISON.** Liaison arrangements will not be altered. The Orderly officer will make the necessary arrangements to connect C/161 with Battalion Headquarters.

6. **ACKNOWLEDGE.**

30th. Jan; 1917.

Lieut.
Adjt., 168th. Brigade, R. F. A.
"B" Group, 32nd Divnl. Artillery.

Copy No 1. A/168.
2. B/168.
3. C/168.
4. D/168.
5. C/161.
6. Hqrs., 32nd Divisional Artillery.
7. Hqrs., 96th. Infantry Brigade.
8. War Diary.
9. War Diary.
10. File.

I ssued at................

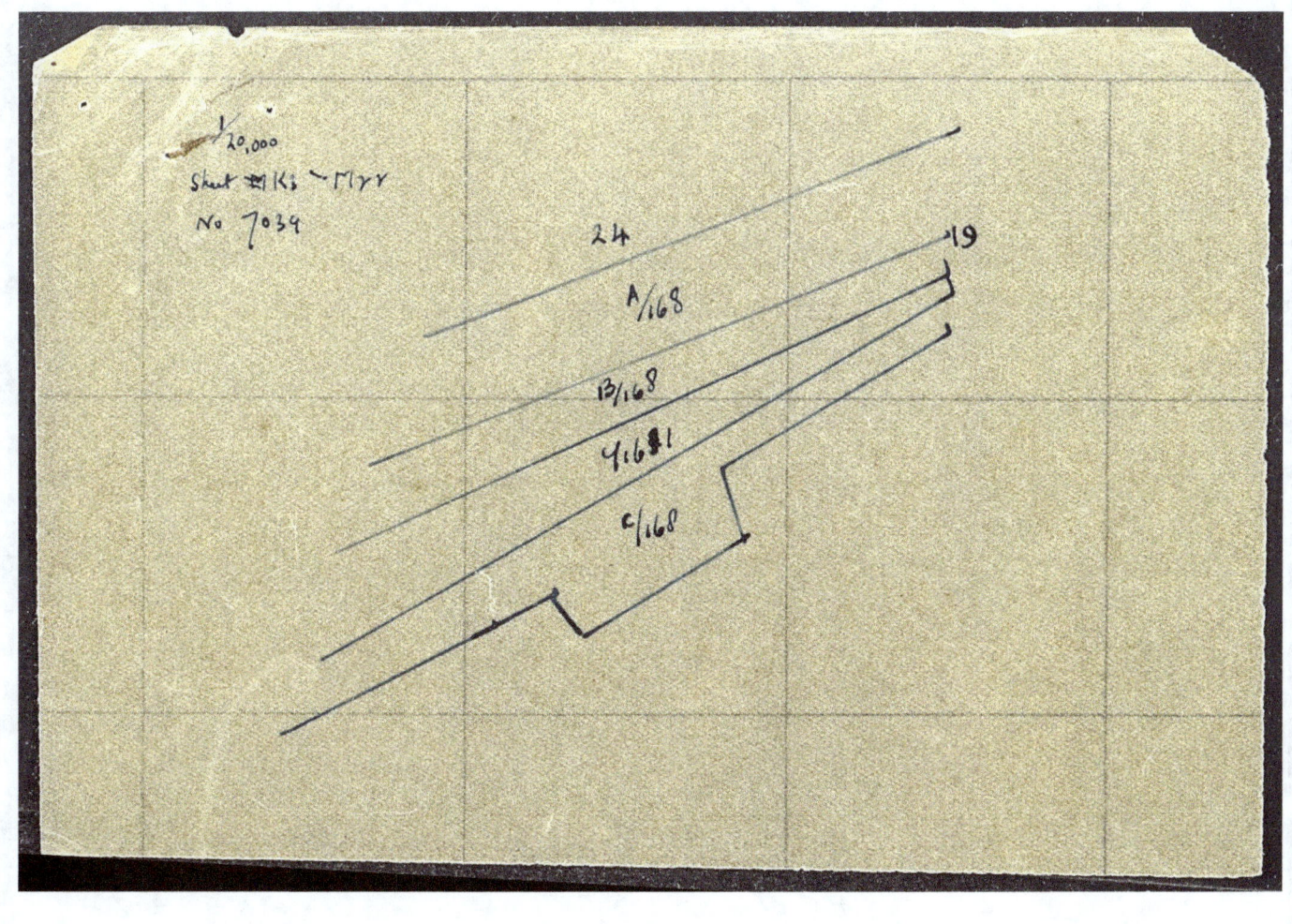

Headquarters Staff — 168th Brigade R.F.A.

Nominal Roll of all ranks.

Officers :— Lt-Col. R. FITZMAURICE.
Lieut. J. C. POOLE.
2/Lieut A. LUMB.
Capt. D. FERGUSON (R.A.M.C).

Other Ranks.:—

L.25839	Cpl	Lee G.
L.28154	"	Thackra J.T.
29811	Bdr	Anderton A.
L.29801	"	Normanton A.
12245	aBdr	Wright J.
L.29430	BdR	Eyre F.
L.25881	"	Gibson H.
L.28042	"	Sugden E
L.28206	Gnr	Ackroyd H.
L.25810	"	Bottomley C.
56777	Gnr	Grindley W.
152003	"	Firth H.
59688	"	Clark B.J.
L.29404	"	Greenwood C.
5645	"	Coles E.
55188	"	Heard H.
L.25480	"	Lucas E.
L.29394	"	Rangeley P.S.
L.25399	"	Ramsden A.
L.25626	"	Slater H.
L.28179	"	Sykes C.A.
L.29296	"	Windle A.T.
L.27531	"	Postlethwaite T.
L.25422	Dvr	Armytage J.R.
L.32440	"	Baker G.
L.32540	"	Blake F.
L.28026	"	Cowham S.
L.32488	"	Dutton J.W.
L.29287	"	Fisher S.
37566	"	Hirons E.
5855	"	Gowan W.
L.32511	"	Iredale A.
L.25825	"	Iredale E.
L.28189	"	Mellor A.
L.29351	"	Newsome A.E.
79511	"	McIntyre A.
L.29424	"	Parker J.
L.29423	"	Pollard W.
L.25853	"	Radley T.
L.29357	"	Reddington M.
L.29389	"	Stansfield P.
6267	S/S	Periera A.T.

Attached :—

A.O.C.625 Stf.Sgt. Barker H.

"A" Battery —:— 168th Bde. R.F.A.

Nominal Roll of all ranks 31/1/17.

- - - - - - - - - -

Officers:— Major Emmet R.
Capt. Brown W.R.
Lieut. Ainley H.W.E.
Lieut. d'Ivry G.C.
2/Lt. Ebbels W.A.
2/Lt. Bell J.G.

Other ranks:—

28514	B.S.M.	Pitchett W.J.
L.28064	B.Q.M.S.	Brearley H.
1105	Sergt.	Witney T.
55261	"	Smith E.F.
25258	"	Williamson A.
L.25426	"	Field P.J.
L.25679	"	Roberts J.
45512	"	McGowan A.H.
L.25445	"	Firth A.
L.25697	Corpl.	Rhodes L.
L.25561	"	Povey J.
L.25619	"	France W.
L.25711	"	Kirkham T.
L.25693	"	Littlewood K.
85294	"	Simpson T.
L.29407	"	Taylor F.
L.25510	Bdr.	
L.32479	Bdr.	Bentley J.
L.28100	"	Pitchforth A.
L.29313	"	Armitage W.B.
L.25708	"	Crawshaw J.S.
L.25574	"	Whiteley C.H.
L.28055	"	Barnes H.
L.25414	"	Wood B.
L.25711	"	Rhodes J.
L.28188	"	Padgett S.H.
L.25464	a/Br	Richardson C.H.
L.32581	"	Williams W.J.
25100	"	Adams E.E.
L.28072	"	Bentley C.
L.32539	"	Penton E.
L.25768	"	Brooksbank
L.25699	"	Oates H.
L.32457	S/C/Br.	Womersley C.
L.28060	"	Kennedy H.
L.25485	"	Williams G.
45525	Far.Sgt.	Spillett H.
L.25785	Cpl.S/S	Town E.
L.28173	S/S	Taylor J.E.
L.25568	"	Sykes J.H.
L.29282	"	Nuttall G.T.
L.28175	"	Waterhouse L.
L.25690	"	Kaye J.T.
L.32485	Sdr	Jackson W.E.
62728	"	Olliver J.E.
147472	Ftr	Hellewell A.
121451	Wh/r	Weaver J.

L.25790	Gnr.	Allot C.V.
L.25595	"	Billington T.
L.28014	"	Bray E.H.
L.28217	"	Bower E.
L.25396	"	Beasley G.
100856	"	Beamish R.
100774	"	Baird S.
L.28180	"	Bolton H.
L.28104	"	Barker N.
L.29379	"	Beaumont L.
L.32471	"	Calvert F.
L.25444	"	Grimlisk M.G.
L.29307	"	Catley F.S.
5556	"	Chappell A.
L.28178	"	Dawson W.
12049	"	Edwards L.
8627	"	Franklin A.
602006	"	Fuller B.
169899	"	Halliday R.
L.25823	"	Ines W.H.
L.25610	"	Hopwood H.
L.25528	"	Hey J.S.
L.28159	"	Hewitt R.
L.28151	"	Hopson T.C.
L.29427	"	Kettle L.J.
L.29411	"	Knoeton J.
L.32512	"	Lumb W.
L.28177	"	Leathem F.
L.28184	"	Lockwood H.
197866	"	McEwing H.
195371	"	McCarthy T.
197865	"	McPherson A.
121010	"	Malpas H.
167120	"	McWilliams T.
167074	"	McGeishie W.
168564	"	Miller W.
150416	"	Mullet E.H.
L.28129	"	Marshall L.
L.25842	"	Marshall H.
L.25536	"	Mansfield W.G.
L.25392	"	Milnes H.
L.29297	"	Noble J.
L.25443	"	Nutall P.
L.28186	"	Parkin J.C.
L.29272	"	Parker W.
L.25776	"	Pearson H.
L.25506	"	Pearson F.
L.28185	"	Proctor R.W.
L.25513	"	Peace A.

L.25584	Gnr. Quanmby W.H.	L.9419	Dr. Bradford H.
L.2565	" Rushworth A.	L.28013	" Sykes W.
L.32451	" Roberts J.	D.99859	" Spencer P.G.
L.28006	" Singleton H.W.	L.25635	" Shaw E.
L.28151	" Slack A.W.	L.25503	" Shaw H.
8610	" Squire A.B.	L.28136	" Shaw N.
12107	" Starinsky J.A.	L.28224	2 Shaw C.A.
L.25781	" Sykes J.	L.25450	" Smith J.R.
52972	" Stocker H.G.	L.25797	" Singleton V.
L.25566	" Shaw J.C.	40554	" Taylor B.
81446	" Slack H.	L.28101	" Taylor T.N.
126074	" Spence B.	L.25460	" Twigg J.
L.25735	" Spencer H.	L.25483	" Varley L.
L.25771	" Thompson J.	L.28214	" Wood W.N.
L.29359	" Townend P.	L.25650	" Wood A.
L.29315	" Townend J.	L.10586	" Westgate P.
L.3255	" Thornber W.H.	L.29331	" Woodcock A.
L.25539	" Thompson J.W.	L.28087	" Walters H.
L.25764	" Wilkinson B.	L.25394	" Wortley T.
L.28018	" Wilkinson T.X	L.25541	" Woodhead E.
L.29500	" Wood P.	L.25819	" Whitehead J.A.
L.32441	" Walker A.	L.25571	" Wilson J.
L.32469	" Wilson J.		
L.25844	" Weldrake E.	Attached:-	
L.29318	" Wood R.		
L.25649	" Wood G.E.		2/Lt. A. C. Miller.
		L.29345	Gnr. Craigie T.
107780	Dr. Archer W.		
81590	" Black A.	S.E.1514 A.V.C.Sgt. Jolly A.J.	
L.25524	" Balmforth H.		
L.28034	" Beaver M.		
L.25525	" Bray H.		
L.25456	" Brearley A.		
L.25587	" Brown H.		
L.25660	" Brooke L.		
L.25395	" Brook G.L.		
L.25658	" Chapman B.		
L.29325	" Cartwright P.		
L.25592	" Crowther J.C.		
5802	" Connor J.		
L.25843	" Digman W.J.		
L.29409	" Dyson W.		
L.28079	" Green F.		
L.25820	" Ganley J.		
L.29316	" Gledhill J.R.		
L.25472	" Green N.		
L.25579	" Griffiths T.C.		
L.25677	" Holroyd H.		
L.28153	" Harrison E.		
L.28201	" Horsfall E.		
L.28075	" Hirst J.		
L.25849	" Holmes E.		
L.29347	" Harncastle S.W.		
L.29417	" Hinchcliffe H.		
L.25519	" Holding J.		
L.32467	" Hirst F.A.		
L.29325	" Jessop E.L.O.		
L.3241	" Kershaw C.		
L.25419	" Kerton B.		
L.28163	" Lodge A.		
L.25384	" Livesey F.C.		
L.28022	" Marsden J.A.		
L.28021	" Millington J.A.		
L.25639	" Millard H.		
L.25641	" Murphy H.		
L.32474	" Malone W.		
L.32464	" Pogson S.		
L.28153	" Priest J.W.		
L.147602	" Orriss H.		
L.25864	" Quinn D.		
L.28074	" Robertshaw G.		
L.28075	" Roe P.		

"B" Battery   - : -   168th Bde. R.F.A.

Nominal Roll of all Ranks 31/1/17.

Officers.   Major F. FitzGibbon.
                 Capt. H. Stead.
                 2/Lt. W. P. Robinson.
                 2/Lt. E. Fisher.
                 2/Lt. L. M. Hastings.
                 2/Lt. W. L. Chamberlain.

Other Ranks.

58482	B.S.M. Stenning T.		L.25382	Gnr Ainley W.H.
L.32457	B.Q.M.S.Lane A.G.		L.25418	" Battye T.
L.32514	Bar.Sgt.Sutcliffe R.		L.32549	" Berry A.
L.25448	Sergt.Beaumont F.		L.25616	" Billington T.
L.29324	" Chambers W.		L.32483	" Binns A.O.
L.25599	" Crooks H.		L.32521	" Bottoms H.
L.25420	" Deakin T.		L.25873	" Broadbent T.
L.29344	" Guthrie A.		L.29265	" Broadley J.
1918	" Harding R.		L.25756	" Broomhead H.
L.25606	" Palframan F.		L.32496	" Burton G.
L.25862	Cpl Hartley J.A.		L.29383	" Dewar W.
L.29357	" Reeves A.		L.25671	" Cocker F.
L.25481	" S/S Sykes A.		L.29363	" Crowland B.
L.29390	Cpl.Taylor H.		79093	" Drewitt H.
L.25871	" Walker S.		L.29392	" Eccles J.
L.25484	" Williams C.		L.29263	" Fowler B.
L.25864	" Mason R.		11578	" Gouldsmith S.C.
L.25716	" Fisher W.W.		L.29262	" Greenwood L.A.
L.25446	Bdr.Bottomley T.		L.29244	" Greenwood A.A.
L.25663	" Holmes L.		L.29380	" Hanson E.
L.29241	" Martin F.		L.25746	" Hargreaves A.
L.25416	" Pullan H.		L.32454	" Hargreaves D.
L.25874	" Shaw L.		111819	" Harris G.
L.25451	" Spendlove T.		L.25554	" Harrison W.
L.28210	" Greenwood M.R.		L.25664	" Hartley A.
L.29326	" Temperton H.K.		L.29399	" Hallos J.W.
L.28138	" Bramley S.M.		L.29242	" Hoyle G.G.
L.29360	" Thornton J.		L.28046	" Holdsworth A.
L.25545	" Turner J.F.		L.25689	" Kenyon J.H.
L.32480	a/Br Bancroft L.		L.25458	" Kiddle F.
L.25756	" Broomhead W.H.		L.32510	" Knight S.
L.28043	" Burch H.		L.25562	" Lawford P.
125511	" Christie H.		L.28220	" Laycock A.
L.28028	" Croft J.H.		L.25623	" Lee F.
16381	" Cawthorne J.		L.25622	" Littlewood A.
L.25547	" Ibbotson M.		28126	" Mallinson F.
L.24990	" Mayers A.		L.29400	" Mitchell D.
L.28213	" Dyson A.		L.32544	" Mitchell R.
5035	S/S Boswell H.		L.28076	" Murray A.
L.29263	" Driver W.		L.29402	" Murray E.
L.25552	" Hoyle C.		L.29395	" Noble F.
L.25510	Gnr.(Cold Shoer) Beadyhough G.W.		L.25632	" Onyon A.
L.25462	S/S Sidebottom J.		L.25836	" Owen W.
L.32552	Gnr.(Cold Shoer) Wilson J.W.		L.25827	" Riddlesden A.
L.25747	Sdlr.Brookspank G.		L.29832	" Riley A.
L.25607	" Stansfield F.		L.25463	" Scott N.
L.25596	Whlr.Yates F.		L.25491	" Sherwood J.N.
L.32456	Fttr.Hill W.		53092	" Scrubbs H.
			L.32473	" Stafford H.

L.29272	Gnr	Tidswell H.G	
11425	"	Thomas O.	
L.25689	"	Thompson J.N.	
L.25629	"	Turner H.	
L.25727	"	Wingtringham B.	
L.29431	"	Wood G.H.	
L.25704	"	Youngman A.	
Dx 5828	"	Spence J.	
18829	"	Brown F.	
15077	"	Woolfe G.H.	
197864	"	McPherson D.	
197862	"	McLennan J.V.	
150377	"	Miller G.W.	
197865	"	MacBried D.	
164025	"	Miller L.	
152712	"	Mason J.	
L.29381	Dvr	Barraclough H.	
L.29258	"	Barraclough T.E.	
L.28213	"	Beaumont H.	
L.28199	"	Beryy A.	
L.29245	"	Berry A.	
L.25857	"	Berry S.	
L.32576	"	Bentley T.	
L.32528	"	Borrisow F.	
L.32566	"	Braithwaite J.N.	
L.25470	"	Brook J.W.	
L.25471	"	Buckley T.	
L.25878	"	Clear A.	
L.32443	"	Crossley A.	
L.28112	"	Crossley F.	
L.28113	"	Crossley J.	
L.32518	"	Crowther J.	
L.25446	"	Davies J.W.	
L.25742	"	Dyson F.	
L.25442	"	Eastwood G	
L.25608	"	Ellis M.	
L.25732	"	Firth H.	
L.32578	"	Gray D.	
L.29367	"	Greenwood J.W.	
L.25728	"	Greenwood C.	
L.25831	"	Hall H.	
L.28204	"	Harrison F.	
L.25479	"	Hattersley F.	
L.32524	"	Hawthornthwaite T.	
L.25822	"	Hinchcliffe A.	
L.25558	"	Hopson A.	
L.32506	"	Holmes W.	
L.29403	"	Horrocks H.	
L.28070	"	Howett J.H.	
L.28132	"	Martin J.	
L.29270	"	Leagard B.	
L.28077	"	Martin L.	
L.28066	"	Mealey O.	
L.28127	"	Mellor H.	
L.29401	"	Moody A.	
L.25870	"	Murray R.	
L.25675	"	Nicholson J.	
L.28194	"	North M	
L.25882	"	Pearson W.	
L.28071	"	Robinson F	
L.25861	"	Robinson T.	
L.29416	"	Robinson W.	
L.25512	"	Robinson W.J.	
L.25730	"	Rushworth B.	
L.25625	"	Scott J.J.	
L.28041	"	Schofield A.	
L.25464	"	Senior G.	
L.32579	"	Shepperd N.	
L.25644	"	Singleton L.N.	
L.25454	"	Snell A.	

L.29397	Dvr	Southwell J.
L.29090	"	Stanton A.
L.31009	"	Sugden C.
L.25569	"	Turner J.
L.25866	"	Townsend H.
L.25598	"	Townsend W.
L.25499	"	Tallis G.
L.25793	"	Tyas J.M.
L.28142	"	Walker J.
L.32567	"	Walker M.
L.25661	"	Wheelwright G.
L.32515	"	Wilkinson L.
L.29257	"	Wilkinson F.
L.29269	"	Wood H.
L.28089	"	Wright F.
97890	"	Butler J.
23748	"	Leckenby J.

Attached.

8949 A.V.C. Sgt. White F.A.

"J" Battery   - : -   168th Bde. R.F.A.

Nominal Roll of all ranks - 31/1/17.

Officers.   Major H. Cottee.
                 Capt. L. G. Firth.
                 Lieut B. T. Groves.
                 2/Lt. H. Lockwood.
                 2/Lt. H. L. James.
                 2/Lt. G.O.J.Barrick.

Other Ranks.

53473	B.S.M. Melone M.J.		4770	Gnr Anderson F.H.
L.2568	B.Q.M.S. Tomlinson S.		14764	" Balls H.M.
L.27727	Sergt Ward A.		L.11994	" Barr J.
L.11952	" Oates R.W.		L.11929	" Brady E.
L.11951	" Townsend W.		L.11966	" Bridgland G.W.
L.19483	" Booth P.P.		L.12026	" Beach J.
L.12004	" Turgoose W.		L.19485	" Briggs E.J.
L.25389	" Kettlewell E.		L.25575	" Booth H?
L.11973	Cpl Booth J.		L.27987	" Broadhead F.
53807	" Keefe J.		L.29303	" Bottomley G.J.
L.11925	" Imms E.		L.28200	" Brook H.
22239	" Fitzgerald W.		L.11981	" Cockell G.
L.29412	" Brown T.		14711	" Creeper H.
6086	" Broderick W.		10790	" Copping H.E.
L.19494	" Marshall H.		L.28147	" Chapman T.
L.19481	Bdr Ward J.S.		60219	" Dennison J.
L.19479	" Wardle L.M.		L.25702	" Denton F.
L.19478	" Todd J.A.		L.11921	" Drabble H.
L.19482	" Barey P.P.		129947	" Deveany F.
L.12055	" " Sanderson G.		L.29414	" Elliott C.
L.27730	" Walton H.		L.25411	" Ellis W.
L.12027	" McGuire J.F.G.		78830	" Frazer J.
L.19484	" Bailey B.C.		L.12017	" Farmery J.W.
L.28121	" Palmer R.		L.12019	" Froggett E.
L.28195	" Garside J.		L.12092	" Garfoot P.W.
L.12028	" Craven W.A.		L.19489	" Gregory H.S.
L.11993	a/Bdr Holroyd T.		16372	" Goddard W.E.
L.11930	" Theobald B.J.		L.11975	" Howarth H.
L.11959	" Ellis W.R.		L.11992	" Halton R.
L.19487	" Carr W.C.		L.12054	" Harrison G.W.
L.19519	" Milnthorpe G.		L.11989	" Howarth R.
10077	" Carruthers T.		88771	" Hall N.
L.25812	" Terry L.		L.19494	" Horner C.
L.25473	" Earnshaw S.		54446	" Hutt R.
L.29308	" Sanderson H.		39444	" Holden F.
37207	" Smith J.W.		L.25751	2 Higgins H.
30751	Far.Sgt.Bishop G.		11074	" Huggett T.
L.11991	Cpl.S/S Halton G.		28102	" Hirst N.
L.11926	S/S Fletcher F.		L.11938	" Hissatt H.
L.27751	" Bailey H.		L.12020	" Inman H
L.25954	" Chappell E.		63915	" Irving W.A.
L.11934	(Cold Shoer) Ismay G.H.		120111	" Jolly W.
L.19518	" Thompson J.		L.19809	" James ".
L.29360	Cpl.Ftr.Hincholiffe J.		L.12201o	" Kenny S.
L.14862	Whlr.Pringle E.		L.25575	" Lee H.
L.11918	Sdlr Iveson J.		L.19514	" Lynes J.
L.11937	" Hall J.		L.12047	" Martin T.
			L.11968	" Mosley C.
			L.11932	" Mulheir J.W.
			L.12002	" Nowell E.M.
			L.11971	" Parkin W.
			134691	" Robinson A.E.
			8864	" Richardson E.A.

L.19496	Gnr	Saberton H.	L.28051	Dvr	Parkin H.
L.27999	"	Spittle T.A.	L.25856	"	Pogson H.
95007	"	Smith C.A.	L.12011	"	Roberts E.W.
L.19907	"	Swinn J.	L.11965	"	Ross G.A.
3802	"	Thompson P.	L.28134	"	Roberts W.
L.25115	"	Taylor J.T.	L.19497	"	Schofield W.
L.19502	"	Wales W.	L.12033	"	Senior E.K.
L.19500	"	Walston L.	12013	"	Shipman H.
L.12009	"	Waldron T.	L.29293	"	Sutcliffe W.
L.19503	"	Watson G.	L.28164	"	Spivey P.
L.19616	"	Waller A.E.	L.28194	"	Scott J.R.
L.12007	"	Wilkinson P.	L.28010	"	Steele J.W.
L.11967	"	Wilcock G.	L.25448	"	Singleton N.
51602	"	Wright H.	L.29309	"	Simpson G.A.
L.19717	"	Wardle G.H.	L.27993	"	Senior J.W.
			L.11920	"	Thompson R.
			L.27747	"	Toothill A.C.
L.12022	Dvr	Ainsworth H.	L.32459	"	Turner H.
L.11919	"	Backhouse G.H.	L.27986	"	Taylor A.E.
L.19504	"	Blackburn J.	L.28095	"	Turner A.B.
L.11942	"	Boulton P.	L.12035	"	Wethey A.
L.12000	"	Brook J.	L.12008	"	Wales A.
L.11935	"	Brooks G.	L.12021	"	Walshaw E.
L.11980	"	Burnley W.S.	L.12006	"	Wrigglesworth F.
L.28116	"	Broadbent J.	L.11940	"	Woollen H.
L.29280	"	Bradley H.	L.11973	"	Williams J.I.
L.11982	"	Clark G.W.	L.28124	"	Walton R.
57926	"	Coles J.	L.27322	"	White L.
L.28197	"	Crawshaw H.	L.1344	"	Young I.
L.25612	"	Clark R.W.	L.28169	"	Williams J.
L.28232	"	Chapman J.			
50755	"	Chapman W.			
L.11969	"	Eubank J.A.			
L.28107	"	Ellis H.			
L.25474	"	Earnshaw B.			
L.12055	"	Farmery T.	Attached:-		
L.19515	"	Firth G.			
L.19506	"	Fretwell H.	2489 A.V.C.Sgt Harding W.		
L.12037	"	Garfitt J.T.			
L.19520	"	Garfoot E.			
L.11922	"	Hulley A.W.			
L.11964	"	Hunter J.			
L.11941	"	Hirst W.			
L.11967	"	Hancock N.			
L.19510	"	Horsfall E.			
L.19519	"	Hudson J.			
L.28054	"	Ingham A.			
L.12041	"	Kershaw H.			
L.11979	"	Kemp R.			
L.19492	"	Lapish J.			
L.19513	"	Lamb M.			
L.29285	"	Lord J.			
L.28051	"	Lawton H.			
85728	"	Maddocks J.			
L.11919	"	Marshall S.			
L.18909	"	Mitchell W.			
77571	"	O'Keefe J.A.			
6074	"	Overland H.			
L.11949	"	Pickard H.			
75445	"	Pipe E.			
L.87691	"	Poynton G.W.			
L.19516	"	Priestley B.			
L.2869	"	Price W.			

779.

"D" Battery   -:-   168th Bde. R.F.A.

Nominal Roll of all ranks - 31/1/17.

Officers:-
        Major D.K. Tweedie.
        Lieut. R. Dunbar.
        Lieut N. Back.
        2/Lt. G.C. Wood.
        2/Lt. A.A. Steward.
        2/Lt. J.J. Caterer.
        2/Lt. E.P. Peel.

Other Ranks:-

No.	Rank	Name	No.	Rank	Name
1370	B.S.M.	Perigo W.	128068	Gnr	Allen C.
100360	Far.Sgt.	Greenwood J.	19896	"	Badger J.
11948	Sgt.	Allen A.J.	26385	"	Bowler H.E.
889548	"	Durrant S.P.	27580	"	Briddock J.A.
35385	"	Hartley B.W.	889514	"	Barker J.A.
265	"	Jefferys S.A.	889522	"	Barker W.
19894	"	Lambley J.		"	Bellamy J.
29329	"	Rothery W.	35665	"	Burke C.
889613	"	Terry W.B.	889513	"	Barker W.H.
78512	Cpl.S/S	Emms A.	25688	"	Caine J.E.
26450	"	Sdlr Mawson J.J.	889536	"	Carmen J.
27618	"	Ftr. Thresh E.	889530	"	Cook B.
35409	"	Dinsdale J.	889521	"	Cook G.F.
19965	"	Hawks T.J.H.	889636	"	Carver J.
27518	"	Holmes G.	19947	"	Dalby E.
889591	"	Philpot J.E.	27596	"	Dixon H.A.
35406	"	Sykes H.F.	889542	"	Dunnett J.
889599	"	Stannard G.	27537	"	Elson G.H.
19914	"	Wooffitt P.E.	27175	"	Fowler A.S.
27756	Bdr	Bonner S.	19950	"	Flannigan J.
27590	"	Bradford J.	12271	"	Fell W.
889568	"	Browse S.A.	40484	"	Goodman A.
35389	"	Dobson J.E.	19848	"	Hellawell G.W.
19930	"	Flannigan P.	97625	"	Howlett S.
27757	"	Hetherington J.	35413	"	Hadley J.
889561	"	Hollingsworth R.	148368	"	Keene T.C.
12257	"	Husband A.	889571	"	Lovvett C.
19840	"	Hempsall J.	889569	"	Lamb S.
889565	"	Jackson A.A.	25317	"	Langford W.G.
889575	"	Last S.	27510	"	Marshall H.
19919	"	Scholey E.	21259	"	MacLennan J.
26400	"	Smith W.	889578	"	Mudd B.
26452	a/Br	Bellamy J.W.	27532	"	Newton L.
889512	"	Bloomsfield S.	19796	"	Parkinson G.H.
19887	"	Foster C.	889585	"	Peck J.W.
35381	"	Guest W.	889590	"	Palmer J.
35195	"	Hamilton T.	28069	"	Ramsden S.
47370	"	McCanesky J.	124923	"	Richardson H.
889607	"	Spinks D.E.	26125	"	Simmons H.A.
86458	"	Voce R.	27520	"	Stacey I.
889533	S/S/Br	Gutteridge A.	27676	"	Starkey E.
27520	S/S	Hellawell A.	26449	"	Shaw F.
27497	"	Innocent R.	129128	"	Smith W.E.
19984	"	Methley J.	889608	"	Simmons W.
27759	"	Popplewell G.		"	Sartbn H.
27612	"	Smith J.	889604	"	Smith F.J.
26447	"	Varney J.	26463	"	Townsend A.B.
78446	Sdlr.	Batley J.	20010	"	Thompson J.
115012	"	Molyneaux D.	35391	"	Trimby J.
26676	"	Schofield J.	889584	"	Todd C.R.
146171	Ftr.	Collar P.A.	889614	"	Thody A.

12044	Gnr	Ward E.		27609	Dvr	Smith J.
5404	"	Williams J.		29405	"	Stewart A.
889623	"	Watling B.		26411	"	Speight A.
889652	"	Woodward F.		26568	"	Spencer C.
889624	"	Wain F.		27505	"	Shone W.
				27600	"	Sykes J.
				889600	"	Smith A.W.
27627	Dvr	Ackroyd T.			"	Skelt E.
27601	"	Archer S.T.		889601	"	Sustins E.
19783	"	Armitage G.		34341	"	Turner A.
5402	"	Bainbridge J.		19736	"	Thompson A.D.
27757	"	Battin W.		24085	"	Tilston R.
26401	"	Bell A.		27566	"	Trafford I.
26524	"	Bellamy F.		71271	"	Thompson J.G.H.
5390	"	Becket E.		889616	"	Theobald W.
12107	"	Bond P.		889611	"	Lampin A.
27615	"	Bowers F.		889612	"	Taylor E.
28059	"	Barker W.		889615	"	Thompson S.
20007	"	Bradley J.		12057	"	Wilkinson J.W.
889511	"	Bell C.		27758	"	Wood J.
889546	"	Bolton E.		27498	"	Wright D.
889521	"	Bunn A.		19794	"	Wheelan J.
889509	"	Brightwell E.		154969	"	Whitaker W.
889510	"	Barton S.		25718	"	Wilson J.
20008	"	Croft J.		889627	"	Watson C.
889529	"	Creed R.		889631	"	Whitehead J.
889581	"	Cocker P.				
889534	"	Chittock A.			Attached:-	
27621	"	Denby F.				
27622	"	Dixon L.		8038	A.V.C.Sgt.	Moore W.
889535	"	Driver R.				
27606	"	Fisher A.				
19799	"	Fisher G.				
19944	"	Flint F.				
889532	"	Fisker C.				
19841	"	Gillman B.T.S.				
19943	"	Green J.				
19803	"	Greenwood J.				
889556	"	Gardner G.E.				
889555	"	Gray S.B.				
20002	"	Hanson C.B.				
1986	"	Hempsall T.				
26422	"	Havenhand H.				
19953	"	Howson W.				
19749	"	Hughes H.				
889563	"	Honeywood B.				
4896	"	Hutchins J.				
27610	"	Jewitt W.				
5411	"	Jackson F.				
51126	"	Johnson P.H.				
5576	"	Lowe G.				
5380	"	Lunn G.				
92590	"	Lewellyn T.				
889570	"	Lay G.				
5379	"	Middleton W.				
5414	"	Padgett J.E.				
19789	"	Peacook J.E.				
25560	"	Palmer J.				
27598	"	Pollard J.				
27222	"	Philips F.				
19939	"	Porter E.				
889587	"	Piper W.				
81641	"	Penny H.				
26410	"	Roper W.				
27594	"	Roebuck L.				
27624	"	Roebuck V.				
889596	"	Reid A.				
889595	"	Raynor H.				
40494	"	Seabrook U.H.				
26406	"	Savage W.				

168th Brigade R.F.A.

Nominal Roll of all ranks who have joined the Brigade during January, 1917.

'A' Battery.

B.25158	Sgt.	Williamson A.
53261	"	Smith E.F.
1103	"	Witney W.
5802	Dvr.	Connor J.
197866	Gnr.	McEwing H.
86276	"	Franklin A.
81590	Dvr.	Black A.
195371	Gnr.	McCarthy B.
197865	"	McPherson A.
121010	"	Malpas H.
12049	"	Edward L.
60200	"	Fuller B.
85294	Cpl.	Simpson C.
167120	Gnr.	McWilliams.
167074	"	McCeashie W.
168564	"	Mellor W.
150416	"	Mallet E.H.

'B' Battery.

1988	Sgt.	Harding E.
150377	Gnr.	Miller L.
152302	"	Milner J.
152742	"	Mason J.
58282	"	Spence J.
14829	"	Brown P.
150477	"	Woolfe C.H.
197861	"	McPherson H.
197862	"	McLennan J.B.
197865	"	McRae D.
97980	Dvr.	Butler J.
23748	"	Lechenby H.

'C' Battery.

2/Lieut. G.O.J. Barrick.

'D' Battery.

889515	Dvr.	Driver R.
889601	"	Whitehead J.
889587	"	Piper W.
889534	"	Chittock A.
889615	"	Thompson S.
889601	"	Sustins E.
4986	"	Hutchins J.

"D" Battery.

263	Sgt.	Jeffery W.
	Lieut.	Back N.
	2/Lt.	Peel E.P.
889613	Sgt.	Terry W.H.
889548	"	Durrant S.P.
889599	"	Stannard G.
889551	Cpl.	Philpots G.E.
889568	Bdr.	Browse S.A.
889561	"	Hollingworth R.
889565	"	Jackson A.A.
889575	"	Last S.
889512	a.Bdr.	Broomfield S.
889607	"	Spinks B.R.
86458	"	Voce R.
889533	S/aBr.	Guttridge A.
889514	Gnr.	Barker J.A.
889522	Gnr.	Barker W.
889571	"	Lovvatt C.
	"	Bellamy G.
889578	"	Mudd B.
889536	"	Curmen G.
889585	"	Peck J.W.
889584	"	Todd C.E.
	"	Surtin H.
889604	"	Smith F.J.
889623	"	Watling B.
889542	"	Dunnitt G.
889590	"	Palmer J.
889550	"	Cook B.
889531	"	Cook G.N.
889614	"	Thody A.
5665	"	Burke C.
889569	"	Lamb S.
889513	"	Barker W.H.
889632	"	Woodward F.
889624	"	Wain F.
889636	"	Carver J.
889608	"	Simmons W.
889616	Dvr.	Theobald W.
889563	"	Honeywood B.
889511	"	Bell C.
889600	"	Smith A.W.
889696	"	Reid A.
889546	"	Bolton E.
889556	"	Garner G.E.
889570	"	Lay G.
889627	"	Watson C.
889521	"	Bunn A.
	"	Skelt E.
889529	"	Creed R.
	"	Penny H.
889511	"	Tampin A.
889595	"	Rayner H.
889532	"	Fisker C.
889612	"	Taylor E.
889509	"	Brightwell E.
889581	"	Cocker B.
889555	"	Gray S.V.
889510	"	Barton S.

168th Brigade R.F.A.

Nominal Roll of all ranks who have left
during January 1917.

'A' Battery

L.32529 Gnr Booth H.
L.25776 Cpl Lewis R.J.
13769 Dr Campey H.
L.28008 " Shaw J.
L.22568 " Sykes J.H.
L.28174 A/Br Tetlow H.
L.28221 Gnr Merriman H.A.
L.32553 Bdr Taylor W.J.
L.25792 aBr Thompson P.S.
49393 Dvr Blake W.
12879 " Ridsdale C.
L.28172 aBr Iredale W.H.

'C' Battery.

L.11939 Gnr Prince W.J.
L.29286 " Fearns P.
L.28115 Sgt.Andrews R.

'B' Battery.

L.25786 Sgt Naylor S.
L.25416 Bdr Pullan H.
26363 Dvr.Wilkins R.C.J.
L.25774 " McVeagh T.
L.25655 Gnr Bentley H.V.
L.25723 Gnr.Scott E.
L.29390 " Ashworth B.
L.29301 " Brooke E.
L.32478 " Wiadop T.
L.25725 " Toothill E.
5035 S/S Boswell H.
L.29286

'D' Battery.

L.19893 Cpl Lomas S.

Headquarters Staff

31508 A/R.S.M. Smith. W.

CONFIDENTIAL.

WAR DIARY

of

168th. BRIGADE, R.F.A.

from 1st. February 1917 to 28th. February 1917.

(Volumne 14.)

Army Form C. 2118.

WAR DIARY
or
INTELLIGENCE SUMMARY.
(Erase heading not required.)

168th Brigade. R.F.A.

Commanded by Lt-Col. R. FITZMAURICE.

Ref. Sheet HEBUTERNE.
57d. N.E. 3 & 4 (Parts of)
1/10,000

Place	Date	Hour	Summary of Events and Information	Remarks and references to Appendices
HEBUTERNE.	1/2/17.	9 a.m.	1/161 reverts to control of its own Brigade. 168th. Brigade R.F.A. covers left Battalion front only, its defensive barrage covering from K.29.d.0.2 to K.25.d.7.5.	
	2/2/17.	12 midnight.	168th Brigade R.F.A. comes under the orders of O.C. 155 th Bde. R.F.A. under 3.B.A., 19th Division. All orders, night lines, etc., issued by O.C. 155th. Brigade, R.F.A.	
	4/2/17.	9 p.m.	Lt-ANLEY of A/168 died from rheumatism caused by severe burns through hut catching fire.	
	5/2/17.	2.15 pm.	Wagon Lines inspected by Lt-Col. R. FITZMAURICE R.F.A.	
	7/2/17.	10 a.m. to 2 p.m.	Enemy shelled 'B' Battery heavily, causing three casualties.	
	9/2/17.	9 p.m.	'A' Battery was shelled with Gas Shells. Five men were gassed and had to be taken to hospital.	
	10/2/17.	8.15 pm.	To assist the 2nd Division on our Right who attacked Ten Tree Alley, 'B' & 'C' Batteries fired in WHITE TRENCH & CHALK ALLEY. The attack was a great success, and 215 prisoners were taken. These batteries also assisted twice during enemy counter attacks.	
	11/2/17.	11.15 pm.	Our batteries covered the 10th. Worcestershire Regt. during a raid on enemy trenches in K.29.b. which unfortunately was unsuccessful.	
	11th to 17th. 2/17.		Brigade still under control of O.C. 155 th Bde. R.F.A. This period was very uneventful.	
	18/2/17.	4 p.m.	The batteries of the 168th Bde R.F.A. withdrawn from the line and proceed to their Wagon Lines, where they again come under the control of O.C. 168th Bde. R.F.A.	

Army Form C. 2118.

WAR DIARY
or
INTELLIGENCE SUMMARY.
(Erase heading not required.)

168th Brigade, R.F.A. Commanded by Lt-Colonel R. FITZMAURICE.

Remarks and references to Appendices:
Ref:- Sheets 1/100,000
LENS 11
AMIENS 17.   66 E. NE. + 66 d. NW.
                         1/20,000

Place	Date	Hour	Summary of Events and Information
WARSNIES	19/2/17	9 a.m.	The Brigade marched to WARSNIES and remained there until the 21st Feb: 1917.
	20/2/17		Lt-Col. FITZMAURICE returned to the brigade after acting C.R.A. 32nd Division for the last month.
ARGOEUVES	21/2/17	9 a.m.	The Brigade marched to ARGOEUVES
	22/2/17	10 a.m.	" " " DOM RT SUR LA LUCE
DOMART	23/2/17	9 a.m.	Battery Commanders visited the positions, O.P's, etc., of batteries being relieved.
	24/2/17	9 a.m.	The Brigade marched to Wagon line at LE QUESNEL and then into action as per Operation Order No. attached.
	26/2/17	10 a.m.	The relief of the 2nd. Regt. Artillery. 27th French Division by 168th. Bde. R.F.A. was completed and to relieved and positions of same as follows :-
			H.Q. 168 — H.Q. 2nd Regt. artillery - L.1.a.2.6.
			A/168. (5 guns) 4th Battery. " L.17.d.7.6.
			A/168. (2 guns) 5th. " " L.8.a.15.19
			B/168. " 6th. " " E.26.b.65.65
			B/168. " 6th. " " E.26.b.15.80.
			C/168. " 9th. " " F.20.d.2.5.
			C/168. " 8th. " " "
			C/168. " 7th. " " F.20.d.4.6
			D/168. 6 Hows. Unoccupied position.
	27/2/17		Brigade H.Q. moved to L.8.d.7.2.
	28/2/17		" " " L.1.a.2.6.

1st March 1917.

M. Purcell Maj. for Lieut-Colonel.
Commanding 168th. Brigade, R.F.A.

SECRET.   Copy No..........

LEFT GROUP
OPERATION ORDER No.17.

Reference Sheet 66c.N.E. & 66d. N.W.   Monday 26th February 1917.

The 168th Brigade R.F.A. less half of 'A' Battery will comprise the Left Group, 32nd Divnl. Artillery under the Command of Lt-Col. E. FITZMAURICE from 10 a.m. on the 26th. February 1917.

1.   Zones and Night Lines of batteries are as follows :-

Position.	Map: Ref.	O.P.	Zones.
A 1.	L.8.a.15.10.	LA HAVATTE.- L.16.c.5.6.	L.17.a. 6.4. to L.11.c. 8.6.
B 1.	F.26.b.65.65	ARRAS - L.10.b.25.80	L.11.c. 8.6. to L.11.b. 2.8.
B 2.	F.26.b.15.80.	DAVOUS. - L.5.c.15.65	L.11.b. 2.8 to L. 6.c. 2.8.
C 1.	L.20.d. 2.3.		L. 6.c. 2.8. to G. 1.b. 3.4.
C 2.	L.20.d. 4.6.		G. 1.b. 3.4. to A.26.d. 8.4.
D.Hows.	L.8.a.70.65	ARRAS - L.10.b.25.80.	L.17.a. 6.4. to A.26.d. 8.4.

Night Lines :-
  18-Pounders - Night lines will be arranged so as to
                 cover the whole zone by sweeping.

  4.5"Hows.   - L.11.d.5.20   - L.11.d. 3.4.
                 G. 1.d.30.65 - A.26.c. 1.2.
  Counter Battery Section.
                 L.11.b.50.75 - L. 6.c. 2.3.

2.   On receiving an S.O.S. Call, the Rates of fire will be as per 32nd Divisional Artillery Instructions of to-day.

3.   As the 18-Pdr. barrage is very thin, the Divisional Front will be divided into barrage zones numbered from one to six - from South to North.
        The three zones on the Left Group front will be covered by batteries as follows on receipt of code call :-

Zone.	Code Call.	Battery.	German Front Line.	Rate of Fire
4.	Barrage Four.	A 1.	L.17.a. 6.4 to L.17.a. 7.7.	
"	" "	A 2.	L.17.a. 7.7. to L.11.c. 7.0	As
"	" "	B 1 & 2.	L.11.c. 7.0 to L.11.c.75.65	
"	" "	C 1 & 2.	L.11.c.75.65 to L.11.a. 9.2	for
"	" "	D. Hows.	Trench Junctions:- L.17.b.00.55 -- L.11.d.00.15 L.17.c.95.92 -- L.17.b.70.48 Counter Bty. Section:- L.11.d. 3.7 -- L.11.d.5.20.	S.O.S.

(Continued)

Zone.	Code Call.	Battery.	German Front Line.	Rate of Fire.
5.	Barrage Five.	A 2.	L.11.a. 9.2 to L.11.b. 1.6	
"	" "	B1 & 2.	L.11.b. 1.6 to L.5.d. 4.4.	As
"	" "	C1 & 2.	L.5.d. 4.4 to L.6.c. 2.8	
"		D.Hows.	Trench Junctions:-	for
			L.11.b. 8.0 -- L.6.c.15.30	
			L.5.d. 7.0 -- L.12.a.20.85.	S. O. S.
			Counter Bty Section:-	
			L.11.b.55.75 -- L.11.b. 3.4.	
6.	Barrage Six.	B1 & 2.	L. 6.c. 2.8 to G. 1.b.22.22	
"	" "	C1 & 2.	G. 1.b.22.22 to A.25.d. 8.4	As
"	" "	D. Hows.	Trench Junctions:-	for
			L. 6.c.85.40 -- G. 1.d.20.63	
			G. 1.b.6.10 -- A.26.c. 1.2	
			Counter Bty Section:-	S. O. S.
			G. 1.b.95.50 -- A.26.c. 3.0	

    18-pdr batteries will sweep their allotted zones in all barrages.
    All S.O.S. Barrages will fall in No Man's Land in front of German Front Line.
    Rates of Fire - As for S.O.S.

    The Section of D/168 detailed for Counter Battery work will in case of S.O.S. fire on barrage until it is called upon for Counter Battery Work.

4.   MUTUAL SUPPORT.
    In case of "Attack Expected or Actual Attack" on Right of 5th Division, B/168 (6 Guns) will fire on German Front Line from A.25.d. 6.3 to A.26.b. 4.5.
    Rate of Fire - as for S.O.S.
    Code Call :- "Defend Centre Division".

5.   A C K N O W L E D G E.

26th February 1917.

                             Alan Lumb.   2/Lieut.
                             Adjt. L E F T   G R O U P,
                             32nd. Divisional Artillery.

Headquarters staff -:o:- 168th Bde. R.F.A.

Nominal Roll of all ranks 28/2/17

Officers:-   Lt-Col. R. FITZMAURICE.
              2/Lieut.A. LUMB.
              2/Lieut.J. G. BELL.
              Capt.   D. FERGUSON (R.A.M.C)

Other Ranks:-

L.25839 Cpl Lee G.
L.28154 " Thackra J.T.
  29811 Bdr.Anderton A.
L.29801 " Normanton A.
  12245 a/Br.Wright J.
L.29430 " Eyre F.
L.25881 " Gibson H.
L.28042 " Sugden E.
L.28206 Gnr Ackroyd H.
L.25810 " Bottomley C.
  59688 " Clark B.J.
   5645 " Coley E.
 152003 " Firth H.
  56777 " Grindley W.
L.29404 " Greenwood C.
  55188 " Heard H.
L.25480 " Lucas E.
L.29394 " Rangeley P.S.
L.25399 " Ramsden A.
L.25626 " Slater H.
L.28179 " Sykes J.A.
L.29296 " Windle A.T.
L.27531 " Postlethwaite.T.
L.25422 Dvr.Armytage J.R.
L.32440 " Baker G.
L.32540 " Blake F.
L.28026 " Cowham S.
L.32488 " Dutton J.W.
L.29287 " Fisher S.
  37566 " Hirons E.
   5855 " Gowan W.
L.32511 " Iredale A.
L.25825 " Iredale B.
L.28189 " Mellor A.
L.29351 " Newsome A.E.
  79511 " McIntyre A.
L.29424 " Parker J.
L.29423 " Pollard W.
L.25853 " Radley T.
L.29357 " Reddington M.
L.29389 " Stansfield P.
   6267 S/S Periera A.T.

A.O.C. 625 Stf.Sgt.Barker H. (Artificer)
L.29307 Gnr.Gatley H.
L.25540 Dvr.Smith R.

"A" Battery   -:-   168th Bde R.F.A.

Nominal Roll of all ranks 28-2-17.

Officers:-   Major R. EMMET
                  Capt. W. R. BROWN.
                  Lieut. O. G. d'IVRY
                  2/Lt. W. A. EBEELS.
                  2/Lt. A. C. MILLER.
                  2/Lt. D. FINNIE.

Other ranks :-

28514	B.S.M.	Patchett W.J.	L.25790	Gnr	Allot C.V.
L.28064	BQMS	Brearley H.	L.25595	"	Billington T.
1105	Sgt.	Witney I	L.28014	"	Bray E.H.
53261	"	Smith E.F.	L.28217	"	Bower E.
L.25258	"	Williamson A.	L.25396	"	Beasley G.
L.25426	"	Field P.J.	100556	"	Beamish R.
L.25679	"	Roberts J.F.	100744	"	Baird S.
43212	"	McGowan A.H.	L.28180	"	Bolton H.
L.25425	"	Firth A.	L.28104	"	Barker N.
L.25697	Cpl.	Rhodes L.	L.29579	"	Beaumont L.
L.25561	"	Povey J.	L.32471	"	Calvert F.
L.25619	"	France W.	L.25444	"	Grimlisk M.J.
L.25711	"	Kirkham T.	L.29345	"	Craigie T.
L.25693	"	Littlewood K.	5556	"	Chappell A.
L.29407	"	Taylor F.	L.28178	"	Dawson W.
L.25479	Bdr.	Bentley J.	L2049	"	Edwards L.
L.28100	"	Aitchforth A.	130451	"	Edwards W.
L.29213	"	Armitage W.B.	8627	"	Franklin A.
L.25708	"	Crawshaw J.I.	602006	"	Fuller B.
L.25574	"	Whiteley C.H.	169899	"	Holliday R.
L.28035	"	Barnes H.	L.25823	"	Hynes W.H.
L.25414	"	Wood B.	L.25610	"	Hopwood H.
L.25731	"	Rhodes J.	L.25528	"	Hey J.I.
L.28188	"	Padgett S.	L.28159	"	Hewitt R.
L.25464	"	Richardson G.H.	L.28151	"	Hopson T.C.
L.32581	"	Williams W.J.	L.29427	"	Kettle L.J.
L.25100	L/Br.	Adams H.E.	L.29411	"	Knocton J.
L.28072	"	Bentley C.	L.32512	"	Lumb W.
L.32539	"	Fenton E.	L.28177	"	Leatham F.
L.25768	"	Brooksbank S.	L.28184	"	Lockwood H.
L.25669	"	Oates H.	197866	"	McEwing H.
L.29297	"	Noble C.	95371	"	McCarthy C.
86310	"	Squires A.E.	97863	"	McPherson A.
L.28060	"	Kennedy H.	L.21010	"	Malpas H.
L.32457	S/aBr	Womersley C.	167120	"	McWilliams T.
L.25485	"	Williams G.	167074	"	McKenzie W.
L.28136	"	Shaw N.	168564	"	Miller W.
L.28034	"	Beavers M.	150416	"	Mallet E.H.
43325	F.rsgt	Spillett H.	L.28129	"	Marshall L.
L.25785	Cpl.S/S	Town H.	L.25536	"	Mansfield W.G.
L.28175	S/S	Taylor J.E.	L.25392	"	Milnes H.
L.29262	"	Nuttall G.I.	6011	"	Myber A.
L.28175	"	Waterhouse L.	112757	"	Negus H.
L.25620	"	Kaye J.T.	L.25443	"	Nuttall P.
L.32435	Sdlr	Jackson W.B.	L.4251	"	Offen F.
62728	"	Oliver J.B.	L.28186	"	Perkins J.C.
147472	Ftr	Hellowell A.	L.29272	"	Parker W.
12245	Whlr	Weaver J.	L.25736	"	Pearson H.
			L.29500	"	Pearson F.
			L.28185	"	Procter R.C.

188590	Gnr	Partridge W.	L.28074	Dvr	Robertshaw G.
L.25513	"	Pearce A.	L.28075	"	Roe F.
L159154	"	Piggott E.J.	94119	"	Radford H.
L.25584	"	Quarmby W.H.	L.28015	"	Sykes W.
L.25653	"	Rushworth A.	99859	"	Spencer P.G.
L.32491	"	Roberts J.	L.25633	"	Shaw E.
L.28006	"	Singleton H.W.	L.25505	"	Shaw H.
L.3815?	"	Slack A.W.	L.28224	"	Shaw J.A.
125107	"	Starinsky A.A.	L.25797	"	Singleton V.
L.25781	"	Sykes J.	1405354	"	Taylor B.
52972	"	Stocker H.G.	L.28101	"	Taylor T.H.
L.25566	"	Shaw J.T.	L.25460	"	Twigg J.
81446	"	Slack H.	L.25482	"	Varley L.
126074	"	Spence R.	L.28214	"	Wood W.N.
L.25755	"	Spencer H.	L.25650	"	Wood A.
L.25771	"	Thornton J.	10586	"	Westgate F.
L.29355	"	Townend J.	L.29321	"	Woodcock W.
L.32525	"	Thomber W.H.	L.28087	"	Walters H.
L.25539	"	Thompson J.W.	L.25394	"	Wortley T.
L.25764	"	Wilkinson B.	L.25541	"	Woodhead E.
L.28018	"	Wilkinson T.	L.25819	"	Whitehead J.A.
L.25575	"	Walker W.T.	781609	"	Watson E.
L.29300	"	Wood F.	159419	"	Whelan W.
L.3241	"	Walker A.	L.21116	"	Wainwright W.
L.25844	"	Weldrake E.			
L.29318	"	Wood R.			attached:-
L.25649	"	Wood G.E.			
M152786	"	Walsh E.	S.E.1514	A/L.Sgt	Jolly A.J.
155715	"	Young W.	50427	Gnr.	Ratcliffe W. (N.I.H)
100780	Dvr	Archer W.			
175551	"	Adams F?			
81590	"	Black A.			
L.25524	"	Bamforth H.			
L.25525	"	Bray H.			
L.25436	"	Brearley A.			
L.25660	"	Brooks L.			
L.25595	"	Brook G.L.			
L.25658	"	Chapman B.			
L.29323	"	Cartwright P.			
L.25592	"	Crowther J.G.			
L 5802	"	Conner J.			
L.25845	"	Digman W.J.			
L.29409	"	Dyson W.			
L.28079	"	Green F.			
L.25820	"	Ganley J.			
L.29216	"	Gledhill J.R.			
L.25579	"	Griffiths J.C.			
L.25677	"	Holroyd H.			
L.28153	"	Harrison F.			
L.28201	"	Horsfall E.			
L.28073	"	Hirst J.			
L.25849	"	Holmes B.			
L.29347	"	Hardcastle J.W.			
L.29417	"	Hinchliffe H.			
L.25519	"	Holding J.			
L.29323	"	Jessop E.L.O.			
L.32541	"	Kershaw C.			
L.25419	"	Kerton E.			
L.28163	"	Lodge A.			
L.25784	"	Livesey S.J.			
L.28022	"	Marsden J.A.			
L.28021	"	Mallinson J.A.			
L.25639	"	Millard F.			
L.25641	"	Murphy H.			
L.32474	"	Malone W.			
101698	"	O'Neill J.			
147602	"	Orriss F.			
L.32464	"	Pogson S.			
L.28153	"	Priest G.W.			
L.25804	"	Quinn D.			

'B' Battery —:o:— 168th Bde. R.F.A.

Nominal Roll of all ranks 28-2-17.

Officers:—
    Major F. FITZGIBBON
    Capt. H. STEAD.
    2/Lt. H. FISHER.
    2/Lt. W.P. ROBINSON.
    2/Lt. L.M. HASTINGS.
    2/Lt. W.L. CHAMBERLAIN.
    2/Lt. J.M. HILL.

Other Ranks:—

58482	BSM	Stenning T.	L.25382	Gnr	Ainley W.H.
L.32437	BQMS	Lane A.C.	L.32549	"	Berry A.
L.32514	Sgt.Far.	Sutcliffe R	L.25616	"	Billington T.
L.25448	Sgt.	Beaumont F.	L.32483	"	Binns A.O.
L.29324	"	Chambers W.	L.32521	"	Bottoms H.
L.25420	"	Deakin T.	L.25873	"	Broadbent T.
L.29344	"	Gutherie A.	L.29265	"	Broadley J.T.
1985	"	Harding R.	L.32496	"	Burton G.
L.25606	"	Palframan F.	L.25671	"	Cocker F.
L.25390	"	Taylor H.	L.29363	"	Crosland E.
L.25862	Cpl	Hartley J.A.	79093	"	Drewitt W.H.
L.25871	"	Walker S.	L.29592	"	Eccles J.L.
L.25484	"	Willans C.	L.29263	"	Fowler B.
L.25864	"	Mason R.	111578	"	Gouldsmith S.C.
L.25716	"	Fisher W.W.	L.29244	"	Greenwood A.A.
L.25874	"	Shaw L.	L.29262	"	Greenwood L.A.
L.29350	"	Thornton J.	L.29380	"	Hanson E.
L.25446	Bdr	Bottomley T.	L.25746	"	Hargreaves A.
L.25863	"	Holmes L.	L.32454	"	Hargreaves D.
L.29241	"	Martin F.	111819	"	Harris G.
L.25416	"	Pullan H.	L.25554	"	Harrison W.
L.25451	"	Spendlove T.	L.25664	"	Hartley A.
L.28210	"	Greenwood M.R.	L.29599	"	Hollas J.H.
L.29326	"	Temperton H.K.	L.29242	2	Hoyle G.G.
L.28138	"	Bramley S.M.	L.29046	"	Houldsworth A
L.25545	"	Turner J.F.	L.25689	"	Kenyon G.H.
L.24990	"	Mayers A.	L.25458	"	Kiddle F.
L.28218	"	Dyson A.	L.32510	"	Knight S.
L.32480	a/Br	Bancroft L.	L.25562	"	Lawford F.
L.25756	"	Broomhead W.H.	L.28220	"	Laycock A.
L.28043	"	Burch H.	L.25623	"	Lee F.
125511	"	Christie H.	L.25622	"	Littlewood A.
L.28203	"	Croft L.H.	L.28126	"	Mallinson F.
16381	"	Cawthorne J.	L.29400	"	Mitchell D.
L.25547	"	Ibbotson M.	L.32544	"	Mitchell R.
15252	"	Wright A.	L.28076	"	Murray A.
L.25491	"	Sherwood J.T.	L.29402	"	Murray E.
505	S/S	Boswell H.	L.29395	"	Noble F.
L.25552	"	Hoyle C.	L.25632	"	Onyon A.
L.25510	"	Readyhough G.W.	L.25836	"	Owen W.
L.25452	"	Sidebottom J.	L.25827	"	Riddlesden A
L.32552	"	Wilson J.W.	L.29382	"	Riley A.
L.25747	Sdlr	Brooksbank G.	L.25463	"	Scott N.
L.25607	"	Stansfield F.	53092	"	Stubbs H.
L.25596	Whlr	Yates F.	L.32473	"	Stafford H.
L.32356	Ftr.	Hill W.	L.29372	"	Tidswell H.T.

11525	Gnr	Thomas O.	L.29416	Dvr	Robinson W.
L.25683	"	Thompson J.T.	L.25512	"	Robinson W.J.
L.25629	"	Turner H.	L.25730	"	Rushworth E.
L.25725	"	Wintringham E.	L.25625	"	Scott J.J.
L.29451	"	Wood G.H.	L.28041	"	Schofield A.
L.25704	"	Youngman A.	L.32579	"	Sheppard N.
5823	"	Spence J.	L.25644	"	Singleton L.M.
18829	"	Brown F.	L.25454	"	Snell A.
150477	"	Woolf C.H.	L.29397	"	Southwell J.
197864	"	McPherson D.	L.28090	"	Stanton A.
197862	"	McLennan J.B.	L.28109	"	Sugden C.
150377	"	Miller C.W.	L.25569	"	Turner J.
197865	"	McCrea D.	L.25866	"	Townsend H.
164025	"	Miller L.	L.25598	"	Townsend W.
152712	"	Mason J.	L.25499	"	Tallis G.
68254	"	Doggett A.	L.25793	"	Ivas J.M.
67772	"	Tanner W.S.	L.28142	"	WALKER J.
2295	"	Coward T.	L.32567	"	Walker M.
156926	"	Gobley J.	L.25651	"	Wheelwright G.
8786	"	Broome H.	L.32515	"	Wilkinson L.
	"	Nightingale	L.29257	"	Wilkinson F.
	"	Leigh	L.29269	"	Wood H.
	"	Platt	L.29089	"	Wright F.
	"	Nash.	97890	"	Butler J.
			152302	"	Milner J.
L.29381	Dvr	Barraclough H.	112192	"	Dennis G.
L.29258	"	Barraclough T.E.		"	Worth
L.28213	"	Beaumont H.		"	Willatt
L.28199	"	Berry A.		"	Whitechurch.
L.25857	"	Berry S.		"	Williams
L.32576	"	Bentley T.			
L.32568	"	Borrisow F.	Attached:-		
L.32566	"	Braithwaite J.F.			
L.25470	"	Brook J.W.	8949 AVC Sgt White F.A.		
L.25878	"	Clear A.			
L.32445	"	Crossley A.			
L.28112	"	Crossley F.			
L.28113	"	Crossley J.			
L.32518	"	Crowther J.			
L.25446	"	Davies J.W.			
L.29383	"	Dewar W.			
L.25742	"	Dyson F.			
L.25422	"	Eastwood G.			
L.25732	"	Firth H.			
L.32578	"	Gray D.			
L.29367	"	Greenwood J.W.			
L.25728	"	Greenwood C.			
L.25831	"	Hall H.			
L.28204	"	Harrison F.			
L.25479	"	Hattersley F.			
L.32524	"	Hawthornthwaite T.W.			
L.25822	"	Hinchcliffe A.			
L.25558	"	Hopson A.			
L.32506	"	Holmes W.			
L.29271	"	Holmes S.			
L.29403	"	Horrocks H.			
L.32447	"	Jackson P.			
L.28070	"	Jowett J.H.			
L.29270	"	Ledgard E.			
L.28132	"	Martin J.			
L.28077	"	Martin L.			
L.28127	"	Mellor H.			
L.29401	"	Moody A.			
L.25870	"	Murray R.			
L.25675	"	Nicholson J.			
L.28194	"	North M.			
L.25882	"	Pearson W.			
L.28071	"	Robinson F.			
L.25861	"	Robinson T.			

"C" Battery   -: o :-   168th Bde R.F.A.

Nominal Roll of all ranks 27/2/17.

Officers :-
    Major H. COTTER
    Capt. L. G. FIRTH
    Lieut. B. T. GROVES.
    2/Lt. H. LOCKWOOD.
    2/Lt. H. L. JAMES.
    2/Lt. G.O.J. BARRICK

Other ranks :-

53475	BSM	Malone M.J.	147564	Gnr	Balls H.N.
L.2568	BQMS	Tomlinson S.	L.11994	"	Barr J.
L.27727	Sgt	Ward A.	L.12026	"	Beach J.
L.11952	"	Oates R.T.	L.11979	"	Brady B.
L.11931	"	Townsend W.	L.19485	"	Briggs E.J.
L.19483	"	Booth P.P.	L.27987	"	Broadhead F.
L.12004	"	Turgoose W.	L.29303	"	Bottomley G.J.
L.11973	Cpl	Booth J.	L.28200	"	Brook J.
53807	"	Keefe J.	L.11981	"	Cockell G.
L.11923	"	Imms E.	L.28147	"	Chapman T.
22239	"	Fitzgerald W.	147114	"	Creeper H.
L.29412	"	Brown T.	60219	"	Davison J.
6083	"	Broderick W.	L.25702	"	DENTON F.
L.19494	"	Marshall H.	L.11921	"	Drabble H.
L.19481	Bdr	Ward J.S.	129947	"	Deveaney F.
L.19479	"	Wardle L.M.	L.29414	"	Elliott C.H.
L.19478	"	Todd J.H.	L.25411	"	Ellis W.
L.12050	"	Sanderson G.	78830	"	Frazer J.
L.12016	"	McGuire T.F.J	L.12017	"	Farmery T.
L.27730	"	Walton H.	L.12019	"	Froggett E.
L.19484	"	Bailey B.C.	L.12092	"	Garfoot J.W.
L.28121	"	Palmer R.	L.19489	"	Gregory H.S
L.12195	"	Garside I.	163727	"	Goddard W.E.
L.12028	"	Craven W.A.	L.11975	"	Howarth H.
L.11930	a/Br	Theobald E.J	L.11992	"	Halton R.
L.11993	"	Holroyd T.	L.11989	"	Howarth R.
L.11959	"	Ellis W.R.	88771	"	Hall N.
L.K19487	"	Carr W.C.	L.19490	"	Homer C.
L.19519	"	Milnthorp G.	34446	"	Hutt R.
105077	"	Carruthers T.	L.594444	"	Holden F.
L.25812	"	Terry L.	L.25751	"	Higgins H.
L.25473	"	Earnshaw S.	L.118744	"	Huggett T.
137207	"	Smith P.W.	145669	"	Heron R.
30671	Far S/Sgt	Bishop G.	167010	"	Hankinson J.
L.11991	Cpl S/S	Halton G.	L.11958	"	Issatt H.
L.11926	S/S	Fletcher F.	L.12026	"	Inman H.
L.27751	"	Bailey H.	63915	"	Irving W.A.
L.25954	"	Chappell E.	120111	"	Jolly W.
L.11934	"	Ismay T.H.	19809	"	James T.
L.19518	"	Thompson J.	122010	"	Kenny S.
107905	"	Copping H.E.	L.25575	"	Lee H.
L.29360	Cpl Ftr	Hinchliffe J.	L.19514	"	Lynes J.
L.14862	Whlr	Pringle E.	L.12017	"	Martin T.
L.11918	Sdlr	Iveson J.	L.11968	"	Mosley O.
L.11937	"	Hall J.	L.11932	"	Mulheir J.W.
			L.12002	"	Nowell E.M.
			L.188587	"	Norman W.

172668	Gnr	Nisbett R.	
188719	"	Poynton A.	
L.11971	"	Parkin W.	
L.13469	"	Robinson A.E.	
L.19496	"	Saburton H.	
L.27999	"	Spittle T.A.	
L.19907	"	Swinn J.	
57802	"	Thompson F.	
L.25715	"	Taylor J.T.	
L.19592	"	Wales W.	
L.19500	"	Walstow L.	
L.12003	"	Waldron T.	
L.19503	"	Watson G.	
L.11967	"	Wilcock G.	
54602	"	Wright H.	
L.19717	"	Wardle T.H.	

L.12022	Dvr	Ainsworth H.
L.11942	"	Boulton P.
L.11980	"	Burnley W.S.
L.11982	"	Clark E.W.
57926	"	Coles J.
L.25012	"	Clark R.W.
L.28232	"	Chapman J.
L.11969	"	Eubank H.A.
L.23107	"	Ellis H.
L.25474	"	Earnshaw E.
L.12055	"	Farmery T.
L.19505	"	Firth G.
L.19506	"	Fretwell H.
L.12037	"	Garfitt J.T.
L.19520	"	Garfoot E.
L.11922	"	Hulley A.W.
L.11964	"	Hunter J.
L.11941	"	Hart W.
L.11969	"	Hancock N.
L.19510	"	Horsfall E.
L.19509	"	Hudson J.
L.12043	"	Kershaw H.
L.11929	"	Kemp R.
L.19492	"	Lapish J.
L.19513	"	Lamb M.
L.29285	"	Lord J.
L.28051	"	Lawton H.
85728	"	Maddox J.
L.19919	"	Marshall S.
18909	"	Mitchell W.
77571	"	O'Keefe J.A.
L.11949	"	Pickard H.
75448	"	Pipe H.
L.27691	"	Poynton G.W.
L.19516	"	Priestley B.
L.2869	"	Pogson H.
L.12011	"	Roberts E.W.
L.11965	"	Ross C.A.
L.28134	"	Roberts W.

L.19497	Dvr	Schofield W.
L.12033	"	Senior E.K.
L.12043	"	Shipman H.
L.29293	"	Sutcliffe W.
L.28164	"	Spivey P.
L.28149	"	Scott J.R.
L.28010	"	Steele J.W.
L.28448	"	Singleton N.
L.27993	"	Senior J.W.
L.27747	"	Toothill A.C.
L.32459	"	Turner H.
L.27966	"	Taylor E.
L.28095	"	Turner A.B.
L.12035	"	Wathey A.
L.12008	"	Wales A.
L.12021	"	Walshaw E.
L.12006	"	Wriglesworth F.
L.11940	"	Woollein H.
L.11973	"	Williams H.
L.28169	"	Williams J.
L.28124	"	Walton R.
L.29322	"	White L.
50414	"	Woolgar C.
51913	"	Whereham E.
47566	"	Wall W.
156908	"	Whitehouse W.
154487	"	Wilson W.
3410	"	Wheeler W.
9304	"	West G.

'D' Battery —:o:— 168th Bde R.F.A.

Nominal Roll of all ranks -28-2-17.

Officers:—
Major D.K. TWEEDIE.
Capt. J.C. POOLE.
Lieut. R. DUNBAR.
Lieut. N. BACK.
2/Lt. G.C. WOOD.
2/Lt. A.A. STEWARD.
2/Lt. B.P. PEEL.
2/Lt. J.J. CATERER.

Other ranks:—

13705	BSM	Perigo W.	
100360	F Sgt	Greenwood J.	
L.11948	Sgt	Allen A.J.	
889548	"	Durrant S.P.	
3583	"	Hartley B.W.	
263	"	Jeffery S.A.	
L.19894	"	Lambley J.	
L.29329	"	Rowley W.	
889613	"	Terry W.S.	
78512	Cpl S/S	Hums A.	
L.26450	Cpl Sdlr	Dawson J.J.	
L.27018	Cpl Ftr	Thresh E.	
35409	Cpl	Dinsdale J.	
L.19965	"	Hawkes T.G.H.	
L.27518	"	Holmes J.	
889591	"	Philpot J.E.	
3406	"	Sykes H.M.	
889599	"	Stannard G.	
L.19914	"	Wooffitt F.E.	
L.27756	Bdr	Bonner S.	
L.27590	"	Bradford J.	
889568	"	Browse S.A.	
35389	"	Dobson J.E.	
L.19930	"	Flannigan P.	
L.27757	"	Hetherington J.	
889561	"	Hollingworth R.	
L.12257	"	Husband A.	
L.19840	"	Kempsall J.	
889565	"	Jackson A.A.	
889575	"	Last S.	
L.19919	"	Scholey E.	
L.26400	"	Smith W.	
L.26452	a/Br	Bellamy J.W.	
889512	"	Bloomfield S.	
L.19887	"	Foster C.	
L.35381	"	Guest W.	
L.35395	"	Hamilton T.	
889607	"	Spinks B.R.	
889555	S/a/Br	Gutteridge A.	
L.27520	S/S	Hellawell A.	
L.27497	"	Innocent R.	
L.27759	"	Popplewell G.	
L.27612	"	Smith J.	
L.26447	"	Varney J.	
L.18446	Sdlr	Batley J.	
	"	Molyneaux D.	
	"	Schofield J.	
L.146171	Ftr	Collar P.A.	
128068	Gnr	Allen C.	
L.19896	"	Badger G.	
L.26385	"	Boler H.E.	
L.27530	"	Briddock J.A.	
889514	"	Barker J.A.	
889522	"	Barker W.	
	"	Bellamy J.	
L.35665	"	Burke C.	
889513	"	Barker W.H.	
L.25688	"	Caine J.E.	
889536	"	Carman J.	
889530	"	Cook B.	
889531	"	Cook G.M.	
889636	"	Calver J.	
L.19947	"	Dalby E.	
L.27596	"	Dixon H.A.	
889542	"	Dunnett J.	
L.27537	"	Elsom J.H.	
L.27075	"	Fowler A.S.	
L.19950	"	Flannigan J.	
40484	"	Goodman A.	
L.19848	"	Hellawell G.W.	
97625	"	Howlett S.	
L.35412	"	Hadley J.	
L.148368	"	Keene T.C.	
889569	"	Lamb S.	
L.25317	"	Langford W.G.	
L.21259	"	McLellan J.	
889578	"	Mudd B.	
L.27532	"	Newton L.	
L.19796	"	Parkinson E.H.	
889585	"	Peek J.W.	
889590	"	Palmer J.	
124923	"	Richardson H.	
L.26125	"	Simmons A.G.	
L.27520	2	Stacey J.	
97676	"	Starkey E.	
L.26449	"	Shaw F.	
L.129128	"	Smith W.E.	
889608	"	Simmons W.	
	"	Sartin H.	
889694	"	Smith J.	
L.26463	"	Townsend A.V.	
L.20010	"	Thompson J.	
L.35391	"	Trimby J.	
889584	"	Todd J.R.	
889614	"	Thody A.	
L.12044	"	Ward E.	
L.35404	"	Williams J.	
889623	"	Watling B.	

889632	Gnr	Woodward S.		L.27624	Dvr	Roebuck V.
889624	"	Waine F.		889596	"	Reid A.
				889595	"	Raynor H.
L.27627	Dvr	Ackroyd T.		40494	"	Seabrook J.H.
L.27601	"	Archer S.L.		L.26406	"	Savage W.
L.19783	"	Armitage G.		L.27609	"	Smith J.
L.35402	"	Baimbridge J.G.		L.29405	"	Stewart A.
L.27757	"	Betting W.		L.26411	"	Speight A.
L.26401	"	Bell A.		L.25568	"	Spencer C.
L.2524	"	Bellamy F.		L.27505	"	Shone W.
L.3590	"	Becket E.		L.27600	"	Sykes J.
1207	"	Bond P.		B889600	"	Smith A.W.
L.27615	"	Bowers F.			"	Skeet W.E.
L.28059	"	Barker W.		889601	"	Sustins E
L.20007	"	Bradley .		L.34341	"	Turner A.
889511	"	Bell C.		L.19736	"	Thompson A.D.
889546	"	Dalton E.		L.24085	"	Tilston R.
889521	"	Bunn A		L.27566	"	Trafford J.
889509	"	Brightwell E.		71271	"	Thompson J.G.H.
889510	"	Barton S.		889616	"	Theobald W.
L.20008	"	Croft J.		889611	"	Tampin A.
889529	"	Creed R.		889612	"	Taylor E.
889581	"	Cocker B.		889615	"	Thompson S.
889534	"	Chitook A.		L.12031	"	Wilkinson J.W.
L.27621	"	Denby F.		L.27758	"	Wood J.
L.27622	"	Dixon L.		L.27498	"	Wright D.
B889535	"	Driver R.		L.19794	"	Whelan J.
L.27606	"	Fisher A.		L.25718	"	Wilson J.
L.19799	"	Fisher G.		889627	"	Watson C.
L.19944	"	Flint F.		889651	"	Whitehead J.
889532	"	Fiske J.		30628	"	Williams C.
L.19841	"	Gilman B.T.S		8038		
L.19943	"	Green J.				
L.19803	"	Greenwood J.				
889556	"	Garner G.		Attached :-		
889555	"	Gray S.V.				
L.20002	"	Hanson C.B.		8038 AVC Sgt Moore W.		
L.1986	"	Hempsall T.				
L.26422	"	Haveland H				
L.19953	"	Howson W.				
L.19749	"	Hughes H.				
889563	"	Honeywood B.				
4896	"	Hutchins J.				
L.27610	"	Jewitt W.				
L.35411	"	Jackson F.				
B.11126	"	Johnson P.H.				
L.3580	"	Lunn G				
92590	"	Lewelyan T.				
889570	"	Lay G.				
L.3579	"	Midleton W.				
L.35414	"	Padgett J.E.				
L.19789	"	Peacock E.				
L.25560	"	Palmer J.				
L.27598	"	Pollard J.				
L.27222	"	Philips F.				
L.19939	"	Porter B.				
889587	"	Piper W.				
889641	"	Pennie H.				
L.26410	"	Robert W.				
L.27595	"	Roebuck L.				

Vol 14

CONFIDENTIAL.

WAR DIARY

of the

168th. Brigade R.F.A.

From 1st. March 1917 to 31st. March 1917.

(Volume XV.)

WAR DIARY or INTELLIGENCE SUMMARY

Army Form C. 2118.

168th. Brigade, R.F.A. Commanded by Lt-Colonel R.FITZMAURICE.

(Erase heading not required.)

Place	Date	Hour	Summary of Events and Information	Remarks and references to Appendices
WARVILLERS.				
	1/3/17.		Wire-cutting carried out by batteries; front very quiet.	(a)
	2/3/17.	11 am.	Corps C.R.A. visited all Battery Commanders.	(a)
		7 pm.	Enemy opened a heavy barrage on our front line, and, under cover of this, came over and took some prisoners leaving a wounded German in our hands. "A" & "B" Batteries were shelled with gas shells.	
	3/3/17.		1 Section B/168 withdrawn from action and proceeded to the 4th Army School at V.UX EN AMIENOIS.	(a)
	4/3/17.	8 pm.	Two Roving Guns sent out, one to F.27.d.8.1 and the other to L.14.b.9.1. These guns are used for Wire-cutting and night-firing on enemy communications.	(a)
	5/3/17.		Wire-cutting carried out all day.	(a)
	6/3/17.		D/168 shelled with Gas Shells; no damage done.	(a)
	7/3/17.		The day was confined to Wire-cutting and registration.	(a)
	9/3/17.	7 pm.	3 Guns of C/168 moved to New position at L.13.c.9.9.	
	10/3/17.	9.30 pm.	Lt-Col. R. FITZMAURICE proceeded on a month's Sick Leave. Major D.K.TWEEDIE D.S.O. assumes Command of the Brigade. Remaining 3 guns of C/168 moved to L.13.c.9.9.	(a)
	11/3/17.		German Front Line wire and trenches in L.17.a. and L.11.a. were systematically fired on all day by 18-pounders, 4.5" Howrs. and 6" Howrs. Re-adjustment of 32nd Divisional Front (see Operation Order No.27.)	(a)
	12/3/17.	6.15 am.	First Raid carried out on German trenches in L.17.3. (See Appendix.)	

Army Form C. 2118.

WAR DIARY
or
INTELLIGENCE SUMMARY.
(Erase heading not required.)

168th Brigade R.F.A.
Commanded by Major D.K. TWEEDIE D.S.O.

Instructions regarding War Diaries and Intelligence Summaries are contained in F. S. Regs., Part II. and the Staff Manual respectively. Title pages will be prepared in manuscript.

Place	Date	Hour	Summary of Events and Information	Remarks and references to Appendices
WARVILLERS	13/3/17.		Wire-cutting carried out.	
	14/3/17.		B/168 moved to New position in L.13.c.	
	16/3/17.		Our guns in conjuction with the French on our right carried out a systematic bombardment on enemy trenches.	
	17/3/17.		The 5th. French Division attacked on our immediate left and met with very little opposition. "A", "B" & "C" batteries 168th Brigade R.F.A. moved to New positions 1000 yards from German front line.	
	18/3/17.		To cover the advance of our Infantry who had found the German lines unoccupied, the Brigade moved into action in the Vicinity of LI GNCOURT covering the 14th Inf. Bde.	
	19/3/17.	9.30.a.m.	The Brigade marched to NESLE and came into action in I.8. and I.9.c. Many civilians found in NESLE.	
	20/3/17.	6.0.a.m.	Took up New positions in I.23.c. Wagon Lines in ROUY LE PETIT. Headquarters at ESMIL ST. NICAISE.	
	21/3/17.	12 noon.	Batteries remained in same positions as yesterday. Headquarters moved to VOYENNES. Batteries moved back to I.23.a.	
	23/3/17.		All horses except 100 sent back to WARVILLERS owing to the difficulty of getting up forage.	
	25/3/17.		Reconnaissance carried out EAST of ESMAINE by Brigade and Battery Commanders.	
	27/3/17.		The horses sent to WARVILLERS on the 23rd. returned to ROUY LE PETIT.	

Army Form C. 2118.

WAR DIARY
or
INTELLIGENCE SUMMARY.

(Erase heading not required.)

168th. Brigade, R. F. A.
Commanded by Major J.K. TWEEDIE D.S.O.

Instructions regarding War Diaries and Intelligence Summaries are contained in F. S. Regs., Part II. and the Staff Manual respectively. Title pages will be prepared in manuscript.

Place	Date	Hour	Summary of Events and Information	Remarks and references to Appendices
	29/3/17	7 am. 4 pm.	The brigade moved to BONY and stayed there all day. Brigade Headquarters moved to 'CHAPAINE. "A", "C" & "D" batteries moved into action near VAUX. "B" battery into action near BEAUVOIS.	
	30/3/17		Registration carried out.	
	31/3/17		Registration by batteries continued. "D" battery MEM (Howitzer) bombarded the village of S.W.	

31st. March 1917.

[signature]
Major.
Commanding 168th. Brigade, R.F.A.

SECRET.

LEFT GROUP - 32nd DIVNL. ARTILLERY.

There will be a Feint Raid on the ~~morning~~ evening of the ~~13th~~ 12th. for the purpose of drawing enemy's fire, and getting information as to his Barrage.

Zero time - ~~4.45 a.m.~~ 6.15 P.M.

C/168 will fire on Front Line from L.11.c.8.1 to L.11.c.8.5.
A/168 " " " " " " L.11.c.85.80 to L.11.a.85.20.
B/168. " " " Support " " L.11.d.1.6 to L.11.b.10.00.
D/168. " " " L.11.d.0.5 " L.11.d.15.70 -- L.11.b.10.00
 L.11.b.1.3 - L.11.b.3.4 -- L.11.d.35.20.

1 Sec. 51st. Siege RGA - will fire on L.17.b.7.5.

Rates of Fire :-

 18-Pounders. - 4 rounds per gun per minute
 4.5" Hows. - 3 " " " " "
 6" Howitzers - 1 " " " " "

Duration of Bombardment - 5 minutes.

It is important that fire should be opened simultaneously.

T.M's and Machine Guns will take part.

Watches will be synchronised by phone on the night of the 12th.

The Officer on duty at the Night O.P. will note and report :-

(1) Volume, duration, and direction of Enemy Fire.
(2) Lights and Rockets.
(3) Area shelled by enemy.
(4) Exact time the enemy puts up a Barrage.

A C K N O W L E D G E.

Alan Lumb. Lieut.
Adjutant - LEFT GROUP.
32nd Divisional Artillery.

12th. March 1917.

Headquarters Staff – ; – 168th. Bde. R. F. A.

Nominal Roll of all Ranks 31/3/1917.

Officers.   Lt-Col. R. Fitzmaurice.
            Lieut. A. Lumb.
            2/Lieut J. G. Bell.
            Capt. D. Ferguson. R.A.M.C.

Other Ranks.

L.25839	Cpl	Lee G.
29811	Bdr.	Anderton A.
L.29801	"	Mormanton A.
12245	a/Br	Wright J.
L.29450	"	Eyre F.
L.25881	"	Gibson H.
L.28042	"	Sugden E.
1305	Sdlr.	Williams T.H.
6267	S/S	Periera A.T.
L.28206	Gnr.	Ackroyd H.
L.25810	"	Bottomley C.
59688	"	Clark B.J.
5645	"	Coley E.
L.29307	"	Catley H.
152003	"	Firth H.
56777	"	Grindley W.
L.29404	"	Greenwood C.
L.25480	"	Lucas E.
L.29394	"	Rangeley P.S.
L.25399	"	Ramsden A.
L.25626	"	Slater H.
L.28179	"	Sykes C.A.
L.29296	"	Windle A.T.
L.27531	"	Postlethwaite T.
L.25422	Dvr.	Armytage J.R.
L.32440	"	Baker G.
L.32540	"	Blake F.
L.28026	"	Cowham S.
L.29287	"	Fisher S.
5855	"	Gowan W.
37566	"	Hirons E.
1873	"	Gutteridge
	"	Greenwood D
198817	"	Foote
L.32511	"	Iredale E.
L.2582	"	Iredale E.
L.28189	"	Mellor Q.
L.29351	"	Newsome A.E.
79511	"	McIntyre A.
L.29424	"	Parker J.
L.29423	"	Pollard W.
L.25853	"	Radley T.
L.29357	"	Reddington M.
165508	"	Reid
L.29389	"	Stansfield P.
L.25540	"	Smith R.

Attached :–

A.O.C.62 Stf.Sgt.Barker H. (Artificer)

"A" Battery -:- 168th. Bde. R.F.A.

Nominal Roll of all Ranks - 31/3/17.

Officers.   Major. R. Emmet.
             Capt. W. R. Brown.
             Lieut. G. O. D'Ivry.
             2/Lt. W. A. Enbels.
             2/Lt. A. C. Miller.
             2/Lt. D. Finnie.
             2/Lt. L. A. Ravald.

Other Ranks.

L.28514	BSM Patchett W.J.	L.25790	Gnr. Allott C.V.
L.28064	BQMS Brearley H.	L.25595	" Billington T.
1105	Sgt. Witney T.	L.28014	" Bray E.H.
53261	" Smith E.F.	L.28217	" Bower E.
25426	" Field P.J.	L.25396	" Beasley G.
L.25679	" Roberts J.F.	100556	" Beamish R.
43512	" McGowan A.H.	100774	" Baird S.
L.2542	" Firth A.	L.28180	" Bolton H.
L.25697	Cpl. Rhodes L.	L.28104	" Barker N.
L.25561	" Povey J.	L.29579	" Beaumont L.
L.25619	" France W.	L.32471	" Calvert F.
L.25693	" Littlewood K.	L.25444	" Crimlisk M.J.
L.29407	" Taylor F.	L.29345	" Craigie T.
L.32581	" Williams W.J.	5556	" Chappell A.
L.25479	Bdr. Bentley J.	L.28178	" Dawson W.
L.28100	" Pitchforth A.	12049	" Edwards L.
L.29513	" Armitage W.B.	130451	" Edwards W.H.
L.25708	" Crawshaw J.I.	86276	" Franklin
L.25574	" Whiteley C.H.	602006	" Fuller B.
L.28015	" Barnes H.	169899	" Holliday R.
L.25414	" Wood B.	L.25823	" Hynes W.H.
L.25701	" Rhodes J.	L.25610	" Hopwood H.
L.28188	" Padgett S.	L.25528	" Hey J.T.
L.25464	" Richardson G.H.	L.28159	" Hewitt R.
L.32553	" Taylor W.J.	L.28151	" Hopson T.C.
L.28072	a/Br. Bentley C.	L.29427	" Kettle L.J.
L.32539	" Fenton E.	L.29411	" Knocton J.
L.25768	" Brookspank G.	L.32212	" Lumb W.
L.25669	" Oates H.	L.28177	" Leathem F.
L.29297	" Noble C.	L.28184	" Lockwood J.
86510	" Squires A.B.	197866	" McEwing H.
L.32457	S/" Womersley C.	95371	" McCarthy C.
L.25485	S/a/Br Williams G.	97863	" McPherson A.
L.28136	" Shaw N.	176126	" McWilliams T.
L.28034	" Beevers M.	167074	" McCreshie G.
43323	Far.Sgt. Spillett H.	168564	" Miller W.
L.25783	Cpl.S/S.Town E.	150416	" Mallett H.
76	" " Parks J.	L.28129	" Marshall L.
L.28173	S/S. Taylor J.E.	L.25536	" Mansfield W.G.
L.29282	" Nuttall G.T.	L.25392	" Milnes H.
L.28175	" Waterhouse L.	6011	" Myler A.
L.25690	" Kaye J.T.	112737	" Negus H.
5882	" Bevington A.	L.25443	" Nuttall P.
L.32485	Sdlr. Jackson W.R.	44251	" Offen F.
62728	" Oliver J.	L.28186	" Parkins J.C.
14747	2.Ftr. Hellawell A.	L.29272	" Parker W.
121451	Whlr. Weaver J.	L.25736	" Pearson H.

L.29306	Dvr. Pearson F.	L.28133	Dvr. Priest G.W.
L.28185	" Proctor A.C.	L.25864	" Quinn D.
188590	" Partridge W.	L.28074	" Robertshaw G.
L.25513	" Pease A.	L.28075	" Roe F.
159154	" Piggott E.J.	9419	" Radford H.
L.25584	" Quarmby W.H.	L.28013	" Sykes W.
L.2563	" Rushworth A.	99859	" Spencer P.J.
L.32491	" Roberts J.	L.25633	" Shaw E.
L.28006	" Singleton H.W.	L.25503	" Shaw H.
L.38151	" Slack A.W.	L.28224	" Shaw C.A.
L.25781	" Sykes Joe.	L.25797	" Singleton V.
52972	" Stocker H.G.	40354	" Taylor B.
L.25566	" Shaw J.C.	L.28101	" Taylor T.H.
81446	" Slack H.	L.25460	" Twigg J.
L.26074	" Spence R.	L.25483	" Varley L.
L.2575	" Spencer H.	L.28214	" Wood W.N.
L.25791	" Thornton J.	L.25650	" Wood A.
L.29255	" Townend J.	105865	" Westgate F.
L.3233	" Thorpper W.H.	L.29331	" Woodcock W.
L.2539	" Thompson J.W.	L.28087	" Walters H.
L.25764	" Wilkinson B.	L.25394	" Wortley T.
L.28038	" Wilkinson T.	L.25541	" Woodhead E.
L.25575	" Walker W.T.	L.25819	" Whitehead J.A.
L.29300	" Wood F.	781609	" Watson E.
L.32441	" Walker a.	159419	" Weedon W.
L.25844	" Weldrake B.	21116	" Wainwright W.
L.29318	" Wood R.		
L.25649	" Wood C.E.		
13371	" Young W.		

attached :-

S.E.1514 Sgt.A.V.C. Jolly A.J.
~~29611-6-~~

107780	Dvr. Archer W.
175251	" Adams F.
81590	" Black A.
L.25824	" Bamforth H.
L.2522	" Bray H.
L.25436	" Brearley A.
L.25660	" Brook L.
L.25305	" Brook G.L.
L.25658	" Chapman B.
L.29323	" Cartwright P.
L.25592	" Crowther W.G.
5802	" Connor J.
L.25843	" Digman W.J.
L.29409	" Dyson W.
L.28079	" Green F.
L.28220	" Ganley J.
L.29316	" Gledhill J.R.
L.25579	" Griffiths J.C.
L.25677	" Holroyd H.
L.28201	" Horsfall E.
L.28073	" Hirst J.
L.25849	" Holmes E.
L.29347	" Hardcastle C.W.
L.29417	" Hinchliffe H.
L.29322	" Jessop E.L.O.
L.3241	" Kershaw C.
L.25419	" Kerton E.
L.28163	" Lodge A.
L.25384	" Livesley F.C.
L.28022	" Marsden J.A.
L.28021	" Mallinson J.A.
L.25639	" Millard H.
L.25641	" Murphy H.
L.32474	" Malone W.
101698	" O'Neill J.
147602	" Orriss H.
L.32464	" Pogson S.

"B" Battery   -:o:-   168th.Bde.R.F.A.

Nominal Roll of all Ranks   -   31/3/1917.
==

Officers.   Major. F. FitzGibbon.
                 2/Lt. W. P. Robinson
                 2/Lt. H. Fisher.
                 2/Lt. L. M. Hastings.
                 2/Lt. W. L. Chamberlain.
                 2/Lt. J. Mitchellhill

Other Ranks.

58462	BSM.	Stenning T.	L.25382	Gnr. Ainley W.H.
L.32457	B.Q.M.S	Lane A.J.	L.32549	" Berry A.
L.32514	Sgt. Farr.	Sutcliffe R.	L.25616	" Billington H.
L.25448	Sgt.	Beaumont F.	L.32483	" Binns A.O.
L.29324	"	Chambers W.	L.32521	" Bottoms H.
L.25420	"	Deakin T.	L.25873	" Broadbent T.
L.29344	"	Gutherie A.	L.29265	" Broadley J.T.
1985	"	Harding R.	8786	" Broom H.
L.25606	"	Palframan F.	18820	" Brown T.
L.25390	"	Taylor H.	L.32496	" Burton G.
L.25871	Cpl.	Walker S.	156926	" Cobley J.A.
L.25484	"	Willans C.	L.25671	" Cocker F.
L.25864	"	Mason R.	L.2295	" Coward T.
L.25716	"	Fisher W.W.	L.29363	" Crosland E.
L.25874	"	Shaw L.	68234	" Doggett A.
L.29350	"	Thornton J.	79093	" Drewitt W.H.
L.25863	"	Holmes L.	L.29392	" Eccles J.L.
	Cpl. S/S	Brennan J.	L.3052	" Earl W.
L.25446	Bdr.	Bottomley T.	L.29263	" Fowler S.B.
L.29241	"	Martin F.	56821	" Gallagher M.
L.25431	"	Spendlove T.	11578	" Gouldsmith S.C.
L.28210	"	Greenwood M.R.	L.29244	" Greenwood A.A.
L.29826	"	Temperton H.K.	L.29262	" Greenwood L.A.
L.28138	"	Bramley S.M.	L.29380	" Hanson E.
L.25545	"	Turner J.F.	L.25746	" Hargreaves A.
L.24990	"	Mayers A.	L.32454	" Hargreaves D.
L.28218	"	Dyson A.	111819	" Harris G.
L.32480	"	Bancroft L.	L.25554	" Harrison W.
L.2756	a/Br.	Broomhead H.	L.25664	" Hartley A.
L.28043	"	Burch H.	L.29399	" Hobbas J.H.
12511	"	Christie H.	5329	" Horan J.S.
L.28208	"	Croft L.H.	L.29242	" Hoyle G.G.
16381	"	Cawthorne J.	L.28046	" Holdsworth A.
L.25547	"	Ibbotson M.	L.25689	" Kenyon J.H.
15224	"	Wright A.	L.25458	" Kiddle F.
L.25491	"	Sherwood J.T.	L.32510	" Knight S.
L.29382	"	Riley A.	L.25562	" Lawford F.
503	S/S	Boswell H.	L.28220	" Laycock A.
L.25552	"	Hoyle G.	L.25623	" Lee F.
L.25510	"	Readyhough G.W.	49118	" Leigh R
L.25452	"	Sidebottom J.	L.25622	" Littlewood A.
L.3252	"	Wilson J.W.	197862	" MacLennan J.B.
L.25747	Sdlr.	Brookspank C.	197864	" Macpherson D.
L.25607	"	Stansfield F.	197865	" MacRea D.
L.25596	Whlr.	Yates F.	L.28126	" Mallinson F.
L.32456	Ftr.	Hill W.	152712	" Mason J.

150377	Gnr.Miller G.W.	20609	Dvr.Ray D.
164023	" Miller L.	L.28071	" Robinson F.
L.29400	" Mitchell D.	5116	" Roberts G.
L.32544	" Mitchell R.	L.25861	" Robinson T.
L.28076	" Murray A.	L.29416	" Robinson W.
L.29402	" Murray E.	L.25512	" Robinson W.J.
188576	" Nash	L.25730	" Rushworth B.
156134	" Nightingale D.	L.25623	" Scott J.J.
L.29395	" Noble F.	L.28041	" Schofield A.
L.25632	" Onyon A.	L.32579	" Shepherd N.
L.25836	" Holling W.	L.25644	" Singleton L.M.
L.25827	" Riddlesden A.	L.25454	" Snell A.
258	" Platt H.	L.29397	" Southwell J.
L.25463	" Scott N.	L.29090	" Stanton A.
5828	" Spence J.	L.28109	" Sugden G.
L.32473	" Stafford H.	L.25569	" Turner J.
67772	" Tanner W.J.	L.25860	" Townsend H.
L.29372	" Tidswell H.T.	L.25598	" Townsend W.
11492	" Thomas O.	L.25499	" Tallis G.
L.25683	" Thompson J.T.	L.25793	" Tyas J.M.
L.25029	" Turner H.	L.28142	" Walker J.
L.25727	" Wintringham E.	L.32567	" Walker M.
150477	" Woolfe C.H.	L.25631	" Wheelwright J.
L.29451	" Wood G.H.	160955	" Whitchurch
L.25704	" Youngman A.	L.32515	" Wilkinson L.
		L.29257	" Wilkinson F.
L.29381	Dvr.Barraclough H.	185398	" Willatt
L.28213	" Beaumont H.	164826	" Williams
L.28199	" Berry A.	L.29269	" Wood H.
L.25827	" Berry S.	141214	" Worth
L.32576	" Bentley T.	L.28069	" Wright F.
L.32528	" Borrisow F.	198809	" Gigg
L.32566	" Braithwaite J.T.	160940	" Ling J.
L.25470	" Brook J.W.		
L.25878	" Clear A.	Attached:-	
L.32443	" Crossley A.		
L.28113	" Crossley J.	S.E.8949 A/J Sgt.White F.A.	
L.32518	" Crowther J.		
L.25446	" Davies J.W.		
112192	" Dennis G.		
L.29383	" Dewar W.		
L.25742	" Dyson F.		
L.25442	" Eastwood G.		
L.25732	" Firth H.		
L.32528	" Gray D.		
L.29367	" Grenwood J.W.		
L.25728	" Grenwood G.		
L.25831	" Hall H.		
L.28204	" Harrison F.		
L.25479	" Hattersley F.		
L.32524	" Hawthornthwaite T.W.		
L.25822	" Hinchliffe A.		
L.25558	" Hopson A.		
L.32506	" Holmes W.		
L.29403	" Horrocks H.		
L.32447	" Jackson F.		
L.28070	" Jowett J.H.		
L.29270	" Ledgard E.		
L.28122	" Martin J.		
L.28077	" Martin L.		
L.28127	" Mellor H.		
152302	" Milner J.		
L.29401	" Moody A.		
L.25870	" Murray R.		
L.25675	" Nicholson J.		
L.28194	" North M.		

"C" Battery -:o:- 168th Bde.R.F.A.

Nominal Roll of all Ranks - 31/3/1917.

Officers.   Major H. Cottee.
             Capt. L. G. Firth.
             Lieut. B. T. Groves.
             2/Lt. H. Lockwood.
             2/Lt. H. L. James.
             2/Lt. G.O. J. Barrick.
             2/Lt. C. A. Annely.

Other Ranks.

53473	BSM.	Malone M.J.		147564	Gnr.	Balls H.N.
L.2568	BQMS	Tomlinson S.		L.11994	"	Barr J.
L.27727	Sgt.	Ward A.		L.12020	"	Beach J.
L.11931	"	Townsend W.		L.11979	"	Brady B.
L.19483	"	Booth P.P.		L.19485	"	Briggs E.J.
L.12004	"	Turgoose W.		L.27987	"	Broadhead F.
L.25682	"	Hartley J.A.		L.29303	"	Bottomley G.J.A.
L.25711	"	Kirkham T.		L.28200	"	Brook J.
35406	"	Sykes H.M.		L.11981	"	Cockell G.
L.11973	Cpl.	Booth J.		L.28147	"	Chapman T.
L.29412	"	Brown T.		147114	"	Creeper H.
L.11923	"	Imns E.		196150	"	Cook F.
22239	"	Fitzgerald W.		60279	"	Davidson J.
53807	"	Keefe J.		L.25702	"	Denton F.
L.19494	"	Marshall H.		L.11921	"	Drabble H.
L.12050	"	Sanderson G.		129947	"	Deveaney F.
L.19481	Bdr.	Ward J.S.		L.25411	"	Ellis W.
L.19479	"	Wardle L.M.		L.12017	"	Farmery J.W.
L.19478	"	Todd J.A.		78830	"	Frazer J.
L.28195	"	Garside I.		L.12019	"	Froggett E.
L.12016	"	Mcguire T.F.J.		78656	"	Fenny F.
L.28121	"	Palmer R.		L.12092	"	Garfoot C.W.
L.27730	"	Walton H.		L.+19489	"	Gregory H.S.
L.19484	"	Bailey S.G.		163727	"	Goddard W.E.
L.12028	"	Craven W.R.		57084	"	Gale S.E.
100077	"	Carruthers T.		163921	"	Gerritt C.W.
L.11993	"	Holroyd T.		150316	"	Gawthorpe A.
L.25812	a/Br.	Terry L.		L.11975	"	Haworth H.
L.25473	"	Earnshaw S.		L.11992	"	Halton R.
37207	"	Smith P.W.		L.11989	"	Haworth R.
L.11959	"	Ellis W.E		88771	"	Hall N.
L.19519	"	Milnthorp G.		L.19490	"	Horner C.
L.19487	"	Carr W.G.		34446	"	Hutt R.
L.11930	"	Theobald E.J.		59444	"	Holdon F.
30751	Far.Sgt.	Bishop G.		L.25751	"	Higgins H.
L.11991	Cpl.S/S.	Halton G.		110744	"	Huggett T.
L.11926	S/S.	Fletcher F.		2933	"	Hesford A.
L.27751	"	Bailey H.		143669	"	Heron R.
L.25954	"	Chappell E.		167010	"	Hankinson J.
L.11938	"	Ismay T.H.		L.11938	"	Hissatt H.
107900	"	Copping H.E.		L.12026	"	Hindman H.
L.29360	Cpl.Ftr.	Hinchliffe J.		63915	"	Irving W.A.
L.14862	Whlr.	Pringle E.		120111	"	Jolly W.
L.119818	Sdlr.	Iveson J.		19809	"	James T.
L.11937	"	Hall J.		L.25575	"	Lee H.
				L.19514	"	Lynes J.

L.12047	Gnr.	Martin T.	85728	Dvr.	Maddocks J.
L.11968	"	Mosley O.	14919	"	Marshall S.
L.11932	"	Mulheir J.W.	L.18009	"	Mitchell W.
L.12002	"	Nowell E.M.	77571	"	O'Keefe J.A.
186587	"	Norman W.	L.11949	"	Pickard H.
172668	"	Nisbit R.	75445	"	Pipe E.
L.11971	"	Parkin W.	L.27691	"	Poynton G.W.
188719	"	Poynts A.	L.19516	"	Priestley B.
134691	"	Robinson A.E.	2869	"	Price W.
L.19496	"	Saburton H.	L.28031	"	Parkin H.
L.27999	"	Spittle T.A.	L.25850	"	Rogson H.
13907	"	Swinn J.	L.12011	"	Roberts E.W.
33802	"	Thompson F.	L.28134	"	Roberts W.
L.23715	"	Taylor J.T.	L.11965	"	Ross C.A.
L.19502	"	Wales W.	L.19487	"	Schofield W.
L.19500	"	Walston L.	L.12033	"	Senior B.K.
L.12003	"	Waldron T.	120413	"	Shipman H.
L.19503	"	Watson G.	L.29293	"	Sutcliffe W.
L.11962	"	Wilcock G.	L.28164	"	Spivey P.
34602	"	Wright H.	L.28149	"	Scott J.R.
L.19717	"	Wardle G.H.	L.28010	"	Steele J.W.
			L.25448	"	Singleton N.
			L.27993	"	Senior J.W.
L.12027	Dvr.	Ainsworth H.	L.11920	"	Thompson R.
L.11919	"	Backhouse G.H.	L.27747	"	Toothill A.C.
L.11942	"	Boulton P.	L.32459	"	Turner H.
L.11935	"	Brooks G.	L.27906	"	Taylor E.
L.11980	"	Burnley W.S.	L.28095	"	Turner A.B.
15220	"	Brury A.	L.12035	"	Wathey A.
L.29280	"	Bradley H.	L.12008	"	Wales A.
L.11982	"	Clark B.W.	L.12021	"	Walshaw E.
57926	"	Coles J.	L.12006	"	Wrigglesworth F.
L.25612	"	Clark R.W.	L.11940	"	Woollin H.
L.28232	"	Chapman J.	L.11973	"	Williams H.
50755	"	Chapman W.	L.28165	"	Williams.
118237	"	Cleaver W.	L.28124	"	Walton R.
L.29291	"	Drake G.	L.29322	"	White L.
L.28107	"	Ellis H.	50414	"	Woolgar C.
L.11969	"	Eubank G.A.	51913	"	Whareham E.
L.25474	"	Earnshaw B.	4366	"	Wall W.
L.12055	"	Farmery T.	L.156968	"	Whitehouse W.
L.19505	"	Firth G.	145487	"	Wilson W.
L.19506	"	Fretwell H.	L.3410	"	Wheeler W.
L.12057	"	Garfitt J.T.	9304	"	West G.
L.19520	"	Garfoot E.	D.1344	"	Young T.
L.11922	"	Mulley W.W.			
L.11964	"	Hunter J.			
L.11941	"	Hart W.			
L.11967	"	Hancock N.			
L.19510	"	Horsfall B.			
L.19509	"	Hudson J.			
L.12041	"	Kershaw			
L.11929	"	Kemp R.			
L.19492	"	Labish J.			
L.19513	"	Lamb M.			
L.28051	"	Lawton H.			
L.29285	"	Lord J.			

Attached :-

2489 Sgt AVC. Harding W.

"D" Battery — :o: — 168th.Bde.R.F.A.

Nominal Roll of all Ranks – 31/3/1917.

Officers :—   Major D.K. Tweedie D.S.O.
               Capt. J.G. Poole.
               Lieut. R. Dunbar.
               Lieut. N. Back.
               2/Lt. G.C. Wood.
               2/Lt. A.A. Steward.
               2/Lt. J.J. Caterer.
               2/Lt. E.P. Peel.

Other Ranks.

13705	BSM.	Perigo W.	128068	Gnr.	Allen C.
100360	Far.Sgt.	Greenwood J.	19896	"	Badger G.
11948	Sergt.	Allen A.J.	26385	"	Boler H.E.
889545	"	Durrant S.P.	27580	"	Briddock J.A.
35383	"	Hartley B.W.	889514	"	Barker J.A.
95107	"	Jeffery S.A.	889522	"	Barker W.
19894	"	Lambley J.T.		"	Bettany J.
L.29329	"	Rowley W.	35665	"	Burke C.
889613	"	Terry W.B.	889513	"	Barker W.H.
78512	Cpl.S/S	Emms A.	25688	"	Caine J.E.
L.26450	Cpl.Sdlr.	Clawson J.J.	889530	"	Cook B.
L.27018	Cpl.Ftr.	Thresh. E.	889531	"	Cook G.M.
35409	Cpl.	Dinsdale J.	889636	"	Calver J.
19965	"	Hawkes T.G.H.	19947	"	Dalby E.
27518	"	Holmes G.	27596	"	Dixon H.A.
889591	"	Philpoth J.B.	889542	"	Dunnett J.
35406	"	Sykes H.M.	27537	"	Elsom G.H.
889599	"	Stannard G.	27175	"	Fowler A.S.
19914	"	Woofitt F.E.	19950	"	Flannigan J.
27756	Bdr.	Bonner S.	40484	"	Goodman A.
27590	"	Bradford J.	55188	"	Heard H.
889568	"	Browse S.A.	19848	"	Helliwell G.W.
35389	"	Dobson J.E.	97625	"	Howlett S.
19930	"	Flannigan P.	35413	"	Hadley J.
27757	"	Hetherington J.	889569	"	Lamb S.
889561	"	Hollingworth R.	25317	"	Langford W.G.
12237	"	Husband A.	21259	"	MacLellan J.
19840	"	Hempsall J.	27532	"	Newton L.
889563	"	Jackson A.A.	19796	"	Parkinson G.H.
889575	"	Last B.	889585	"	Peck J.W.
19919	"	Scholey E.	124923a	"	Richardson H.
26400	"	Smith W.	26125	"	Simmons A.G.
26452	a/Br.	Bellamy J.W.	27220	"	Stacey J.
889512	"	Bloomfield S.	97676	"	Starkey B.
35381	"	Guest W.	26449	"	Shaw F.
35395	"	Hamilton T.H.	129128	"	Smith W.E.
889607	"	Spinks B.R.	889608	"	Simmons W.
889535	S/a/Br	Guttridge C.		"	Sartin H.
27533	S/S	Hellawell A.	889604	"	Smith F.J.
27497	"	Innocent R.	26463	"	Townsend A.V.
27729	"	Popplewell G.	20010	"	Thompson J.
27612	"	Smith J.	35391	"	Trimoy J.
26447	"	Varney J.	889584	"	Todd C.R.
78446	Sdlr.	Batley J.	889514	"	Thody A.
113012	"	Molyneaux D.	12044	"	Ward E.
26076	"	Schofield J.	35404	"	Williams J.
146171	Ftr.	Collar P.A.	889623	"	Watling B.
			889632	"	Woodward F.

889624	Gnr.	Wainoe F.	

27627	Dvr.	Akroyd T.		27609	Dvr.	Smith J.
27601	"	Archer S.L.		29403	"	Stewart G.
19783	"	Armitage G.		26411	"	Speight A.
35402	"	Bainbridge J.G.		27505	"	Shone W.
27757	"	Batten W.		27600	"	Sykes J.
26401	"	Bell G.		889600	"	Smith A.W.
26524	"	Bellamy F.			"	Skeet E.
35390	"	Beckett E.		889601	"	Sustins E.
12107	"	Bond P.		34341	"	Turner A.
27615	"	Bowers F.		19736	"	Thompson A.D.
28059	"	Barker W.		24085	"	Tilston R.
20007	"	Bradley J.		27566	"	Trafford J.
889511	"	Bell J.		71271	"	Thompson J.G.H.
L.32514	"	Dutton J.		889616	"	Theobald W.
889546	"	Dalton B.		889612	"	Taylor E.
889521	"	Bunn G.		889615	"	Thompson S.
889509	"	Brightwell E.		12031	"	Wilkinson J.W.
889510	"	Burton S.		27758	"	Wood J.
20008	"	Croft J.		27498	"	Wright D.
889591	"	Cocker B.		19794	"	Whelan J.
889534	"	Chittock A.		25718	"	Wilson J.
27621	"	Denby F.		889631	"	Whitehead J.
276212	"	Dixon L.		36628	"	Williams G.
889535	"	Driver R.				
27606	"	Fisher A.				
19799	"	Fisher G.		Attached :-		
19944	"	Flint F.				
19841	2	Gilman D.L.S.		SE.8038 AVC Sgt. Moore W.		
19943	"	Green J.				
19803	"	Greenwood J.				
889556	"	Garner G.E.				
889555	"	Gray S.V.				
20002	"	Hanson G.B.				
1986	"	Hempsall T.				
26422	"	Havenand H.				
19953	"	Howson W.				
19749	"	Hughes H.				
889563	"	Honeywood B.				
27610	"	Jewitt W.				
35411	"	Jackson F.				
35380	"	Lunn G.				
92590	"	Llewelyan T.				
889570	"	Lay G.				
35579	"	Middleton W.				
35414	"	Padgett J.E.				
19789	"	Peacock G.E.				
25560	"	Palmer J.				
27598	"	Pollard J.				
27222	"	Philips F.				
19939	"	Porter E.				
889587	"	Piper W.				
81641	"	Penny H.				
27595	"	Roebuck L.				
27624	"	Roebuck V.				
889596	"	Reid A.				
889595	"	Raynor H.				
40494	"	Seabrook J.H.				
26406	"	Savage W.				

SECRET.

FRIDAY 9th March 1917.

LEFT GROUP - 32nd DIVNL. ART'Y

OPERATION ORDER No. 21.

Reference Sheet 66c.N.E. & 66d.N.W.(Parts of) 1/20.000

1. The 5th. Division will extend its right and relieve the 32nd. Division in that portion of its front as far South as O.B.5 Communication Trench exclusive, on the night of March 10/11th. 1917.

2. The 97th. Infantry Brigade will extend its right to BOXALL DUMP on the night of March 11/12th.

3. The Left Group R.F.A. will cover the front L.21.d.9.5 to L.5.d.5.5 from 6 p.m. on the 11th. March 1917.

   Zones of batteries will be as follows :-

Battery.	Map: Ref.	Zone.	
C/168.(6 Gns)	L.13.c.9.9	L.21.d.9.5	to L.17.c.0.2.
A/168.(6 Gns)	{L.8.a.15.10 / L.7.a.5.5	L.17.c.0.2 L.11.c.75.70	to L.11.c.75.70
B/168.(4 Gns)	P.26.b.15.80.	~~Hollandscheur~~	to L.5.d.5.5
D/168.(6 Howrs)	L.8.a.70.60.	L.21.d.9.5	to L.5.d.5.5.

   Night lines.

   18-Pounders - will be arranged so that the whole zones are covered by sweeping.

   4.5"Hows. - L.22.c.8.6   L.22.b.9.7
                L.17.c.75.52   L.17.b.0.5
                L.11.d.35.20   L.5.d.7.0

4. LIAISON. Liaison officers will be provided by :-
   C/168. with Right Battalion at AGNEW L.15.b.7.7.
   B/168. "   Left   "   " WHY L.10.a.5.3.

   They will report to their respective Battalion Headquarters on the afternoon of the 11th. March 1917.

5. AMMUNITION. Ammunition in the present gun-pits of C/168 will be handed over to relieving battery and a receipt obtained; amounts handed over to be wired to this office.

(Continued.)

(Continued)

6. From the completion of Reliefs on the 10/11th inst., the Divisional Front will be divided into Four Barrage Zones, numbered from One to Four from South to North.

The ones affecting the Left Group will be fired on by batteries on receipt of Code Call as follows :-

Zone.	Code Call.	Battery.	German Front Line.	
2.	Barrage Two.	C/168.	L.35.b.4.7	to L.22.c.0.2
		A/168 (3 Guns)	L.22.c.0.2	to L.22.c.4.8
3.	Barrage Three.	C/168.	L.22.c.4.8	to L.22.b.45.55
		A/168.	L.22.b.45.55	to L.17.c.3.6
		B/168.	L.17.c.3.6	to L.17.a.6.4
		Right Group. (12 18-Pounders) 4.8		
			L.22.c.4.8	to L.17.a.6.4.
		D/168. (Hows) Trench Junctions :-		
			L.22.c.5.1	L.22.d.80.95
			L.23.a.6.7	L.17.c.45.20
			L.17.c.75.80	L.17.b.7.5.
4.	Barrage Four.	C/168.	L.17.a.6.4	to L.11.c.8.6.
		A/168.	L.11.c.8.6	to L.11.b.15.75
		B/168.	L.11.b.15.75	to L.5.d.5.5
		Right Group (6 18-Pounders)		
			L.17.a.6.4	to L.5.d.5.5
		D/168. (Hows) Trench Junctions :-		
			L.17.b.7.5.	L.11.d.5.20
			L.11.b.3.4.	L.11.b.65.55
			L.5.d.9.3	L.6.c.85.40

<u>18-Pounders</u> will sweep their allotted zones in all barrages.

<u>Rates of Fire.</u> The Rate of Fire for the above will in all cases be the same as for S.O.S., unless otherwise ordered.

7. <u>Registration.</u>- must be carried out immediately.

8. Acknowledge by wire.

9th. March 1917.

Alan Lumb
2/Lieut.
Adjutant – LEFT GROUP.
32nd. Divisional Artillery.

CONFIDENTIAL.

WAR DIARY

of the

168th. Brigade, R. F. A.

from 1st. April 1917 to 30th. April 1917.

(Volume 16.).

Army Form C. 2118.

WAR DIARY
or
INTELLIGENCE SUMMARY.

(Erase heading not required.)

168th Brigade R.F.A.
Commanded by Lt-Col. E. FITZMAURICE R.F.A.

Instructions regarding War Diaries and Intelligence Summaries are contained in F. S. Regs., Part II. and the Staff Manual respectively. Title pages will be prepared in manuscript.

Place	Date	Hour	Summary of Events and Information	Remarks and references to Appendices
	1/4/17.	8 a.m.	The 168th Brigade R.F.A. moved to positions in F.12.c. and took part in an attack on the village of SAVY and the SQ18 SAVY which was very successful. Headquarters at PUZEAUX.	
		6 p.m.	Batteries moved to positions in F.6.d.	
	2/4/17.	5 a.m.	The Brigade covered the 14th Inf. Bde. in an attack on FRANCILLY - SELENCY which was very successful, one battery of 77 m.m. guns captured.	
	3/4/17.	2.30 p.m.	Batteries fired as per appendix (a) to assist the French who attacked on our immediate right.	
	4/4/17.	1.0 p.m.	Batteries moved into action in X.12., H.Q. at DALLILY. Many horses died from fatigue.	
	5/4/17.		Registration carried out.	
	6/4/17.	9.0 p.m.	The Brigade covered the 183rd Brigade 61st Division in an attack on FRESNOY le PETIT. (see appendix (b).)	
	7/4/17.		4.5"Howrs. bombarded enemy's strong points, 18-pdrs carried out wire-cutting.	
	8/4/17.	5.0 p.m.	Bombardment of enemy posts by 18-pdrs and 4.5" Hows.	
	9/4/17.		4.5"Hows. bombarded the ST QUENTIN defences.	
	10/4/17.	8 pm to 5 a.m.	Night firing on enemy roads and defences.	
	11/4/17.		The usual bombardment of enemy trenches carried out.	
	12/4/17.		Registration carried out. 4.5" Hows. fired at ST QUENTIN station where train was reported to have arrived.	
	13/4/17.	2.0 a.m.	To assist the French who attacked BOCOURT, our 18-pdrs & 4.5"Hows.bombarded the HINDENBURG LINE at the North West corner of ST QUENTIN.	

Lt-Col E Fitzmaurice returned from leave

Army Form C. 2118.

168th Brigade R.F.A. Commanded by Lt-Col R. FITZMAURICE R.F.A.

WAR DIARY
or
INTELLIGENCE SUMMARY.
(Erase heading not required.)

Instructions regarding War Diaries and Intelligence Summaries are contained in F. S. Regs., Part II. and the Staff Manual respectively. Title pages will be prepared in manuscript.

Place	Date	Hour	Summary of Events and Information	Remarks and references to Appendices
	14/4/17.	4.30.a.m.	Attack & Capture of LAYET. (see appendix (9)) This was a very successful operation, and 400 prisoners were taken.	
		5.0.pm.	Batteries moved forward to positions in the vicinity of FOLMON.	
	15/4/17.	4.0.a.m.	To assist the 35th Division in an attack on CHICOURT the Brigade placed a standing barrage on enemy trenches in M.24.d. Lt-Col M.Fitzmaurice proceeded on Senior Officers Conference.	
		2.0.pm.	Brigade H.Q. moved to BOIS De HOMON.	
	16/4/17.		Front very quiet. Nothing happened.	
	17/4/17.		Shoots on enemy trenches carried out.	
	18/4/17.		The ordinary day shooting on enemy trenches carried out, also night firing on enemy communications.	
	19/4/17.	11.0.a.m.	O.P's heavily shelled. Large fires in ST QUENTIN.	
	20/4/17.	9.0p.m.	'D' Battery moved forward to M.33.	
	21/4/17.		Front very quiet.	
	22/4/17.	4.0.a.m.	Night firing on enemy roads N. of ST QUENTIN. 32nd Division Infantry go out to rest and are relieved by 61st Division.	
	23/4/17.	9.0.pm.	'A' Battery moved forward to M.33.c.8.7. Notification received that No.L.29363 Gnr. CROSLAND E. 'B' Battery has been granted the Military Medal.	
	24/4/17.		Front very quiet. The usual daily firing took place.	
	25/4/17.		— ditto —	

Army Form C. 2118.

WAR DIARY
or
INTELLIGENCE SUMMARY.
(Erase heading not required.)

168th Brigade R.F.A.
Commanded by Lt-Col. R. FITZMAURICE R.F.A.

Instructions regarding War Diaries and Intelligence Summaries are contained in F. S. Regs., Part II. and the Staff Manual respectively. Title pages will be prepared in manuscript.

Place	Date	Hour	Summary of Events and Information	Remarks and references to Appendices
	26/4/17.		Lt-Col. FITZMAURICE returned and took over Command of the Brigade.	
	27/4/17.		Front very quiet.	
	28/4/17.	4.20.a.m.	A successful raid was carried out on the enemy trenches in M.30.b.3.6 by the 2/4th OXFORDS. One prisoner and 3 Machine Guns captured. The Brigade took part as per attached Appendix (d).	
	29/4/17.		Brigade H.Q. moved to X.11.a.5.4. 2/Lieut. L.A.H.HASTINGS 'D' Battery awarded the Military Cross.	
		12 noon 6.0 p.m.	'D' Battery heavily shelled.	
	30/4/17.		Bursts of fire at irregular intervals throughout the day on the woods running from M.36.b.1.5 to M.36.a.9.7.	

1st May 1917.

[signature] Lt-Colonel.
Commanding 168th. Brigade, R.F.A.

APPENDIX 'A'

SECRET.

O.C. /168th. Bde. R.F.A.

"A", "B", & "D" Batteries, 168th Brigade R.F.A. will fire this afternoon as below, to assist the French who are going to attack CHEVREUX, LOIVRE and l'EPINE DE CHEVREUX.

Zero hour will be 3.pm.

Battery.	Time.	Object.	Rate.	No. of rds.
A/168	2.30.pm. to 3.15.pm.	Enfilade Railway S.24.d.0.2 to S.19.c.0.6	1 rd. per gun per minute.	270
B/168.	2.30.pm. to 3.15.pm.	Enfilade Road S.24.a.0.2 to S.24.b.0.5	1 rd. per gun per minute.	270

The above batteries will lift their fire Eastwards at the rate of 100 yards every five minutes, so as to keep pace with main barrage.

Ammunition will be used in the proportion 50% A and 50% AX.

D/168 will bombard the village CHEVREUX in A.5.b. - A.6.a. - and S.29.d. (Ammunition Expenditure - 100 rds.) and the village of LOIVRE A.6.c. and d. (Ammunition Expenditure - 50 rds.)

Time - from 2.30.pm. to 3.15.pm.

ACKNOWLEDGE.

3/4/1917.

Lieut.
Adjt. 168th. Brigade R.F.A.

SECRET.

Copy No. 7.

32nd DIVISIONAL ARTILLERY INSTRUCTIONS
-: No: 2. :-
Reference 1/40,000 Sheets 62.B; & 66.C; 66.D;
-: and 62.C. :-

1. The 32nd Divisional Artillery and 62nd H.A.G. will fire as follows on the 3rd instant to assist the FRENCH.

2. The Heavy Artillery and 4.5" Howitzers will bombard the following areas from 2.30.pm. to 3.15.pm.

Target.	Nature of Guns & No: of Rds fired.			4.5" How: Battery.
	4.5" Howitzers.	6" Howitzers.	60. Pounders.	
FAUBOURG D' ISLE, T.21; 22 & 27.	-	100.	-	-
Village OESTRES, A.5.b; A.6.a.&.S.29.d.	100.	-	50.	D/168.
Enemy works in S.24.a.&.b.	200.	-	100.	D/161.
Village of GAUCHY A.6.c. and.d.	50.	-	50.	D/168.

3. (a). 159th Brigade R.F.A. will form an attack barrage as follows to deceive enemy and draw hostile fire:-

No:& nature of Guns.	Time during which fire rests on each objective.	Objective.	Rate of fire.	No:of rounds.
3 - 18.Pdr. Batteries.	2.30. - 2.50.pm.	S.30.b.0.6. to S.23.b.8.3.	1 round per gun per min:	360.
-do-	2.50. - 3.0.pm.	S.30.b.2.8. to S.24.a.0.5.	3 rounds per gun per min:	540.
-do-	3.0.pm - 3.5.pm.	S.30.b.3.9. to S.24.a.15.	2 rounds per gun 50. per min:	180.
-do-	3.5. - 3.10.pm.	S.24.d.5.0. to S.24.a.30.	2 rounds per gun 65. per min:	180.
-do-	3.10. - 3.15.pm.	S.24.d.7.0. to S.24.a.45.	2 rounds per gun 75. per min:	180.

(b). 1 - 4.5" Howitzer Battery will fire on above objectives lifting off each objective 5 minutes in advance of 18 - Pounder barrage.

RATES OF FIRE. 2:50. - 3.0.pm. 2 rounds per How: per minute.
3.0.pm - 3.15.pm. 1 round per How: per minute.

4. SPECIAL TASK FOR 18 - Pounder Batteries.

Battery.	Time.	Objective.	Rate of fire.	No: of rounds.
A/168.	2.30.to 3.15.pm.	Enfilade Railway, S.24. d.0.0. to T.19.c.0.5.	1 round per gun per minute.	270.
B/168.	2.30.to 3.15.pm.	Enfilade Road S.24.a.0.0 to S.24.b.0.2.	1 round per gun per min:	270.
				540.

NOTE.
Above two batteries will lift their fire Eastwards at the rate of 100 yards every 5 minutes. *so as to keep pace with main barrage.*

5. 18 - Pounder Ammunition.

50% Sprapnel & 50% H.E. for all barrages.

6. Registrations for the above Programme will be carried out on morning of 3rd instant as far as circumstances permit.

7. Fire will cease at 3.15.pm. unless orders to continue are received from this office.

8. Watches will be synchronised from this office at 1.0.pm.

9. ACKNOWLEDGE.

(sd). A.J.GIBBS. Capt.RA.

Brigade Major, 32nd Divisional Artillery.

3/4/17.

ISSUED AT... *9 am.*

Copy No. 1. H.Q., 32nd Division.
2. -do-
3. -do-
4. -do-
5. -do-
6. 161st Brigade R.F.A.
7. 168th Brigade R.F.A.
8. 159th Brigade R.F.A.
9. 62nd H.A.G.
10. IV. Corps R.A.
11. Retained.
12. Diary.
13. Diary.
14. 14th Inf: Bde.
15. 26th Inf: Bde.
16. 97th Inf: Bde.

SECRET.

168th. Brigade, R.F.A.

OPERATION ORDER No. 25.

6th. April 1917.

Reference Sheet attached.

The 61st Division will attack the village of FRESNOY LE PETIT to-night.

Zero time 9 pm.

The 168th. Brigade R.F.A. will take part, tasks of batteries as follows :-

18-Pounders

(a) O plus 10 to O plus 15. C/168   M.27.b.5.2 to M.27.b.0.3.   ) 2 rds
                             A/168 (3 guns) M.27.b.0.3 to M.27.a.85.50) per
                             B/168   M.27.a.85.50 to M.27.a.75.70) gun
) per
) minute

(b) O plus 15 to O plus 18   C/168   M.27.b.5.2 to M.27.b.4.4.   ) 2 rds.per
                             A/168 (3 guns) M.27.b.4.4. to M.27.b.2.6) gun per
                             B/168   M.27.b.2.6 to M.27.b.05.80) minute.

(c) O plus 18 to O plus 23   C/168   M.28.a.2.0 to M.27.b.7.4   ) 2 rds.per
                             A/168 (3 guns) M.27.b.7.4 to M.27.b.50.65) gun per
                             B/168   M.27.b.50.65 to M.27.b.3.9) minute.

(d) O plus 23 to O plus 45   C/168   M.34.b.8.0 to M.34.b.2.7.   ) 1 rd. per
                             A/168 (3 guns) M.34.b.2.7 to M.28.c.9.2   ) gun per
                             B/168   M.28.c.9.2 to M.28.c.5.6   ) minute.

(e) O plus 45 to O plus 1 hr.   - ditto -   ½ rd per gun per
                                                              minute.

In barrage (d) and (e), batteries will search back to trench in M.28.d. and M.34.b.

Howitzers.

O plus 10 to O plus 23 D/168 (2 guns) on Strong Point M.28.a.3.8.
                              (1 gun) on Cross Roads   M.21.d.4.0
                              (1 gun)   M.28.d.6.3.
                              (1 gun)   M.28.d.35.30

O plus 23 to O plus 1 hr. D/168. (2 guns) search and sweep GRICOURT
                                  (2 guns) search Wood in M.28.d.
                                  (1 Gun) trench M.28.d.35.30

Watches will be synchronised from this office by telephone.

A C K N O W L E D G E.

6th. April 1917.   Lieut.
                                       Adjt. 168th. Brigade, R.F.A.

SECRET.   Copy No......

168th. Brigade, R.F.A.
OPERATION ORDER No.26 d/-10/4/17.

Reference 1/B.000 sheet 62b. S.W.

1. The 97th. Infantry Brigade will attack and capture the
   village of PAINE and its defences.
   This will be carried out by the 2nd.K.O.Y.L.I. on the left,
   and the 16th. H.L.I. on the right.
   The dividing line between Battalions will be a line from
   the Cottages (N.4.a.2.1) to PAINE CHATEAU (Road Triangle
   N5.a.8.8 and chateau inclusive to 2nd. K.O.Y.L.I.)
   The first objective will be a N. & S. line drawn down
   through PAINE CHATEAU.
   The second objective will be the Sunken Road running through
   squares M.30 and N.6 and all in M.30.a. inclusive and the
   high ground to the North on a line M.5.a.0.0 to M.5.b.9.3.

2. The Left Battalion will be supported by the 168th Brigade,
   R. F. A. as shown in attached Maps A & B.

3. At Zero plus 75 a Protective Barrage will be formed on the
   2ND LINE. Fire will be continued on this line until Zero
   plus 85 at one round per gun per minute, after which time
   it will cease until further orders are issued.

4. The S.O.S. Barrage will be :-

   18-Pdrs.   on the Protective Barrage.
                     in M30C + Southern Exits of GRICOURT
   4.5" Hows.   Woods ~~~~~~~~~~~~
   Ammunition Shrapnel.

5. 2/Lt. G. C. Wood, B/168, will be Liaison Officer with the
   2nd. K.O.Y.L.I.

6. Zero Day and time will be notified later.

7. Watches will be synchronised from this Headquarters.

8. A C K N O W L E D G E.

                                                          Lieut.
10th. April 1917.   Adjt. 168th Brigade, R.F.A.

O.C.   /168th Bde. R.F.A.

Herewith New Map "A". This cancels the previous one issued with Operation Order No. 26.

Please do not destroy the old Map "A".

As the exact position of the Trench is not known, it has been put in Barrage Map approximately.

Batteries must carefully register the portion of the Trench on which they will fire from Zero to Zero plus 10.

[signature] Lieut.

12/4/17.   Adjt. 168th Brigade, R.F.A.

"A" Form.
MESSAGES AND SIGNALS.

Army Form C.2121
(in pads of 100).
No. of Message ....

Prefix ...... Code ...... m.	Words	Charge	This message is on a/c of :	Recd. at .... m.
Office of Origin and Service Instructions.				Date ....
	Sent		.... Service.	From ....
	At .... m.			
	To			
	By	(Signature of "Franking Officer.")	By ....

TO { O.C D/168 R.F.A

Sender's Number.	Day of Month.	In reply to Number.	AAA
* A.M. 26	13/4/17		

Ref. Operation Order No. 26 dated 10/4/17.
Para 4.
The S.O.S. for D/168 given therein is
cancelled, and the following
substituted.

Wood in M 30 c
Southern Exits of GRICOURT.

From: Alan Lumb Lt
Place: Adj 168th Brigade R.F.A.
Time:

The above may be forwarded as now corrected. (Z)

MS 6 Speeches etc.
3 Speeches, 3
2 AHC 30 Sept

Map A.

18 Pdr Creeping Barrage.

Times given are those at which
Barrage **OPENS** on each line

━━━ Protective Barrage

Rates of fire in Green figures

━━━ { ZERO+48 to ZERO+70 — 1 Rd per gun per min
      ZERO+70 to ZERO+75 — 3 Rds per gun " "

4.5 HOW TASKS.

TIME	TASK		MAP B.
ZERO to ZERO+8	3 Guns: Trench S4b99 to S4b7.6 to S5a3.5 1 " : Church 1 " : S4b9.6 to S4b9.9		
ZERO+8 to ZERO+74	As per SKETCH.		

RATE OF FIRE: 1 Round per Gun per min.

Times given are those at which Barrage OPENS on each LINE.

M S

Officer Commanding
/16th Bde. R.F.A.

Reference Sheet 19. IV.Corps Topo.Section. 1/20,000.

In the Raid to be carried out at zero on the morning of the 28th. the tasks of batteries will be as follows :-

Task.	Battery.	Time	
(1)	'A' Bty.	Zero to Zero + 12.	Barrage trench from M.30.d.2.7 to M.30.b.6.0 to M.30.d.8.8
	'A' Bty.	Zero + 12 to Zero + 60.	Barrage trench from M.24.d.4.4 to M.19.c.2.6

Rates of Fire:-
    Zero to Zero + 9   2 rds per gun per minute.
    Zero + 9 to Zero + 12   3 " " " " "
    Zero + 12 to Zero + 30   1½ " " " " "
    Zero + 30 to Zero + 60   1 " " " " "

(2)	"B" Bty,	Zero to Zero + 4	Barrage trench from M.30.d.2.0 to M.30.d.2.7.
	"B" Bty,	Zero + 4 to Zero + 60.	Barrage Trench from M.30.a.9.9. to M.24.d.4.4.

Rates of Fire:-
    Zero to Zero + 4   2 rds per gun per minute
    Zero + 4 to Zero + 7   3 rds " " " "
    Zero + 7 to Zero + 30   1½ " " " " "
    Zero + 30 to Zero + 60   1 " " " " "

(3)	"C" Bty	Zero to Zero + 7	Barrage trench from M.36.b.0.7 to M.30.d.5.2.
	"C" Bty	Zero + 7 to Zero + 60	Barrage trench from M.30.b.4.5 to M.30.a.9.9.

Rates of Fire:-
    Same as "B" Battery.

(4)	"D" Bty	Zero to Zero + 7 (6 Hows)	Search and sweep L.WOOD M.30.c
	"D" Bty	Zero + 7 to Zero + 60. (6 Hows)	Cutting and Crater M.24.d

Rates of Fire:-
    Zero to Zero + 7   1½ rds per gun per minute.
    Zero + 7 to Zero + 60   ½ " " " " "

Ammunition.- Expenditure will be in the proportion of 50% A. and 50% AX.
No AX will be used until Zero + 10.

Zero time will be notified later.

Watches will be synchronised from this office by telephone.

A C K N O W L E D G E.

27th. April 1917.

Lieut.
Adjt. 16th. Brigade, R.F.A.

Headquarters Staff -:0:- 168th Brigade R.F.A.

Nominal Roll of all ranks 30/4/17.
------ ooOoo ------

Officers;-   Lt - Col FITZMAURICE.R.
              Lieut Alan Lumb
              2/Lieut H.Fisher
              Capt D.Ferguson(R.A.M.C)

Other Ranks;-   L.25839.   Corp'l   Lee G.
                     29811.   Bomb   Anderton A.
                   L.29801.   "   Normanton A.
                     12245.   a/Bmbr   Wright J.
                   L.29430.   "   Eyre F.
                   L.25881.   "   Gibson H.
                   L.28042.   "   Sugden E.
                     79511.   Mc Intyre
                   L.28206.   Gnr   Ackeroyd E.
                   L.25810.   "   Bottomley G.
                     59688.   "   Clark B.J.
                      5645.   "   Colley E.
                     15200.   "   Firth H.
                     50777.   "   Grindley W.
                   L.29404.   "   Greenwood G
                   L.25480.   "   Lucas E.
                   L.29394.   "   Rangeley P.S.
                   L.25399.   "   Ramsden A.
                   L.25626.   "   Slater H.
                   L.28179.   "   Sykes C.A.
                   L.29296.   "   Windle A.T.
                   L.27531.   "   Postlethwaite F.
                   L.25422.   Dvr   Armitage J.R.
                   L.32440.   "   Baker G.
                   L.32540.   "   Blake F.
                   L.28026.   "   Cowham S.
                      5742.   "   Dickenson J.
                   L.29287.   "   Fisher S.
                    198817.   "   Foote G.
                      1573.   "   Gutheridge H.
                     13104.   "   Greenwood G.D.
                     37566.   "   Hirons E.
                      5855.   "   Gowam W.
                   L.32511.   "   Iredale A.
                   L.2825.   "   Iredale H.
                   L.28189.   "   Mellor A.
                   L.29381.   "   Newsome A.E.
                   L.28732.   "   Martin J.
                   L.29424.   "   Parker J.
                   L.29423.   "   Pollard W.
                   L.25833.   "   Radley T.
                   L.29357.   "   Reddington M.
                    165508.   "   Reed S.
                   L.29389.   "   Stansfield P.
                      6267.   s/s   Pereira A.T.
                              Sadd'r   Williams.

                 A.O.C. 625   staff Sergt Barker H. (Artificer)

A Battery — ; — 168th Brigade R.F.A.

Nominal Roll of all ranks 30/4/17.
————oooOooo————

Officers ;—
    Major R.EMMET
    Capt W.R.Brown
    Lieut O.G.d'Ivry
    2/Lieut Bowels W.R.
    2/Lieut J.G.Bell.
    2/Lieut A.G.Miller.
    2/Lieut Ravald L.A.

Other Ranks;—

28514.	B.S.M.	Patchet W.J.	L29307	Gnr	Oatley H.
28064.	Q.M.S.	Brearley H.	190397.	"	Cross F.
110.	Sergt	Witney F.	28178.	"	Dawson W.
53261.	"	Smith E.F.	12049.	"	Edwards L.
25426.	"	Field P.J.	130461.	"	Edwards W.H.
2679.	"	Roberts J.F.	86276.	"	Franklin
43312.	"	McGowan A.H.	190415.	"	Foote C.
2425.	"	Firth A.	602006.	"	Fuller S.
2697.	Corpl	Rhodes L.	132061.	"	Fearn H.
2561.	"	Povey J.	169899.	"	Halliday R.
2619.	"	France W.	2823.	"	Hynes W.H.
83394.	"	Simpson C.	2610.	"	Hopwood H.
2693.	"	Littlewood K.	28159.	"	Hewit R.
29407.	"	Taylor F.	28151.	"	Hopson T.C.
32281.	"	Williams W.C.	29427.	"	Kettle L.J.
2479.	Bombr	Bentley J.	29411.	"	Knockton J.C.
28100.	"	Pitchforth A.	32512.	"	Lumb W.
29313.	"	Armitage W.B.	28177.	"	Leatham F.
2708.	"	Crawshaw J.I.	28184.	"	Lockwood H.
2574.	"	Wood B.	197866.	"	McErving H.
2731.	"	Rhodes J.	95371.	"	McCarthy C.
28188.	"	Padgett S.	97863.	"	McPherson A.
2464.	"	Richardson C.H.	167120.	"	McWilliams T.
32553.	"	Taylor W.J.	167074.	"	McHieshie W.
28072.	a/Bdr	Bentley C.	150416.	"	Mallett H.
3239.	"	Fenton B.	28129.	"	Marshall L.
2768.	"	Brooksbank S.	25536.	"	Mansfield W.G.
2669.	"	Oates H.	25392.	"	Milnes H.
29297.	"	Noble B.	6011.	"	Myler A.
83010.	"	Squires A.E.	112737.	"	Negus H.
25485.	Sa/Bdr	Williams C.	25443.	"	Nuttall P.
28136.	"	Shaw N.	44251.	"	Offer F.
28034.	"	Beavers M.	28186.	"	Perkins J.C.
167423.	"	Sweet J.	29272.	"	Parker W.
25783.	Cpl s/s	Town B.	2736.	"	Pearse H.
76.	"	Packs J.	29306.	"	Pearson F.
28173.	S.S.	Taylor J.E.	28185.	"	Proctor R.C.
29282.	"	Nuttal J.T.	25513.	"	Peace A.
28175.	"	Waterhouse L.	2584.	"	Quarmby W.H.
2690.	"	Kaye J.T.	2663.	"	Rushworth A.
5882.	"	Bevington A.	32491.	"	Roberts J.
32485.	Sadd'r	Jackson W.R.	28006.	"	Singleton H.W.
62728.	"	Olliver J.E.	2781.	"	Sykes Jow.
147472.	Fitter	Helliwell E.	52972.	"	Stocker H.C.
121451.	Wheeler	Weaver J.	2566.	"	Shaw J.C.
25790.	Gnr.	Allott J.V.	81446.	"	Shaw H.
25595.	"	Billington T.	148166.	"	Smith A.
28014.	"	Bray E.H.	126074.	"	Spence R.
28217.	"	Bower B.	5889.	"	Shoesmith W.
100556.	"	Beanish R.	2573.	"	Spencer A.
100774.	"	Baird S.	51733.	"	Spellany F.
28180.	"	Bolton H.	2791.	"	Thornton J.
29379.	"	Beaumont L.	2935.	"	Townend J.
32471.	"	Calvert F.	323.	"	Thornber W.H.
2934.	"	Craigie T.	2764.	"	Wilkinson B.
5556.	"	Cappell A.			

28038	Gnr	Wilkinson T.
25575	"	Walker W.T.
29300	"	Wood F.
32441	"	Walker A.
25844	"	Weldrake H.
29318	"	Wood R.
25649	"	Wood G.H.
133713	"	Young W.
107780	Dvr	Archer W.
17521	"	Adams F.
81590	"	Black A.
25524	"	Balmforth H.
2552	"	Bray H.
25436	"	Brearley A.
25395	"	Brook G.L.
25608	"	Chapman B.
29323	"	Cartwright P.
25592	"	Crowther Ch.G.
5802	"	Connor J.
109981	"	Chapman H.
41489	"	Crisp E.
25843	"	Digman W.J.
29409	"	Dyson W.
28079	"	Green F.
2820	"	Ganly J.
29316	"	Gledhill J.R.
25579	"	Griffiths I.C.
25677	"	Holdroyd H.
28201	"	Horsfall H.
28073	"	Hirst J.
25849	"	Holmes H.
29347	"	Hardcastle C.W.
29417	"	Hincliffe H.
32541	"	Kershaw C.
25419	"	Kerton H.
28163	"	Lodge A.
25384	"	Liversey I.C.
28022	"	Marsden J.A.
28021	"	Mallinson J.A.
25639	"	Millard H.
25641	"	Murphy H.
826369	"	Morse L.
101698	"	O'neill H.
147602	"	Parryiss H.
32464	"	Pogson S.
28133	"	Priest G.W.
75864	"	Quinn D.
28074	"	Robershaw G.
28075	"	Roe H.
28013	"	Sykes W.
49859	"	Spencer G.
25633	"	Shaw E.
25503	"	Shaw H.
28224	"	Shaw C.A.
25797	"	Singleton V.
28101	"	Taylor I.H.
25460	"	Twigg J.
25483	"	Varley L.
28214	"	Wood W.H.
2560	"	Wood A.
10576	"	Westgate F.
29331	"	Woodcock W.
28087	"	Walters H.
25394	"	Wortley T.
25541	"	Woodhead H.
25819	"	Whitehead J.A.
159419	"	Weedon W.
21116	"	Wainwright W.
25540	"	Smith J.H.

attached:-

S.E.1514. Sgt Jolley A.J. A.V.C.

"B" Battery.   ---ooOoo---   168th Brigade R.F.A.

Nominal Roll of all ranks 1st 30/4/17.
---ooOoo---

Officers:-   Major F. FITZGIBBON.
                2/Lieut W.P.Robinson.
                2/Lieut L.M.Hastings M.C.
                2/Lieut W.L.Chamberlain.
                2/Lieut J.Mitchelhill
                2/Lieut C.P.Basnett.
                2/Lieut A.E.Marriott.

Other Ranks:-

58482.	B.S.M.	Stenning T.	18820.	Gnr	Brown F.
L.32437.	Q.M.S.	Lane A.C.	L.32496.	"	Burton G.
L.3214.	F.Sgt	Sutcliffe R.	L.25671.	"	Cocker F.
L.25448.	Sergt	Beaumont F.	2295.	"	Coward T.
L.25428.	"	Deckin T.	L.29263.	"	Crosland W.(M.M.)
L.29344.	"	Guthrie A.	68234.	"	Doggett A.
L.1985.	"	Harding R.	79093.	"	Drewitt W.H.
L.25606.	"	Palframan F.	L.29392.	"	Eccles J.L.
L.25390.	"	Taylor H.	3052.	"	Earl W.
L.25871.	Corpl	Walker S.	L.29263.	"	Fowler B.
L.25484.	"	Wilans G.	56821.	"	Gallaher M
L.25864.	"	Mason R.	11578.	"	Goldsmith S.C.
L.25716.	"	Fisher W.W.	L.29244.	"	Greenwood A.A.
L.25874.	"	Shaw L.	L.29262.	"	Greenwood L.A.
L.29350.	"	Thornton J.	L.29380.	"	Hanson E.
L.25863.	"	Holmes L.	L.25746.	"	Hargreaves A.
6	s/s Cpl	Brennan J.	L.32454.	"	Hargreaves D.
L.25446.	Bombr	Bottomley T.	111819.	"	Harris G.
L.25451.	"	Spendlove T.	L.25504.	"	Harrison W.
L.28210.	"	Greenwood M.R.	L.25664.	"	Hartley A.
L.29826.	"	Temperton H.K.	5329.	"	Horan J.S.
L.28138.	"	Bramley S.M.	L.29242.	"	Hoyle G.G.
L.2545.	"	Turner J.E.	L.28046.	"	Holdsworth A.
L.24990.	"	Mayers A.	L.25689.	"	Kenyon J.H.
L.28218.	"	Dyson A.	L.25458.	"	Kiddle F.
L.32480.	"	Bancroft L.	L.3210.	"	Knight S.
L.5961.	"	Hurst W.	L.2562.	"	Lawford F.
L.25808.	a/Bmbr	Broomhead W.H.	L.28220.	"	Laycock A.
L.28043.	"	Birch H.	L.25623.	"	Lee F.
L.2511.	"	Christy H.	L.25622.	"	Littlewood A.
L.28208.	"	Croft L.H.	197862.	"	McLennan J.B.
16381.	"	Cawthorne J.	197864.	"	McPhearson D.
L.25475.	"	Ibootson M.	197865.	"	McRea D.
15224.	"	Wright A.	L.28126.	"	Mallinson F.
L.2491.	"	Sherwood J.T.	L.25712.	"	Mason J.
15273.	"	Holmes N.	30377.	"	Miller C.W.
503.	s/s	Boswell H.	16402.	"	Miller L.
L.2552.	"	Hoyle C.	L.29400.	"	Mitchell D.
L.2510.	"	Readyhough G.W.	L.3244.	"	Mitchell R.
L.2492.	"	Sidebottom J.	L.28076.	"	Murray A.
L.3252.	"	Wilson J.W.	L.29402.	"	Murray E.
L.2747.	Sadd'r	Brocksbank G.	18876.	"	Nash T.J.
L.25607.	"	Stansfield F.	156134.	"	Nightingale D.
L.2596.	Wheel'r	Yates F.	L.29395.	"	Noble F.
L.32456.	Fitter	Hill W.	L.25632.	"	Onyon A.
L.25382.	Gnr	Ainley W.H.	L.25836.	"	Owen W.
	"	Bury A.	2558.	"	Platt H.
L.3249.	"	Billington H.	L.25827.	"	Riddlesden A.
L.25616.	"	Binns A.O.	L.25463.	"	Scott N.
L.32483.	"	Bottoms H.	5828.	"	Spence J.
L.3521.	"		L.32473.	"	Stafford H.
L.25873.	"	Broadbent T.	67772.	"	Tanner W.C.
L.29261.	"	Broadley J.T.	L.29372.	"	Tidswell H.T.
8786.	"	Broom H.	11462.	"	Thomas O.

L.2683.	Gnr	Thompson J.T.		L.2598.	Dvr	Townsend W.
L.2629.	"	Turner H.		L.2499.	"	Tallis G.
L.2727.	"	Winteringham E.		L.28142.	"	Walker J.
150477.	"	Wolf H.		L.3267.	"	Walker M.
L.29431.	"	Wood G.H.		L.2631.	"	Wheelwright G.
L.2704.	"	Youngman A.		160955.	"	Whitchurch
198809.	"	Gigg B.		L.3215.	"	Wilkinson L.
160946.	"	Ling J.		L.29257.	"	Wilkinson F.
67704.	"	Tunstall A.		185398.	"	Willatt.
46249.	"	Scott F.		164826.	"	Williams
				L.29269.	"	Wood H.
L.29381.	Dvr	Barraclough H.		141214.	"	Worth
L.29258.	"	Barraclough T.E.		L.28089.	"	Wright E.
L.28213.	"	Beaumont H.		930739.	"	Matthis M.C.
L.28199.	"	Bury A.		213085.	"	Newns A.
L.2837.	"	Bury S.		216330.	"	Cork F.
L.3276.	"	Bentley T.		18573.	"	Chesters D.
L.3228.	"	Barrisow F.				
L.3266.	"	Braithwaite J.F.				
L.2470.	"	Brook J.W.				
L.2878.	"	Clear A.				
L.32443.	"	Crossley A.				
L.28113.	"	Crosley J.				
L.3218.	"	Crowther J.				
L.2446.	"	Davis J.W.				
112192.	"	Dennis G.				
L.29383.	"	Dewar W.				
L.2742.	"	Dyson F.				
L.2442.	"	Eastwood G.				
L.2732.	"	Firth H.				
L.3238.	"	Grey D.				
L.29367.	"	Greenwood J.W.				
L.2729.	"	Greenwood C.E.				
L.2831.	"	Hall H.				
L.28214.	"	Harrison F.				
L.2479.	"	Hattersley F.				
L.3224.	"	Hawthornthwaite T.W.				
L.2822.	"	Hinscliffe A.				
L.2558.	"	Hobson A.				
L.3206.	"	Holmes W.				
L.29403.	"	Horrocks H.				
L.32447.	"	Jackson F.				
L.28070.	"	Jowett J.W.				
L.29270.	"	Ledgard H.				
L.2747.	"	Leckenby J.				
L.28132.	"	Martin J.				
L.28077.	"	Martin L.				
L.28127.	"	Miller H.				
152302.	"	Milner J.				
L.29401.	"	Moody A.				
L.2870.	"	Murray R.				
L.2675.	"	Nicholson J.				
L.28194.	"	North M.				
20609.	"	Ray D.				
L.28071.	"	Robinson F.				
5116.	"	Roberts G.				
L.2861.	"	Robinson T.				
L.2512.	"	Robinson W.J.				
L.2730.	"	Rushworth E.				
L.262.	"	Scott J.J.				
L.28041.	"	Schofield A.				
L.3279.	"	Shepard N.				
L.2644.	"	Singleton L.M.				
L.2454.	"	Snell A.				
L.29797.	"	Southwell J.				
L.28090.	"	Stanton A.				
L.28109.	"	Sugden G.				
L.2569.	"	Turner J.				
L.2866.	"	Townsend H.				

Attached:-
8949. Vety.Sergt White F.A.

"C" Battery.　　　---ooOoo---　　　168th Brigade R.F.A.

Nominal Roll of all ranks 30/4/17.

---ooOoo---

Officers:-　　　Major H.Cottee.
　　　　　　　　Capt L.G.Firth.
　　　　　　　　Lieut B.T.Groves
　　　　　　　　2/Lieut H.L.James
　　　　　　　　2/Lieut G.O.J.Barrick
　　　　　　　　2/Lieut C.A.Anelay
　　　　　　　　2/Lieut S.J.Hinton.
　　　　　　　　2/Lieut C.A.Browne

Other Ranks:-

53473.	B.S.M.	Malone M.J.	L.28200.	Gnr	Brook J.
L.268.	Q.M.S.	Tomlinson S.	L.11981.	"	Cockle G.
L.27727.	Sergt	Ward A.	L.28147.	"	Chapman T.
L.11931.	"	Townsend W.	L.147114	"	Creeper H.
L.12004.	"	Turgoose W.	196154.	"	Cooke F.
L.2711.	"	Kirkham T.	138478.	"	Cannell W.
35406.	"	Sykes H.M.	60219.	"	Davison H.
22239.	"	Fitzgerald W.	L.25702.	"	Denton F.
L.29412.	"	Brown T.	129947.	"	Divaney F.
L.11973.	Corpl	Booth J.	L.25411.	"	Ellis W.
L.11923.	"	Imms E.	L.12017.	"	Farmery J.W.
L.19494.	"	Marshall H.	78830.	"	Fraser J.
L.12050.	"	Sanderson G.	L.12019.	"	Froggett B.
L.19481.	"	Ward J.S.	78656.	"	Penny F.
L.28195.	"	Garside I.	163727.	"	Goddard W.E.
L.28121.	"	Palmer R.	37084.	"	Gale S.E.
L.19489.	Bomb'r	Wardle L.M.	163921.	"	Gerritt S.W.
L.19478.	"	Todd J.A.	150316.	"	Gawthorpe A.
L.12016.	"	McGuire T.F.J.	L.11973.	"	Howarth H.
L.27730.	"	Walton H.	L.11992.	"	Halton R.
L.19484.	"	Bailey B.C.	88771.	"	Hall N.
L.12028.	"	Craven W.A.	L.19490.	"	Homer C.
L.05077.	"	Caruthers T.	3446.	"	Hut R.
L.11993.	"	Holdroyd T.	304444.	"	Holdern F.
L.25473.	"	Earnshaw S.	L.2751.	"	Higgins H.
L.25812.	"	Terry L.	L.10744.	"	Huggett T.
L.29414.	"	Elliott C.H.	2933.	"	Hisford A.
37207.	a/"	Smith P.W.	143669.	"	Heron R.
L.11959.	"	Ellis W.R.	167010.	"	Hankinson J.
L.19519.	"	Milnthorpe G.	L.12020.	"	Inman H.
L.19487.	"	Carr W.C.	63915.	"	Irving W.A.
L.11962.	"	Wilcock G.	120111.	"	Jolley W.
L.27987.	"	Broadhead D.	19809.	"	James T.
L.28010.	"	Steele J.W.	L.19514.	"	Lines J.
L.25775.	"	Lee H.	2285.	"	Lewis E.W.
L.12035.	"	Wathey A.	L.12047.	"	Martin T.
30751.	Far Sgt	Bishop G.	L.11932.	"	Mulheir J.W.
L.11991.	s/s Cpl	Halton G.	L.12002.	"	Nowell E.M.
L.11926.	s/s	Fletcher F.	188587.	"	Norman W.E.
L.27751.	"	Bailey H.	172668.	"	Nesbitt R.
L.2954.	"	Chappel H.	L.11971.	"	Parkin W.
L.11934.	"	Ismay T.H.	188719.	"	Poynts A.
L.19518.	"	Thompson J.	134691.	"	Robinson A.E.
10790.	"	Copping H.E.	185827.	"	Spink G.
L.29360.	Cpl Ft'r	Hincliffe G.	L.19496.	"	Saberton H.
L.14862.	Wheel'r	Pringle B.	L.27909.	"	Spittle T.A.
L.11927.	Sadd'r	Hull J.	13907.	"	Swinn J.
147364.	Gnr	Balls H.N.	1268.	"	Sellars G.
L.11954.	"	Burr J.	67727.	"	Smith J.
L.12026.	"	Beach J.	37802.	"	Thompson J.
L.11979.	"	Brady D.	L.25715.	"	Taylor J.T.
L.19485.	"	Briggs E.J.	L.19502.	"	Wailes W.

L.12003	Gnr.	Waldron T.	
L.19503	"	Watson G.	
34602	"	Wright H.	
L.19717	"	Wardle G.H.	

L.12022	Dvr.	Ainsworth E.
L.11919	"	Backhouse G.H.
L.11949	"	Boulton P.
L.11985	"	Burnley W.S.
L.15220	"	Brury A.
L.11982	"	Clark E.W.
57926	"	Coles J.
L.25612	"	Clark R.W.
L.28232	"	Chapman J.
50755	"	Chapman W.
L.119327	"	Cleaver E.R.
840589	"	Clough G.
L.29291	"	Drake G.Z.
L.28107	"	Ellis H.
L.11969	"	Eubank J.A.
L.25474	"	Earnshaw E.
L.12055	"	Fannery T.
L.19505	"	Firth G.
L.19506	"	Fretwell H.
L.12037	"	Garfitt J.T.
L.19520	"	Garfoot E.
L.11922	"	Hulley A.W.
L.11962	"	Hunter J.
L.11941	"	Hart W.
L.11967	"	Hancock N.
L.19510	"	Horsfall E.
L.19509	"	Hudson J.
L.12041	"	Kershaw H.
L.11929	"	Kemp R.
L.19492	"	Lapish J.
L.19513	"	Lamb M.
L.28015	"	Lawton H.
L.29285	"	Lord J.
85728	"	Maddox J.
L.14919	"	Marshall S.
L.18919	"	Mitchell W.
77571	"	O'Keefe J.A.
6074	"	Overland H.
L.11949	"	Pickard H.
75445	"	Pipe E.
L.27691	"	Poynton G.W.
L.19516	"	Priestley B.
L.2869	"	Price W.
L.28031	"	Parkin H.
L.25850	"	Pogson H.
L.12011	"	Roberts E.W.
L.11965	"	Ross J.A.
L.19487	"	Schofield W.
L.12033	"	Senior E.K.

L.20413	Dvr.	Shipman H.
L.29293	"	Sutcliffe S.
L.28164	"	Spivey P.
L.28149	"	Scott J.R.
L.25448	"	Singleton N.
L.27993	"	Senior J.W.
L.11920	"	Thompson R.
L.27747	"	Toothill A.C.
L.32459	"	Turner H.
L.27906	"	Taylor E.
L.28095	"	Turner A.B.
L.12068	"	Wales A.
L.12021	"	Walshaw E.
L.12006	"	Wrigglesworth F.
L.28169	"	Williams J.
L.28124	"	Walton R.
L.29322	"	White L.
50414	"	Woolgar G.
51913	"	Wareham E.
156918	"	Whitehouse W.
145487	"	Wilson W.
L.3416	"	Wheeler W.
9304	"	Wist G.
344	"	Young T.

Attached. Sgt. A.V.C. Harding

'D' Battery — 168th Bde. R.F.A.

Nominal Roll of all ranks — 1/5/1917.

OFFICERS.
Major D. K. Tweedie.
Capt. J. C. Poole.
Lieut. R. Dunbar.
2/Lt. G. C. Wood.
2/Lt. A. A. Steward.
2/Lt. J. J. Caterer.
2/Lt. E. P. Peel.

Other Ranks.

13705	BSM.	Perigo W.	128068	Gnr	Allen C.
3922	BQMS	Le page H.	19896	"	Badger G.
100360	Far.Sgt.	Greenwood J.	5005	"	Ball G.C.
11948	Sgt.	Allen A.	26385	"	Boler H.E.
889548	"		25789	"	Blood J.
35383	"	Hartley B.W.	27580	"	Briddock J.A.
950107	"	Jeffrey S.A.	889514	"	Barker J.A.
19894	"	Lambley J.T.	889522	"	Barker W.
78512	Cpl.S/S	Emms A.		"	Bettane J.
26460	"	Sadlr Lawson J.J.	3566	"	Burke C.
27618	"	Ftr. Thresh E.	889513	"	Barker W.H.
35409	"	Dinsdale J.	25688	"	Caine J.E.
19930	"	Flannigan P.	889530	"	Cook B.
19965	"	Hawkes T.G.H.	889531	"	Sock G.M.
889591	"	Philpoth J.E.	19947	"	Dalby E.
889599	"	Stannard J.	27596	"	Dixon H.E.
19914	"	Wooffitt F.E.	889542	"	Dunnett J.
28146	Bdr.	Boothroyd W.	911227	"	Day F.E.
27756	"	Bonner S.	27537	"	Esom G.H.
27590	"	Bradford J.	27175	"	Fowler A.S.
889568	"	Browse S.A.	19950	"	Flannigan J.
35389	"	Dobson J.E.	179512	"	Garnham A.C.
27757	"	Hetherington J.	40484	"	Goodman A.
19840	"	Hempsall J.	104591	"	Howard A.
88956	"	Jackson A.A.	55188	"	Heard H.
889575	"	Last S.	19848	"	Hellawell G.W.
19919	"	Scholey E.	97625	"	Howlett S.
26400	"	Smith W	35413	"	Hadley J
26452	a/Br	Bellamy J.W.	148368	"	Keone F.C.
35381	"	Guest W.	889569	"	Lamb S.
35795	"	Hamilton H.	25317½	"	Langford W.G.
889607	"	Spinks B.R.	2129	"	McLennan J.
889533	S/a/Br	Gutteridge A.	5079	"	McLaughton T.
27533	S/S	Hellawell A.	27532	"	Newton L.
27497	"	Innocent R.	19796	"	Parkinson G.H.
27759	"	Popplewell G.	1307	"	Petchley C.
27612	"	Smith J.	889585	"	Peck J.W.
26447	"	Varney J.	124923	"	Richardson H.
78446	Sdlr	Batye J.	138484	"	Sagar R.
113012	"	Molyneaux D.	26125	"	Simmons A.G.
26676	"	Schofield J.	4005	"	Sugar F.
116171	Ftr.	Collar P.A.	27520	"	Stacey J.
			97676	"	Starkey E.
			26449	"	Shaw F.
			129128	"	Smith W.E.
			889608	"	Simmons W.
				"	Sartin H.
			889604	"	Smith F.J.
			26463	"	Townsend A.V.

20010.	Gnr	Thompson J.
889584.	"	Podd C.R.
889614.	"	Shoddy A.
12044.	"	Ward E.
35404.	"	Williams J.
889623.	"	Watling B.
889632.	"	Woodward F.
889624.	"	Waine F.
27627.	Dvr	Ackeroyd T.
27601.	"	Archer S.L.
19783.	"	Armitage G.
35402.	"	Bainbridge J.G.
27757.	"	Batten W.
26401.	"	Bell A.
26524.	"	Bellamy F.
35390.	"	Beckett E.
12107.	"	Bond P.
28059.	"	Barker W.
20007.	"	Bradley J.
889511	"	Bell J.
32488.	"	Dutton J.
889546.	"	Doughton E.
88952l.	"	Bunn A.
889509.	"	Brightwell E.
271225.	"	Collins J.R
20008.	"	Croft J.
889581.	"	Cocker B.
889534.	"	Chittock A.
13985.	"	Doulavy W.
27621.	"	Denby F.
10522.	"	Dowd L.
27622.	"	Dickson L.
44891.	"	Drapper A.
889537.	"	Driver R.
27606.	"	Fisher A.
19799.	"	Fisher G.
19944.	"	Flint F.
19943.	"	Green J.
19803.	"	Greenwood J.
889556.	"	Garner G.E.
889555.	"	Gray S.V.
19865.	"	Hempsall T.
26422.	"	Havenand H.
19953.	"	Howson W.
19749.	"	Hews H.
889563.	"	Honeywood B.
27610.	"	Jewitt W.
35411.	"	Jackson F.
35380.	"	Lunn G.
92590.	"	Lewellyn T.
14011.	"	Male F.G.
889570.	"	Lay G.
47044.	"	McCormick A.
35379.	"	Middleton W.
2151.	"	Miller A.J.
35414.	"	Padgett A.G.
19789.	"	Peacock J.E.
2560.	"	Palmer J.
27222.	"	Phillips F.
19939.	"	Parker E.
889587.	"	Piper W.
81641.	"	Penny H.
2759.	"	Roebuck L.
889596.	"	Red A.
889595.	"	Rainer H.
40494.	"	Seabrook J.H.
26406.	"	Savage W.

27609.	Dvr	Smith J.
29405.	"	Stewart A.
26411.	"	Speight A.
27505.	"	Shone W.
27600.	"	Sykes J.
889600.	"	Smith A.W.
	"	Skeet E.
889601.	"	Suspins E.
34341.	"	Turner A.
19736.	"	Thompson A.D.
24085.	"	Tilston R.
27566.	"	Trafford J.
71271.	"	Thomson J.G.H.
889616.	"	Theobold W.
889612.	"	Taylor E.
889615.	"	Thompson S.
12031.	"	Wilkinson J.W.
27498.	"	Wright D.
19794.	"	Whelan J.
27718.	"	Wilson J.
889631.	"	Whitehead J.
36628.	"	Williams C.
		Westrop

attached;—

8038.   Vet'y Sergt Moore W.

CONFIDENTIAL.

WAR DIARY

of the

168th. BRIGADE, R. F. A.

from 1st. May 1917 to 31st. May 1917. (Volume 17.)

———————-oooooOooooo-———————

WAR DIARY or INTELLIGENCE SUMMARY.

(Erase heading not required.)

Army Form C. 2118.

168th. Brigade, R.F.A.
Commanded by Lt-Col. R. FITZMAURICE.

Instructions regarding War Diaries and Intelligence Summaries are contained in F. S. Regs., Part II. and the Staff Manual respectively. Title pages will be prepared in manuscript.

Place	Date	Hour	Summary of Events and Information	Remarks and references to Appendices
	1/5.17.	9 pm.	One section per battery withdrawn to Wagon Line.	
	2/5.17.	9 pm.	Remainder of Batteries withdrawn to Wagon Line. Front taken over by 306th. Brigade R.F.A. Headquarters move to M.T.11Y.	
	3/5/17.		Brigade in rest; day spent in general overhauling and cleaning up.	
	4/5/17.		Major F. FITZJEBSON, 'B' Battery awarded D.S.O.	
	6/5.17.	10.30 am.	G.O.C., Division inspected the Brigade.	
	7/5.17.	9 p.m.	One section per Battery return to action.	
	8/5.17.	9 p.m.	Remainder of Battery's return to action (see Appendix)	
	9/5.17.	10 am.	Lt-Col. R. FITZMAURICE takes over Command of the Left Group 61st Div. Artillery.	
	10/5/17.	3 pm.	Army shoot on enemy's trenches; XXXX XXX and attack on Observation Balloons. No balloons brought down on our front.	
		5.15 pm.	'C' & 'D' Batteries heavily shelled. Positions damaged but no casualties.	
	11/5/17.	2 pm.	'A' Battery heavily shelled. 2 guns damaged but no casualties.	
	12/5/13	Night.	4th GLOUCESTERS 183rd Infantry Brigade, 61st Division, raided CEPY FARM, supported by B/168, C/168, D/168, 2/161 and 2 guns B/306th Bde R.F.A.. Artillery fire reported "very accurate" by Infantry.	
	13/5/17.		C.R.A., 26th French Division reconnoitred the sector.	
	14/5/17.		F... Group Commander and subordinate Group Commanders reconnoitred the Sector.	
	16/5/17.	12 midnight.	Counter Battery Section of D/168 withdrawn to Wagon Line.	

Army Form C. 2118.

WAR DIARY
or
INTELLIGENCE SUMMARY.
(Erase heading not required.)

Instructions regarding War Diaries and Intelligence Summaries are contained in F.S. Regs., Part II. and the Staff Manual respectively. Title pages will be prepared in manuscript.

168th Brigade R.F.A.

Commanded by Lt-Col. R. FITZMAURICE.

Place	Date	Hour	Summary of Events and Information	Remarks and references to Appendices
	17/5/17	4 a.m.	1 section of 'A', 'B' & 'C' 168 Bde R.F.A., C/161, relieved by 1 section of Batteries of French 16 Reg. A.C. 26th French Division.	
		11 p.m.	Remaining 4 guns of D/168 withdrawn from action. Remainder of A, B, and C/168 relieved by French 16 Reg. A.C. 26th French Division. All Batteries withdrawing to Wagon Lines at TILLY. Command taken over by French Lt-Col. ZAMBEAUX at 11.30 p.m.	
	18/5/17	7 a.m.	Brigade marched from TILLY to LANGEVOISIN.	
	19/5/17		" " LANGEVOISIN to BOUCHOIR.	
	20/5/17		" " BOUCHOIR " IGNAUCOURT.	
	21/5/17		Lt-Col. R. FITZMAURICE to bed with trench fever. Major F. FITZGIBBON DSO took Command of Brigade.	
	22/5/17		Batteries made preparations for entrainment.	
	23/5/17		Lt-Col. R. FITZMAURICE went into hospital. Brigade marched by batteries from IGNAUCOURT and entrained at GUILLAUCOURT. Lieut (a/Capt) J.R.J GOLD awarded the Military Cross. Sergeant B. W. HARTLEY (D/168) awarded the D.C.M.	
	24/5/17		Brigade detrained at BAILLEUL and marched to Wagon Lines in 36th (ULSTER) Divnl area, coming under Command of G.O.C. 36th Division, 9th Corps, Second Army.	
	25/5/17		Major FITZGIBBON (Commdg. Brigade) and Battery Commanders reconnoitred Battery positions opposite WYTSCHAETE.	
	26/5/17		Major D.K. TWEEDIE DSO returned from 42nd Division and took over Command of the Brigade from Major F. FITZGIBBON DSO.	
	27/5/17		Lt-Col. R. FITZMAURICE returned from hospital and assumed Command of the Brigade. Heavy shelling on the front. 'B' Battery mess cart blown up. 1 man killed, 1 wounded and 2 horses killed.	

Army Form C. 2118.

WAR DIARY
or
INTELLIGENCE SUMMARY.
(Erase heading not required.)

168th Brigade R.F.A.
Commanded by Lt-Col. R. FITZMAURICE.

Instructions regarding War Diaries and Intelligence
Summaries are contained in F. S. Regs., Part II.
and the Staff Manual respectively. Title pages
will be prepared in manuscript.

Place	Date	Hour	Summary of Events and Information	Remarks and references to Appendices
	28/5/17		1 gun of each battery taken into action.in N.29.a. (reference Sheet 28 S.W. 1/20,000) There was much shelling and difficulty was experienced in getting them into position.	
	29/5/17		A further gun of each battery taken into action.	
	30/5/17		1 section of each battery taken into action.	
	31/5/17		Registration carried out. Remainder of guns go into action.	

31st May 1917.

A.H.M^c...
Lieut-Colonel.
Commanding 168th. Brigade, R.F.A.

Headquarters Staff -;0;- 168th Brigade R.F.A.

Nominal Roll of all ranks 31/5/17.

Officers :- Lt-Col.R.FITZMAURICE.
             Lieut A.LUMB.
             Lieut H.FISHER.

             Capt.D.FERGUSON. (R.A.M.C.)

Other Ranks:-
```
       1362. B.S.M. Mc.Gowan R.H. (M.C.)
    L.25839. Corpl. Lee G.
    L.29801.   "    Normanton A.
      29811. Bdr  Anderton A.
    L.25881.  "   Gibson H.
    L.29430. a/Bdr Eyre E.
      1224?.  "    Wright J.
    L.28042.  "    Sugden E.
      79511.  "    Mc Intyre A.
    L.28206. Gnr  Akroyd A.
    L.25810.  "   Bottomley C.
      59688.  "   Clark B.J.
       5645.  "   Colley E.
     152003.  "   Firth H.
       5677?. "   Grindley W.
    L.29404.  "   Greenwood C.
      55188.  "   Bengeley P.S.
    L.29394.  "   
    L.25480.  "   Lucas E.
    L.25399.  "   Ramsden A.
    L.25626.  "   Slater H.
    L.28179.  "   Sykes C.A.
    L.29296.  "   Windle A.T.
    L.27531.  "   Postlethwaite T.
    L.25422. Dvr  Armitage J.R.
    L.32440.  "   Baker G.
    L.32540.  "   Blake F.
    L.28026.  "   Cowham S.
       5742.  "   Dickenson J.
    L.29287.  "   Fisher S.
     198817.  "   Foote G.
       1573.  "   Gutteridge H.
      37566.  "   Hirons E.
       5855.  "   Gowam W.
      13104.  "   Greenwood C.D.
    L.32511.  "   Iredale A.
    L.2582?.  "   Iredale H.
    L.28189.  "   Mellor A.
    L.28132.  "   Martin J.
    L.2935l.  "   Newsome A.E.
    L.29424.  "   Parker J.
    L.29423.  "   Pollard W.
    L.25853.  "   Radley T.
      16508.  "   Reed S.
    L.29357.  "   Reddington M.
    L.29389.  "   Stansfield P.
       6207.  s/s Periera A.T.
              Saddler Williams

             A.O.C. 625. Staff Sergt Barker H. (Artificer).
```

"A" Battery   -;-   168th Brigade R.F.A.

Nominal Roll of all ranks 31/5/17.

Officers:- Major R. EMMET.
Capt O. d'IVRY.
2/Lieut W... EBBELS.
2/Lieut RAVALD L.A.
2/Lieut J.G. BELL.
2/Lieut A.C. MILLER.
2/Lieut I.W. WEEDON

Other Ranks -

L.28514.	B.S.M.	Patchett W.J.	L.28014.	Gnr	Bray E.H.
L.28064.	Q.M.S.	Broarley H.	100556.	"	Beamish R.
1105.	Sgt	Witney T.	100774.	"	Baird S.
53261.	"	Smith E.R.	L.28180.	"	Ballon H.
L.25426.	"	Field R.J.	L.29379.	"	Beaumont L.
L.25679.	"	Roberts J.	L.32471.	"	Calvert F.
43312.	"	McGowan A.R.	L.29345.	"	Craigie T.
L.25425.	"	Firth A.	5556.	"	Chappel A.
L.32181.	"	Williams W.J.	L.29307.	"	Catley H.
L.25697.	Cpl	Rhodes L.	L.190397.	"	Cross F.
L.25561.	"	Povey J.	L.28178.	"	Dawson W.
L.25619.	"	France W.	12049.	"	Edwards L.
83394.	"	Simpson C.	130451.	"	Edwards W.H.
L.25093.	"	Littlewood K.	8627 6.	"	Franklin A.
L.29407.	"	Taylor F.	190415.	"	Foote G.
L.32479.	Bdr	Bentley J.	60200.	"	Fuller B.
L.28100.	"	Pitchforth A.	15261.	"	Fearn H.
L.29313.	"	Armitage W.B.	L.25823.	"	Hynes W.H.
L.25708.	"	Crawshaw J.I.	L.25610.	"	Hopwood H.
L.25574.	"	Whiteley C.H.		"	Keighley F.
L.25414.	"	Wood B.	L.32512.	"	Lumb W.
L.25731.	"	Rhodes J.	184485.	"	Lewis E.J.
L.28188.	"	Padget C.	L.28177.	"	Leatham F.
L.25464.	"	Richardson G.H.	197866.	"	McEwing H.
L.32553.	"	Taylor W.J.	195371.	"	McCarthy C.
L.28072.	a/Bdr	Bentley C.	97863.	"	McKeshie A.
L.32527.	"	Fenton E.	168564.	"	Miller W.
L.27768.	"	Brocksbank S.	150416.	"	Mallett H.
L.25669.	"	Oates H.	L.28129.	"	Marshall L.
L.29297.	"	Noble C.	L.25392.	"	Milnes H.
86310.	"	Squires W.E.	6011.	"	Myler A.
L.28136.	"	Shaw N.	L.25443.	"	Nuttall P.
L.28034.	"	Beevers M.	44251.	"	Offon F.
80791.	s/a/Bdr	Stratton T.	L.28186.	"	Perkins J.C.
L.25536.	"	Mansfield W.G.	L.25736.	"	Pearson H.
L.25513.	"	Pearse A.	L.25584.	"	Quarmby W.H.
169899.	"	Holliday G.	L.25653.	"	Rushworth A.
L.28217.	"	Bower B.	L.32491.	"	Roberts J.
L.29306.	"	Pearson F.	L.25781.	"	Sykes J.
167074.	"	McGeachie I.E.	52972.	"	Stocker H.G.
167423.	"	Sweet J.	L.25766.	"	Shaw J.C.
L.32449.	Far Sergt	Andrews R.	148166.	"	Smith A.
L.25783.	s/s Cpl	Towne E.	126074.	"	Spence R.
76.	"	Penks J.	5889.	"	Shoesmith W.
L.29282.	"	Nuttal G.T.	81446.	"	Slack H.
L.28175.	"	Waterhouse L.	L.25735.	"	Spencer H.
L.25690.	"	Kaye J.T.	51733.	"	Spelissy F.
			L.25771.	"	Thornton J.
L.32485.	Saddler	Jackson W.E.	L.29355.	"	Townend J.
6 2728.	"	Oliver J.E.	L.32535.	"	Thornber W.H.
154173.	"	Skipp J.N.	L.28008.	"	Wilkinson T.
147472.	Fitter	Hellawell A.	L.25575.	"	Walker W.T.
7246.	"	Barnborough R.	L.29300.	"	Wood F.
121451.	Wh'l'r	Weaver J.	L.32441.	"	Walker A.
L.25740.	Gnr	Allott G.V.	L.25844.	"	Weldrake E.
L.2559.	"	Billington T.	L.29318.	"	Wood R.

L.25649.	Gnr	Wood C.E.	
L.25485.	"	Williams G.	
L.133713.	"	Young W.	
107780.	Dvr	Archer W.	
175251.	"	Adams E.	
81590.	"	Black A.	
L.25524	"	Balmforth H.	
L.2552.	"	Bray H.	
L.25436.	"	Brearley A.	
L.25395.	"	Brook G.L.	
L.25658.	"	Chapman B.	
L.29323.	"	Cartwright P.	
L.25592	"	Crowther J.E.	
5802	"	Connor J.	
109981.	"	Chapman H.	
41489.	"	Crisp E.	
L.29409.	"	Dyson W.	
L.28079.	"	Green F.	
L.25820.	"	Ganlby J.	
L.29316.	"	Gledhill H.	
L.25779.	"	Griffiths T.C.	
L.25677.	"	Holdroyd H.	
L.28201.	"	Horsfall E.	
L.28073.	"	Hirst J.	
L.25849.	"	Holmes E.	
L.29347.	"	Hardcastle C.W.	
L.29417.	"	Hincliffe H.	
L.32541.	"	Kershaw C.	
L.25419.	"	Kerton E.	
L.28163.	"	Lodge A.	
L.25384.	"	Livesey F.C.	
L.28021.	"	Mallinson J.A.	
L.25639.	"	Millard H.	
826369.	"	Morse L.	
L.28151.	"	Hobson T.C.	
101689.	"	O'neil J.	
147602.	"	Harris H.	
L.32464.	"	Pogson S.	
L.28135.	"	Priest G.W.	
L.25864.	"	Quinn D.	
L.28074.	"	Robershaw G.	
L.28075.	"	Roe F.	
L.28013.	"	Sykes W.	
99859.	"	Spencer P.G.	
L.25633.	"	Shaw E.	
L.25503.	"	Shaw H.	
L.28224.	"	Shaw C.A.	
L.25797.	"	Singleton V.	
L.25450.	"	Smith J.R.	
217881	"	Shot en N.	
219990.	"	Tall F.	
742190.	"	Tanner A.	
L.28101.	"	Taylor D.H.	
L.25460.	"	Twigg J.	
L.25483.	"	Valey L.	
L.28214.	"	Wood W.N.	
L.25650.	"	Wood A.	
10586.	"	Westgate F.	
L.29331.	"	Woodcock W.	
L.28087.	"	Walters H.	
L.25394.	"	Wortley T.	
L.25541.	"	Woodhead E.	
L.25819.	"	Whitehead J.A.	
159419.	"	Wedon W.	

1677.	Gnr	Steveson G.W.	
821657.	"	Swadling H.	
2236.	"	Seed A.	
150668.	"	Schaefer A.E.	
38812.	"	Symonds H.	
156164.	"	Sargent C.	

S.E. 1514. Sergt Jolley A.G. Attached.

'B' Battery.   -;-   168th Brigade R.F.A.

Nominal Roll of all ranks 31/5/17.

Officers:-   Major F. FITZGIBBON. D.S.O.
                Capt L.M.HASTINGS M.C.
                2/Lieut W.P.ROBINSON.
                2/Lieut.W.L.CHAMBERLAIN.
                2/Lieut. MITCHELHILL J.
                2/Lieut. C.P.BASNETT.
                2/Lieut. A.E.MARRIOTT.

Other ranks:-

58482.	B.S.M.	Stenning T.	L.29363.	Gnr	Crosland H.
L.32437.	Q.M.S.	Lane A.C.	68234.	"	Doggett J.
L.32314.	Far sgt	Sutcliffe R.	79093.	"	Drewitt W.H.
L.25448.	Sergt	Beaumont F.	L.29392.	"	Eccles J.
L.25420.	"	Deakin T.	3052.	"	Earl W.
L.29344.	"	Gutherie A.	L.29263.	"	Fowler B.
1985.	"	Harding R.	56821.	"	Gallaher M.
L.25606.	"	Palframan F.	198809.	"	Gigg B.
L.25390.	"	Taylor H.	11578.	"	Gouldsmith S.O.
L.25484.	"	Willans C.	L.29244.	"	Greenwood A.A.
L.25871.	Cpl.	Walker S.	L.29262.	"	Greenwood L.A.
L.25864.	"	Mason R.	L.29380.	"	Hanson B.
L.25716.	"	Fisher W.W.	L.25746.	"	Hargreaves A.
L.25874.	"	Shaw L.	111819.	"	Harris G.
L.29330.	"	Thornton J.	L.25554.	"	Harrison W.
L.25863.	"	Holmes L.	L.25664.	"	Hartley A.
L.28210.	"	Greenwood M.R.	4329.	"	Horan J.S.
98737.	s/s Cpl	Brennan J.	L.28046.	"	Holdsworth A.
L.25446.	Bdr	Bottomley T.	L.25488.	"	Kiddle F.
L.25451.	"	Spendlove T.	L.25562.	"	Lawford F.
L.29826.	"	Temperton H.K.	L.28220.	"	Laycock A.
L.28138.	"	Bramley S.M.	L.25623.	"	Lee F.
L.25545.	"	Turner J.F.	160940.	"	Leng J.
L.24990.	"	Mayers A.	L.25622.	"	Littlewood A.
L.28218.	"	Dyson A.	197862.	"	McLennan J.B.
L.32480.	"	Bancroft L.	197864.	"	McPherson D.
L.5961.	"	Hirst W.	197865.	"	McRea D.
15224.	"	Wright A.	L.28126.	"	Mallinson F.
L.28043.	"	Burch H.	15272.	"	Mason J.
L.25808.	a/Bdr	Broomhead W.H.	150377.	"	Miller C.W.
L.25411.	"	Christie H.	16402.	"	Miller L.
16381.	"	Cawthorne J.	L.29400.	"	Mitchell D.
L.25547.	"	Ibbotson M.	L.32444.	"	Mitchell R.
L.25491.	"	Sherwood J.	197395.	"	Mullard C.H.
15273.	"	Holmes N.	L.28076.	s/a/Bdr	Murray M.
L.25742.	"	Dyson F.	L.29402.	Gnr	Murray B.
503.	s/s	Boswell H.	188576.	"	Nash T.J.
L.25552.	"	Hoyle C.	156134.	"	Nightingale D.
L.25510.	"	Readyhough G.W.	L.25632.	"	Onyon A.
L.25452.	"	Sidebottom J.	L.25836	"	Owen W.
L.32552.	"	Wilson J.W.	258.	"	Platt H.
L.25747.	Sadd'r	Brooksbank C.	L.25827.	"	Riddlesden A.
L.25607.	"	Stansfield T.	46249.	"	Scott F.T.
L.25596.	Wh'l r.	Yates E.	L.25463.	"	Scott N.
L.25382.	Gnr	Ainley W.H.	159803.	"	Shaw J.A.
L.32549.	"	Berry A.	5828.	"	Spence J.
L.25616.	"	Billington H.	16748.	"	Stanage J.W.
L.32483.	"	Binns A.O.	L.32473.	"	Stafford H.
L.32421.	"	Bottoms H.	67772.	"	Tanner W.C.
L.25873.	"	Broadbent T.	L.29572.	"	Tidswell H.T.
L.29265.	s/a/Bdr	Bradley J.T.	11452.	"	Thomas O.
L.32496.	Gnr	Burton C.	L.25683.	"	Thompson J.T.
8786.	"	Broome H.	67704.	"	Tunstall A.
18820.	"	Brown F.	L.25629.	"	Turner H.
L.25671.	"	Cocker F.	L.25727.	"	Winteringham B.
2295.	"	Coward T.	150477.	"	Wolfe H.

Continued.

L.29431.	Gnr	Wood G.H.	
L.27044.	"	Youngman A.	
L.29381.	Dvr	Barraclough H.	
L.29258.	"	Barraclough T.E.	
L.28213.	"	Beaumont H.	
L.28199.	"	Berry A.	
L.25837.	"	Berry S.	
L.32376.	"	Bentley T.	
L.32328.	"	Borrisow F.	
L.32366.	"	Braithwaite J.F.	
L.25470.	"	Brook J.W.	
L.25878.	"	Clear A.	
18673.	"	Chesters D.	
L.32443.	"	Crossley A.	
216330.	"	Cook F.	
L.28113.	"	Crosley J.	
L.32318.	"	Crowther J.	
L.25446.	"	Davis J.W.	
112102.	"	Dennis G.	
L.29383.	"	Dewar W.	
L.25442.	"	Eastwood G.	
L.25782.	"	Firth H.	
L.32338.	"	Gray D.	
L.29367.	"	Greenwood J.W.	
L.25728.	"	Greenwood G	
L.25831.	"	Hall H.	
L.28204.	"	Harrison F.	
L.25479.	"	Hattersley F.	
L.32524.	"	Horthornthwaite T.	
L.25882.	"	Hincliffe A.	
L.25558.	"	Hobson A.	
L.32306.	"	Holmes W.	
L.29403.	"	Horrocks H.	
L.32447.	"	Jackson P.	
L.28070.	"	Jowett J.H.	
L.29270.	"	Ledgard B.	
L.25748.	"	Leckenby J.	
L.28077.	"	Martin L.	
L/930739	"	Matthis M.C.	
815569.	"	Mayers F.	
L.28129.	"	Mellor H.	
L.29401.	"	Moody A.	
152302.	"	Milner J.	
L.25870.	"	Murray R.	
213085.	"	Newns A.	
L.25675.	"	Nivholson J.	
L.28194.	"	North M.	
20609.	"	Ray D.	
L.28071.	"	Robinson F.	
5116.	"	Roberts G.	
L.25861.	"	Robinson T.	
L.25512.	"	Robinson W.J.	
L.25730.	"	Rushworth B.	
L.25625.	"	Scot J.J.	
L.28041.	"	Scholefield A.	
L.32379.	"	Shepherd N.	
L.25644.	"	Singleton L.M.	
L.25454.	"	Snell A.	
180180.	"	Tooth V.S.	
L.29397.	"	Southwell J.	
L.28090.	"	Stanton A.	
L.28109.	"	Sugden O.	
L.25569.	"	Turner J.	
2088.	"	Turner J.	
L.25866.	"	Townsend H.	
L.25598.	"	Townsend W.	
L.25499.	"	Tallis G.	
160935.	"	Whitchurch T. wounded 27/5/17	
L.32315.	"	Wilkinson L.	
L.29237.	"	Wilkinson H.	
185398.	"	Willat W.	

164826.	Dvr	Williams
L.29269.	"	Wood H.
14124.	"	Worth
L.28089.	"	Wright F.

8949. Vet Sergt White F.A.

A.V.C. (attached).

"B" Battery.   168th Brigade R.F.A.

Nominal Roll of all ranks 31/5/17.

Officers:-   Major H. COTTER.
             Capt   B.T. GROVES.
             2/Lieut James H.L.
             2/Lieut G.I. Barrick
             2/Lieut C.A. Anelay.
             2/Lieut S.J Hinton.
             2/Lieut Ronaldson H.R.M.
             2/Lieut C.A Browne.

Other Ranks.:-

53473.	B.S.M.	Malone M.J.		138478.	Gnr	Carmell W.
L.5688.	C.M.S.	Tomlinson S.		60219.	"	Davison J.
L.2727.	Sergt	Ward A.		L.2702.	"	Denton F.
L.19483.	"	Booth P.P.		L.2411.	"	Ellis W.
L.12004.	"	Turgoose W.		L.12019.	"	Farmery J.W.
L.2771.	"	Kirkham T.		98830.	"	Fraser J.
5406.	"	Sykes H.M.		L.12019.	"	Froggett E.
22239.	"	Fitzgerald W.		7866.	"	Fenny F.
L.29412.	"	Brown T.		37084.	"	Gale S.E.
L.11973.	Cpl.	Booth J.		163921.	"	Gerrett G.W.
L.11923.	"	Imms E.		L.11975.	"	Haworth H.
L.19484.	"	Marshall		L.11992.	"	Halton R.
L.12050.	"	Sanderson G.		L.11989.	"	Haworth R.
L.19481.	"	Ward J.S.		88771.	"	Hall N.
L.28195.	"	Garside I.		L.19490.	"	Horner C.
L.28121.	"	Palmer R.		34446.	"	Foot R.
L.19479.	Bdr	Wardle L.M.		89444.	"	Holdern F.
L.19478.	"	Todd J.H.		L.25751.	"	Higgins H.
L.12016.	"	Maguire T.F.G.		110744.	"	Huggett T.
L.27730.	"	Walton H.		2933.	"	Hesford A.
L.19484.	"	Bailey B.G.		143609.	"	Heron R.
L.19830.	"	Goldsborough		167010.	"	Hankinson J.
L.11993.	"	Holdroyd T.		L.12020.	"	Inman H.
105077.	"	Carruthers T.		L.20111.	"	Jolley W.
L.2812.	"	Terry L.		19809.	"	James T.
L.2473.	"	Earnshaw S.		L.19514.	"	Lines J.
L.29414.	"	Elliott C.H.		L.22285.	"	Lewis S.W.
L.11959.	a/Bdr	Ellis W.R		L.12047.	"	Martin T.
L.19519.	"	Milnthorpe G.		L.11932.	"	Mulheir J.W.
L.19487.	"	Carr W.C.		L.12002.	"	Nowell E.M.
L.11962.	"	Wilcocks G.		172668.	"	Nesbitt R.
L.27987.	"	Broadhead F.		L.11971.	"	Parkin W.
L.28010.	"	Steel J.W.		188719.	"	Poynts
L.2775.	"	Lee H.		134691.	"	Robinson A.E.
L.12015.	"	Wathey A.		185837.	"	Spinks G.
50751.	Far Sergt	Bishop G.		L.19496.	"	Saberton H.Y.
L.11991.	S/s Cpl	Halton G.		L.27999.	"	Spittle T.A.
L.11926.	"	Fletcher W.		13907.	"	Swinn J.
L.27751.	"	Bailey F.		1228.	"	Sellar G.
L.2954.	"	Chappel E.		67727.	"	Smith J.
L.11934.	"	Ismay T.H.		37207.	"	Smith P.W
10790.	"	Copping H.E.		1296.	"	Smith W.E.
63915.	"	Irving W.A.		56143.	"	Smith T.
L.29366.	Cpl Ftr.	Hincliffe J.		95803	"	Smith W.R.
L.14862.	Whl'r	Pringle B.		32207.	"	Smith A.
L.11937.	Sad'r	Hall J.		201541.	"	Seedhouse S.
147564.	Gnr	Balls H.W.		33802.	"	Thompson F.
L.11994.	"	Barr J.		L.2715.	"	Taylor J.I.
L.19485.	"	Briggs B.J.		L.19502.	"	Wailes W.
L.11979.	"	Brady B.		L.12003.	"	Waldron T.
L.28200.	"	Brock J.		L.19717.	"	Wardle C.H.
L.11981.	"	Cockle G.				
L.28147.	"	Chapman T.				
147114.	"	Creeper H.				
196150.	"	Cock F.				

Continued.

L.12022.	Dvr	Ainsworth H.
L.11919.	"	Backhouse G.H.
L.11942.	"	Bolton P.
L.11980.	"	Burnley W.S.
15229.	"	Bury A.
L.11982.	"	Clark S.W.
L.28232.	"	Chapman J.
L.18327.	"	Cleever E.L.
L.29291.	"	Drake G.E.
L.28107.	"	Ellis H.
L.11969.	"	Eubank J.A.
L.25474.	"	Earnshaw H.
L.12055.	"	Farmery T.
L.19506.	"	Fretwell H.
L.12037.	"	Garfitt J.I.
L.19520.	"	Garfoot H.
L.11964.	"	Hunter J.
L.11941.	"	Hart W.
L.11969.	"	Hancock N.
L.19510.	"	Horsfall E.
L.19509.	"	Hudson J.
L.12041.	"	Kershaw H.
L.11929.	"	Kemp R.
L.19492.	"	Lapish J.
L.19513.	"	Lamb M.
12051.	"	Lawton H.
L.29285.	"	Lord J.
85729.	"	Maddocks J.
L.18009.	"	Mitchel W.
L.14919.	"	Marshall S.
77571.	"	O'Keefe J.A.
6074.	"	Overland H.
75445.	"	Pipe H
L.27691.	"	Poynton G.W.
L.19516.	"	Priestly B.
2869.	"	Price W.
L.28031.	"	Parkin H.
L.28850.	"	Pogson H.
L.12011.	"	Roberts E.W.
L.11965.	"	Ross C.A.
L.19487.	"	Schofield W.
L.12033.	"	Senior B.K.
120413.	"	Shipman H.
L.29293.	"	Sutcliffe W.
L.28164.	"	Spivey P.
L.28149.	"	Scott J.R.
L.25448.	"	Singleton N.
L.27993.	"	Senior J.W.
186618.	"	Stride W.
185364.	"	Speak J.W
93604.	"	H.Seymour
L.27747.	"	Toothill A.C.
32459.	"	Turner H.
L.27906.	"	Taylor H.
L.28095.	"	Turner A.B.
L.12008.	"	Wailes A.
L.12021.	"	Walshaw H.
L.12006.	"	Wrigglesworth F.
L.28169.	"	Williams J.
L.28124.	"	Walton R.
L.29322.	"	White H.
51913.	"	Whareham H.
4487.	"	Wilson W.
13400.	"	Wheeler W.
1344.	"	Young T.
2489.	A.V.C. Sergt	Harding W.

'D' Battery. -:O:- 168th Brigade R.F.A.

Nominal roll of all ranks 31/5/17.

Officers:- Major D.K.TWEEDIE.D.S.O.
A/Capt J.C.POOLE.M.C.
Lieut Dunbar R.
Lieut G.C.Wood
2/Lieut A.R. Stewart.
2/Lieut J.J.Caterer
2/Lieut E.F.Peel.

Other ranks:-

1305.	B.S.M.	Perigo W.	3665.	Gnr	Burke G.
3922.	Q.M.S.	Le Page H.	2688.	"	Cain J.E.
100360.	Farr Sgt	Greenwood J.	889530.	"	Cook B.
11948.	Sergt	Allen J.	889531.	"	Cock G.M.
35409.	"	Dinsdale J.	19947.	"	Dally E.
19930.	"	Flannagan P.	27596.	"	Dixon H.A.
35383.	"	Hartley B.W.	889542.	"	Dunnett J.
950107.	"	Jeffrey S.A.	911227.	"	Day F.E.
19894.	"	Lambley J.T.	44891.	"	Draper A.
78512.	S/S Cpl	Emms A.	2757.	"	Elsom G.H.
26450.	Sadd'r	Clawson J.J	27175.	"	Fowler A.S.
27618.	Ftr	Thresh E.	19950.	"	Flannagan J.
35389.	Corpl	Dobson J.E.	179512.	"	Garnham A.E.
19965.	"	Hawkes T.G.H.	40484.	"	Goodman A.
27757.	"	Hetherington J.	27518.	"	Holmes G.
19840.	"	Hempsall J.	104591.	"	Howard A.
889566.	"	Jackson A.A.	55188.	"	Heard H.
889691.	"	Philpot J.E.	901238.	"	Hendley H.
19914.	"	Wooffitt F.B.	19848.	"	Hellewell G.W.
27756.	Bdr	Bonner S.	9762.	"	Howlett S.
27590.	"	Bradford J.	35413.	"	Hadley J.
889568.	"	Browse S.A.	148368.	"	Keene T.C.
26452.	"	Bellamy J.W.	2317.	"	Langford W.G.
35395.	"	Hamilton T.H.	21239.	"	McLennan J.
889575.	"	Last S.	5079.	"	McLaughton T.
19919.	"	Scholey S.	889284.	"	Poad G.R.
26400	"	Smith W.	19796.	"	Parkinson J.H.
27601.	a/Bdr	Archer S.T.	1307.	"	Petchley.
35390.	"	Beckett E.	901599.	"	Richardson H.
27580.	"	Braddock J.A.	138484.	"	Sugar R.
	"	Bettany	2612.	"	Simmons A.G.
1986.	"	Hempsall T.	4002.	"	Sugar F.
14511.	"	Male F.G.	27520.	"	Stacey I.
124923.	"	Richardson H.	97676.	"	Starkey E.
930380.	"	Stafford P.O.	26449.	"	Shaw F.
88953.	s/a/Bdr	Cutteridge A.	129128.	"	Smith W.E.
27533.	s/s	Hellewell A.	970798.	"	Sandford G.
27497.	"	Innocent R.		"	Sartin H.
27759.	"	Popplewell G.	20422.	"	Stones S.A.
27612.	"	Smith J.	889604.	"	Smith F.J.
26447.	"	Varney J.	26463.	"	Townsend A.V.
78446.	Sadd	Butley J.	20010.	"	Thompson J.
113012.	"	Molyneaux D.	889614.	"	Thody A.
26676.	"	Schofield J.	12044.	"	Ward E.
146171.	Ftr.	Collar P.A.	25404.	"	Williams G.
128068.	Gnr	Allen E.	889623.	"	Watling B.
19896.	"	Badger G.	889632.	"	Woodward F.
5003.	"	Bull G.S.	889624.	"	Wain F.
2638.	"	Boler H.E.	19783.	Dvr	Armitage G.
27589.	"	Blood J.	35402.	"	Bainbridge J.G.
201448.	"	Board A.	27757.	"	Battin W.
889514.	"	Barker J.A.	26401.	"	Bell A.
889522.	"	Barker W.	26244.	"	Bellamy F.

Continued.   'D' Battery.

12107.	Dvr	Bond P.
28019.	"	Barker W.
20007.	"	Bradley J.
889511.	"	Bell C.
889521.	"	Burn A.
889509.	"	Brightwell B.
27122.	"	Collins J.R.
20008.	"	Croft J.
889581.	"	Cocker B.
889534.	"	Chittock A.
L32488.	"	Dutton J.W.
889546.	"	Dalton B.
889548.	"	Durrant S.P.
13985.	"	Donleavy W.
27621.	"	Denby F.
10023.	"	Dowd F.
27622.	"	Dixon L.
88953.	"	Driver R.
2162.	"	Evans S.
19799.	"	Fisher G.
8982.	"	Flack A.
31333.	"	Faulkner A.
35381.	"	Guest W.
19943.	"	Green J.
19803.	"	Greenwood J.
889556.	"	Garner G.E.
889555.	"	Gray S.V.
26422.	"	Havenhand H.
19353.	"	Howson W.
19749.	"	Hughes H.
889563.	"	Honeywood B.
27610.	"	Jewwitt W.
35411.	"	Jackson F.
35380.	"	Lunn G.
9290.	"	Lewellyn T.
889570.	"	Lay G.
47044.	"	McCormick A.
35379.	"	Middleton W.
2151.	"	Miller A.G.
35414.	"	Padget J.B.
19789.	"	Peacock J.B.
27222.	"	Phillips F.
19939.	"	Porter B.
889587.	"	Piper W.
889596.	"	Reade A.
889595.	"	Rayner H.
40494.	"	Seabrook J.H.
26406.	"	Savage W.
27609.	"	Smith J.
29400.	"	Stewart A.
26411.	"	Speight A.
27505.	"	Stone W.
27600.	"	Sykes J.
889600.	"	Smith A.W.
889601.	"	Sustins B.
202441.	"	Turner A.
19736.	"	Thompson A.D.
202430.	"	Townsend A.
24085.	"	Tilston R.
12232.	"	Tyler H.
71271.	"	Thompson J.G.H.
191541.	"	Twist G.
889616.	"	Thoebald W.
83586.	"	Toms R.
40493.	"	Tandy P.
889612.	"	Taylor E.
864518.	"	Thompson C.
12031.	"	Wilkinson J.W.
27498.	"	Wright D.
19794.	"	Whelan J.

2718.	Dvr	Wilson J.
889631.	"	Whitehead J.

8038. Sergt Moore W. A.V.C.

(attached.)

SECRET.

Copy No. 8

168th Brigade R.F.A.

OPERATION ORDER No. 30.

Ref Sheet 62b S.W. 1/20,000

Monday 7th May 1917.

1. The 168th Brigade R.F.A. will go into action on the nights 7/8th and 8/9th May as per attached Tables 'A' & 'B'.

2. On completion of this move, the 168th Brigade R.F.A. and 'A' Battery 161st Brigade R.F.A. will constitute the Left Group. Zones of batteries will be as follows:-

   A/161.   S.12.b.7.7   to   T.1.c.3.5   to   S.6.b.9.6
   C/168.   S.6.b.9.6   to   M.36.b.4.3
   B/168.   M.36.b.4.2   to   M.30.c.5.1
   A/168.   M.30.c.5.1   to   M.30.a.65.00

3. Batteries being relieved will move out with echlons empty and will fill from the wagons of the batteries relieving them.
   Receipts to be given and taken and amounts wired to this office on completion of relief.

4. The Wireless operator attached to D/168 will take over from the operator of D/161 on the 8th inst, at the section attached to Counter Battery Group.

5. An officer of A/168 will relieve the Liaison officer at Battalion H.Q. at 4.p.m. on the 8th.

6. Battery Boards, registrations, telephone lines, defence schemes, etc will be handed over by batteries being relieved, to the incoming batteries.

7. The Command of the Left Group will be taken over by O.C. 168th Brigade R.F.A. at 10.a.m. on the 9th inst.
   Headquarters at X.18.a.

8. After noon on the 8th inst all batteries will indent on officer in charge 32nd D.A.C. V.A.D. for ammunition.
   Guides will be sent with each indent, and will guide the D.A.C. wagons to battery positions after dusk.

9. ACKNOWLEDGE.

Alan Thumb
Lieut.
Adjt 168th Brigade R.F.A.

7th May 1917.

Copy No. 1.   A/168
"   "   2.   B/168
"   "   3.   C/168
"   "   4.   D/168
"   "   5.   O.C. 161st Bde R.F.A.
"   "   6.   H.Q. 32nd Div Art'y
"   "   7.   War Diary
"   "   8.   File.
           9.   H.Q. 61st Bde
          10. 306th Arc R.F.A.

TABLE "A"

Night 7/8th.

1 Section A/16 will relieve 1 Section A/306 at N.33.a.9.8
1 Section B/16 will go into position at G.2.b.5.5 (at present unoccupied)
1 Section C/16 will go relieve 1 Section B/161 at G.3.d.
1 Section D/16 will relieve 1 Section D/161 at G.8.b.2.2
1 Howitzer D/16 " " 1 Howitzer D/161 at G.10.a.2.0

TABLE "B"

Night 8/9th.

Remainder of A/16 will relieve the remainder A/306
 " " B/16 will go into position at G.2.b.5.5
 " " C/16 will relieve the remainder B/161
1.Howitzer D/16 " " " " D/161 at G.8.b.2.2
1. " D/16 " " " " D/161 at G.10.a.2.0

There must be no movement East of HOLNON WOOD until after dark.

CONFIDENTIAL.

WAR DIARY

of

168th Brigade R.F.A.

from 1st. June 1917 to 30th. June 1917.

(Volume 18.)

Army Form C. 2118.

WAR DIARY
or
INTELLIGENCE SUMMARY.
(Erase heading not required.)

168th. Brigade R.F.A.
Commanded by Lt-Col. R. FITZM.URICE.

Instructions regarding War Diaries and Intelligence Summaries are contained in F.S. Regs., Part II. and the Staff Manual respectively. Title pages will be prepared in manuscript.

Place	Date	Hour	Summary of Events and Information	Remarks and references to Appendices
	1917.			
	June 1st.		All batteries registered on WYTSCHAETE Church. (remains of)	B.
	2nd.		Strengthening of gun-pits and dug-outs continued.	B.1.
	3rd.		Corpl. L. HAW of B/168 awarded the CROIX de GUERRE.	A.2.
	4th.	4 pm.	Brigade H.Q. moved to Battle H.Q. at N.34.c.6.6. Batteries carried out registration by aeroplane observation.	A.3.
	6th.		Lt-Col. FITZMAURICE commanding 168th Bde. R.F.A. and Major COTTER commanding 'C' Battery 168th. Bde. R.F.A. awarded the D.S.O.	B.2.
	7th.	3.10 am.	Attack on the MESSINES – WYTSCHAETE RIDGE by the 36th. Division. which was very successful. All objectives and a large number of prisoners taken. The 3 18-pdr. Batteries of the 168th Brigade R.F.A. assisted by barraging Back Areas. (See appendix "A") D/168 was attached to Heavy Artillery for Counter Battery work.	A.4.
		3.10 pm.	Successful attack on the OOSTTAVERNE LINE by the 11th. Division. The 3 18-pdr batteries of the 168th. Brigade R.F.A. assisted by playing a Creeping Barrage in front of the Infantry. (See appendix "B") D/168 was under the orders of O.C. 173rd. Brigade R.F.A.	B.A.
		9.40 pm.	Enemy counter attack on VAN HOVE FARM beaten off. The casualties of the Brigade during the above operations were – 1 sergt. and 1 man killed. – 1 sergt. and 1 man wounded.	B.A.
	8th.	11 a.m. 9.45 pm.	Batteries fired several times on the enemy reported to be massing. Counter-attack beaten off.	C.A.

Army Form C. 2118.

WAR DIARY
or
INTELLIGENCE SUMMARY.
(Erase heading not required.)

Instructions regarding War Diaries and Intelligence Summaries are contained in F.S. Regs., Part II. and the Staff Manual respectively. Title pages will be prepared in manuscript.

168th Brigade R.F.A. Commanded by Lt-Colonel R. FITZMAURICE D.S.O.

Place	Date	Hour	Summary of Events and Information	Remarks and references to Appendices
	9/5/17	7.p.m.	Batteries withdrew to Wagon Lines. The total amount of ammunition expended during the past three days is:- 16,211 Rounds 18-pdr. Ammn. and 5,176 4.5 Howr. Ammunition.	
	10/6/17		Day spent in General Overhauling and Cleaning up.	
	11/6/17	7.a.m.	The Brigade marched to STEENVOORDE.	
	12/6/17		Brigade remained at STEENVOORDE.	
	13/6/17	9.a.m.	The C.O. inspected all the Brigade	
	14/6/17	7.a.m.	The Brigade marched to WORMHOUDT	
	15/6/17	7.a.m.	Commanding Officer and Battery Commanders proceeded by Motor Bus to the H.Q. of the 29th French Divisional Artillery, and visited Battery positions in the vicinity of NIEUPORT.	
	16/6/17	11.30.a.m.	Brigade marched to LEYSELE.	
	17/6/17	8.30.a.m. 5.p.m.	Brigade marched to LOMBARTZYDE. One Section per 18-pdr Battery marched into action in the vicinity of NIEUPORT and relieved 5 Sections of the 29th Divisional Artillery.	
	18/6/17	5.a.m. 5.p.m	Headquarters moved to COST DUNKIRK. A 2nd Section per Battery moved into action.	
	19/6/17	5.p.m.	Remaining Sections moved into action.	
	20/6/17	9.a.m.	Lt-Colonel FITZMAURICE D.S.O. 168th Brigade R.F.A. took over command of the Artillery covering t. LOMBARTZYDE - ST GEORGES Sectors (see Appendix "C")	
	21/6/17	10.p.m. 9.30 to 10.p.m.	1 Section of each French Battery withdrew from action see Appendix Bombardment of Enemy Support line opposite LOMBARTZYDE.	

Army Form C. 2118.

WAR DIARY
or
INTELLIGENCE SUMMARY.
(Erase heading not required.)

168th Brigade R.F.A.

Commanded by Lt-Col. R. FITZMAURICE. D.S.O.

Instructions regarding War Diaries and Intelligence Summaries are contained in F.S. Regs., Part II. and the Staff Manual respectively. Title pages will be prepared in manuscript.

Place	Date	Hour	Summary of Events and Information	Remarks and references to Appendices
	22/6/17	10.p.m.	Remaining French sections withdrawn.	OL
	23/6/17			OL
	24/6/17	9.a.m.	Command of the Artillery covering the LOMBARTZYDE Sector passes from Lt-Col. B. FITZMAURICE. D.S.O. to Lt-Col. COTTON D.S.O.	OL
	25/6/17		'B' Battery attached to Corps H.A. for Counter Battery Work.	
	26/6/17			OL
	27/6/17		Enemy's Artillery very active against our front and back areas, our artillery replied hotly.	OL
	28/6/17	1.20.a.m.	What appeared to be an attempted Raid on our trenches opposite LOMBARTZYDE, stopped by our artillery fire.	OL
		10.30.p.m.	Changes in the dispositions of Batteries. see Appendix "D"	OL
	29/6/17		Enemy Artillery (heavy) very active all day on our back areas.	
	30/6/17		Very wet and stormy. Front very quiet.	

1st July 1917.

[signature]
Lieut-Colonel.
Commanding 168th Brigade R.F.A.

Appendix "A".

SECRET.   "A" Group.   36th Divisional Artillery.   Copy No.........

OPERATION ORDER No. 7.

Reference Secret Sheet 2.1.N.2. 1/40,000.

The Tasks allotted to the 3 18-pdr Batteries of "A" Group (16th Brigade R.F.A.) From zero until zero plus 5 hours 15 minutes will be as follows:—

Bty.	Time.	Task.	Rate of Fire.	Ammunition.
(a) B/16.	Zero to zero plus 35 minutes	Will cover with smoke the front of WYTSCHAETE along the line CORBOUR TRENCH — OBVIOUS DRIVE. from O19c95.40	4 rds per gun per minute	All smoke.
"	Zero plus 35 mins to zero plus 4 hours	Search CORBOUR — SOUTONY from O.20.a.0.7 to O.14.d.3.15.	2 rds per gun per minute	
"	Zero plus 4 hours to zero plus 5 hours	Search and sweep OOSTTAVERNE WOOD.	2 rds per gun per minute	
"	Zero plus 5 hours to zero plus 5 hours 15 mins	Barrage from O.15.c.6.1 to O.15.c.9.5.	2 rds per gun per minute	
(b) A/16.	Zero to zero plus 3 hours 40 mins.	Search OOSTTAVERNE TRENCH. from O.14.c.43.15 to O.15.c.cc.95.	2 rds per gun per minute.	90% shrapnel 10% H.E.
"	Zero plus 3 hours 40 mins to zero plus 5 hours 15 mins	Search OIL TRACK. from O.21.a.3.2 to O.21.a.2.8.	2 rds per gun per minute.	
(c) C/16.	Zero to zero plus 3 hours 40 mins.	Search CRYSTAL ALLEY from O.13.b.78.82 to O.14.c.3.3.	2 rds per gun per minute.	
"	Zero plus 3 hours 40 mins to zero plus 5 hours.	Search and sweep OOSTTAVERNE WOOD.	2 rds per gun per minute.	
"	Zero plus 5 hours to zero plus 5 hours 15 mins.	Barrage from O.21.a.2.8 to O.15.c.6.1.	2 rds per gun per minute.	

At zero plus 5 hours 15 mins, after the capture of the BLACK LINE, 3/168 Bde R.F.A. will cease to do Counter Battery work and will come under orders of O.C. 1/1 left manion Bde R.F.A.

The S.O.S. signal will remain RED I GRA. cartridges.

"G" day and zero hour will be notified later.

The tasks after zero plus 5 hours 15" minutes will be allotted later.

A C K N O W L E D G E.

5th June 1917.

Alan Shunt Lieut.
Adjt 1 G.B. Brigade R. F. A.

SECRET.

Appendix "B"

O.C. /16th Bde. R.F.A.

Reference Map A.6 attached.

(1) The 18-pounder batteries of the 16th Brigade R.F.A. will open fire at zero plus 318 minutes on the first Barrage line in front of the BLACK LINE.

(2) The time shown on that line will therefore read 318 to 320 as altered on the map. Subsequently, the batteries will conform to the times laid down on the map up to the period of consolidation on the BROWN LINE, viz:- 351 to 390 (inclusive).

(3) The batteries will again open on this line at New zero minus 15, lifting off that line at New zero onto the next line; subsequent lifts will be as shown in Green figures viz:-

zero to zero plus 3.
zero plus 3 to zero plus 6.
zero plus 6 to zero plus 9.
zero plus 9 to zero plus 12.
zero plus 12 to zero plus 20.
zero plus 20 to zero plus 25.
zero plus 25 to zero plus 30.
zero plus 30 to zero plus 45.

(4) These Batteries will take up S.O.S. and L.L. Calls if sent to them during the following times :-

From zero to zero plus 315 (except 'B' Bty when firing smoke Barrage.)

From zero plus 351 to zero plus 390

From zero plus 390 to New zero minus 15.

After firing on any S.O.S. or L.L. Call, they will immediately continue their allotted task.

(5) Should an S.O.S. Call go up when our Infantry are on the BLACK LINE, Batteries will open fire on the 318 to 320 line.

(6) 'B' Battery will have an officer at O.P.10 from first zero minus 15 onwards throughout the operations.

(7) 'C' Battery will have an officer at P.2 from the same time.

Alan Thumb Lieut.
6th June 1917.   Adjt. 16th. Brigade, R.F.A.

Ref Sheet 28 S.W.
1/10,000

O

28

27

— CORPS MAUVE LINE.

20   26

BLACK LINE

A.6

SECRET.   Copy No...........

Appendix "C".

168th Brigade R.F.A.

Operation Order No. 39. – 18/6/17.

Reference plan Directeur 1/10,000 Region de NIEUPORT.

1. At 9.a.m. on the 20th June 1917, the Command of the Field Artillery on the ST GEORGE'S and LOMBARTZYDE sectors passes to Lt – Col. R.FITZMAURICE.D.S.O. Commanding 168th Bde R.F.A. The ST GEORGE'S Sector is that called YSER sector by the French.
   The LOMBARTZYDE sector is that called NIEUPORT – VILLE by the French.

2. These two sectors are held by the 14th Infantry Brigade with the following Regiments in the Front Line – from Right to Left;– The Royal Scots, The Manchester Regt., The Dorsets.

   In support is the H.L.I.

   The H.Q. of the Royal Scots is at VACHE CREVEE.
   That of the Manchester's at SARDINERIE.
   That of the Dorsets at REDAN.
   That of the H.L.I. also near REDAN.

3. (a) The Artillery covering the Infantry in the ST GEORGE'S sector is the 168th Brigade R.F.A., less D/168 and B/161.

   (b) The Artillery covering the LOMBARTZYDE sector is the 2nd French Artillery Groupe (Commandant Major LAUJIER at BOIS TRIANGULAIRE.) To this Group is attached D/168 and A/161.
   There is a single gun at TERREUR which enfilades the centre of this sector, and another at RAGHUSE which enfilades the northern portion. There is also another at MAISON DU MARIN which is only to be used should the enemy break through, as it is laid so as to fire within our present line.

   None of these 3 enfilading guns are to be fired unless directly asked for by the Commandant 2nd French Artillery Group.

4. There is also an enfilading gun at REDAN which is never to be fired unless asked for by the Commandant NIEUPORT BAINS Group, as it is only to be used should the enemy break through, being laid on the ground within our own lines.

5. The Artillery in the LOMBARTZYDE sector, from 9.a.m. on the 20th instant, will form a barrage exactly as it now does, along the front from about 250 meters E of Mon. de MARAIS to about 250 meters S.E. of Mon de LYS.
   A/161 reinforcing this barrage.

Continued.

Reference Map TB No.1. 1/20,000 Y Corps Topo Sect.

D/168, in case of S.O.S. LOMBARTZYDE sector will fire on the following points viz:-

  M.23.b.5.6 - M.23.a.85.70. - M.16.d.35.20
  M.23.b.9.9 - M.23.a.32.76 - M.17.c.1.5

Should S.O.S. ST GEORGE'S sector be received D/168 will fire on the following points:-

  N.32.c.1.4 - N.32.c.80.85 - N.32.c.20.85
  N.32.a.5.6 - N.19.c.9.7 - N.19.c.25.55

5. The Artillery of the ST GEORGE'S sector is allotted Barrage Lines as follows:-

  A/168. From a point 200 yards S.E. of ROOD POORT Fe (N.25.b.0.3.) to N.25.b.0.6 to N.19.c.0.0.

  B/168. From a point N.19.c.0.0. to M.24.d.3.5 to M.24.d.0.6

  C/168. N.31.d.8.4. to N.32.c.1.9. to N.32.a.4.7

  B/161. ~~xxxxxxxxxxxxxxx~~
    (Reinforcing Battery)
    2 guns. N.31.d.8.4 to N.32.a.4.7
    4 guns. N.19.c.4.0. to M.24.d.0.6

6. LIAISON.

  C/168 will provide an officer to do Liaison with the Royal Scots Regt. At once.
  B/168 will provide an officer to do Liaison with the Manchester Regt. At once.
D/168. will provide an officer to do Liaison with the Dorset Regt from 9.a.m. on the 20th inst.
'D' battery will find a Liaison officer with the Commandant, French Field Artillery Colonel GIVIERGM.D.S.O at R.36.a.3.9 from 12.noon 19th to 9.a.m. on the 20th.

7. TELEPHONES.

  D/168 will find a telephonists party at the Headquarters of the 2nd French Artillery Group from 9.a.m. on the 20th to work D.3. telephones.
  The telephone Exchange at the PELICAN will be manned by telephonists from 168th Brigade R.F.A. H.Q. from 12.midnight on the 19th.

8. S.O.S. SIGNAL.

  Until 9.a.m. on the 20th one Rocket bursting into 6.red lights.
  After 9.a.m. on the 20th until further orders two Green rockets fired in quick succession.

9. A C K N O W L E D G E.

                Lieut.
19th June 1917.   Adjt 168th Brigade R.F.A.

A.B.C./168.
14th Infantry Brigade
H.Q. 32nd Div Artillery
161st Brigade R.F.A.

1. The following changes and reliefs will take place to-night the 28/29th June 1917.

   (a) A/168 will move the ~~two guns~~ Section now in a forward position to the position being prepared at M.34.c.93.75.

   (b) C/168 will move the ~~two guns~~ Section which ~~are~~ is in the most westerly position (D) to 'A' Battery's present position at s.1.b.69.65.

   (c) 1 gun of B/168 will relieve the gun of A/168 in position at M.35.b.1.4. The gun of A/168 will then be placed in position at M.34.c.93.75, arrangements being made for 'B' Battery's team to do this.

   Times of reliefs:- (a) & (b) Teams will not pass East of M.31.d.2.3 before 10.15.p.m.

   (c) This gun will leave 'B' Battery position at midnight.

2. On completion of the above, the front will be covered as follows:-

   C/168. 4 guns in positions F & F'.   N.31.d.9.3. to N.32.c.22.85 to N.32.a.3.6 (omitting the portions under water 2 guns on Northern portion.)

   C/168. 2 guns   "   "   s.1.b.69.65)   N.19.c.5.0 to N.19.c.0.0
   A/168. 3   "   "   "   s.1.b.69.65)   (With one gun playing round ROOD POORT to N.&.E.)

   B/168. 5   "   N.19.c.0.0 to M.24.d.3.5

   A/168. 3   "   "   "   (M.34.c.93.75) on Support Line N.19.c.4.3 to N.19.a.0.0

   B/168. 1   "   "   "   Take over duties of RACEUGE Gun.

   D/168.   As at present.

3. The sections of A & C/168 will take their Ammunition with them.

   The Ammunition at RACEUGE will be handed over to B/168.

4. The section of C/168 going into 'A' Battery's position will be under the orders of O.C. A/168 until further orders.

5. Reports by telephone when reliefs are complete.

6. ACKNOWLEDGE.

28th June 1917.   Alan Thumb.
                           Adjt 168th Brigade R. F. A.
                           Lieut.

Headquarters Staff - "O" :- 168th Brigade R.F.A.

Nominal Roll of all ranks 30/6/17.

Officers:-   Lt-Col. R.FITZMAURICE.D.S.O.
             Lieut. Ian LUMB.
             Lieut. H.FISHER.
             Capt. D. FERGUSON. (R.A.M.C)

Other Ranks:- 1362.R.S.M.McGowan M.C.
              L.2839. Cpl Lee G.
              L.29801. " Normanton A.
              L.2881. Bdr Gibson H.
              29811. " Anderton A.
              1224. a/Bdr Wright J.
              L.29430. " Ayre F.
              L.28042. " Sugden H.
              L.28206. Gnr Akroyd A.
              L.2810. " Bottomley G.
              59688. " Clark B.J.
              564. " Colley H.
              152003. " Firth H.
              36777. " Grindley W.
              L.29404. " Greenwood G.
              L.2480. " Lucas H.
              L.29394. " Rangeley P.S.
              L.2399. " Ramsden A.
              L.2626. " Slater H.
              L.28179. " Sykes C.A.
              L.2926. " Windle W.T.
              L.27531. " Postlethwaite T.
              13404. " Greenwood G.D.
              L.2422. Dvr Armitage J.
              L.32440. " Baker G.
              L.3240. " Blake F.
              L.28026. " Cowham S.
              5742. " Dickenson J.
              L.29287. " Fisher B.
              198817. " Foote G.
              1573. " Gutteridge W.
              57466. " Hirons B.
              2855. " Gowan W.
              L.3211. " Iredale A.
              L.282. " Iredale H.
              L.8189. " Mellor A.
              L.28132. " Martin J.
              L.7911. a/Bdr McIntyre A.
              L.2931. Dvr Newsome A.B
              L.29424. " Parker J.
              L.29423. " Pollard W.
              L.285. " Radley T.
              L.2917. " Reddington M.
              L.29389. " Stansfield P.
              6267. s/s Periera A.T.
                    Sdlr Williams G.
              16168. Dvr Reed B.
              A.O.D. 62. Str Sgt Barker H. (Artificer).

"C" Battery.

Nominal Roll of all ranks   30/6/17.

Officers:- Major R. KNIGHT.
          a/Capt G.O. d'IVRY.
          2/Lieut. W. TEBBELS.
          2/Lieut. L. R. WILD.
          2/Lieut. J.G. BELL.
          2/Lieut. C. MILLER.

Other ranks:-

28514.	B.S.M.	Patchett W.J.		L.2595.	Gnr	Billington T.
L.28064.	Q.M.S.	Broadley H.		L.28014.	"	Brigg D.H.
1105.	Sergt	Whitney H.		100556.	"	Beamish R.
33061.	"	Smith H.T.		100774.	"	Baird S.
L.2426.	"	Field F.J.		L.28180.	"	Bolton H.
L.2679.	"	Roberts J.R.		L.29379.	"	Beaumont L.
43312.	"	McGowan H.		L.32471.	"	Calvert E.
L.2542.	"	Firth H.		L.2934.	"	Craigie T.
L.3281.	"	Williams W.J.		132564.	"	Curd W.N.
L.2697.	Cpl.	Rhodes L.		5556.	"	Chappell A.
L.2561.	"	Povey J.		190397.	"	Cross F.
L.2619.	"	France W.		L.28178.	"	Dawson W.
8594.	"	Simpson G.		12049.	"	Edwards L.
L.2693.	"	Littlewood K.		130431.	"	Edwards W.H.
L.29407.	"	Taylor M.		8626.	"	Franklin
L.32479.	Bdr	Bentley J.		190413.	"	Foote G.
L.28100.	"	Pitchforth		15261.	"	Fearn H.
L.29313.	"	Armitage W.B.		L.2472.	"	Green N.
L.2708.	"	Crawshaw J.I.		L.2823.	"	Hynes W.H.
L.2574.	"	Whiteley C.H.		L.2610.	"	Hopwood H.
L.2414.	"	Wood B.		735.	"	Keighley E.
L.2731.	"	Rhodes A.		L.3212.	"	Lumb W.
L.28188.	"	Padgett S.		164485.	"	Lewis P.J.
L.2464.	"	Richardson H.		L.28177.	"	Leatham
L.3253.	"	Taylor W.J.		197866.	"	McEwing H.
L.28072.	a/Bdr	Bentley G.		19377.	"	McCarthy C.
L.3239.	"	Fenton E.		197863.	"	McPherson A.
L.2768.	"	Brooksbank S.		168864.	"	Miller W.
L.2669.	"	Oates H.		150416.	"	Mallett H.
L.29297.	"	Noble G.		L.28129.	"	Marshall L.
86310.	"	Squires H.B.		L.2392.	"	Milnes H.
L.28136.	"	Shaw N.		L.2443.	"	Nuttall P.
L.28034.	"	Bevors M.		4421.	"	Offen E.
80741.	s/a/Bdr	Stratton T.		L.28186.	"	Perkins J.C.
L.2536.	"	Mansfield W.G.		L.2736.	"	Pearson H.
L.2513.	"	Peace		L.2653.	"	Rushworth A.
L.72096.	"	Smith L.		21170.	"	Robinson H.
169899.	"	Halliday R.		199083.	"	Raskilly R.
L.28217.	"	Bower M.		2815.	"	Rice H.E.
L.29306.	"	Pearson F.		224342.	"	Rockett B.
160074.	"	McGoudie M.		66262.	"	Rhodes H.
167423.	"	Sweet J.		32491.	"	Roberts J.
L.32449.	Far sgt	Andrews R.		L.2781.	"	Sykes J.
L.2783.	Corpl s/s	Town H.		L.2566.	"	Shaw J.G.
76.	"	Parks J.		14866.	"	Smith
L.29282.	"	Nuttall G.T.		126074.	"	Spence R.
L.28175.	"	Waterhouse L.		5889.	"	Shoesmith W.
L.2690.	"	Kaye J.T.		81446.	"	Slack H.
L.28151.	"	Hopson T.G.		L.273.	"	Spencer H.
L.32485.	Sadd'r	Jackson W.R.		51733.	"	Spaliey F.
6228.	"	Oliver J.H.		221089.	"	Soloman
154173.	Ftr	Kipp J.W.		1677.	"	Stevenson G.W.
147472.	Ftr	Hellawell		82167.	"	Swadling H.
7246.	"	Bambrough R.		2236.	"	Speed
42831.	"	Norton		150668.	"	Schaefer H.B.
121401.	Whlr	Weaver J.		38812.	"	Symonds H.
L.2790.	Gnr	Illot O.V.		156164.	"	Sargent O.

A.

Attached.

2/Lieut. Weedon J.W.
S.E.1514. Sgt Jolley A.J. A.V.C.

L.2771.	Gnr	Thornton J.
30526.	"	Thorpe W.J.
L.29 .	"	Townend J.
L.32 .	"	Thornber W.H.
L.28088.	"	Wilkinson T.
L.29500.	"	Wood F.
L.32441.	"	Walker J.
L.2846.	"	Weldrake .
L.29318.	"	Wood R.
L.2649.	"	Wood G.H.
L.248 .	"	Williams G.
133713.	"	Young W.
107780.	Dvr	Archer W.
17521.	"	Adams F.
L.2 24.	"	Bamforth H.
L.2 2.	"	Bray H.
L.2436.	"	Brearley .
L.2618.	"	Chapman B.
L.29323.	"	Cartwright T.
L.2592.	"	Crowther J.G.
2802.	"	Connor J.
109981.	"	Chapman H.
41489.	"	Crisp H.
L.29409.	"	Dyson W.
L.28079.	"	Green F.
L.2820.	"	Ganley J.
L.29316.	"	Gledhill J.G.
L.2579.	"	Griffiths T.G.
L.28201.	"	Horsfall H.
L.28073.	"	Hirst J.
L.2849.	"	Holmes M.
L.281 .	"	Harrison F.
L.29347.	"	Hardcastle G.W.
93514.	"	Hartley .
L.3241.	"	Kershaw J.
L.2419.	"	Kerton H.
L.28163.	"	Lodge A.
L.2384.	"	Liversey F.G.
L.28021.	"	Mallinson J.
L.2639.	"	Millard H.
826369.	"	Morse L.
101698.	"	O'Neill J.
147602.	"	Orriss H.
32464.	Dvr	Pogson S.
L.28136.	"	Priest G.W.
35864.	"	Quinn D.
L.28074.	"	Robertshaw G.
L.28075.	"	Roe F.
L.28013.	"	Sykes W.
99869.	"	Spencer P.G.
L.2633.	"	Shaw H.
L.2505.	"	Shaw H.
L.28224.	"	Shaw G.
L.2797.	"	Singleton V.
L.240.	"	Smith J.P.
16514.	"	Smith J.W.
217881.	"	Shotton R.
960541.	"	Salmon S.J.
219990.	"	Tall F.
741290.	"	Tanner .
L.28101.	"	Taylor T.H.
L.2460.	"	Twigg J.
L.2483.	"	Varley L.
L.28214.	"	Wood W.N.
L.2 0.	"	Wood .
10 86.	"	Westgate .
L.29331.	"	Woodcock W.
L.28087.	"	Walters H.
L.2594.	"	Wortley T.
L.2 41.	"	Woodhead B.
L.2819.	"	Whitehead J.
159419.	"	Weedon W.
21116.	"	Wainwright W.G.

'B' Battery.   Nominal roll of all ranks. 30/6/17.

Officers:-   Major F.FitzGibbon D.S.O.
              Capt. L.M.Hastings M.C.
              Lieut. W.P.Robinson.
              2/Lieut. W.L.Chamberlain.
                  "   J.Mitchelhill.
                  "   C.F.Basnot.
                  "   Marriott A.E.

Other ranks:-

58482.	B.S.M.	Stenning T.		L.2926.	s/a/Bdr	Broadley J.T.
L.32437.	Q.M.S.	Lane A.C.		8786.	Gnr	Broome H.
L.3214.	Far Sgt	Sutcliffe R.		18820.	"	Brown F.
L.2420.	Sergeant	Deakin T.		L.32496.	"	Burton G.
L.2448.	"	Beaumont H.		L.2671.	"	Cocker F.
L.29344.	"	Guthrie A.		2295.	"	Coward F.
1985.	"	Harding R.G.		L.29363.	"	Crosland. (M.M)
L.2590.	"	Taylor H.		L.29385.	"	Dewar W.
L.2484.	"	Williams G.		68230.	"	Doggett J.
L.2599.	"	Crooks H.		79093.	"	Brewit W.C.
L.2871.	Corporal	Walker S.		L.29392.	"	Eccles J.
L.2864.	"	Mason R.		5052.	"	Earl W.
L.2716.	"	Fisher W.W.		L.29263.	"	Fowler B.
L.2874.	"	Shaw L.		5682.	"	Gallagher N
L.2920.	"	Thornton J.		198809.	"	Gill B.
L.2863.	"	Holmes L.		L.29244.	"	Greenwood A.
L.28210.	"	Greenwood M.R.		L.29262.	"	Greenwood L.
9873.	Cpl s/s	Brenner J.		L.29386.	"	Hanson E.
L.2446.	Bombr	Bottomley T.		L.2746.	s/a/Bdr	Hargreaves A.
L.2451.	"	Spendlove T.		L.3244.	Gnr	Hargreaves D.
L.29826.	"	Temperton H.K.		111819.	s/a/Bdr	Harris G.
L.2838.	"	Bradley S.		L.2664.	Gnr	Hartley A.
L.2524.	"	Turner J.T.		15329.	"	Horan J.S.
L.2524.	"	Mayers A.		L.28046.	"	Holdsworth A.
L.24990.	"	Dyson A.		L.2668.	"	Kiddle F.
L.28218.	"	Bancroft L.		L.3210.	"	Knight S.
L.32480.	"	Hirst W.		L.2562.	"	Lawford F.
L.2960.	"	Wright A.		L.28220.	"	Laycock A.
1824.	"	Burch H.		L.2623.	"	Lee F.
L.28043.	a/Bdr	Broomhead W.H.		100940.	"	Ling J.
L.2808.	"	Christie H.		L.2622.	"	Littlewood A.
12511.	"	Hawthorne J.		197862.	"	McLennan J.B.
16381.	"	Ibbotson M.		197864.	"	McPherson D.
L.2547.	"	Sherwood J.		197868.	"	McRen D.
L.2491.	"	Holmes N.		L.28126.	"	Mallinson F.
1573.	"	Dyson F.		15712.	"	Mason J.
L.2742.	"	Murray A.		15377.	"	Miller G.W.
L.2807.	"	Gouldsmith S.O.		16402.	"	Miller L.
11578.	"	Boswell H.		L.29400	"	Mitchell D.
503.	s/s	Hoyle C.		L.3244	"	Mitchell R.
L.2552.	"	Readyhough G.W.		19535.	"	Mullard G.H.
L.2510.	"	Sidebottom J.		L.29402.	"	Murray E.
L.2462.	"	Wilson J.W.		18876.	"	Nash T.J.
L.3252.	Saddler	Brooksbank G.		15634.	"	Nightingale D.
L.2747.	"	Stansfield P.		L.2632.	"	Onyon A.
L.2607.	Wheeler	Yates F.		L.2856.	"	Owen W.
L.2596.	Fitter	Hill W.		258.	"	Platt H.
L.3246.	Gunner	Ainley W.H.		L.2827.	"	Riddlesdon A.
L.2382.	"	Berry A.		L.2827.	"	Scott F.T.
L.3249.	"	Billington H.		L.2463.	"	Scott N.
L.2616.	"	Binns A.O.		19803.	"	Shaw J.A.
L.32485.	"	Bottoms H.		5828	"	Spence J.
L.3221.	"	Broadbent T.				
L.2873.						

B.

16748. Gnr Stonage J.W.	L.2569. Dvr Turner J.
L.32473. " Stafford H.	2088. " Turner J.
L.29372. " Tidswell H.T.	L.2866. " Townsend H.
11452. " Thomas O	L.2598. " Townsend W.
L.2683. " Thompson J.T.	L.2499. " Tallis G.
67704. " Tunstall A.	L.3215. " Willinson L.
L.2629. " Turner H.	L.2927. " Wilkinson F.
L.2727. " Winteringham B.	L.2927. " Willet W.
L.29431. " Wood G.H.	18398. " Williams B.
L.2704. " Youngman	L.29209. " Wood G.H.
208386. " Rix H.	L.29209.
221070. " Rogers S.B.	141214. " Worth W.D.
176283. " Ritchie G.	L.28089. " Wright F.

L.29381. Dvr Barraclough L.H.
L.2928. " Barraclough T.E.
L.2928. " Beaumont H
L.28199. " Berry
L.2837. " Berry S.
L.3276. s/a/Bdr Bentley T.
L.3266. Dvr Braithwaite W.T.
L.3228. " Bardisow A.
L.2470. " Brook J.W.
18373. " Chesters D.
L.2878. " Clegg
L.28113. " Crosley J.
L.3218. " Crowther J.
L.2446. " Davies J.W.
112102. " Dennis B.
L.2442. " Eastwood G.
L.2732. " Firth H.
L.3238. " Gray D.
L.29307. " Greenwood F.W
L.2728. " Greenwood J.
L.2831. " Hall H.
L.28204. " Harrison F
L.25479. " Hattersley F.
L.3224. " Horthornthwaite T.
L.2822. " Hincliffe A.
L.2558. " Hobson A.
L.3206. " Holmes W.
L.29463. " Horrocks H.
L.32447. " Jackson P.
L.28070. " Jowett J.H.
L.29270. " Ledgard H.
L.25748. " Leckenby J.
L.28077. " Martin L.
930759. " Mathis M.G.
81569. " Mayers F.
L.28127. " Mellor H.
m15 2302. " Milner J.
L.29411. " Moody
L.2870. " Murray R.
213085. " Newns A.
L.2675. " Nicholson J.
L.2675. " North M.
20609. " Ray D.
L.28071. " Rollinson F.
5116. " Roberts G.
L.2861. " Robinson T.
L.2512. " Robinson W.J.
L.2730. " Rukworth E.
L.262. " Scott J.J.
L.28041. " Schofield W.
20373. " Sharples J.B.
L.3279. " Shepard N.
L.2644. " Singleton L.M.
L.2454. " Snell
180180 " Tooth V.S.
L.29397. " Southwell J.
L.28090. " Stanton A.

8949. Sergt White F.W. (.V.C).

"B" Battery. Nominal Roll of all Officers and Other Ranks. 30/6/17.

Officers:-
            Major H.COTTER.D.S.O.
            /Capt GROVER B.T.
            2/Lieut.JAMES H.L.
            2/Lieut.BARRICK G.C.I
            2/Lieut.NELLY C...
            2/Lieut.HINTON S.J.
            2/Lieut.RONALDSON H.R.M.
            2/Lieut.BROWNE C...

Other Ranks:-

53473.	B.S.M.	Malone M.J.		60219.	Gnr Davison J.
L.5688.	Q.M.S.	Tomlinson S.		L.2702.	" Dean F.
L.19483.	Sergt.	Booth F.F.		L.2411.	" Ellis E.
L.12004.	"	Turgoose W.		L.12017.	" Farmery J.W.
5406.	"	Sykes H.M.		78850.	" Fraser J.
L.2711.	"	Kirkham T.		L.12019.	" Froggett E.
22239.	"	Fitzgerald W.		78636.	" Fenny H.
L.29412.	"	Brown T.		57084.	" Gale S.H.
L.11973.	Corpl	Booth J.		16292l.	" Gerrott G.W.
L.11923.	"	Innes H.		197894.	" Grummitt
L.19494.	"	Marshall S.		11975.	" Haworth H.
L.12000.	"	Sanderson G.		L.11992.	" Halton R.
L.19481.	"	Ward J.S.		L.11989.	" Haworth R.
L.28195.	"	Garside I.		88771.	" Hall N.
L.28121.	"	Palmer R.		L.19490.	" Horner C.
L.27727.	"	Ward...		34446.	" Hutt R.
L.19479.	Bdr	Wardle L.M.		86444.	" Holden F.
L.19478.	"	Todd J...		L.2521.	" Higgins H.
L.12016.	"	Maguire T.F.G.		110744.	" Huggett T.
L.19484.	"	Bailey B.C.		3922.	" Hesford...
	"	Gouldsborough L.		143669.	" Heron R.
L.11993.	"	Holdroyd T.		167010.	" Hankinson J.
16077.	"	Carruthers T.		57518.	" Heath W.H.
L.2812.	"	Terry L.		7534.	" Harb J.H.
L.2473.	"	Burnshaw S.		L.12020.	" Inman H.
L.29414.	"	Elliott G.H.		120111.	" Jolley W.
L.27730.	"	Walton H.		19809.	" James T.
L.11919.	/	Ellis W.R.		L.19314.	" Lynes J.
L.19319.	"	Milnthorpe G.		L.2285.	" Lewis B.W.
L.19487.	"	Carr W.C.		L.12047.	" Martin T.
L.11962.	"	Wilcock G.		L.11932.	" Mulheir J.W.
L.27987.	"	Broadhead B.		L.12002.	" Nowell H.M.
L.28010.	"	Steele J.W.		172668.	" Nesbit R.
L.2775.	"	Lee H.		L.11971.	" Parkin W.
L.1203.	/	Watney...		188719.	" Poynts...
93644.	A/a/Bdr	Seymour W.		14369.	" Robinson A.E.
48296.	Far Sgt	Key		219279.	" Stockton P.
L.11991.	Cpl S/S	Halton G.		184085.	" Sheppard W.
L.11926.	S/S	Fletcher F.		190804.	" Shaw N.
L.2751.	"	Bailey H.		185837.	" Spink J.
L.2914.	"	Chappell B.		L.19496.	" Saberton H.
L.11934.	"	Ismay T.H.		L.27999.	" Spittle T.
10790.	"	Copping H.L.		15907.	" Swinn J.
6391.	"	Irving W...		1268.	" Sellar G.
L.29360.	Cpl Ftr	Hinoliffe J.		67727.	" Smith J.
L.14862.	Whlr	Prince B.		1296.	" Smith W.B.
L.11937.	Sdlr	Hall J.		30143.	" Smith T.
147164.	Gnr	Bellis H.W.		93803.	" Smith W...
L.11994.	"	Barr J.		32207.	" Smith...
L.12026.	"	Booth J.		57207.	" Smith F.W.
L.11979.	"	Brady B.		201541.	" Goodhouse S.
L.1948.	"	Briggs M.J.		68714.	" Skelland R.
L.28200.	"	Brook J.		123842.	" Sutton H.T.
L.11981.	"	Cockell G.		20788.	" Stevenson S.
L.28147.	"	Chapman T.		23802.	" Thompson...
147114.	"	Creeper H.		L.2713.	" Taylor J.T.
196150.	"	Cooke...		L.10717.	" Wardle G.H.
				L.19502.	" Wales W.

6.

L.12003.	Gnr	Waldron T.
L.12022.	Dvr	Ainsworth H.
200790.	"	Bell J.T.
533420.	"	Backhouse G.H.
L.11919.		
821420.	"	Beale W.W.
L.11942.	"	Boulton P.
221666.	"	Brown J.T.
L.11980.	"	Burnley W.S.
15220.	"	Berry J.
L.11982.	"	Clarke H.W.
L.28252.	"	Chapman J.
1832.	"	Cleaver S.R.
L.29291.	"	Drake G.
4344.	"	Davis J.
L.28107.	"	Ellis H.
L.11969.	"	Eubank J.
L.25474.	"	Earnshaw H.
L.12055.	"	Farmery T.
L.19506.	"	Fretwell H.
22242.	"	Fitch E.J.
L.12037.	"	Garfitt J.T.
L.19520.	"	Garfoot H.
L.11964.	"	Hunter J.
L.11941.	"	Hart W.
L.11967.	"	Hancock H.
L.19510.	"	Horsfall B.
L.19509.	"	Hudson J.
L.12041.	"	Kenshaw H.
L.11929.	"	Kemp R.
L.19492.	"	Lapish J.
L.19513.	"	Lamb M.
L.28011.	"	Lawton H.
L.29285.	"	Lord J.
85728.	"	Maddocks J.
L.14919.	"	Marshall S.
L.18909.	"	Mitchell W.
85571.	"	O'Keefe J.M.
6074.	"	Overland J.
75445.	"	Pipe H.
L.27691.	"	Poynton G.W.
L.11916.	"	Priestley B.
2869.	"	Price W.
L.28031.	"	Purkin H.
L.2850.	"	Pogson H.
L.12011.	"	Roberts H.W.
L.1196.	"	Ross C.
1265.	"	Schilling R.M.
117610.	"	Scott H.
	"	Studley F.
L.19487.	"	Schofield W.
L.12033.	"	Senior E.K.
120413.	"	Shipman H.
L.29295.	"	Sutcliffe W.
L.28164.	"	Spivey P.
L.28149.	"	Scott J.H.
L.25448.	"	Singleton N.
L.27993.	"	Senior J.W.
86618.	"	Stride W.
8364.	"	Speak J.W.
L.27727.	"	Toothill W.G.
32459.	"	Turner H.
L.27906.	"	Taylor H.
L.28095.	"	Turner A.B.
L.12008.	"	Wales A.
L.12021.	"	Walshaw H.
L.12006.	"	Wrigglesworth F.
L.28169.	"	Williams J.
L.28124.	"	Walton R.
L.29322.	"	White L.
51913.	"	Wareham H.
149487.	"	Wilson W.
2410.	"	Wheeler W.
L.1344	"	Young T.

'D' Battery.   Nominal Roll of All Ranks. 30/6/17.

Officers.   Major D.K.Tweedie D.S.O.
            Capt J.C. Poole M.C.
            Lieut. R.Dunbar.
            Lieut. J.C.Wood.
            2/Lieut. A.A.Steward.
            2/Lieut. H.P.Peel.
            2/Lieut. J.Caterer.
            2/Lieut. H.W.Briscoe.(attached T.M's)

Other Ranks:-

137601.	B.S.M.Perigo.	889630.	Gnr Cook B.
3922.	Q.M.S.Le Page.	889631.	" Cook G.M.
100560	Sergt Greenwood J.(Farr)	19047.	" Dally B.
11948.	" Allen W.J.	7596.	" Dixon H.
1409.	" Dinsdale J.	889543.	" Dunnet J.
1966.	" Hawkes T.J.H.	2537.	" Elsom G.H.
50107.	" Howden Geffrey S.	931081.	" Dredge G.F.
1996.	" Hawkes T.G.H.	2917.	" Fowler A.S.
L.2606.	" Palfreman F.	179512.	" Gatham A.E.
19914.	" Woolfitt F.C.	40484.	" Goodman A.
78512.	Cpl S/S Emms A.	27518.	" Holmes J.
26450.	Cpl Sadd Clawson J.J.	104291.	" Howard A.
42.	Cpl Whlr Derbyshire W.	55188.	" Heard H.
27706.	Cpl Bonner S.	19848.	" Helliwell G.W.
27580.	" Briddock J.	3413.	" Hadley J.
3380.	" Dobson J.H.	148368.	" Keene F.C.
27577.	" Hetherington J.	19707.	" Lancaster G.
19840.	" Hempsall J.	889584.	" Podd G.R.
8806.	" Jackson A.	19796.	" Parkinson G.H.
889291.	" Philpot J.H.	1307.	" Petchley C.
27290.	Bdr Bradford J.	901599.	" Richardson C.H.
889108.	" Browse A.	144699.	" Sprat J.
3392.	" Hamilton T.H.	138484.	" Sugar R.
88875.	" Last R.	851331.	" Stirrett R.F.
19919.	" Scholey B.	2612.	" Simmons E.
20400.	" Smith W.	103314.	" Samuels S.
27601.	a/Bdr Archer S.T.	4005.	" Sugar F.J.
889122.	" Barker W.	960164.	" Slyfield W.J.
3590.	" Beckett H.	27520.27265	" Stacey E.
31981.	" Bethany J.	16473.	" Sherwin L.
20008.	" Croft J.	97676.	" Starkey H.
1986.	" Hempsall T.	297097.	" Smith P.
1411.	" Mole F.G.	190802.	" Sykes J.W.
124923.	" Richardson H.	970798.	" Sandford G.
930380.	" Stafford P.O.	889608.	" Simmons W.
24083.	" Tilson B.		" Sartins H.
889135.	s/s/Bdr Gutteridge A.	20422.	" Stones S.
27555.	s/s Halliwell A.	889604.	" Smith F.G.
27497.	" Innocent	199489.	" Tomlin J.W.
27759.	" Popplewell	26463.	" Townend A.W.
27612.	" Smith J.	92001.	" Talley I.
20447.	" Varley J.	20010.	" Thompson J.
78446.	Sadd Batley	965804.	" Tarrant A.B.
26076.	" Schofield	38810.	" Tinsley G.
140171.	Fbr Collar P.	190088.	" Taylor A.
120860.	Gnr Allen J.	696070.	" Thomas J.
19876.	" Badger C.	3404.	" Williams J.
3603.	" Bell G.J.	889632.	" Woodward F.
26589.	" Boler H.H.	889624.	" Wain F.
27589.	" Blood J.		
201448.	" Board A.		
889114.	" Barker J.	19783.	DVR Armitage G.
3663.	" Burke C.	3402.	" Bainsbridge G J
180893.	" Clarke J.S.	27757.	" Battin W.
20688.	" Cain J.B.	26401.	" Bell A.

D.

20524.	Dvr Bellamy E.	12232.	Dvr Tyler H.
12107.	" Bond P.	71271.	" Thompson G.G.
80802.	" Barnforth P.	171541.	" Twist A
20019.	" Baker W.	889616.	" Theobald W.
200771.	" Birch G.	8386.	" Toms R.
20007.	" Bradley J.	40493.	" Tandy P.
217097.	" Bush H.H.	889612.	" Taylor E.
889011.	" Bell J.	864518.	" Thompson C.
889021.	" Bunn A.	12051.	" Wilkerson J.W.
889009.	" Brightwell B.	27498.	" Wright D.
27125.	" Collins J.R.	19794.	" Whelan J.
889081.	" Cocker B.	5718.	" Wilson J.
889054.	" Kitcock ..	889631	" Whitbread J.
32488.	" Dutton J.W.		
889046.	" Dalton H.		
889048.	" Durrant S.F.		
1598.	" Bon-Leavy W.		
27621.	" Denby M.		
10522.	" Dowd T		
27622.	" Dixson S.		
8890..	" Driver R.		
2592.	" Evans D.		
8902.	" Flook ..		
1523.	" Faulkner ..		
3581	" Guest W.		
19943.	" Green J.		
19803.	" Greenwood J.		
889056.	" Garner J.H		
889055.	" Gray S.V.		
2422.	" Haverhand H.		
19153.	" Howson W.		
19749.	" Hughes H		
889063.	" Honeywood B.		
27010.	" Jewitt W.		
3411.	" Jackson F.		
3580.	" Sunn G.		
9290.	" Lewellyn T.		
889070.	" Law G.		
3579.	" Middleton W.		
5079.	" McLaughlin S.		
27598.	" Pollard G.		
3414.	" Padgett J.H.		
19789.	" Peacock J.H.		
27222.	" Phillips F.		
19939.	" Porter M.		
889087.	" Piper W.		
2691.	" Rigg J.		
889096.	" Read ..		
81641.	" Penny H.		
88909.	" Raynor L.		
150962.	" Smith J.		
40494.	" Seabrook J.H.		
26406.	" Savage W.		
27609.	" Smith J.		
2940.	" Stewart ..		
219001.	" Southam ..		
26411.	" Speight ..		
2750.	" Shone W.		
80050.	" Stokes H.		
27690.	" Sykes J.		
82603.	" Shortlands A.H.		
889001.	" Sustins H.		
202441.	" Turner ..		
19736.	" Thompson A.D.		
202430.	" Townend ..		

"J" Battery   168th. Brigade R.F.A.

Nominal Roll of all Ranks posted to above Unit during June 1917.

Regtl. No. & Name	Posted from.	Date
42821 Btr. Norton A.	32 D.A.C.	9/6/1917.
L.2472 Gnr. Green N.	"	"
132304 Gnr. Curd W.H.	"	"
96047 Dvr. Salmon S.J.	"	"
9314 " Hartley "	"	12/6/1917.
166114 " Smith J.W.	"	21/6/1917.
21702 Gnr. Robinson H.	"	"
30024 " Thorpe W.J.	"	"
199283 " Rascilly F.	"	"
2815 " Rice E.J.	"	"
224342 " Rockett B.	"	"
66262 " Rhodes A.E.	"	19/6/1917.
72090 a/B.Smith L.		
221089 Gnr. Solomon L.		

-----ooooo0ooooo-----

"A" Battery —:— 168th Bde. R.F.A.

Nominal Roll of all ranks who have left the above unit during June 1917.

Regtl. No. & Name.	Reason	Date.
6011 Gnr. Myler A.	Evacuated "Sick"	20/5/1917
5297 2 " Stocker G.	" "	2/6/1917
L.2575 " Walker W.T.	" "Wounded"	3/6/1917
L.2584 " Quarmby W.H.	" "	3/6/1917
L.29307 " Cutler H.	" "	
L.2815 9 Dvr. Harrison H.	" "	
L.3252 A/Br. Taylor W.J.	" "	2/6/1917
5802 Dvr. Connor J.	To T.M's.	2/6/1917
4421 Gnr. Offen F.		

———————oooooOooooo———————

"B" Battery —:— 168th Bde. R.F.A.

Nominal Roll of all ranks posted to above unit during June 1917.

Regtl No. & Name.			posted from.	Date.
280586	Gnr	Rix H.M.	32 D.A.C.	21/6/1917.
221070	"	Rodgers S.R.	"	"
176283	"	Ritchie H.	"	"
L.2599	Sgt.	Crooks H.	Base.	1/6/1917.

"B" Battery   168th Brigade R.F.A.

Nominal Roll of All Ranks who have been evacuated from Unit during June 1917.

Regtl No. & Name	Reason	Date
L.28109 Dvr. Sugden G.	Evacuated "Sick"	13/6/1917
L.32443 " Crossley .	" "	"
L.2606 Gnr. Wolfe C.H.	Transferred to 32 T.M's.	25/6/1917
216330 Dvr. Cooke F.	" " "	"

"C" Battery — 168th. Bde. R.F.A.

Nominal Roll of all ranks posted to above unit during June 1917.

Regtl. No. & Name.	Posted from.	Date.
94317 Gnr. Dean E.	32 D.A.C.	8/6/1917.
137518 " Heath W.H.	"	"
7334 " Hart J.H.	"	"
197894 " Grummett	"	"
132104 Dvr. Studley F.	"	"
221666 " Browne G.T.	"	"
200790 " Bell J.T.	"	"
821420 " Beale W.A.	"	"
4344 " Davis J.	"	12/6/1917.
820635 " Schilling R.M.	"	"
177610 " Scott H.	"	"
22242 " Fitch E.J.	"	18/6/1917.
48296 Far.Sgt. Kev	"	21/6/1917.
685715 Gnr. Skelland R.	"	"
190804 " Shaw N.	"	"
123842 " Sutton H.T.	"	"
219279 " Stockton P.	"	"
184082 " Sheppard W.	"	"
207858 " Stevenson S.	"	"

"C" Battery -:- 168th Bde. R.F.A.

Nominal Roll of all ranks who have left above Unit during June 1917.

Regtl. No. & Name	Reason	Date.
138478 Gnr. Carmalt W.	Evacuated "Sick"	6/6/1917.
147504 " Balls F.	Transferred to 32 T.M's.	25/6/1917.
196150 " Cocke F.	" " "	"

'D' Battery — : — 168th Bde. R.F.A.

Nominal Roll of all ranks who have been posted to above unit during June 1917.

Regtl. No. & Name.	Posted from.	Date.
82663 Dvr. Shorthand A.H.	32 D. A. C.	12/6/1917.
42 Cpl.Whlr.Derbyshire W.	"	10/6/17.
130962 Dvr. Smith J.	"	12/6/1917.
185893 Gnr. Clarke J.S.	"	9/6/17.
931081 " Dredge J.S.	"	"
197075 " Lancaster J.	"	"
144699 " Spratt J.	"	"
95804 " Tarrant A.E.	"	"
80182 Dvr. Barmforth F.	"	"
200771 " Birch G.	"	"
217907 " Bush H.H.	"	"
72096 a/Bdr Smith D.	"	"
95 6164 Gnr. Slyfield W.G.	"	21/6/1917.
196862 " Sikes J.W.	"	"
199489 " Tomlin T.W.	"	"
92601 " Talley J.	"	"
69070 " Thomas J.	"	"
58810 " Tinsley G.	"	"
190082 " Taylor H.	"	"
81641 Dvr. Penny H.	"	"
27598 " Pollard J.	"	"

"D" Battery - : - 168th Bde. R.F.A.

Nominal roll of all ranks who have left above unit during June 1917.

Regtl. No. & Name.	Reason.	Date.
113012 Sdlr. Molyneux D.	Evacuated "Sick"	27/5/1917.
19894 Sgt. Longley J.T.	" "	29/5/1917.
19799 Dvr Fisher G.	" "Wounded"	4/6/1917.
911227 Gnr Day E.B.	" "Sick"	6/6/1917.
3383 Sgt. Hartley B.W.	" "Wounded"	7/6/17.
129128 Gnr. Smith W.H.	" "	"
2317 " Longford W.G.	Killed in action.	7/6/17.
19930 Sgt. Flannigan P.	" "	"
889600 Dr. Smith A...	Transferred to R.C.Co.R.E's	8/6/17.
106866 Gnr Scratchard G.	Evacuated "Sick"	20/6/17.
26449 " Shaw F.	" "	"
901238 " Handley H.	" "	"
930380 A/Bdr Stafford P.O.	Transferred to 32nd D.T.M's.	2/6/1917.
889530 Gnr. Cook B.	" " "	"

CONFIDENTIAL.

WAR DIARY

of the

168th. BRIGADE R.F.A.

from 1st. JULY 1917 to 31st. JULY 1917.

(Volume 19.)

Army Form C. 2118.

WAR DIARY
or
INTELLIGENCE SUMMARY.
(Erase heading not required.)

16th. Brigade R.F.A. Commanded by Lt-Col R. FITZMAURICE D.S.O.

Place: Reference Sheet NIEUPORT 1/40,000

Date	Hour	Summary of Events and Information	Remarks and references to Appendices
1-7-17.	1.40 a.m.	The Brigade supported the 2nd Manchesters in a raid on enemy trenches in N.19.o. (See Appendix 1) The Raiding Party wandered round the enemy's trenches and searched six dug-outs, but all the enemy had fled.	OL.
2-7-17.		Great activity of enemy aeroplanes. Our batteries carried out several bombardments of enemy trenches.	OL.
3-7-17.	12.30 a.m. 2.30 pm.	Enemy bombarded our trenches in N.30.b. Our batteries replied vigourously. 'A' Battery heavily shelled. No damage done.	OL.
4-7-17.		Work commenced on a large number of Battery positions in and around NIEUPORT.	OL.
5-7-17.	12 pm.	"D" Battery heavily shelled. No damage done.	OL.
6-7-17.		14th. Inf. Bde. relieved by 96th. Inf.Bde. in the Sector covered by the 16th Bde R.F.A.	OL.
7-7-17.		NIEUPORT heavily shelled all day.	OL.
9-7-17.		Enemy Artillery very active. Our batteries carried out Retaliation schemes during the day.	OL.
10-7-17.		After a heavy bombardment lasting 12 hours, the Germans attacked from the Coast to LOMBARTZYDE. The 1st Division on our left was driven to the South side of the YZER. The 97th. Inf. Bde. lost a little ground at first, but retook it later. The enemy's fire on back areas and batteries was very heavy. Bde.R.F.A. was not attacked, so assistance was given by concentrating all batteries on the front attacked. Ammunition expended - 18-Pdr. 5,500. 4.5 Hows. 2,570. Casualties - 3 killed and 9 wounded	OL.

Army Form C. 2118.

WAR DIARY
or
INTELLIGENCE SUMMARY.

(Erase heading not required.)

168th. Brigade R.F.A.

Commanded by Lt-Col. R. FITZMAURICE DSO

Instructions regarding War Diaries and Intelligence Summaries are contained in F.S. Regs., Part II. and the Staff Manual respectively. Title pages will be prepared in manuscript.

Place	Date	Hour	Summary of Events and Information	Remarks and references to Appendices
	11-7-17.		The enemy kept up a desultory fire on our trenches opposite LOMBARTZYDE.	ak
	12-7-17		"C" Battery shelled. 1 gun-pit blown in. Casualties - 2 killed and 3 wounded.	ak
			Our batteries carried out bombardments of enemy trenches and wire-cutting "B" Battery very heavily shelled. 2 gun-pits blown in - 3 guns damaged, and ammunition blown up. Casualties - 1 killed and 3 wounded.	ak
	13-7-17.		Our batteries carried out wire-cutting and bombardments of enemy trenches south of LOMBARTZYDE.	ak
		7 p.m.	Enemy attempted an attack on our trenches opposite LOMBARTZYDE but was beaten off.	
	14-7-17. 15-7-17. 16-7-17.		The 3rd Australian Army Field Artillery Brigade came into action, and was placed under the command of Lt-Col. R. FITZMAURICE D.S.O. the 168th. and 3rd. Australian Brigades R.F.A. comprising "A" Group. Bombardment of enemy trenches and wire carried out all day.	ak
	17-7-17. 18-7-17.		"C" Battery heavily shelled. Several direct hits were obtained on gun-pits, but they were not blown in. 1 man wounded. 96th. Infantry Brigade relieved by the 146th. Infantry Brigade in the sector covered by the 168th. Brigade R.F.A.	ak
	19-7-17.	2 a.m.	Enemy attack on our trenches opposite LOMBARTZYDE broken up by our barrage; Many dead were left on our wire. Our batteries carried out bombardments on enemy trenches.	ak
	20-7-17.		"C" Battery heavily shelled - no guns damaged and no casualties. Lt-Col. FITZMAURICE D.S.O. proceeds on leave. Major FITZGIBBON D.S.O. assumes command of the Brigade.	ak

Army Form C. 2118.

WAR DIARY
or
INTELLIGENCE SUMMARY.
(Erase heading not required.)

16th. Brigade R.F.A.
Commanded by Lt-Col. R. FITZMAURICE D.S.O.

Instructions regarding War Diaries and Intelligence Summaries are contained in F. S. Regs., Part II. and the Staff Manual respectively. Title pages will be prepared in manuscript.

Place	Date	Hour	Summary of Events and Information	Remarks and references to Appendices
	21-7-17.		"A" Battery heavily shelled all morning, 3 guns put out of action and much ammunition exploded. No casualties. "B" Battery shelled all afternoon. Much damage done to the position but no guns damaged. No casualties. "C" Battery had 7 Gas Casualties. NIEUPORT shelled with Gas Shells.	O.K.
	22-7-17. 11 p.m.		"B" & "C" Batteries heavily shelled. The usual bombardment of enemy trenches and wire continued. Enemy attempted to come over to our lines, but was driven back by our barrage.	O.K.
	23-7-17.		Enemy's Heavy Artillery very active. "C" Battery was shelled continuously for 4 hours. Gun-pits badly damaged. 2.9.O.S. Calls replied to: It is thought the enemy meant to attack but were kept back by our barrage.	O.K.
	24-7-17.		Rained. Quiet all day.	O.K.
	25-7-17		"D" Battery received its first lot of 106 fuzes, and carried out very effective wire-cutting with them.	O.K.
	26-7-17.		The 245th. Brigade R.F.A. took over the defence of MT GEORGE'S SECTOR and moved into our H.Q. at X.6.a.2.2., 182d Brigade R.F.A. H.Q. moved to MAISON CARREE – S.3.9.7.3. (see Appendix 2.) "C" Battery moved into Battle position at M.34.d.47.81.	O.K.
	27-7-17.		"A" Battery moved into new position at S.3.a.75.00.	O.K.
	28-7-17. 11 p.m. & 12 a.m.		In connection with Raids which were carried out, Batteries fired on Enemy trenches (see Appendix III) Enemy shelled Batteries and back areas heavily for some hours with Gas shell.	O.K.
	29-7-17. 1.35.a.m.		Gas bombardment carried out. Our batteries took part (see Appendix 4. –) Enemy's retaliation was very heavy;	O.K.

Army Form C. 2118.

WAR DIARY
or
INTELLIGENCE SUMMARY.
(Erase heading not required.)

16th. Brigade R.F.A.

Commanded by Lt-Col.R.F.TZMAURICE D.S.O.

Place	Date	Hour	Summary of Events and Information	Remarks and references to Appendices
	30-7-17.	2 am. 8 pm.	Gas bombardment as on the 29th. carried out. Practice Barrage carried out on the whole of the Corps front.	ae.
	31-7-17.		A quiet day. Lt-Col.FITZMAURICE D.S.O. returned from leave and assumed Command of the Group. The undermentioned have been awarded the Military Medal:- No. L.28079 Dvr. Green F. 12-6-17 " 147602 " Curtiss E. " " 27756 Bdr. Bonner A. 6-7-17 " L.2615 O Gnr. Bolton E. 29-6-17 " 107905 A/S Copping H.H. " " 34751 Str. Sgt. Fearn Bishop G." " " L.39 Cpl. Dobson J.H. " " L.2091 Cpl Normanton A. "	ae.

1st. August 1917.

M Newinn
Lt-Colonel.

Commanding 16th. Brigade, R.F.A.

SECRET.

O.C. /168th Brigade R.F.A.
14th Infantry Brigade.
H.Q. 52nd Division Artillery.

SCHEME 'C'.

1. Sepia will carry out a raid on the enemy's trenches at zero hour on the night of 30th / 1st July.

2. The Artillery will form a box barrage whilst the infantry are entering and in the trenches, and covering fire for the withdrawal.

3. When the Raiding party gets into the position, ready to start the Raid, the Code Word "GUARD" will be sent to the Artillery.

4. Bangalore Torpedoes will be used to cut the wire at zero hour; When this has been done, the Raiding party will move forward and the Artillery will open fire.

5. The Code Word for the Artillery to open fire will be "COSSACK" The action then will be as follows:-

   A/168. 2 guns in forward position on N.25.a.40.95
           4 guns from N.19.c.4.0 to N.19.c.65.45.

   B/168. Enfilade Trenches from M.24.d.90.18 to N.19.c.45.40

   D/168.
           1 gun M.24.d.5.3.
           1 gun M.24.d.8.4.
           1 gun M.24.d.9.4.
           1 gun M.24.d.93.36
           1 gun M.24.d.95.32
           1 gun N.19.c.9.8.

   This fire will be kept up until the Raiding party leaves the trenches and is sufficiently clear to admit of covering fire along the front line of enemy's trench.
   It will last from 10 to 20 minutes.

   Rates of fire:-

           18-pdrs. 3 rounds per gun per minute for 4 minutes
                     then 2 Rds per gun per min.
           4.5" Hows. 2 rounds per gun per minute all through.

6. On receipt of the Code Word "BANG" the Artillery action will be as follows:-

   D/168.   As before.

   A/168.   from N.2.a.40.95 to N.19.c.40.05 to N.19.c.0.0

   B/168.   from N.19.c.2.0 to M.24.d.9.2.

   Rates of fire:-

           18-pdrs and 4.5" Hows - 2 rounds per gun per minute.

   This rate will continue until Code Word "SLOW" is sent, when it will be halved until Code Word "CHASE" is received.
   The Code Word "BANG" will be duplicated by a rocket bursting into SILVER RAIN.

7. D/168 will find Liaison officer, Telephone and 2 Telephonists to be with The O.C. Raiding party.
The Liaison officer will be responsible that all communications are in good working order, and that he and all his telephonists know the pre-arranged Code Words.
Battery Commanders will also see that their telephonists who will be on duty at the time, know the Code Words, so that there will be no element of confusion.

8. Visual signalling will also be arranged.

9. ACKNOWLEDGE.

30th June 1917.

Alan Thumb Lieut.
Adjt 168th Brigade R.F.A.

SECRET   Copy No.............

"A" GROUP R.F.A.

OPERATION ORDER No. 42.
WEDNESDAY 25th July 1917.

Reference Sheet LOMBARTZYDE 1/20.000.

1.   The task of covering the ST GEORGE'S Sector, (D & E Sub-sectors) at present done by "A" Group, will be carried out by "F" Group from 10.0 a.m. to-morrow the 26th. July 1917.

2.   The S.O.S. lines of "A" Group from the above hour will be as follows :-

B/168.		M.24.d. 3.8	to	M.24.a. 5.1
A/168.		M.24.a. 5.1	to	M.24.a. 0.3
C/168.		M.24.a. 0.3	to	M.23.b. 5.4
7th Bty.	2 guns.	M.18.a. 9.1	to	N./3.a. 0.8
	4 guns.	M.23.b. 6.7	to	M.17.d. 7.7 to M.18.c.7.9.
8th.Bty.	6 guns.	M.24.a.85.00	to	M.24.a.75.40 to
		M.24.b. 2.9	to	M.18.d. 4.5
9th.Bty.	3 guns.	N.19.c. 0.8	to	N.14.c.00.25
	3 guns.	N.19.c. 3.5	to	N.19.b. 6.2 to N.20.a. 0.1

3.   All necessary registration will be carried out at once.

4.   D/168 will be directly under the orders of O.C., "F" Group.

5.   LIAISON. The liaison officers at present with Nos. 1 & 2 Battalions will be relieved by Officers of "F" Group at 10.0 a.m. on the 26th.July 1917.

6.   A C K N O W L E D G E.

                                                    Alan Kuumb   Lieut.
25th. July 1917.   Adjutant - "A" GROUP.

O.C.   /168th. Bde. R.F.A.

1. In connection with two raids which are to take place to-night "A" Group will carry out the following bombardments :-

   TIME.
   11 pm.   C/168. (4 guns)   Front Line M.23.b.6.4 to M.23.b.3.5
   to   "   (2 guns)   LADIES LANE M.23.b.30.45 to M.23.b.6.8.
   11.15 pm.   A/168. (4 guns)   C.T. M.23.b.6.4 to M.23.b.95.90
                   B/168. (4 guns)   C.T. M.24.a.10.85 to M.24.a.30.65

   12 midnight
   to   ditto   ditto.
   12.15 a.m.

   Rate of Fire - 2 rds. per gun per minute. 50% A + 50% A.X.

2. The points of entry of the raids are as follows :-

   11 pm.   ROSE TRENCH from its junction with the CRIQUE DE NIEUWENDAMME to a point 50 yards South.

   12 mid-night.   M.23.b.85.30 to M.23.b.63.30.

3. Please ACKNOWLEDGE.

                                          Alan Thumb. Lieut.
   28-7-1917.   Adjutant - "A" GROUP.

SECRET. Copy No..........

"A" GROUP R.F.A.

OPERATION ORDER NO. 44.

FRIDAY 27th. July 1917.

Reference 1/20,000 LOMBARTZYDE Edn.1.A.

1. There will be a Gas Bombardment of the following points in the enemy's lines by Special Companies R.E. at 1.35 a.m. 28th. July 1917.

    GROOTE BAMBURGH FARM,
    M.24.a.4.2., M.23.b.6.5., LOMBARTZYDE.,
    HEUVRIDAGE FORT., & M.19.0.

2. This bombardment will be dependent on the wind.

3. "A" GROUP will fire as follows :-

Zero + 30 to Zero + 40 and Zero + 65 to Zero + 75.

A/168.	(2 guns)	Search Communication Trenches M.24.a.4.1 to M.24.a.7.4 and M.24.a.2.2 to M.24.a.4.6.
B/168.	(4 guns)	BAMBURGH TRENCH. M.24.d.3.8 to M.24.a.4.1.
C/168.	(2 guns)	Search Communication Trench M.23.b.6.4 to M.24.a.0.9.
7th.Bty. - A.F.A.		BAMBURGH WALK. M.24.b.1.0 to M.24.a.6.5.
8th.Bty.A.F.A.		BAMBURGH WALK. M.24.a.6.5 to M.24.a.0.9.
9th.Bty.A.F.A.		BAMBURGH TRENCH. M.24.a.4.1 to M.23.b.8.3.

4. Rate of Fire - 2 rds. per gun per minute.

5. Ammunition. - 50 % Shrapnel and 50 % H.E.

6. Watches will be synchronised by telephone from this Office not before 11 p.m.

7. Zero hour will be 1.35 a.m.

8. About 8 pm. 27th., Batteries will be informed if the operation is to take place by the following code:-

    To take place - KICK.
    NOT TO take place - DUD.

    If the attack is decided on and subsequently postponed, Batteries will be informed by wire

    CANCEL KICK.

9. ACKNOWLEDGE.

27th. July 1917.

Alan Lumb Lieut.
Adjutant - "A" GROUP.

Headquarters Staff : 168 Bde.R.F.A.

Nominal Roll of all ranks as at July 1st 1917.

OFFICERS.
Lt-Col.R.FITZMAURICE.D.S.O.
Lieut. A. Lumb.
Lieut. H. FISHER.
2/Lt. H.L.JAMES.
Capt. D. FERGUSON R.A.M.C.(attached)

OTHER RANKS.
```
     1362 aRSM McGowan R.H. M.C.
   L.25839 Cpl.Lee G.
   L.29801 Cpl.Normanton A.
   L.25881 Bdr.Gibson H.
   L.29811  "  Anderton A.
    12245 a/Br.Wright J.
   L.28042  "  Sugden E.
   L.29430  "  Eyre F.
   L.28026 Gnr.Ackroyd H.
   L.25810  "  Bottomley C.
   L.59688  "  Clark B.J.
     5645  "  Celley H.
   152003  "  Firth H.
    56777  "  Grindley W.
   L.29404  "  Greenwood C.
   L.25480  "  Lucas E.
   L.29394  "  Rangeley P.S.
   L.25399  "  Ramsden A.
   L.25626  "  Slater H.
   L.28179  "  Sykes C.A.
   L.29296  "  Windle A.T.
   L.27531  "  Postlethwaite T.
   131004  "  Greenwood C.D.
   L.25422 Dvr.Armytage J.R.
   L.32440  "  Baker G.
   L.32540  "  Blake F.
   L.28026  "  Cowham S.
     5742  "  Dickensen J.
   L.29287  "  Fisher S.
   198817  "  Foote G.
     1573  "  Gutteridge W.
    37566  "  Hirons E.
     5855  "  Gowan W.
   L.32511  "  Iredale A.
   L.25825  "  Iredale E.
   L.28189  "  Meller A.
   L.28132  "  Martin J.
    79511  "  McIntyre A.T.
   L.29351  "  Newsome A.E.
   L.29424  "  Parker J.
   L.29423  "  Pollard W.
   L.25853  "  Radley T.
   L.29357  "  Reddington M.
   L.29389  "  Stansfield P.
     6267 S/S Periera A.T.
          Sdlr.Williams J.
   163508 Dvr.Reed S.
      625.Stf.Sgt.Artificer Barker H. (AOC)
```

Nominal Roll of all ranks who have joined during July 1917

```
   221398 Gnr.Smith C.
```

Nominal Roll of all ranks who have been evacuated during July 1917

```
     5645 Dvr.Celley E.
   165508  "  Reed S.
```

"A" BATTERY -:o:- 168th.BDE.R.F.A.

Nominal Roll of all ranks as at July 1st. 1917.

Officers:-
        Major R.Emmet.
        a/Capt. G.O.d'Ivry.
        2/Lt. W.A.Ebbels.
        2/Lt. L.A.Ravald.
        2/Lt. J.G.BEll.
        2/Lt. A.C.Miller.
        2/Lt. J.W.Weeden.

Other ranks:-

28514	BSM	Patshett W.J.	L.25790	Gnr.	Allet C.V.
L.28084	QMS	Brearley H.	L.25595	"	Billington T.
1105	Sgt.	Whitney T.	L.28014	"	Bray E.H.
53061	"	Smith E.F.	100556	"	Beamish R.
L.25426	"	Field P J.	100774	"	Baird S.
L.25679	"	Roberts J.F.	L.28180	"	Bolton H.
43312	"	Mc.Gowan A.H.	L.29379	"	Beaumont L.
L.25425	"	Firth A.	L.32471	"	Calvert F.
L.32581	"	Williams W.J.	L.29345	"	Craigie T.
L.25697	Cpl.	Rhodes L.	132364	"	Curd W.N.
L.25561	"	Pevey W.	5556	"	Chappell A.
L.25619	"	France W.	190397	"	Cross F.
83594	"	Simpson C.	L.28178	"	Dawson W.
L.25693	"	Littlewood K.	12049	"	Edwards L.
L.29407	"	Tayler F.	L30451	"	Edwards W.H.
L.32479	Bdr.	Bentley J.	86276	"	Franklin A.
L.28100	"	Pitchforth A.	190415	"	Foote G.
L.29313	"	Armitage W.B.	152561	"	Fearn H.
L.25708	"	Crawshaw J.T.	L.25472	"	Green N.
L.25574	"	Whiteley C.H.	L.25823	"	Hynes W.H.
L.25414	"	Wood B.	L.25610	"	Hopwood H
L.25731	"	Rhodes J.	7733	"	Keighley F.
L.28188	".	Padgett S.	L.32512	"	Lumb W.
L.25464	"	Richardson H.	184485	"	lewis P.J.
L.32553	"	Tayler W.J.	L.28177	"	Leathem F.
L.28072	a/Br.	Bentley C.	197866	"	McEwing H.
L.32539	"	Fenton E.	159371	"	McCarthy C.
L.25768	"	Brooksbank S.	197863	"	McPherson A.
L.25669	"	Oates H.	168564	"	Miller W.
L.29297	"	Noble C.	150416	"	Mallett H.
83610	"	Squires A.E.	L.28129	"	Marshall L.
L.28136	"	Shaw N.	L.25392	"	Milnes H.
L.28034	"	Beavers M.	L.25433	"	Nuttall P.
80741	S/M/Br	Stratton T.	44251	"	Offen F.
L.25536	"	Mansfield W.G.	L.28186	"	Perkins J.C.
L.25768	"	Peace A.	85736	"	Pearson H.
L.72096	"	Smith L.	L.25653	"	Rushworth A.
169899	"	Halliday R.	211715	"	Robinson H.
L.28217	"	Bower E.	199083	"	Raskilly R.
L.29306	"	Pearson F.	L.2815	"	Rice E.F.
167704	"	McGeashie M.	224342	"	Reckett B.
167423	"	Sweet J.	66262	"	Rhodes A.F.
L.32499	Farr.Sgt.	Andrews R.	L.32491	"	Roberts J.
L.25783	S/S.Cpl.	Town E.	L.25781	"	Sykes J.
765	S/S.	Parks J.	L.25566	"	Shaw J.C.
L.29282	"	Nuttall G.T.	148166	"	Smith A.
L.28175	"	Waterhouse L.	126074	"	Spence R.
L.25690	"	Kaye J.T.	5889	"	Shoesmith W.
L.28151	"	Hopson T.C.	81446	"	Slack H.
L.32485	Sdlr,	Jackson W.R.	L.25735	"	Spencer H.
62728	"	Oliver J.E.	51733	"	Spellissy F.
154173	"	Skipp J.W.	221089	"	Solomon J.
147472	Ftr.	Hellawell A.	16577	"	Stevenson G.W.
72465	"	Bamborough R.			
42831	"	Norton A.			
	Whlr,	Weaver J.			
12145	Whlr.				

821657	Gnr.	Swadling H.		L.28075	Dvr.	Roe F.
22365	"	Speed A.		L.28013	"	Sykes W.
150668	"	Schaefer A.E.		99859	"	Spencer P.G.
38812	"	Simmons H.		L.25633	"	Shaw E.
156164	"	Sargents E.		L.25503	"	Shaw H.
L.25771	"	Thornton J.		L.28224	"	Shaw C.A.
E.30326	"	Thorpe F.		L.25797	"	Singleton V.
L.29355	"	Townend J.		L.25450	"	Smith J.P.
L.32535	"	Thornber W.H.		166514	"	Smith J.W.
L.28088	"	Wilkinson T.		217881	"	Shotton R.
L.29300	"	Wood F.		960540	"	Salmon S.G.
L.32441	"	Walker A.		219990	"	Tall F.
L.25646	"	Waldrake E.		741290	"	Tanner A.
L.29318	"	Weed R.		L.28101	"	Taylor T.H.
L.25649	"	Wood C.E.		L.25460	"	Twigg J.
L.25485	"	Williams G.		L.25463	"	Varley L.
133713	"	Young W.		L.28214	"	Wood W.A.
				L.25650	"	Wood A.
107780	Dvr.	Archer W.		10586	"	Westgate F.
175251	"	Adams F.		L.29331	"	Woodcock W.
L.25524	"	Bamforth H.		L.28087	"	Walters H.
L.25525	"	Bray H.		L.25394	"	Wortley T.
L.25436	"	Brearley A.		L.25541	"	Woodhead E.
L.25659	"	Chapman B.		L.25899	"	Whitehead J.A.
L.29323	"	Cartwright P.		159419	"	Weeden W.
L.25592	"	Crowther J.G.		21116	"	Wainwright W.O.
L 9802	"	Conner J.				
109981	"	Chapman E.				
? 41489	"	Crisp E.				
L.29409	"	Dyson W.				
L.28079	"	Green F.				
L.25820	"	Ganley J.				
L.29316	"	Gledhill J.G.				
L.25579	"	Griffiths T.C.				
L.28201	"	Horsfall F.				
L.28073	"	Hirst J.				
L.25499	"	Holmes F.				
L.28153	"	Harrison F.				
L.39347	"	Hardcastle C.W.				
X.93514	"	Hartley A.				
L.32541	"	Kershaw C.				
L.25419	"	Kirton E.				
L.28163	"	Lodge A.				
L.25384	"	Livesey F.C.				
L.28021	"	Mallinson J.A.				
L.25639	"	Millard H.				
826369	"	Morse L.				
101698	"	O'Neill J.				
147602	"	Orriss H.				
L.32464	"	Pogson S.				
L.28136	"	Priest G.W.				
L.35864	"	Quinn D.				
L.28074	"	Robertshaw C.				

Attached.
S.E.1514 AVC Sgt. Jally A.J.

"A" Battery :   168th.Bde.R.F.A.

Nominal Roll of all ranks posted to Battery during July 1917.

```
  1985   Cpl.Harding R.
226903   Gnr.Hancock J.G.
 28006    "  Singleton H.W.
152789    "  Wildsmith H.
 18757    "  Hart O.
192477    "  Ormiston A.
 32523   a/Br.Philipsen H.
 54101    "  Perkins T.
204732   Dvr Malburn H.
 55046    "  Marshall R.
 12171    "  Lewis L.
212321    "  Crawford C.
```

Nominal Roll of all ranks evacuated during July 1917.

```
RSM.
 28514  BSM.Patchett W.J.
L.25693  Cpl.Littlewood K.
L.25464  Bdr.Richardson H.
L.32553   "  Tayler W.J.
L.28072 a/Bdr Bentley C.
L.25669   "  Oates H.
L.28151  S/S Hopson T.C.
L.25781  Gnr.Sykes J.
  5889    "  Shoesmith W.
  5802  Dvr.Conner J.
L.28073   "  Hirst J.
L.28214  Dvr Wood W.N.
```

"B" BATTERY —:o:— 168 Bde.R.F.A.

Nominal Roll of all ranks as at 1-7-17

Officers:—
    Major F. FitzGibbon. D.S.O
    Capt. L.M. Hastings. M.C
    Lieut. W.P. Robinson.
    2/Lt. W.L. Chamberlain.
    2/Lt. J. Mitchelhill.
    2/Lt. C.P. Basnett.
    2/Lt. A.E. Marriott.

Other ranks:—

58482	BSM	Stenning T.	L.29265	Gnr.	Broadley J.T.
L.32437	QMS	Lane A.C.	8786	"	Broom H.
L.32514	Far.Sgt.	Sutcliffe R.	18820	"	Brown F.
L.25420	Sgt.	Deakin T.	L.32496	"	Burton G.
L.25448	"	Beaumont F.	L.25671	"	Cooker F.
L.29344	"	Gutherie A.	L.2295	"	Coward F.
1985	Sgt.	Harding R.C.	L.29363	"	Cresland E. M.M.
L.25390	"	Taylor H.	L.29383	"	Dewar W.
L.25484	"	Willans C.	68336	"	Doggett J.
L.25599	"	Crooks H.	79093	"	Drewitt W.C.
L.25871	"	Walker S.	L.29392	"	Eccles J.
L.25864	"	Mason R.C.	3052	"	Earl W.
L.25716	"	Fisher W.W.	L.29263	"	Fowler B.
L.25874	"	Shaw L.	56821	"	Gallagher N.
L.29350	"	Thornton J.	198809	"	Gigg B.
L.25863	"	Holmes L.	L.29244	"	Greenwood A.A.
L.28210	"	Greenwood M.R.	L.29262	"	Greenwood L.A.
98737	S/S.Cpl.	Brennan J.	L.29386	"	Hansen E.
L.25446	Bdr.	Bottomley T.	L.25746	"	Hargreaves A.
L.25451	"	Spendlove T.	L.32454	"	Hargreaves D.
L.29826	"	Temperton H.K.	L.111819	"	Harris G.
L.28138	"	Bramley S.	L.25664	"	Hartley A.
L.25545	"	Turner J.T.	15329	"	Horan J.E.
L.24998	"	Mayers A.	L.28046	"	Holdsworth A.
L.28218	"	Dyson F.	L.25658	"	Kiddle F.
L.32480	"	Bancroft L.	L.32510	"	Knight S.
5960	"	Hurst W.	L.25562	"	Lawford F.
152524	"	Wright A.	L.28220	"	Laycock A.
L.28023	Bdr.	Burch H.	L.25623	"	Lee F.
L.25808	a/Br.	Broomhead W.H.	160940	"	Ling J.
L.25511	"	Christie H.	L.25622	"	Littlewood A.
16381	"	Cawthorne J.	197862	"	McLennan J.B
L.25547	"	Ibbetson M.	197864	"	Mc.Pherson E.
L.25491	"	Shirwood J.	197865	"	McCrea D.
152735	"	Holmes N.	L.28126	"	Mallinson F.
L.25742	"	Dyson F.	152712	"	Mason J.
L.28076	"	Murray A.	150377	"	Miller C.W.
L.11578	"	Gouldsmith S.C.	164025	"	Miller L.
5035	S/S.	Boswell H.	L.29400	"	Mitchell D.
L.25558	"	Hoyle C.	L.32544	"	Mitchell R.
L.25510	"	Readyhough G.W.	199395	"	Mullard G.H.
L.25452	"	Sidebottom J.	L.29402	"	Murray E.
L.32552	"	Wilson J.W.	188576	"	Nash T.J.
L.25747	Sdlr.	Brooksbank G.	156134	"	Nightingale D.
L.25607	"	Stansfield F.	L.25632	"	Onyon A.
L.25396	Whlr.	Yates F.	L.25836	"	Owen W.
L.32456	Ftr.	Hill W.	2358	"	Platt H.
L.25382	Gnr.	Ainley W.H.	L.25827	"	Riddlesden A.
L.32549	"	Berry A.	46249	"	Scott F.T.
L.25616	"	Billington H.	L.25463	"	Scott N.
L.32485	"	Binns A.O.	159803	"	Shaw J.A.
L.32521	"	Bottoms H.	5828	"	Spence J.
L.25873	"	Broadbent T.			

165478	Gnr. Stanage U.W.	L.28070	Dvr. Jewett J.H.
L.32473	" Stafford H.	L.29270	" Ledgard H.
L.29372	" Tidswell H.T.	L.23748	" Leckenby J.
114525	" Thomas O.	L.28077	" Martin L.
L.25683	" Thompson J.T.	930739	" Mathis M.C.
67704	" Tunstall A.	815569	" Mayers F.
L.25629	" Turner H.	L.28127	" Meller H.
L.25727	" Wintringham E.	152302	" Milner J.
L.29431	" Wood G.H.	L.29411	" Moody A.
L.25704	" Youngman A.	L.25870	" Murray R.
208386	" Rix H.	L.213085	" Newns A.
221070	" Rodgers SR.	L.25675	" Nicholson J.
176283	" Ritchie J.	L.28194	" North M.
L.29381	Dvr. Barraclough L.H.	L.20609	" Ray D.
L.29258	" Barraclough T.E.	L.28071	" Robinson F.
L.28213	" Beaumont H.	5116	" Roberts G.
L.28199	" Berry A.	L.25861	" Robinson T.
L.25837	" Berry S.	L.25512	" Robinson W.J.
L.32576	" Bentley T.	L.25730	" Rushworth E.
L.32566	" Braithwaite J.T.	L.25625	" Scott J.J.
L.32528	" Berrisow F.	L.28041	" Schofield A.
L.25470	" Brook J.W.	203373	" Sharples J.E.
185733	" Chesters D.	L.32579	" Sheppard N.
L.25878	" Clear A.	L.25644	" Singleton L.M.
L.28113	" Crossley J.	L.25454	" Snell A.
L.32518	" Crowther J.	180180	" Teeth V.S.
L.25446	" Davies J.W.	L.29397	" Southwell J.
112102	" Dennis S.	L.28090	" Stanton A.
L.25442	" Eastwood G.	L.25569	" Turner J.
L.25732	" Firth H.	2088	" Turner J.
L.32538	" Gray D.	L.25866	" Townsend H.
L.29367	" Greenwood J.W.	L.25598	" Townsend W.
L.25728	" Greenwood C.	L.25499	" Tallis G.
L.25831	" Hall H.	L.32515	" Wilkinson L.
L.28204	" Harrison F.	L.29257	" Wilkinson F.
L.25479	" Hattersley F.	185398	" Willatt W.
L.32524	" Hawthornethwaite T.	164826	" Williams E.
L.25822	" Hinchcliffe A.	L.29269	" Wood G.H.
L.23558	" Hobson A.	141214	" Worth W.D.
L.32506	" Holmes W.	L.28089	" Wright F.
L.29463	" Horrocks H.	Attached:-	
L.32447	" Jackson P.	8949 AVC.Sgt. White F.A.	

"B" BATTERY : 168 Bde.R.F.A.

Nominal Roll of all ranks posted during July 1917

L.32523   a/Bdr.   Philipson H.
125275   "   Leach A.
218427   Gnr.   Irvine R.
93752   "   Farmer F.
17044   Dvr.   McCormack A.
219144   "   Markham C.
219070   "   Kirk H.
217555   "   Mackie J.
L.25624   "   Senior G.

Nominal Roll of all ranks evacuated during July 1917.

         2/Lieut.W.L.Chamberlain
         1985 Sgt.Harding R.
L.25390   "   Tayler H.
L.25484   "   Willans C.
L.29350 Cpl.Thornton J.
L.25863   "   Holmes L.
L.28218 Bdr.Dyson A.
L.32496 Gnr.Burton G.
L.29392   "   Eccles J.
152732   "   Mason J.
L.25463   "   Scott N.
L.28127 Dvr Moller H.
L.25512   "   Robinson W.J.

"C" BATTERY   -:o:-   168th.Bde.R.F.A.

Nominal Roll of all ranks as at 1-8-17.

Officers:-
          Major H. COTTEE.D.S.O.
          Capt. B.T.GROVES.
          2/Lt. G.O.J.BARRICK.
          2/Lt. C.A.ANELAY.
          2/Lt. S.J.HINTON.
          2/Lt. H.R.M.RONALDSON.
          2/Lt. C.A.BROWNE.

Other ranks:-

53473	BSM Malone M.J.	L.28200	Gnr.Brook J.
L. 5688	QMS.Tomlinson S.	L.11981	" Cockell G.
L.19483	Sgt.Booth J.P.	L.28:47	" Chapman T.
L.12004	" Turgoose W.	147114	" Creeper H.
35406	" Sykes H.M.	196150	" Cooke F.
L.25711	" Kirkham T.	60219	" Davison J.
22239	" Fitzgerald W.	L.25702	" Dean F.
L.29412	" Brown T.,M.M.	L.25411	" Ellis E.
L.11973	Cpl.Booth J.	L.12017	" Farmery J.W.
L.11923	" Imms E.	78830	" Fraser J.
L.19404	" Marshall H.	L.12019	" Froggett E.
L.12050	" Sanderson G.	78656	" Fenny F.
L.19481	" Ward J.S.	37084	" Gale S.E.
L.28195	" Garside I.	163921	" Gerrett G.W.
L.28121	" Palmer R.	197894	" Grummitt A.
L.27727	" Ward A.	D.11975	" Haworth H.
L.19479	Bdr.Wardle J.M.	L.11992	" Halton R.
L.19478	" Todd J.S.	L.11989	" Haworth R.
L.12016	" McGuire T.F.J	88771	" Hall N.
L.19484	" Bailey B.C.	L.19490	" Horner C.
19830	" Goldsborough L.	34446	" Hutt R.
L.11993	" Holdroyd T.	80444	" Holden F.
115077	" Carruthers T.	L.25751	" Higgins H.
L.25812	" Terry L.	110744	" Huggett E.
L.25473	" Earnshaw S.	3933	" Hesford A.
L.29414	" Elliott C.H.	143669	" Heron R.
L.27730	" Walton H.	167010	" Hankinson J.
L.11959a	/Br.Ellis W.R.	37518	" Heath W.A.
L.19519	" Milnthorpe G.	7334	" Hart J.
L.19487	" Uarr W.C.	L.12020	" Inman H.
L.11962	" Wilcock G.	120111	" Jowett W.
L.27987	" Broadhead F.	L.19809	" James T.
L.28010	" Steele J.W.	L.19514	" Lynes J.
L.25775	" Lee H.	2285	" Jewis E.W.
L.12035	" Wathey A.	L.12047	" Martin T.
935644	S/a/Br.Seymour W.	L.11932	" Mulheir J.W.
48296	Farr.Sgt.Key J.	L.12002	" Nowell E.M.
L.11991	Cpl.S/S.Halton G.	172668	" Nesbit R.
L.11926	S/S.Fletcher F.	L.11971	" Parkin W.
L.27751	" Bailey H.	188719	" Poynts A.
L.25954	" Chappell E.	14369	" Robinson A.M.
L.11934	" Ismay T.H.	219279	" Stockton F.
107905	" Copping H.E.	184085	" Sheppard W.
63915	" Irving W.A.	190804	" Shaw N.
L.29360	Cpl.Fhtr.Hinchcliffe J.	185837	" Spink J.
L.11937	Cpl.Whlr.Prince E.	L.19496	" Saburton H.
147564	Sdlr.Hall J. L.11937.	L.27999	" Spittle T.
L.11994	Gnr.Balls J.W.	13907	" Swinn J.
147564	" Balls H.W.	1268	" Sellar G.
L.12026	" Beach J.	67727	" Smith J.
L.11979	" Brady B.	L.12965	" Smith W.A
L.19485	" Briggs E.J.		

50143	Gnr.	Smith T.	L.29285	Dvr. Lord J.
935803	"	Smith W.A.	85728	" Maddocks J.
32267	"	Smith A.	L.14919	" Marshall S.
37207	"	Smith P.W.	L.18909	" Mitchell W.
201541	"	Seedhouse S.	85571	" O'Keaffe J.A.
685715	"	Skelland R.	6074	" Overland J.A.
123842	"	Sutton E.T.	75545	" Pipe E.
207858	"	Stevenson S.	L.27691	" Poynton G.W.
33802	"	Thompson B.	L.11951	" Priestley B.
L.25715	"	Tayler J.T.	2869	" Price W.
L.19717	"	Wardle G.H.	L.28031	" Parkin H.
L.19502	"	Wales W.	L.25850	" Pogson H.
L.12003	"	Waldren T.	L.12011	" Roberts E.W.
L.12022	Dvr.	Ainsworth H.	L.11965	" Rose C.A.
200790	"	Bell J.T.	12665	" Schilling R.M.
L.11919	"	Backhouse G.H.	117610	" Scott H.
821420	"	Beale W.A.	132504	" Studley F.
L.11942	"	Boulton P.	L.19487	" Schofield W.
221666	"	Brown J.T.	L.12033	" Senior B.K.
L.11980	"	Burnley W.S.	120413	" Shipman H.
15520	"	Berry A.	L.29293	" Sutcliffe W.
L.11982	"	Clarke E.W.	L.28164	" Spivey P.
L.28232	"	Chapman J.	L.28149	" Scott J.R.
18327	"	Cleaver S.R.	L.25448	" Singleton N.
L.29291	"	Drake G.	D.27993	" Senior J.W.
4344	"	Davis J.	86618	" Stride W.
L.28107	"	Ellis H.	83564	" Speak J.W.
L.11969	"	Eubank J.A.	L.27727	" Toothill A.C.
L.25474	"	Earnshaw E.	L.32459	" Turner H.
L.12055	"	Farmery T.	L.27906	" Tayler H.
L.19506	"	Fretwell H.	L.28095	" Turner A.B.
22242	"	Fitch E.J.	L.12008	" Wales A.
L.12037	"	Garfitt J.T.	L.12021	" Walshaw E.
L.15520	"	Garfoot E.	L.12006	" Wrigglesworth F.
L.11964	"	Hunter J.	L.28169	" Williams J.
L.11941	"	Hart W.	L.28124	" Walton R.
L.11967	"	Hancock N.	L.29322	" White L.
L.19510	"	Horsfall E.	51913	" Watsham E.
L.19509	"	Hudson J.	143487	" Wilson W.
L.12041	"	Kershaw H.	2410	" Wheeler W.
L.11929	"	Kemp R.	1344	" Young T.
L.19492	"	Lapish J.		
L.19513	"	Lamb M.		
L.28051	"	Lawton H.		

Attached.
AVC.Sgt.Harding T.

"C" BATTERY : 168th.Bde.R.F.A.

Nominal Roll of all ranks posted during July 1917.

```
115097  a/Br.Muste W.
L.32657 Gnr. Herder W.
205331   "   Imeson C.E.
L.25702  "   Denton F.
163727   "   Goddard W.E.
L.11978 Dvr. Williams H.
218502   "   Leeves G.J.
```

Nominal Roll of all ranks evacuated during July 1917.

```
L.19483 Sgt.Booth P.P.
 35406   "  Sykes H.M.
 15077 Bdr.Carruthers T.
L.11991 Cpl.S/S Halton G.
L.11981 Gnr.Cockell G.
 60219   "  Davison J.
L.11992  "  Halton R.
  7334   "  Hart J.H.
172668   "  Nesbitt R.
L.25474 Dvr.Earnshaw E.
 83364   "  Speak J.W.
```

"D" BATTERY   -:o:-   168th.Bde.R.F.A.

Nominal Roll of all ranks as at July 1st. 1917.

Officers.   Major D.K.Tweeddle D.S.O.
                 Capt. J.C.Peele M.C.
                 Lieut. R.Dunbar.
                 Lieut. J.C.Weed.
                 2/Lt. A.A.Steward.
                 2/Lt. E.P.Peel.
                 2/Lt. J.J.Caterer.
                 2/Lt. E.W.Briscoe.

Other ranks:-

13705	BSM Perigo W.	889530	Gnr.Cook B.
3922	QMS.Le Page	35893	" Clarke J.S.
100360	Sgt.Far.Greenwood J.	L.25688	" Cain J.E.
11948	" Allen J.	889531	" Cook C.M.
35409	" Dinsdale J.	19947	" Dalby E.
19965	" Hawkes T.G.H.	27596	" Dixon H.A.
50107	" Jeffrey S.A.	889543	" Dunnett J.
L.25606	" Palframan P.	27537	" Elsom G.H.
19914	" Weeffitt F.C.	951081	" Dredge E.F.
78312	Cpl.S/S.Emms A.	29175	" Fowler A.S.
26450	" Sdlr Derbyshire W.	179512	. Garnham A.E.
27756	" Benner S.	40484	" Goodman A.
42	Cpl.Whlr.Derbyshire.	27518	" Holmes J.
27580	Cpl.Briddock J.A.	104591	" Howard A.
35380	" Dobson J.E.	55188	" Heard H.
27577	" Hetherington J.	19848	" Hellewell G.W.
19840	" Hempsall J.	35413	" Hadley J.
889565	" Jackson A.A.	148362	" Keene F.C.
889591	" Philpot J.E.	197075	" Lancaster G.
27590	Bdr.Bradford J.	889584	" Podd C.R.
889508	" Browse S.A.	19796	" Parkinson C.H.
35395	" Hamilton T.H.	144699	" Spratt J.
889575	" Last S.	138484	" Sagar R.
19919	" Scholey E.	851331	" Stirratt R.F.
26400	" Smith W.	26125	" Simmons E.
27601	aBr.Gutteridge A.	103314	" Samuels R.
	Archer S.T.	4005	" Sugar F.J.
889522	" Barker W.	956164	" Slyfield W.J.
35390	" Beckett E.	27520	" Stacey R.
31981	" Bettany J.	156473	" Sherwin E.
20008	" Croft J.	97676	" Starkey E.
1986	" Hempsall T.	297097	" Smith P.
14511	" Make F.G.	196862	" Sykes J.W.
124923	" Richardson H.	970798	" Sandford G.
930380	" Stafford P.S.	889608	" Simmons W.
24083	" Tilson R.		" Sartins H.
889535	s/aBr.Gutteridge A.	20422	" Stones S.A.
27533	S/S Hellawell A.	889604	" Smith F.G.
27497	" Innocent J.	199489	" Tomlin J.W.
27759	" Popplewell J.	26463	" Townend A.W.
27652	" Smith J.	92601	" Talley I.
26447	" Varney J.	20010	" Thompson J.
78446	Sdlr.Batley J.	955804	" Tarrant A.E.
26676	" Schofield	38810	" Tinsley G.
146171	Ftr.Collar P.A.	190085	" Taylor A.
120840	Gnr.Allen C.	696070	" Thomas J.
19876	" Badger G.	35404	" Williams J.
50035	" Ball G.C.	889632	" Woodward F.
26385	" Beler H.E.	889624	" Wain F.
27589	" Blood J.A.		
201448	" Beard A.		
889514	" Barker J.A.		
35665	" Burke C.		

19783	Dvr.	Armitage G.	35379	Dvr. Middleton W.
35402	"	Bainbridge G.J.	5079	" Mclaghlin S.
27757	"	Battin W.	27598	" Pollard G.
26401	"	Bell A.	35414	" Padgett J.E.
26524	"	Bellamy F.	19789	" Peacock J.
12107	"	Bond P.	27222	" Phillips F.
805852	"	Bamforth P.	19939	" Porter E.
28059	"	Barker W.	889587	" Piper W.
200771	"	Birch D.	25691	" Rigg J.
20007	"	Bradley J.	889596	" Reid A.
217097	"	Bush H.	81641	" Penny H.
889511	"	Bell C.	889595	" Rayner L.
889521	"	Bunn A.	130962	" Smith J.
889509	"	Brightwell E.	40494	" Seabrooke J.H.
271255	"	Collins J.A.	26406	" Savage W.
889581	"	Cocker B.	27609	" Smith J.
889534	"	Chittock A.	29405	" Stewart A.
32438	"	Dutton J.W.	219001	" Souphan A.
889546	"	Durrant S.P.	26411	" Speight A.
13985	"	Donleavey W.	275505	" Shone W.
27621	"	Denby F.	806150	" Stokes H.
105225	"	Dowd T.	27600	" Sykes J.
27682	"	Dixon S.	826653	" Shortlands A.H.
889535	"	Driver R.	889601	" Sustins E.
2562	"	Evans S.	202441	" Turner A.
8982	"	Flock A.	19736	" Thompson A.D.
31333	"	Faulkner A.	202430	" Townend A.
35381	"	Guest W.	122325	" Tyler H.
19943	"	Green J.	71271	" Thompson G.G.
19803	"	Greenwood J.	171541	" Twist C.
889556	"	Garner J.E.	889616	" Theobald W.
889555	"	Gray S.V.	83586	" Toms R.
26422	"	Havehand H.	40493	" Tandy P.
19953	"	Howson W.	889612	" Taylor E.
19749	"	Hughes H.	864518	" Thompson G.
889563	"	Honeywood B.	12031	" Wilkinson J.W.
27610	"	Jewett W.	27498	" Wright D.
35411	"	Jackson F.	19794	" Whelan J.
35380	"	Lunn G.	25718	" Wilson J.
92590	"	Llewelyn T.	889631	" Whitehead J.
889570	"	Lay G.		

"D" Battery : 168th.Bde.R.F.A.

Nominal Roll of all ranks posted during July 1917.

```
 26452 Cpl.Bellamy J.W.
221608 a/Br.Percy K.
 21259 Gnr.McLellan J.
106866  "  Scatchard G.
207185  "  Snell W.S.
209455  "  Snewing J.W.
208236 Dvr.Keates C.
696667  "  Lewis G.J.
 18380  "  Lumm W.
 78643  "  Marshall R.E.
 88935  "  Kearnan J.P.
 27624  "  Roebuck V.
```

Nominal Roll of all ranks evacuated during July 1917.

```
        Major D.K.Tweedie D.S.O.
        2/Lieut. J.J. Caterer.
        2/Lieut. E.W.Briscoe.

  3922 BQMS LePage
 25606 Sgt.Palframan F.
889508 Bdr.Browse S.A.
 31981 aBr.Bettany E.
 93320  "  Stafford P.O.
889534 Gnr.Cook B.
 19947  "  Dalby E.
931081  "  Dredge G.F.
 27518  "  Holmes J.
 35413  "  Hadley J.
 20422  "  Stones S.A.
271255 Dvr.Collins J.R.
889548  "  Durrant S.P.
 27598  "  Pollard G.
826653  "  Shetlands A.H.
```

CONFIDENTIAL.

WAR DIARY

of the

168th. BRIGADE R.F.A.

from 1-8-17 to 31-8-1917.

Volume XVIII.

Army Form C. 2118.

WAR DIARY
or
INTELLIGENCE SUMMARY.
(Erase heading not required.)

Instructions regarding War Diaries and Intelligence Summaries are contained in F. S. Regs., Part II. and the Staff Manual respectively. Title pages will be prepared in manuscript.

Place: Ref. LOMBARTZYDE SHEET Scale 1/20000

168th Brigade R.F.A.
Commanded by Lt-Colonel R. FITZMAURICE D.S.O.

Date	Hour	Summary of Events and Information	Remarks and references to Appendices
1/8/17.	3.a.m.	In connection with a Raid on our left, our batteries fired on Enemy Front and support Trenches S.W. of LOMBARTZYDE.	A.
		Very wet day, front quiet.	
2/8/17.	9.a.m.	Daylight Raid carried out on our left, our Batteries assisted by Barraging Enemy Front and support Trenches S.W. of LOMBARTZYDE.	A.
3/8/17.		Rained all day. Batteries in action in the Low Lying Country, flooded out.	A.
4/8/17.	8.p.m.	B/168 and D/168 batteries heavily shelled with 5.9" How, over 200 rounds being fired on them. No damage done. Fourth occasion on which a destructive shoot has been attempted on B/168 in its present position.	A.
5/8/17.		Thick ground mist all day. Enemy artillery inactive.	A.
6/8/17.	3.30.pm	Practice Barrage under direction of Group Commander, Lt - Col. R. FITZMAURICE D.S.O carried out by batteries of Group "A" on front line trenches S.E. of LOMBARTZYDE.	A.
7/8/17.		The usual shooting on enemy trenches carried out. Enemy very quiet.	A.
8/8/17.	1.a.m.	In conjunction with a Raid on enemy trenches in N.22.b. "A" Group carried out a feint bombardment in N.24.b. (see Appendix A.) 5 prisoners and 1 Machine gun were captured in the Raid.	A.
9/8/17.	1.3.a.m.	Gas Bombardment carried out on enemy trenches (see Appendix B. Weather continued to be very showery.	A.

Army Form C. 2118.

WAR DIARY
or
INTELLIGENCE SUMMARY.
(Erase heading not required.)

16th Brigade R.F.A.
Commanded by Lt - Colonel R. FITZMAURICE D.S.O.

Place	Date	Hour	Summary of Events and Information	Remarks and references to Appendices
	10/8/17.		Wet day Front quiet.	OL
	11/8/17.		Brigade Headquarters shelled during the night with high velocity gun.	OL
	12/8/17.		Brigade Headquarters shelled during the night with gas shell.	OL
	13/8/17.		A/168.R.F.A. Wagon Lines CONYEW, shelled - 14 horses killed and 15 wounded.	OL
	14/8/17.		Batteries withdrawn from action to the Wagon Lines for a rest.	OL
	15/8/17.		Brigade Headquarters moved to ST IDENBAIGH.	OL
	16/8/17.		Batteries remained in rest.	OL
	17/8/17. to 23/8/17.			OL
	24/8/17.		2/Lieut S.J HINTON. C/168 R.F.A. awarded the Military Cross.	OL
	25/8/17.		Batteries return into action as per Appendix C	OL
	26/8/17.		Brigade Headquarters moved to MAISON CARREE S.3.c.7.3. and took over the defence of the front held by the 98th Infantry Brigade at 6.p.m. in the absence of Lt - Colonel FITZMAURICE.D.S.O. who was acting O.R.A. Major F. FITZGIBBON. D.S.O. Commanded the Group.	OL
	27/8/17.1.a.m		Gas Bombardment of Enemy's trenches South of LOMBARTZYDE. See Appendix D 8th Australian Battery withdrawn from action.	OL

Army Form C. 2118.

WAR DIARY
or
INTELLIGENCE SUMMARY.
(Erase heading not required.)

168th Brigade R.F.A.
Commanded by Lt-Col. R. FITZMAURICE D.S.O.

Place	Date	Hour	Summary of Events and Information	Remarks and references to Appendices
	28/8/17.		Batteries carried out Day and Night firing on enemy's communications. Day very wet and stormy.	OK
	29/8/17.		98th Infantry Brigade relieved by 97th Infantry Brigade. 7th and 9th Australian Batteries withdrew from action.	OK
	30/8/17.		Very wet and stormy, the front exceedingly quiet. Batteries carried out Day and Night firing on enemy approaches.	OK
	31/8/17.		Weather remained wet and stormy.	OK

Major.
Commanding 168th Brigade R. F. A.

Headquarters Staff. ---oOo--- 168th Brigade R. F. A.

NOMINAL ROLL OF ALL RANKS 31/8/17. [1/9/4]

Officers :-   Lt - Colonel.R.FITZMAURICE.D.S.O.
              Captain.ALAN LUMB.
              Lieut HAROLD FISHER.
              Lieut.HAROLD.L.JAMES
              Captain D.FERGUSON. (R.A.M.C.)

Other Ranks:-
         1362. R.S.M. McGowan.M.C.
    L.25839. Cpl. Lee G.
    L.29801.   "   Normanton A.
    L.25881. Bdr   Gibson.H.
      29811.   "   Anderton.A.
      12245. a/Bdr Wright J.
    L.29430.   "   Eyre F.
    L.28042.   "   Sugden.E.
    L.28206. Gnr   Akroyd.A.
    L.25910.   "   Bottomley.C.
      59688.   "   Clark.B.J.
    L.29404.   "   Greenwood.C.
     152003.   "   Firth H.
      56777.   "   Grindley W.
    L.25480.   "   Lucas E.
    L.29394.   "   Rangeley P.S.
    L.25399.   "   Ramsden.A.
    L.25626.   "   Slater H.
    L.28179.   "   Sykes.C.A.
    L.29296.   "   Windle A.T.
    L.27531.   "   Postlethwaite T
      13164.   "   Greenwood C.D.
    L.25422. Dvr   Armitage.J.
    L.32440.   "   Baker G.
    L.32540.   "   Blake F.
    L.28026.   "   Cowham S.
    L.5742.   "   Dickenson J.
    L.29287.   "   Fisher S.
     198817.   "   Foote G.
       1573.   "   Gutteridge W.
      35766.   "   Hirons E.
    L.5855.   "   Gowman W.
    L.32511.   "   Iredale A.
    L.25825.   "   Iredale E.
    L.28129.   "   Mellor A.
    L.28132.   "   Martin J.
      79511.   "   McIntyre A
    L.29351.   "   Newsome A.
    L.29424.   "   Parker J.
    L.29423.   "   Pollard W.
    L.25853.   "   Radley T.
    L.29357.   "   Reddington M.
    L.29389.   "   Stansfield P.
       6267. S/S   Periera A.T.
       1305. Sadd Williams T.
              Gnr   Smith.C.

         A.O.C. 625.Staff Sgt Barker H. (Artificer).

'A' Battery.   ---oOo---   168th Brigade R.F.A.

NOMINAL ROLL OF ALL RANKS. 31/8/17.

Officers.   Major. R. EMMET.
             Capt. G.O. d'IVRY.
             Lieut L.A. RAVALD.
             2/Lieut W.A. EBBELS.
             "   A.C. MILLER.
             "   J.W. WEEDON.
             "   J.G. BELL.

Other Ranks.:-

L.18467.	B.S.M.	Stephenson.C.	154173.	Sadd	Skipp J.W.
L.28064.	BQMS.	Brearley H.	72465.	Ftr	Bambrough R.
L.25426.	Sergt	Field P.J.	42821.	"	Norton.A.
L.25679.	"	Roberts L.F.	147472.	"	Hellewell A.
43312.	"	McGowan H.	121451.	Whlr	Weaver J.
L.25425.	"	Firth A.	L.25790.	Gnr	Allott C.V.
53261.	"	Smith E.F.	10574.	"	Alford C.
L.32581.	"	Williams W.H.	L.25575.	"	Billington.T.
L.25697.	Cpl.	Rhodes L.	L.28014.	"	Bray E.H.
L.25561.	"	Povey J.	L.28180.	"	Bolton.H.
L.25619.	"	France W.	100556.	"	Beamish R.
L.29407.	"	Taylor F.	100774.	"	Baird S.
L.29313.	"	Armitage W.B.	L.29379.	"	Beaumont L.
1985.	"	Harding R.C.	L.25768.	"	Brooksbank S.
1105.	"	Whitney T.	202446.	"	Birrell W.
L.32479.	Bdr	Bentley J.	92721.	"	Black.W.
L.28100.	"	Pitchforth A.	116349.	"	Buckley L.
L.25708.	"	Crawshall J.	222460.	"	Birks F.
L.25574.	"	Whiteley C.H.	L.32471.	"	Calvert F.
L.25514.	"	Wood B.	L.29345.	"	Craigie T.
L.25731.	"	Rhodes J.	132364.	"	Curd W.A.
L.28188.	"	Padjett S.	5556.	"	Chappell A.
L.25464.	"	Richardson.G.H.	190397.	"	Cross F.
83594.	"	Simpson C.	212321.	"	Crawford C.
L.28034.	"	Beevers M.	L.28176.	"	Dawson W.
86310.	"	Squires A.E.	L.12049.	"	Edwards L.
L.32539.	a/Bdr	Fenton.E.	130451.	"	Edwards W.H.
54101.	"	Perkins T.J.	86276.	"	Franklin A.
L.29297.	"	Noble E.	190415.	"	Foote G.
32523.	"	Phillipson.R.	152561.	"	Fearn.H.
L.28136.	"	Shaw N.	L.25472.	"	Green.N.
72096.	"	Smith L.	L.25823.	"	Hynes W.H.
L.28174.	"	Tetlow H.	226903.	"	Hancox H.P.
L.28217.	"	Bower E.	18757.	"	Hart C.
L.25513.	"	Pease A.	733.	"	Keighley F.J.
167074.	"	McGeachie J.	L.32512.	"	Lumb H.
169899.	s/a/Bdr	Halliday R.	L.25610.	"	Hopwood H.
L.25536.	"	Mansfield W.G.	184485.	"	Lewis E.J.
167423.	"	Sweet J.	L.28177.	"	Leatham F.
L.32449.	Far Sgt	Andrews R	197866.	"	McEwing H.
L.25783.	Cpl s/s	Town E.	159371.	"	McCarthy E.
765.	" "	Parks J.	197863.	"	McPherson.A.
L.29282.	S/S	Nuttall G.T.	168568.	"	Miller W.
L.28175.	"	Waterhouse L.	150416.	"	Mallett H.
L.25690.	"	Kaye J.	L.28129.	"	Marshall L.
173878.	"	Ackeroyd C.	L.25392.	"	Milnes H.
L.32485.	Sadd	Jackson W.R.	L.25443.	"	Nuttall P.
62728.	"	Olliver J.E.	44251.	"	Offen.F.

192477.	Gnr	Ormiston.A.	204732.	Dvr	Malbain.H.
L.25736.	"	Pearson.H.	101698.	"	O'Neil J.
L.29306.	"	Pearson.F.	147602.	"	Orriss H.
L.28126.	"	Perkins J.C.	L.32464.	:	Pogson,S.
L.25653.	"	Rushworth.A.	L.28136.	"	Priest.G.W.
211705.	"	Robinson.H.	35864.	"	Quinn.D.
199083.	"	Raskilly P.	L.28074.	"	Robertshaw S.
W.2815	"	Rice.E.F.	L.28075.	"	Roe.F.
224342.	"	Rockett B.	L.28013.	"	Sykes.W.
66262.	"	Rhodes A.E.	960541.	"	Salmon.S.J.
L.32491.	"	Roberts J.	99859.	"	Spencer.P.S.
L.25566.	"	Shaw J.E.	L.25633.	"	Shaw.E.
148166.	"	Smith.A.	L.25503.	"	Shaw.H.
L.28006.	"	Singleton.H.V.	L.28224.	"	Shaw.C.A.
L.26074.	"	Spencer R.	L.25797.	"	Singleton.V.
81446.	"	Slack.H.	L.25450.	"	Smith.J.R.
L.25735.	"	Spencer H.	166514.	"	Smith.W.J.
221089.	"	Soloman L.	217881.	"	Shotton.R.
821657.	"	Swadling A.	219990.	"	Tall.F.
16577.	"	Stevenson,G.W.	741490.	"	Tanner.A.
22365.	"	Speed.A.	L.28101.	"	Taylor.T.H.
150668.	"	Schaefer.A.E.	L.25460.	"	Twigg.J.
38812.	"	Symonds H.	L.25483.	"	Varley.L.
156164.	"	Sargent C.	L.25650.	"	Wood.A.
L.25771	"	Thornton J.	10586.	"	Westgate.F.
30526.	"	Thorpe W.J.	L.29331.	"	Woodcock.W.
L.29355.	"	Townend J.	L.28087.	"	Walters.H.
L.32535.	"	Thonner W.H.	L.25394.	"	Wortley,T
L.25844.	"	Weldrake E.	L.25541.	"	Woodhead.E.
L.28088.	"	Wilkinson T.	L.25819.	"	Whitehead.J.A.
L.29300.	"	Wood F.	159419.	"	Weedon.W.
L.32441.	"	Walker A.	21116.	"	Wainwright.W.
L.29318.	"	Wood.R.	L.28214.	"	Wood.W.
L.25649.	"	Wood.C.E.			
L.25485.	"	Williams G.			
133713.	"	Young W.	Attached.		
234892.	"	Wooff F.L.	S.L.1514.Sgt Jolly.A.J.		
19805.	"	Yates W.			

107780.	Dvr	Archer W.
175251.	"	Bamforth H.
L.25525.	"	Bray H.
L.25436.	"	Brearley A.
L.25483.	"	Brook.G.L.
L.25658.	"	Chapman.B.
L.29323.	"	Cartwright.P.
L.25592.	"	Crowther.J.
109981.	"	Chapman.H.
41489.	"	Crisp E.
L.29409.	"	Dyson.W.
L.28079.	"	Green.F.
L.25820.	"	Ganley.J.
L.29316.	"	Gledhill.J.R.
L.25579.	"	Griffiths.T.C.
L.28201.	"	Horsfall E.
L.25849.	"	Holmes.E.
L.28153.	"	Harrison.F.
L.29347.	"	Hardcastle.C.W.
93514.	"	Hartley.A.
L.32541.	"	Kershaw.C.
L.25419.	"	Kerton.E.
L.28163.	"	Lodge.A.
L.25384.	"	Livesey.F.C.
12171.	"	Lewis.
L.28021.	"	Mallinson.J.A.
L.25639.	"	Millard.H.
826369.	"	Morse L.
L.35046.	"	Marshall.A.

'B' Battery. —oOo— 168th Brigade R.F.A.

NOMINAL ROLL OF ALL RANKS. 31/8/17.

Officers:- Major FITZGIBBON.F. D.S.O.
Capt. HASTINGS.L.M. M.C.
Lieut ROBINSON.W.P.
2/Lieut CHAMBERLAIN.W.L.
" MITCHELHILL.J.
" BASNETT.C.P.
" MARRIOTT.A.E.

Other Ranks:-

58482.	B.S.M.	Stenning.T.	L.25382.	Gnr Ainley W	
L.32437.	BQMS.	Lane.A.C.	L.32449.	Gnr Berry A.	
L.32514.	Far Sgt	Sutcliffe R.	L.25616.	"	Billington.H.
L.25420.	Sergt	Deakin T.	L.32483.	"	Binns A.O
L.25448.	"	Beaumont.F.	L.32521.	"	Bottoms.H.
L.29344.	"	Gutherie A.	L.29265.	"	Broadley J.T.
L.25599.	"	Crooks H.	L.25873.	"	Broadbent F.
L.25716.	"	Fisher W.W.	8786.	"	Broome H,
L.28210.	"	Greenwood M.R.	18820.	"	Brown F.
L.25871.	Corpl.	Walker S.	8993.	"	Blake A.
L.25693.	"	Littlewood K.	87766.	"	Brown.G.
L.29826.	"	Temperton.H.K.	211667.	"	Bone.E.W.
L.25864.	"	Mason.R.	211574.	"	Cartwright H.W.
L.25863.	"	Holmes.L.	205152.	"	Cook.W.
L.28076.	"	Murray A.	182839.	"	Cousins A.T.
98737.	s/s Cpl.	Brennan J.	L.29313.	"	Crosland .E.
L.28218.	Corpl	Dyson,A.	211662.	"	Cheeseman P.G.
L.25446.	Bdr	Bottomley T.	120237.	"	Charman H.
L.25451.	"	Spendlove.T.	L 25671.	"	Cocker F.
L.28138.	"	Bramley S.	2295.	"	Coward.T.
L.25545.	"	Turner J.	L.29383.	"	Dewar W
L.24990.	"	Mayers A.	68234.	"	Doggett J.
L.32480.	"	Bancroft L.	3052.	"	Earl.W.
L.25491.	"	Sherwood J.	L.29263.	"	Fowler B.
125511.	"	Cristie.H.	56821.	"	Gallaher M.
L.5961.	"	Hurst W.	L.29244.	"	Greenwood A.A.
152524.	"	Wright A.	93752.	"	Farmer H.
L.28043.	"	Burch H.	198809.	"	Gigg B.
L.25808.	a/Bdr	Broomhead W.H.	L.29262.	"	Greenwood L.A.
16381.	"	Cawthorne J.	L.29380.	"	Hanson.E.
L.25547.	"	IBBotson.M.	L.32454.	"	Hargreaves D.
152735.	"	Holmes N.	L.25664.	"	Hartley A.
L.25742.	"	Dyson,F.	5329.	"	Horan.J.S.
11578.	"	Gouldsmith S.	111819.	"	Harris G.
L.25746.	"	Hargreaves A.	L.28046.	"	Holdsworth.A.
L.25463.	"	Scott.N.	218427.	"	Irvine,L,
79093.	"	Drewitt W.C.	L.25458.	"	Kiddle F.
115275.	"	Leach A.	L.32510.	"	Knight S.
5035.	S/S	Boswell H.	L.28220.	"	Laycock.A.
L.25510.	"	Readyhough G.W.	L.25562.	"	Lawford.F.
L.25452.	"	Sidebottom.J.	L.25623.	"	Lee F.
L.25552.	"	Hoyle C.	160940.	"	Leng J.
L.32552.	"	Wilson,J.	L.25622.	"	Littlewood H.
L.25747.	Sadd	Brooksbank G.	197864.	"	Mc Pherson.D.
L.25607.	"	Stansfield F.	197862.	"	Mc Lennan J.B.
L.25596.	Whlr	Yates F.	197865.	"	Mc Rae D.
L.32456.	Ftr	Hill W.	150377.	"	Miller C.W.
			L.28126.	"	Mallinson.F.

164025.	Gnr	Miller F.	L.28066.	Dvr Medley.O.
L.29400.	"	Mitchell D	152302.	" Milner J.
L.32544.	"	Mitchell R.	47044.	" Mc Cormick A.
L.29402.	"	Murray E.	L.29401.	" Moody A.
197395.	"	Mullard G.H.	121959.	" Morley A.T.
188576.	"	Nash.T.J.	L.25870.	" Murray R.
156134.	"	Nightingale D.	213085.	" Newns A.
L.25632.	"	Onyon.A.	L.25675.	" Nicholson.J.
L.25836.	"	Owen.W.	L.28194.	" North.M.
2358.	"	Platt H.	73229.	" Parnaby W.
L.25827.	"	Riddlesden.A.	20609.	" Ray D.
46249.	"	Scott.F.J.	L.28071.	" Robinson.F.
159803.	"	Shaw J.A.	5116.	" Roberts G.
5824.	"	Spence C.	L.25861.	" Robinson.T.
165748.	"	Stannage J.W.	L.25512.	" Robinson.W.J.
L.32473.	"	Stafford.H.	L.25730.	" Rushworth.E.
L.29372.	"	Tidswell H.F.	L.25625.	" Scott J.J.
114525.	"	Thomas O.	L.28041.,	" Scholefield.A
L.25683.	"	Thompson.J.T.	L.25624.	" Senior.G.
67704.	"	Tunstall A.	203373.	" Sharples.J.F.
L.25629.	"	Turner H.	L.32579.	" Sheppherd N.
150477.	"	Wolfe C.H.	L.25644.	" Singleton.L.M.
208386.	"	Rix H.	L.25454.	" Snell.A.
221070.	"	Rogers S.R.	180180.	" Tooth.V.S.
176283.	"	Ritchie G.	L.29397.	" Southwell.J.
L.29431.	"	Youngman.A.	L.28090.	" Stanton.A.
			L.25569.	" Turner J.
			2088.	" Turner J.
			L.25866.	" Townsend H.
L.29381.	Dvr	Barraclough H.	L.25598.	" Townsend W.
L.29258.	"	Barraclough T.E.	L.25499.	" Tallis.G.
L.28213.	"	Beaumont. H.	L.32515.	" Wilkinson.L.
L.28199.	"	Berry A.	L.29257.	" Willat.W.
L.25837.	"	Berry S.	164829.	" Williams,E
L.32576.	"	Bentley T.	L.29431.	" Wood.G.H.
L.32538.	"	Barrisow.F.	L.29269.	" Wood.H.
L.32566.	"	Braithwaite J.F.	141214.	" Worth.W.D.
L.25470.	"	Brook.J.W.	L.28089.	" Wright.F.
185735.	"	Chesters D.		
L.25878.	"	Clear A.		
L.28113.	"	Crossley J.	8949.	Sergt.White.F.A. (A.V.C.) attd
L.32518.	"	Crowther J.		
L.25446.	"	Davies J.		
112102.	"	Dennis S.		
L.25442.	"	Eastwood.G.		
L.25732.	"	Firth.H.		
L.32538.	"	Gray D.		
L.29367.	"	Greenwood.J.W.		
L.25728.	"	Greenwood.C.		
L.25831.	"	Hall.H.		
L.28204.	"	Harrison.F.		
L.25479.	"	Hattersley F.		
L.32524.	"	Hawthornthwaite.T.W.		
L.25822.	"	Hincliffe A.		
L.25558.	"	Hobson.A.		
L.32506.	"	Holmes.W.		
L.29403.	"	Horrocks.H.		
L.32447.	"	Jackson.P		
L.28070.	"	Jowett.J.H.		
L.29270.	"	Ledgard.E.		
L.23746.	"	Leckenby J.		
79005.	"	Lynch P.		
217555.	"	Mackie J.		
L.28077.	"	Martin.L.		
219114..	"	Markham C.		
930739.	"	Matthis M.C.		
815569.	"	Mayers.F.		

'C' Battery.　　—oOo—　　168th Brigade R.F.A.

NOMINAL ROLL OF ALL RANKS – 1/8/17.

Officers:- Major COTTEE.H.D.S.O.
　　　　　　Capt　GROVES B.J.
　　　　　　2/Lieut BARRICK.G.J.
　　　　　　　"　　ANELAY.C.A.
　　　　　　　"　　HINTON.S.J.
　　　　　　　"　　RONALDSON.H.R.M.
　　　　　　　"　　BROWN.C.A.

Other Ranks:-

53473.	B.S.M.	Malone.M.J.	45372.	Gnr Anderson.F.C.
L.5686.	BQMS	Tomlinson.S.	170432.	" Arnold J.T.
L.12004.	Sergt.	Turgoose W.	L.11973.	" Booth J.
L.25711.	"	Kirkham.T.	147564.	" Balls.H.W.
L.29412.	"	Brown.T.	L.11994.	" Barr J.
L.12050.	"	Sanderson.G.	L.19485.	" Briggs.E.J.
22339.	"	Fitzgerald.W.	L.11979.	" Brady B.
L.28195.	"	Garside.I.	L.12026.	" Beach J.
L.19481.	Cpl.	Ward.A.S.	129105.	" Bolster W.G.
L.28121.	"	Palmer.R.	43449.	" Burbridge W.S.
L.27727.	"	Ward.A.	6521.	" Braid J.K.
L.19484.	"	Bailey B.C.	45377.	" Baker J.
L.11993.	"	Holdroyd.T.	L.28167.	" Chapman.T.
L.25473.	"	Earnshaw.S.	147114.	" Cruper H.
L.19479.	Bdr	Wardle L.M.	196180.	" Cooke F.
L.19478.	"	Todd.J.A.	830528.	" Carter G.H.
L.12016.	"	Maguire T.F.J.	L.25762.	" Denton.F.
L.27730.	"	Walton.H.	L.25411.	" Ellis W.
L.19830.	"	Goldsborough.L.	L.12019.	" Farmery J.W.
L.25812.	"	Terry L.	28830.	" Fraser J.
L.29414.	"	Elliott B.H.	L.12019.	" Froggett E.
L.19510.	"	Milnthorpe G.	37084.	" Gale S.E.
L.19487.	"	Carr W.C.	191894.	" Grummitt A.
L.11962.	"	Wilcox G.	163727.	" Goddard W.E.
L.27987.	"	Broadhead F.	163921.	" Gerritt J.W.
L.11959.	a/Bdr	Ellis.W.R.	88771.	" Hall N.
L.28010.	"	Steele J.W.	L.19490.	" Horner C.
L.12035.	"	Wathy A.	L.11975.	" Haworth H.
935644.	"	Seymour W.	L.11989.	" Haworth R.
L.28200.	"	Brook.J.	14446.	" Hutt R.
L.2265.	"	Lewis E.W.	89444.	" Holden F.
50143.	"	Smith.T.	L.25751.	" Higgins.H.
115097.	"	Musto W.	10744.	" Huggett A.H.
L.25775.	"	Lee H.	167010.	" Hankinson J.
94317.	"	Dean E.	37518.	" Heath W.H.
138424.	"	Kirkham T.	2933.	" Hesford A.
48296.	Far Sgt	Key J.	32657.	" Horder W.
L.11926.	S/S	Fletcher F.	205331.	" Imeson.J.E.
L.27751.	"	Bailey H.	L.12020.	" Inman H.
L.25954.	"	Chappel E.	L.12111.	" Jolley W.
L.11934.	"	Ismay T.H.	L.19809.	" James T.
107905.	"	Copping.H.	L.19514.	" Lynes.J.
63915.	"	Irving W.A.	L.11932.	" Mulheir J.W.
L.12041.	"	Kershaw H.	L.12002.	" Mowell S.M.
L.29360.	Cpl Ftr	Hincliffe J.	L.12047.	" Martin.J.
L.11991.	Cpl S/S	Halton.G.	L.11971.	" Parkin.W.
L.14862.	Whlr	Pringle E.	188719.	" Poynts A.
L.11937.	Sadd	Hall J.	134691.	" Robinson.A.E.
143669.	–	Heron.R.	L.19496.	" Saberton.H.

219279.	Gnr	Stockton.P.		L.28031.	Dvr	Parkin.H.
184085.	"	Shepphard.W.		L.25850.	"	Pogson.H.
19804.	"	Shaw N.		40357.	"	Powell B.A.
L.27999.	"	Spittle T.		41796.	"	Peckham L.
13907.	"	Swinn J.		L.12011.	"	Roberts E.W.
1228.	"	Sellars G.		L.11965.	"	Ross C.A.
67727.	"	Smith J.F.		L.19467.	"	Schofield W.
185837.	"	Spink.J.		L.12033.	"	Senior E.K.
12965.	"	Smith W.E.		120413.	"	Shipman H.
935803.	"	Smith.W.A.		L.29293.	"	Sutcliffe W.
32267.	"	Smith A.		L.12033.	"	
37207.	"	Smith.P.W.		L.28164.	"	Spivey.p.
20154.	"	Seedhouse S.		L.28149.	"	Scott J.R.
685715	"	Skeland R.		L.25448.	"	Singleton N.
207858.	"	Stevenson.S.		L.27993.	"	Senior J.W.
33802.	"	Thompson.F.		186618.	"	Stride W.
123842.	"	Sutton.E.T.		132504.	"	Studley F.
L.25712.	"	Taylor J.T.		177610.	"	Scott.H.
L.19502.	"	Wales W.		826655.	"	Schilling R.M.
L.12003.	"	Waldron.T.		L.27906.	"	Taylor E.
L.19717.	"	Wardell G.H.		L.27747.	"	Toothill A.C.
219005.	"	Ward L.T		32459.	"	Turner H.
208477.	"	Woodman H.		L.28095.	"	Turner A.B.
229565.	"	Wall A.		L.12008.	"	Wales.A.
46846.	"	Young F.J.		L.12021.	"	Walshaw E.
L.12022.	Dvr	Ainsworth H.		L.12006.	"	Wrigglesworth F.
L.11919.	"	Backhouse G.H.		L.28169.	"	Williams J.
L.11942.	"	Boulton.P.		L.28142.	"	Walton.R.
L.11985.	"	Burnley W.S.		L.29322.	"	White.L.
15229.	"	Bury A.		51913.	"	Wareham.E.
221666.	"	Brown.G.T.		45487.	"	Wilson.W.
220790.	"	Bell J.T.		1340.	"	Wheeler W.
821420.	"	Beale W.A.		L.11978.	"	Williams.H.
L.11982.	"	Clarke.E.W.		L.1344.	"	Young.T.
L.28232.	"	Chapman.J.				
L.18327.	"	Cleaver E.		2489.	Sergt	Harding.W. (A.V.C)
L.29291.	"	Drake.G.				
L.28017.	"	Ellis H.				
4344.	"	Davis J.				
L.11969.	"	Ewbank J.A.				
L.12055.	"	Farmery T.				
L.19506.	"	Fretwell H.				
22242.	"	Fitch E.J.				
L.12037.	"	Garfitt J.T.				
L.19520.	"	Garfoot E.				
L.11964.	"	Hunter J.				
L.11941.	"	Hart W.				
L.11967.	"	Hancock.N.				
L.19513.	"	Horsfall E.				
L.19509.	"	Hudson.J.				
L.11929.	"	Kemp R.				
L.19492.	"	Lapish.J.				
L.19513.	"	Lamb.M.				
L.29285.	"	Lord.J.				
L.28152.	"	Leeves A.E.				
L.28051.	"	Lawton.H.				
85728.	"	Maddocks J.				
L.18907.	"	Mitchell W.				
L.14919.	"	Marshall S.				
77571.	"	O'keefe J.W.				
6074.	"	Overland H.				
75445.	"	Pipe E.				
L.27691.	"	Poynton.G.W.				
L.19516.	"	Priestly B.				
2869.	"	Price.W.				

NOMINAL ROLL OF ALL RANKS POSTED TO 'B' BATTERY.
DURING MONTH. AUGUST 1917.

211574.	Gnr	Cartwright H.W.	Posted from 32nd D.A.C.	9/8/17.
205152.	"	Cook W.	Ditto.	"
182839.	"	Cousins A.T.	"	"
8993.	"	Blake A.	"	"
211662.	"	Cheeseman P.G.	"	"
120237.	"	Charman.H.	"	"
97766.	"	Brown.G.	"	"
211657.	"	Bone E.W.	"	"
121959.	Dvr	Morley A.T.	"	15/8/17.
79905.	"	Lynch P.	"	"
13229.	"	Parnaby W.	"	"
115275.	Gnr	Grace H	"	1/8/17
93762.	Dvr	Gorman	"	"
218424.	Dvr	Irving	"	"
170245.	Dvr	McCormack A	219144 Dvr Barkley	"
214055.	"	Mackie	219070 " Kirk H	"

NOMINAL ROLL OF ALL RANKS EVACUATED DURING MONTH.

152524.	a/Bdr	Wright A.	Evacuated Sick.	8/8/17.
L.25728.	Dvr	Greenwood C.	Evacuated Wounded	25/8/17.

D Battery

NOMINAL ROLL OF ALL RANKS EVACUATED DURING MONTH

```
Lieut  Dunbar R.      Wounded in action.  4/8/17.
40058, Dvr Sugar F.J.                    15/8/17.
2562.   "  Evans S.   Evacuated Sick.       "
35379.  "  Middleton.W.    "       "     9/8/17.
```

'D' Battery.   ---oOo---   168th Brigade R.F.A.

NOMINAL ROLL OF ALL RANKS. 1/9/17.

Officers:-   Captain. JC.POOLE.M.C.
             Lieut R. DUNBAR.
             Lieut G.C.WOOD.
             2/Lieut E.P.PEEL.

Other Ranks.:-

13705.	B.S.M.	Perigo.W.	
100360.	Farr Sgt	Greenwood.J.	
11948.	Sergt	Allen.G	
27580.	"	Briddock.J.A.	
35409.	"	Dinsdale.J.	
19965.	"	Hawkes.F.G.H.	
27577.	"	Hetherington.J.	
950107.	"	Jeffrey S.A.	
19914.	"	Wooffitt F.E.	
L.25606.	"	Palframan.F.	
27601.	Cpl	Archer S.T.	
27756.	"	Bonner S.	
26452.	"	Bellamy J.W.	
35389	"	Dobson.J.E.	
889565.	"	Jackson.S.A.	
19919.	"	Scholey E.	
27590.	Bdr	Bradford.J.	
889522.	"	Barker.W.	
35390.	"	Beckett E.	
20008.	"	Croft J.	
35395.	"	Hamilton.T.H.	
1986.	"	Hempsall.T.	
889575.	"	Last S.	
14511.	"	Male F.G.	
35414.	"	Padjett J.E.	
26400.	"	Smith W.	
97676.	"	Starkey.E.	
35665.	a/Bdr	Burke C.	
25688.	"	Cain.J.E.	
27622.	"	Dixon.L.	
8982.	"	Flack.A.	
124923.	"	Richardson.H.	
27520.	"	Stacey.J.	
26411.	"	Speight .A.	
24083.	"	Tilston.R.	
221602.	"	Percy K.	
889535.	s/a/Bdr	Gutteridge.A.	
55188.	"	Heard.H.	
27533.	S/S	Helliwell.A.	
27497.	"	Innocent R.	
27759.	"	Popplewell G.	
27612.	"	Smith.J.	
26447.	"	Varney.J.	
78446.	Sadd	Batley.A.	
26676.	"	Schofield.J.	
146171.	Ftr	Collar P.A.	
78512.	Cpl S/S	Emms A.	
26450.	" Sadd	Clawson.J.J	
42.	" Whr	Derbyshire W.	
128068.	Gnr	Allen.C.	
2097.	"	Blythe W.	
19896.	"	Badger G.	
46330.	"	Brow.P.H.	
50035.	"	Ball G.H.	
889514.	Gnr	Barker J.A.	
192042.	Gnr	Bishop H.H.	
26385.	"	Boler H.E.	
27589.	"	Blood.J.	
201448.	"	Board.A.	
15049.	"	Cavanah J.	
185893.	"	Clarke.J.S.	
889531.	"	Cook.G.M.	
27596.	"	Dixon.H.A.	
889542.	"	Dunnett J.	
931081.	"	Dredge.G.F.	
27537.	"	Elsom.G.	
27175.	"	Fowler A.S.	
179512.	"	Garnham A.E.	
104581.	"	Howard.A.	
19848.	"	Hellewell G.W.	
148368.	"	Keene T.C.	
40484.	"	Goodman A.	
197075.	"	Lancaster J.	
21259.	"	Mc Lellan J.	
212536.	"	New H.	
840470.	"	Pitcher R.S.	
889584.	"	Podd C.R.	
86332.	"	Powell H.	
19796.	"	Parkonson.G.H.	
131526.	"	Philcox A.J.	
35052.	"	Powley F.A.	
1307.	"	Pitchley.C.	
212552.	"	Robins.A.S.	
20270.	"	Robinson.J.	
901599.	"	Richardson.C.H.	
209455.	"	Snewing J.W.	
144699.	"	Spratt.J.	
4005.	"	Sugar F.G.	
207185.	"	Snell.W.H.	
138484.	"	Sagar R.	
851331.	"	Stirrat R.F.	
26125.	"	Simmons E.G.	
103314.	"	Samuels R.	
956164.	"	Slyfield W.J.	
156473.	"	Sherwin L.	
297097.	"	Smith S.J.	
196862.	"	Sykes.J.W.	
889608.	"	Simmons W.	
	"	Sartin.H.	
889604.	"	Smith F.J.	
199489.	"	Tomlin T.W.	
26463.	"	Townsend A.V.	
92601.	"	Tully J.	
166866.	"	Scatchard J.	
20016.	"	Thompson.J.	
696070.	"	Thomas J.	
955604.	"	Turrant E.	
38810.	"	Tinsle G.	
190065.	"	Taylor E.	
35404.	"	Williams.J.	

889632.	Gnr	Woodward.E.
889624.	"	Wain.F.

19783.	Dvr	Armitage.G.
35402.	"	Bainbridge J.G.
27757.	"	Battin.W.
26401.	"	Bell.A.
26524.	"	Bellamy F.
12107.	"	Bond.P.
805852.	"	Barnforth.P.
20859.	"	Barker W.
200771.	"	Birch.G.
20007.	"	Bradley J.
217907.	"	Bush.H.H.
889511.	"	Bell E.
889521.	"	Bunn A.
889509.	"	Brightwell E.
889581.	"	Cocker B.
889534.	"	Chittock A.
32488.	"	Dutton.J.W.
889546.	"	Donleavy W.
105225.	"	Dowd T.
27621.	"	Denby F.
889535.	"	Driver R.
31333.	"	Faulkner A.
2562.	"	Evans.S.
35381.	"	Guest W.
19943.	"	Green J.
19803.	"	Greenwood J.
889556.	"	Garner J.E.
889555.	"	Gray S.V.
26422.	"	Havenhand H.
19953.	"	Howson.W.
19749.	"	Hughes H.
889563.	"	Honeywood B.
27610.	"	Jewitt W.
35411.	"	Jackson.F.
88935.	"	Kearson.J.
208238.	"	Keates C.
35380.	"	Lunn G.
18380.	"	Lund W.
92590.	"	Lewellyn T.
696267.	"	Lewis D.
889570.	"	Lay G.
78643.	"	Marshall R.E.
35379.	"	Middleton,W.
20085.	"	Luxford.R.T.
5079.	"	Mc Laughlin.S.
8328.	"	Lindley A.
19789.	"	Peacock J.E.
12939	"	Porter E.
27222.	"	Phillips.F.
889587.	"	Piper W.
27624.	"	~~Penny~~ Roebuck.V.
25691.	"	Rigg.J.
81641.	"	Penny H.
889596.	"	Read.A.
889595.	"	Rayner L.
130962.	"	Smith,J.
40494.	"	Seabrook J.H.
29405.	"	Stewart A.
26406.	"	Savage W.
219001.	"	Soupham.E.A.
27505.	"	Shone.W.
606150.	"	Stokes.H.
27609.	"	Smith.J.
27600.	"	Sykes.J.W.

889601.	Dvr	Sustins E.
202441.	"	Turner A.
19736.	"	Thomson.A.D.
202430.	"	Towsend A.
71271.	"	Thompson.J.G.H.
171541.	"	Twist G.
122325.	"	Tyler H.
889616.	"	Theobald W.
83586.	"	Toms R.
40493.	"	Tandy P.
889612.	"	Taylor E.
12031.	"	Wilkinson.J.W.
27498.	"	Wright .D.
19794.	"	Whelan.J.
846510.	"	Thompson.C.
889631.	"	Whitehead.J.
25718.	"	Wilson.J.

8038.	Sergt	Moore.W.	A.V.C.

NOMINAL ROLL OF ALL RANKS POSTED TO 'C' BATTERY DURING MONTH AUGUST 1917.

115097.	a/Bdr	Maste W.	Posted from 32nd.D.A.C.	1/8/17.
32657.	Gnr	Herder W.	Ditto	"
20533.	"	Imeson.T.E.	"	"
281052.	"	Leeves A.E.	"	"
L.3449.	"	Berbridge W.G.	"	9/8/17.
45372.	"	Anderson.F.	"	"
138424.	a/Bdr	Kirkham T.	"	"
208477.	Gnr	Woodman.H.	"	"
219005.	"	Ward.T.	"	"
830528.	"	Carter G.H.	"	"
45377.	"	Baker J.	"	"
229565.	"	Wall A.	"	"
6521.	"	Braid J.K.	"	"
46845.	"	Young F.J.	"	"
129105.	"	Belsorr A.G.	"	"
174034.	"	Arnold J.T.	"	"
685266.	"	Brown.T	"	29/8/17.
225293.	"	Bentley A.	"	"
168329.	"	Bevan J.G.	"	"

NOMINAL ROLL OF ALL RANKS EVACUATED DURING MONTH.

L.12050.	Sgt	Sanderson.G.	Killed in action 3/8/17.	
185837.	Gnr	Spink J.	Wounded in action	"
32267.	"	Smith.A.	" " "	"
L.28095.	Dvr	Turner A.B.	Evacuated Shell Shock.	11/8/17.
85728.	"	Maddocks J.	" Sick	15/8/17.
L.11964.	"	Hunter J.	" "	"
L.25711.	Sgt	Kirkham T.	" "	18/8/17.
168719.	Gnr	Poynts A.	" "	21/8/17.
L.28164.	Dvr	Spivey.F.	" "	30/8/17.
30754.	Far Sgt	Bishop.G.	" To England to Cadet Unit.	26/8/17.

NOMINAL ROLL OF ALL RANKS POSTED TO 'A' BATTERY, DURING AUGUST, 1917.

L.28174.	a/Bdr	Tetlow.H.	Posted from B/162 Bde R.F.A. 1/8/17.
54101.	"	Perkins.	Posted from 32nd D.A.C. 1/8/17.
52525.	"	Phillipson.	Ditto
13171.	Dvr	Lewis	"
35046.	"	Marshall.	"
152782.	Gnr	Wildsmith	"
204732.	Dvr	Malbon	"
18757.	"	Hart	"
212321.	"	Crawford	"
192472.	"	Ormiston	"
234892.	Gnr	Wooff.F.L.	"
19805.	"	Yates.W.	" 9/8/17.
10574.	"	Alford.C.	"
221345.	"	Ackeroyd C.	"
202446.	"	Birrell W.	"
9272l.	"	Black.W.	"
116349.	"	Buckley L.	"
222460.	"	Birks F.	"
651912.	"	Brunton.A.G.	" 29/8/17.
225242.	"	Breeze G.H.	"
211547.	"	Bush A.J.	"

NOMINAL ROLL OF ALL RANKS EVACUATED DURING MONTH.

	2/Lieut	A.C.Miller.	Posted to 39th Brigade R.F.A. 1/8/17.
L.28150.xGnrxxBaitonxW.			
L.25574.	Bdr	Whiteley C.H.	Evacuated Sick 3/8/17.
L.25384.	Dvr	Livesey F.	" 4/8/17.

NOMINAL ROLL OF ALL RANKS POSTED TO 'D' BATTERY
DURING MONTH, AUGUST 1917.

221602.	a/Bdr	Percy K.	Posted from 32nd D.A.C.	1/8/17.
207185.	Gnr	Snell W.P.	Ditto	"
209445.	"	Snewing J.W.	"	"
78643.	Dvr	Marshall R.E.	"	"
86935.	"	Kearnon J.P.	"	"
208238.	"	Keates C.	"	"
696267.	"	Lewis C.J.	"	"
18380.	"	Lund W.	"	"
840470.	Gnr	Pitcher R.S.	"	9/8/17
212552.	"	Robins A.S.	"	"
212536.	"	New H.	"	"
86332.	"	Powell H.	"	"
131526.	"	Philcox A.J.	"	"
20270.	"	Robinson J.	"	"
15049.	"	Cavanagh J.	"	"
2097.	"	Blythe W.	"	"
46330.	"	Braw P.H.	"	"
192402.	"	Bishop H.H.	"	"
35052.	"	Powley F.A.	"	"
20085.	Dvr	Luxford J.	"	"
8328.	"	Lindley J.	"	20/8/17.

Appendix A

ARTILLERY PROGRAMME FOR FEINT RAID.
to be carried out in conjunction with 'B' Group.

1.   'F' Bty R.H.A.   M.23.b.07.50 to M.23.b.07.72.

       A/168.   Enfilades   M.23.b.6.4. to M.23.b.75.62.

       1 How 'D' Group.   M.23.b.69.56 to M.23.b.40.73

       1 How 'G' Group.   M.23.b.40.73 to M.23.b.07.72

       8th Bty Aus F.A.

           Zero to Zero plus 4.   M.23.b.60.40 to M.23.b.07.50
           Zero plus 4 to Zero plus 8   Lift 50 yards
           Zero plus 8 to Zero plus 12.   Lift 50 yards
           Zero plus 12 to Zero plus 40   M.23.b.69.50 to M.23.b.07.72
                                             on LORRY WALK.

       C/168   M.23.a.6.4. to M.23.b.07.50

2. Rates of fire.   Zero to Zero plus 12.

                       18-Pdrs - 3 rds per gun per min
                       4.5" How - 2 rds per gun per min

                 Zero plus 12 to Zero plus 40

                       18-Pdrs - 2 rds per gun per min
                       4.5" Hows - 1 rd per gun per mins

                 Zero plus 40   - CEASE FIRE.

3. Zero time will be 1.a.m. on the night of 7/8th August 1917.

4. Watches will be synchronised from this Headquarters at 9.30.p.m on the 7th August 1917.

5. ACKNOWLEDGE.

                                                           Lieut.
                                     Adjutant - 'A' Group.

6th August.1917.

Copy No.1.   A/168
  "   No.2.   8th Bty A.F.A.
  "   No.3.   G.Group.
  "   No.4.   "
  "   No.5.   "
  "   No.6.   D   "
  "   No.7.   H.Q.32nd D.A.
  "   No.8.   War Diary.
  "   No.9.   B.Group.
  "   No.10. File.

SECRET. Appendix B Copy No..........

'A' GROUP R. F. A.
OPERATION ORDER No.49.

Wednesday 8th August 1917.

1. The No.1.and 'K' Special Companies R.E. will carry out a projector and Stokes Mortar Gas attack on LOMBARTZYDE Village and GROOT BAMBURGH FARM on the night August 8/9th if the wind is favourable.

2. (a) 100 projectors will be fired into LOMBARTZYDE Village.

   (b) 500 4" Stokes Mortars Gas shells into GROOT BAMBURGH FARM.

3. ZERO HOUR.

   In order to allow for change in the wind during the night there will be two alternative hours for Zero i.e.

   FIRST ZERO - 11.30.p.m. August 8th

   SECOND ZERO - 1.30.a.m. August 9th

4. CODE.

   The following code will be used to notify if the Operation is or not to take place, and the hour of Zero:-

Operation will take place Zero 11.30.p.m. August 8th.	DERBY
Operation will take place Zero 1.30.a.m. August 9th.	BALFOUR
Operation will not take place at 11.30.p.m.	CANCEL DERBY
Operation will not take place at 1.30.a.m.	CANCEL BALFOUR
Operation will not take place on night August 8/9th	SMITH

5. The attack will be carried out as follows:-

   (a) At Zero 100 projectiles will be fired into LOMBARTZYDE Village round the area, M.17.c.0.0 M.17.c.3.2 - M.17.c.3.7 - m M.16.d.7.3 and 250 Stokes Mortar Shells into GROOT BAMBURGH FARM.

   (b) At Zero plus 45 250 Stokes Mortar Shells will be fired into GROOT BAMBURGH FARM

6. 'A' Group will co-operate as shown in TABLE 'A'.

7. A wire will be sent to all concerned in code (vide para 4.) at 8.p.m. on August 8th notifying if the attack is or is not to take place.

Continued.

Continued.

8. In order to obviate any risk from a projector falling short into our lines, all men in that portion of the LOMBARTZYDE Sector East of NOSE ALLEY and North of NASAL Support will put on their Respirators five minutes before Zero and keep them on till Zero plus 5.

Two Golden Rain Rockets will be fired from the REDAN at Zero minus 15 to warn the troops concerned to put on their Respirators.

G.O.C. 147th Infantry Brigade will be responsible for having the 2 Golden Rain Rockets fired at Zero - 15.

9. Watches will be synchronised from this office.

10. ACKNOWLEDGE.

Alan Lumb.
8th August 1917.   Adjutant - 'A' Group. Lieut.

Copy No.1. A/163
  "   No.2. B/168
  "   No.3. C/168
  "   No.4. 7th Bty A.F.A.
  "   No.5. 8th Bty A.F.A.
  "   No.6. File.

TABLE 'A'.

TIME.	UNIT.	TASK.
Zero plus 2 to zero plus 15.	A/168	S.O.S.LINES
	C/168	S.O.S.LINES
	8th Bty.A.F.A.	M.24.a.8.4. to M.24.a.6.7. to M.18.c.7.0
	7th Bty A.F.A.	M.18.c.7.0 to M.18.c.9.7

Ammunition:- Shrapnel.

Rate of fire:- 1 Rd per gun per minute.

NOTE:- No shells to fall nearer the objectives than the limits above laid down before Zero plus 10 as they xxx break up the gas clouds.

Zero plus 10 to Zero plus 15.	B/168.	GROOTEBAMBURGH FARM.

Ammunition:- Shrapnel.

Rate of fire:- 3 Rds per gun per minute.

Zero plus 47 to Zero plus 65.	A/168.) C/168.) 8th Bty A.F.A) 7th " A.F.A)	Same as for Zero plus 2 to Zero plus 15

Zero plus 55 to Zero plus 65.	B/168	Same as for Zero plus 10 to Zero plus 15

Zero plus 65 to 4.a.m.		All the above mentioned Batteries will keep up intermittent Shrapnel fire on the above Tasks at the rate of 25 rds per Battery per hour.

SECRET.   Copy No..........

168th Brigade R.F.A.

OPERATION ORDER No.51.

                                    FRIDAY AUGUST 24th 1917.

Appendix C

1. Batteries of the 168th Brigade R.F.A. will proceed into action from rest on the night 25/26th August 1917 as shewn on attached Table 'A'

2. From 6.p.m on the 26th, A.B.& C.Batteries 168th Bde R.F.A. and the 7th 8th 9th Batteries 3rd Australian Brigade will constitute 'A' GROUP and will be commanded by Major F FITZGIBBON.D.S.O.

3. O.C. 'A' GROUP will take over the defence of ST GEORGE'S Sector (D.& E.Sub-sectors) which is held by the 98th Infantry Brigade from 6.p.m.on the 26th.

    The S.O.S.Lines of Batteries from this hour will be as follows:-

    (E Sub-sector.)

    A/168.   N.31.d.9.3 to N.32.c.22.85 to N.32.a.3.6.
              (Omitting the portions under water.)

    (D Sub-sector.)

    C/168.   N.19.c.4.0 to M.24.d.85.20
    B/168.   M.24.d.85.20 to M.24.d.26.40
    7th Aus   1 gun on Sap N.25.a.40.95
      " "   1 gun sweeping from N.25.b.2.5. to N.25.b.3.1.
      " "   2 guns N.19.c.4.0 to M.24.d.85.20
    8th Aus   M.24.d.85.20 to M.24.d.28.40
    9th Aus   2 guns N.19.c.2.5. to N.19.d.00.85
    9th Aus   2 "   M.24.d.70.55 to N.19.c.1.9

4. B/168 will be under the orders of O.C. 'G' Group but in the event of S.O.S.will fire on 'A' Group front as follows:-

    M.24.d.55.60 to M.24.d.75.45
    M.24.d.95.25. to M.24.d.62.50

5. Six guns per Battery will be in position but four only will be manned, the detachments of the remaining two guns will be resting at the Wagon Lines.

6. LIAISON.
   An officer from A/168 will take over Liaison with the Battalion at VACHE CREVEE at 6.p.m.on the 26th.
   An officer from the 7th Aus Battery will take over Laison with the Battalion at the BRIQie at the same hour.
   They will report at Battalion H.Q.at 5.p.m.

7. Any necessary registration must be carried out as early as possible on the 26th.

8. Group H.Q. will be established at.............. at 4.p.m on the 26th.

9. ACKNOWLEDGE.

                                         Captain.
                             Adjutant 168th Brigade R.F.A.

25/8/17.

TABLE 'A'.

Unit.	Time of start.	Destination.	Route.
B/168.	7 – 30.p.m.	Action.	Main COXYDE – NIEUPORT Road.
C/168.	7 – 45.p.m.	"	WULPEN – PELICAN Road.
A/168.	8 – 0.p.m.	"	Cross country track running from GROOT LABEUR FARM to Position.

A distance of 250 yards must be maintained between Sections through-out the march, and no vehicle must pass East of the Line OOST DUNKERQUE – WULPEN before dark.

H.Q. 33rd Divisional Artillery.
H.Q. 32nd Divisional Artillery
H.Q. 168th Brigade R.F.A

Reference para 8 of OPERATION ORDER No. 51. of yesterday's date.

Brigade Headquarters will be situated at S.3.d.7.3.

25/8/17.

Blackcumb Captain.
Adjt 168th Brigade R. F. A.

Appendix D

O.C. A.B.&.C.168th Brigade R.F.A.
O.C. 7.8.9th Batteries.A.F.A.

1. A Gas Bombardment from projectors on RAT TRENCH area will take place to-night the 26/27th August if conditions are favourable.

2. 'A' Group will take part as follows:-

   Zero plus 5 to Zero plus 10.   8th Aus. N.19.c.57.35 to N.19.c.4.4
                                  9th Aus. N.19.c.4.4   to N.19.c.3.5
                                  7th Aus. N.19.c.3.5. to N.19.c.25.60
                                  C/168.   N.19.c.25.60 to N.19.c.2.7
                                  B/168.   N.19.c.2.7   to N.19.c.1.9

   Zero plus 10 to Zero plus 15. C/168.   N.19.c.35.10 to N.19.c.2.0
                                  9th Aus N.19.c.2.0   to N.19.c.05.05
                                  8th Aus N.19.c.05.05 to M.24.d.9.2.
                                  B/168.   N.19.c.1.5. to M.24.d.90.35
                                  7th Aus M.24.d.90.35 to M.24.d.70.55

   Zero plus 30 to Zero plus 35.   As for Zero plus 10 to Zero plus 15

   Zero plus 35 to Zero plus 38   As for Zero plus 5 to Zero plus 10

   Zero plus 38 to Zero plus 40   As for Zero plus 10 to Zero plus 15

   Zero plus 40   All guns Cease Fire.

   Rates of Fire.

   Zero plus 5 to Zero plus 10) Each Battery 3 bursts of Fire of 2
   Zero plus 10 to Zero plus 15) rounds per gun at irregular intervals.
   Zero plus 30 to Zero plus 35)

   Zero plus 35 to Zero plus 38) Each Battery 2 bursts of Fire of 2 rds
   Zero plus 38 to Zero plus 40) per gun at irregular intervals.

3. There will be two alternative ZERO hours for this operation, one two hours after the other, in case conditions are unsuitable, for the first:-
        First ZERO   11.p.m 26th August 1917.
        Second ZERO   1.a.m. 27th August 1917.
   The wind is considered safe from West to South West to South South East.

4. All concerned will be notified in the following code at 7.p.m on 26/8/17 as to whether the gas attack is, or is not to take place, and subsequently if any alteration in the programme is made:-

        Gas attacks will take place   Sandbags will be required.
        ZERO 11.p.m.August 26th

        Gas attacks will take place   Shovels will be required.
        ZERO hour 1.a.m.August 27th

        Gas attacks will not take place   Cancel order for Sandbags.
        at 11.p.m.

        Gas attacks will not take place   Cancel order for shovels.
        at 1.a.m.

        Gas attacks will not take place
        on the night Aug 26/27th   Cancel order for material.

5. ACKNOWLEDGE.

                                          Alan Thumb   Captain.
26/8/17.   Adjutant 'A' GROUP.

CONFIDENTIAL.

WAR DIARY

of the

168th. BRIGADE R.F.A.

from 1st.Sept.1917 to 30th.Sept.1917.

Volume XXI

WAR DIARY
or
INTELLIGENCE SUMMARY.

(Erase heading not required.)

Army Form C. 2118.

163th Brigade R.F.A.
Commanded by Lt.- Colonel R FITZMAURICE.
D.S.O.

Place	Date	Hour	Summary of Events and Information	Remarks and references to Appendices
	1/9/17.		Day very wild and wet, front very quiet.	AL
	2/9/17.	11.30.pm	Practice S.O.S. Barrage carried out. Enemy carried out vigorous Counter Battery Work.	AL
	3/9/17.		Enemy carried out his Sixth destructive shoot on B/163.R.F.A. position with 8" Hows. Many direct hits were obtained on Gun Pits, and two guns put out of action.	AL
	4/9/17.	1.pm to 3.pm	Enemy Heavy Artillery very active. Destructive shoot carried out on A/163.R.F.A. Ammunition exploded and two guns scorched.	AL
	5/9/17.		Our Batteries carried out destructive bombardments on enemy trenches. Enemy shelled and destroyed PELICAN BRIDGE.	AL
	6/9/17.		Lt.-Col. FITZMAURICE returned to the Brigade and assumed command of 'A' GROUP R.F.A. which consists of A.B.C.&.D. Batteries 163th Brigade R.F.A.	AL
	8/9/17.	10.pm	Batteries fired in conjunction with a Gas Projector and Stokes Mortar Bombardment on enemy trenches, S.E. of LOMBARTZYDE.	AL
	11/9/17.	9.30.pm	14th Infantry Brigade Raided 'GROOTE BAMBURGH FARM'. B & D/163.R.F.A.took part Many Germans were killed and two taken prisoners, but they were killed whilst coming across No Man's Land. Enemy obtained direct hits on gun pits of B & D 163.R.F.A. Casualties. (B) 2 Gunners killed, 1 Sergt, and 1 Gunner Wounded (D) 1 Gunner killed, 1 Sergt, and 2 Gunners Wounded.	AL
	13/9/17.	10.45.am	Batteries fired in conjunction with a Gas Projector and Stokes Mortar Bombardment on enemy trenches S.E. of LOMBARTZYDE. Enemy Artillery very active on roads and back Areas.	AL
	15/9/17.		Sergt TURGOOSE C/163.R.F.A. awarded the MILITARY MEDAL. 16th H.L.I relieved 2nd K.O.Y.L.I.and XIth Border Regt relieved 17th.H.L.I. in the Sector covered by 'A' GROUP.	AL

Army Form C. 2118.

WAR DIARY
or
INTELLIGENCE SUMMARY.
(Erase heading not required.)

163rd Brigade R. F. A.
Commanded by Lt.-Col. R. FITZMAURICE. D.S.O.

Instructions regarding War Diaries and Intelligence Summaries are contained in F. S. Regs., Part II. and the Staff Manual respectively. Title pages will be prepared in manuscript.

Place	Date	Hour	Summary of Events and Information	Remarks and references to Appendices
	16/9/17.		Sergeant HAWKES. D/168.R.F.A. awarded the MILITARY MEDAL.	ok.
	17/9/17.	5.25.am	After a heavy bombardment the enemy attempted a raid on our trenches South of LOMBARTZYDE. Only one man of the enemy reached our trenches and was killed.	ok.
		10.30.am	The DIVISIONAL Commander visited Battery Positions. Remarkable decrease in enemy Artillery Fire. Front very quiet.	ok.
	18/9/17.	7.30.am	A single gun placed in a forward position to be used for Sniping. D/168.R.F.A. carried out Registration by Aeroplane Observation.	ok.
		10.am.	Commenced to rain and continued all day. Front very quiet.	
	19/9/17.	11.am	D/168. Shelled for 4 hours by 15.c.m.Hows, 1 gun destroyed. Casualties 1 Gunner Killed 1 " Wounded	ok.
	20/9/17.		Enemy Artillery much more active than usual on Battery Positions.	ok.
	21/9/17.	3.30.am	Enemy bombarded our trenches in ST GEORGE'S, our Batteries retaliated. Enemy Heavy Artillery very active all day. Bombs were dropped by Enemy Aircraft near A/168.R.F.A.Position wounding 2 N.C.O's	ok.
	22/9/17.		Front quiet. The enemy carried out night firing on Roads and Bridges. Lt.G.C.WOOD, D/168, awarded the Military cross.	ok.
	23/9/17.	9.30.am	Enemy Aircraft very active, they were attacked by our machines and driven off, no more were seen until V.p.m.	ok.
	24/9/17.	12.30.pm	D/168.R.F.A. carried out shoots by Aeroplane Observation on enemy Bridges in the vicinity of NIEUWENDAMME FORT. Enemy fired Gas into ST GEORGE'S, our Batteries retaliated on enemy front line opposite. DORSETS relieved the 15th H.L.I. - ROYAL SCOTS relieved 2nd MANCHESTER'S in the Sector covered by the 163rd Brigade R. F. A.	ok.
	25/9/17.		Remarkably quiet day, enemy artillery fire, practically NIL, until dark when bursts of fire were directed on all the roads W. of NIEUPORT.	ok.

Army Form C. 2118.

WAR DIARY
or
INTELLIGENCE SUMMARY.
(Erase heading not required.)

166th Brigade R. F. A.
Commanded by Lt-Colonel R FITZMAURICE.D.S.O.

Place	Date	Hour	Summary of Events and Information	Remarks and references to Appendices
	26/9/17.	4.pm	Practice Counter Preparation and S.O.S.Barrage on the Divisional Front.	OK.
	27/9/17.	6.a.m.	Enemy Bombarded our trenches heavily opposite LOMBARTZYDE, our Artillery replied.	OK.
	28/9/17.		D/168.R.F.A.carried out Shoots by Aeroplane Observation on enemy Bridges in the vicinity of NIEUWENDAMME FORT. 1 Bridge destroyed - 1 damaged.	OK.
	29/9/17.		Weather continued to be fine. Aircraft very active. Enemy Aeroplanes bombed back Areas.	OK.
	30/9/17.	10.30 to 1.30.am	The enemy carried out his 9th Destructive Shoot on B/168.R.F.A. with 8" and 11" Hows firing about 150 rounds. Two Gun Pits were blown in. 1 man slightly wounded.	OK.

Lieut - Colonel.
Commanding 168th Brigade R. F. A.

Headquarters Staff.   -:0:-   168th Brigade R.F.A.

NOMINAL ROLL OF ALL RANKS FOR MONTH OF SEPTEMBER 1917.

Officers:- Lt - Colonel. R.FITZMAURICE.D.S.O.
           Captain.ALAN LUMB.
           Lieut HAROLD FISHER.
           Lieut HAROLD.L.JAMES.
           Captain.D.FERGUSON.(R.A.M.C.)

Other Ranks:-.

    1362.R.S.M.Mc Gowan.M.C.
L.25839.Corpl Lee G.
L.25881.Bdr Gibson.H.
  29811. " Anderton.A.
  12245.a/Bdr Wright.J.
L.29430. " Sugden.E.
L.28042. " Eyre F.
L.28206.Gnr Akroyd.A.
L.25910. " Bottomley C.
  59688. " Clark.B.J.
L.29404. " Greenwood.C.
  56777. " Grindley.W.
L.25626. " Slater.H.
L.29296. " Windle A.T.
L.27531. " Postlethwaite.T.
L.25422.Dvr Armitage.G.
L.32440. " Baker.G.
L.32540. " Blake.F.
L. 5742. " Dickenson.J.
  19817. " Foote.G.
   1573. " Gutteridge.A.
  35766. " Hirons.E.
L. 5855. " Gowan.W.
L.32511. " Iredale.A.
L.25825. " Iredale.E.
L.28129. " Mellor.A.
L.28132. " Martin.J.
  79511. " Mc Intyre.A.
L.29424. " Parker.J.
L.25853. " Radley.T.
L.29357. " Reddington.M.
L.29389. " Stansfield.P.
   6267. s/s Periera A.T.
   1305. Sadd.Williams.T.

    A.O.C. 625.Staff Sergt Barker.H. (Artificer).

'A' Battery.   -:0:-   168th Brigade R.F.A.

NOMINAL ROLL OF ALL RANKS.   1/10/17.

Officers:- Major.R.EMMET.
Capt.G.O.d'IVRY.
Lieut L.A.RAVALD.
" W.A.EBBELS.
2/Lieut J.W.WEEDON.
" F.J.CLARKE. Posted from 32nd D.A. 2/9/17.

Other ranks:-

L.18467.	B.S.M.	Stephenson.C.	
L.28066.	BQMS.	Brearley.A.	
L.25426.	Sergt	Field.P.J.	
L.25679.	"	Roberts.J.F.	
43312.	"	McGowan.A.H.	
L.25425.	"	Firth.A.	
53261.	"	Smith.A.	
L.32581.	"	Williams.W.J.	
L.25697.	Cpl	Rhodes.L.	
L.25561.	"	Povey.J.	Wounded Admitted to hospital. 21/9/17.
L.25619.	"	France W.	
L.29407.	"	Taylor.F.	
L.29313.	"	Armitage.W.B.	
1985.	"	Harding.R.C.	
1105.	"	Witney.T.	
L.32479.	Bdr	Pitchforth.A.	
L.25708.	"	Crawshaw.J.F.	
L.25574.	"	Whiteley.C.H.	Returned from hospital taken on Strength 3/9/17.
L.25414.	"	Wood.B.	
L.25731.	"	Rhodes J.	
L.28188.	"	Padgett S.	
L.25464.	"	Richardson.G.H.	
83594.	"	Simpson.C.	
L.28034.	"	Beevers.M.	
86310.	"	Squires.A.E.	
L.32539.	a/Bdr	Fenton.E.	
54101.	"	Perkins.F.J.	
L.29297.	"	Noble.C.	
L.32523.	"	Philipson.R.	
L.28126.	"	Shaw N.	
72096.	"	Smith.L.	Admitted to hospital Evacuated 6/9/17.
L.28174.	"	Tetlow.H.	
L.28217.	"	Beaver.E.	
L.25513.	"	Peace A.	Wounded Admitted to Hospital. 21/9/17.
167074.	"	McGeashie.J.	
169899.	s/a/Bdr	Halliday.R.	
L.25536.	"	Mansfield.W.G.	
167422.	"	Sweet.J.	
L.32449.	Far"Sgt	Andrews.R.	
L.25783.	Cpl s/s	Town.E.	
765.	"	Parks.J.	
L.29282.	S/S	Nuttall E.T.	
L.28175.	"	Waterhouse L.	
L.35690.	"	Kaye.J.T.	
173878.	"	Ackeroyd.C.	
L.32495.	Saddlr	Jackson.W.R.	
62728.	"	Oliver.J.	
154173.	"	Skipp.J.W.	
147472.	Ftr.	Hellewell.A.	
72465.	"	Bambrough.A.	
42821.	"	Norton.A.	
121451.	Whlr	Weaver.J.	
L.25790.	Gnr	Allott.W.	
221345.	"	Alston.J.D.	

10574.	Gnr	Alford.C.	
L.25575.	"	Billington.T.	
L.25014.	"	Bray.E.H.	Posted to T.M's. 22/9/17.
100556.	"	Beamish.R.	
100774.	"	Baird.S.	
L.29379.	"	Beaumont.L.	
L.25768.	"	Brooksbank.S.	
202446.	"	Berrill.W.	
92721.	"	Black.W.	
116349.	"	Buckley.L.	To Base Dental Treatment. Evacuated. 3/9/17.
651912.	"	Brunton.A.G.	Posted from 32nd.D.A.C. 29/8/17.
222460.	"	Birks.F.	
225242.	"	Breeze.T.H.	Posted from 32nd.D.A.C. 29/8/17.
L.32471.	"	Calvert.F.	
L.29345.	"	Craigie.T.	
132364.	"	Curd.W.A.	
5556.	"	Chappel.A.	
190397.	"	Cross.F.	
212321.	"	Crawford.C.	
28178.	"	Dawson.W.	
12049.	"	Edwards.L.	
130451.	"	Edwards.W.H.	
82676.	"	Franklin.M.	
190415.	"	Foote.G.	
15256.	"	Fearn.H.	
L.25472.	"	Green.N.	
L.25823.	"	Hynes.W.H.	
226903.	"	Hancox.H.R.	
18757.	"	Hart.C.	
733.	"	Keighley.F.J.	
L.32512.	"	Lumb.W.	
184485.	"	Lewis.E.J.	
L.28177.	"	Leatham.F.	
197866.	"	Mc Ewing.H.	
159371.	"	Mc Carthy.E.	
197863.	"	Mc Phearson.D.	
168568.	"	Miller.W.	
150416.	"	Mallett.H.	
L.28129.	"	Marshall.L.	
L.25392.	"	Milnes.H.	
L.25443.	"	Nuttall.P.	
44251.	"	Offen.F.	
192477.	"	Ormiston.A.	
L.29306.	"	Pearson.F.	
L.28186.	"	Perkins.J.C.	
L.25653.	"	Rushworth.A.	
211705.	"	Robinson.H.	
199803.	"	Raskilly.R.	
2815.	"	Rice.E.F.	
224362.	"	Rockett.B.	
66262.	"	Rhodes.A.E.	
L.32491.	"	Roberts.J.	
L.25566.	"	Smith.A.	
L.28006.	"	Singleton.H.W.	
L.26074.	"	Spencer.R.	
81446.	"	Slack.H.	
L.25735.	"	Spencer.H.	
221039.	"	Soloman.L.	
821657.	"	Swadling.A.	
22365.	"	Speed.A.	
150668.	"	Schaefer.A.E.	
38812.	"	Symonds.H.	
156164.	"	Sargent.C.	
L.25771.	"	Thornton.J.	
30526.	"	Thorp.W.J.	
L.29355.	"	Townend.J.	
L.32535.	"	Thornber.W.H.	
L.28038.	"	Wilkinson.T.	
L.29300.	"	Wood.F.	
L.32441.	"	Walker.A.	
L.29319.	"	Wood.R.	
L.25649.	"	Wood.C.E.	
L.25485.	"	Williams.C.	

123713. Gnr Young.W.
 19605. " Yates.W.
234892. " Wooff.F.J.

175251. Dvr Adams.F.
L.25524. " Bamforth.H.
L.25525. " Bray.H.
L.25436. " Brearley.A.
L.25395. " Brook G.L.   Posted from 32.d.D.A.C.   13/9/17.
L.25658. " Chapman.B.
L.29323. " Cartwright.P.
L.25592. " Crowther.J.T.
109981. " Chapman.H.
 41489. " Crisp.B.
L.29409. " Dyson.W.
L.28079. " Green.F.
L.25820. " Ganley.J.
L.29316. " Gledhill.J.R.
L.25579. " Griffiths.T.C.
L.28201. " Horsfall.E.
L.25849. " Holmes.L.
L.28153. " Harrison.F.
L.29347. " Hardcastle.C.W.
 93514. " Hartley.A.
 82541. " Kershaw.C.
L.25419. " Kerton.E.
L.28163. " Lodge.A.
L.25384. " Livesey.F.C.   Evacuated 30/8/17.
 12171. " Lewis.   "   "
L.28021. " Mallinson.J.A.
L.25639. " Millard.H.
826369. " Morse.L.
 35046. " Marshall.R.
204732. " Malbon.H.
101698. " O'Neill.J.
147602. " Orris.H.
L.32464. " Pogson.S.
L.28136. " Priest.E.W.
 35864. " Quinn.D.
L.28074. " Robertshaw G.
L.28075. " Roe.F.
L.28013. " Sykes.W.
 99859. " Spencer.P.G.
L.25633. " Shaw.E.
L.25502. " Shaw.H.
L.28224. " Shaw.C.A.
L.25797. " Singleton.V.
L.25450. " Smith.J.R.
166514. " Smith.W.J.
217881. " Shotton.R.
219990. " Fall.F.
741290. " Tanner.A.
 26101. " Taylor.T.H.
L.25463. " Varley.L.
L.25650. " Wood.A.
 10586. " Westgate.F.
L.29331. " Woodcock W.
L.28067. " Walters.H.
L.25394. " Wortley.T.
L.25541. " Woodhead B.
L.25819. " Whitehead.J.A.
159419. " Weedon.W.
 21116. " Wainwright.W.C.
L.28214. " Wood.W.A.

S.E.1514. Sgt Jolly.A.J. (Attached).

'B' Battery.   —:0:—   168th Brigade R.F.A.

NOMINAL ROLL OF ALL RANKS SEPTEMBER 1917.

Officers:- Major.F.FITZGIBBON.D.S.O.
Capt.L.M.HASTINGS.M.C.
Lieut W.B.ROBINSON.
2/Lieut.CHAMBERLAIN.W.L
  "   J.MITCHELHILL
  "   C.P.BASNETT.

Other ranks:-

55432.	B.S.M.	Stenning.T.	
L.32437.	BQMS.	Lane.A.C.	
L.32514.	Far Sgt	Sutcliffe.R.	
L.25548.	Sergt	Beaumont.F.	
L.25599.	"	Crooks.H	
L.25716.	"	Fisher.W.W.	Evacuated (Wounded) 27 Sept.1917.
L.29344.	"	Gutherie.A.	
L.28210.	"	Greenwood.M.R.	
L.25374.	"	Shaw.L.	
98737.	Cpl s/s	Brennan J.	
L.28138.	Cpl	Bramley S.M.	
L.25693.	"	Littlewood.K.	
L.23076.	"	Murray A.	
24990.	"	Mayers.A.	
L.25491.	"	Sherwood.J.T.	
L.28326.	"	Temperton.H.K.	
L.12243.	"	Vincent A.	Posted from 32nd D.A.C. 19/9/17.
L.25871.	"	Walker S.	
L.25446.	Bdr	Bottomley T.	
L.32430.	"	Bancroft L.	
125511.	"	Christie.H.	
79093.	"	Drewitt.W.C.	
L.25472.	"	Dyson.F.	
L.25746.	"	Hargreaves A.	
L.25545.	"	Turner J.F	
L.25451.	"	Spendlove.T.	
L.25608.	s/Bdr	Broomhead.W.H.	
16331.	"	Cawthorne.I.	
L.32576.	"	Bentley.T.	
152375.	"	Holmes.N.	
L.29503.	"	Horrocks.H.	
L.25547.	"	Ibbotson.M.	
11578.	"	Gouldsmith.S.O	
115275.	"	Leach A.	
L.29382.	"	Riley.A.	Posted from O.C.Reinforcements HAVRE. 19/9/17
L.25463.	"	Scott.N.	
5035.	s/s	Boswell.H.	
L:32549.	"	Berry.A.	
L.25552.	"	Hoyle.C.	
L.25510.	"	Readyhough.G.W.	
L.25453.	"	Sidebottom.J.	
L.32552.	"	Wilson.J.	
L.25747.	Sdlr	Brooksbank.G.	
L.25607.	"	Stansfield.F.	
L:25596.	Whlr	Yates.F.	
L.32456.	Ftr	Hill.W.	
765047.	Gnr	Ball T.H.	
162912.	"	Allen.T.W.	Posted from 32nd.D.A.C. 19/9/17.
229157.	"	Bellfield.G.	
156556.	"	Benton.H.J.	
169329.	"	Bevan J.G.	
L.25616.	"	Billington.H.	
L.32463.	"	Binns.A.O.	
L.32521.	"	Bottoms.H.	
L.29265.	"	Broadley.J.T.	

18820.	Gnr.	Brown.F.	
8993.	"	Blake.A.	
57766.	"	Brown.G.	
211607.	"	Bone.E.W.	
211547.	"	Bush.A.J.	
211574.	"	Cartwright H.V.	
120237.	"	Charman.H.	
211662.	"	Cheeseman.A.	
162927.	"	Clarke.H.	Posted from 32nd.D.A.C.19/9/17.
205152.	"	Cooke.W.	
162339.	"	Cousins.A.T.	
L.25671.	"	Cocker.F.	
2295.	"	Coward.T.	
L.29383.	"	Dewar W.	
68234.	"	Doggett.J.	
L.29263.	"	Fowler.B.	
93752.	"	Farmer.H.	
198809.	"	Gigg.B.	
L.29262.	"	Greenwood L.A.	
L.29380.	"	Hanson.E.	
L.32454.	"	Hargreaves D.	
11619.	"	Harris.G.	
L.28046.	"	Holdsworth A.	
218427.	"	Irvine.L.	
L.25459.	"	Kiddle.F.	
L.32510.	"	Knight.S.	
L.28220.	"	Laycock.A.	
L.25623.	"	Lee.F.	
160940.	"	Ling.G.	
L.25622.	"	Littlewood.H.	
197864.	"	Mc Phearson.D.	
197865.	"	Mc Rae..D.	Killed in action 12.9.17.
L.28126.	"	Mallinson.F.	
164025.	"	Miller.L.	
L.29400.	"	Mitchell.D.	
L.32544.	"	Mitchell. R.	
221036.	"	Mole. T.	Posted from 32nd.D.A.C. 19/9/17.
199395.	"	Mullard.G.H.	
188576.	"	Nash.T.J.	
156134.	"	Nightingale.D.	
L.25632.	"	Onyon.A.	
2358.	"	Plate.H.	
L258727.	"	Riddleston.A.	
46249.	"	Scott.F.J.	
159803.	"	Shaw.J.A.	
5624.	"	Spence C.	
165748.	"	Stanage.J.W.	
L.33473.	"	Stafford.H.	
L.29372.	"	Tidswell.H.T.	
L.25683.	"	Thomspon.J.T.	
67704.	"	Tunstall.A.	
L.25629.	"	Turner.H.	
208386.	"	Rix.H.	
221070.	"	Rodgers.E.R.	
176283.	"	Ritchie.G.	
L.25727.	"	Winteringham.F.	
L.25716.	"	Woof.G.H.	Killed in action 12/9/17.
150477.	"	Woolf.C.H.	

L.29381.	Dvr	Barraclough.H.	
L.29258.	"	Barraclough.T.E.	
L.28213.	"	Beaumont.T.E.	
L.28199.	"	Berry.A.	
L.25837.	"	Berry.S.	
L.32528.	"	Borissaw.F.	
L.32566.	"	Braithwaite.J.F.	
L.25470.	"	Brook.J.W.	
185735.	"	Chesters.D.	
L.25878.	"	Clear.A.	
L.28113.	"	Crossley.J.	
L.32518.	"	Crowther.J.	
L.25446.	"	Davis.J.	
112102.	"	Dennis.S.	
L.25442.	"	Eastwood.G.	
L.25732.	"	Firth.H.	
L.32538.	"	Gray D.	
L.29367.	"	Greenwood.J.W.	
L.25728.	"	Greenwood.C.	Posted to Battery from D.A.C. 1/9/17.
1396.	"	Green.R.	Posted from 32nd D.A.C. 1/9/17.
L.25831.	"	Hall.H.	
L.28204.	"	Harrison.F.	
L.25479.	"	Hattersley.F.	
L.32524.	"	Hawthornthwaite.T.W.	
L.25822.	"	Hincliffe.A.	
L.25558.	"	Hobson.A.	
L.32506.	"	Holmes.W.	
L.32447.	"	Jackson.P.	
L.28070.	"	Jowett.J.H.	
L.29270.	"	Ledgard.E.	
L.23748.	"	Leckenby J.	
79005.	"	Linch P.	
217555.	"	Mackie.J.	
L.28077.	"	Martin.L.	
219114.	"	Markham.C.	
930739.	"	Mathis.M.C.	
815569.	"	Mayers.F.	
L.28066.	"	Medley.O.	
152302.	"	Milnes.J.	
47044.	"	Mc Cormick.A.	
L.29401.	"	Moody.A.	
121959.	"	Morley.A.T.	
L.28127.	"	Mellor.H.	Posted from 32nd.D.A.C. 1/9/17.
L.25870.	"	Murray.R.	
213085.	"	Newnes.A.	
L.25675.	"	Nicholson.J.	
L.28194.	"	North M.	
733229.	"	Parnaby W.	
20609.	"	Ray D.	
L.28071.	"	Robinson.F.	
5116.	"	Roberts.G.	
L.25861.	"	Robinson.T.	
L.25512.	"	Robinson.W.J.	
L.25730.	"	Rushworth.E.	
L.25625.	"	Scott.J.J.	
L.28041.	"	Scholefield.A.	
L.25624.	"	Senior.G.	
203373.	"	Sharples.J.E.	
L.32579.	"	Shaphard.N.	
L.25644.	"	Singleton.E.	
L.25454.	"	Snell.A.	
180180.	"	Tooth.V.S.	
L.29397	"	Southwell.J.	
L.28090.	"	Stanton.A.	
L.25569.	"	Turner.J.	
2088.	"	Turner.J.	
L.25866.	"	Townsend.H	
L.25598.	"	Townsend.W.	
L.25499.	"	Tallis.G.	
L.32515.	"	Wilkinson.L.	
L.29257.	"	Wilkinson.L.F.	

185398.	Dvr Willatt.W.	
164826.	" Williams.E.	
L.29269	" Wood.H.	
141214.	" Worth.W.D.	
L.28089.	" Wright.F.	

8949. Vet Sergt.White.F.A.   A.V.C. attached.

'C' Battery.   168th Brigade R.F.A.

                Officers.   Major.H.COTTEE.D.S.O.
                            Capt.B.J.GROVES.
                            2/Lieut.C.J.BARRICK.
                                "   C.A.ANELAY.
                                "   S.J.HINTON.M.C.
                                "   H.R.M.RONALDSON.
                                "

Other ranks.

    53473.   B.S.M.Malone.M.J.
   L.5688.   B.Q.M.S.Tomlinson.S.
  L.12004.   Sergt Turgoose.W.
    22339.   "   Fitzgerald.W.
  L.23195.   "   Garside.J.
  L.19461.   Cpl Ward.J.S.
  L.23121.   " Palmer.R.
  L.27727.   " Ward.A.
  L.19484.   " Bailey.B.C.
  L.11993.   " Holdroyd.T.
  L.25473.   " Earnshaw.S.
  L.25812.   " Terry.L.
  L.19479.   Bdr Wardle.L.M.
  L.19479.   " Todd.A.
  L.12016.   " Maguire.J.T.
    19830.   " Gouldsborough.L.
  L.22730.   " Walton.H.
  L.29414.   " Elliott.C.H.
  L.19519.   " Milnthorpe.J.
  L.19487.   " Carr.W.C.
  L.11962.   " Wilcox.G.
  L.28010.   " Steele.J.W.
  L.28200.   " Brook.J.
   138424. a/Bdr Kirkham
  L.11959.   " Ellis.W.D
  L.12035.   " Wathy.A.
    93564.   " Seymour.W.
   L.3235.   " Lewis.E.W.
    50143.   " Smith.T.
   115097.   " Musto.W.P.
    48296.   Far Sgt Key.J.
  L.25954.   Cpl.S/S Chappel.E.
  L.11926.   s/s Fletcher.F.
  L.27751.   " Bailey.H.
  L.11934.   " Ismay.T.H.
   109905.   " Copping.H.E.
    63915.   " Irving.W.A.
  L.12041.   " Kershaw.H.
  L.29360.   Cpl Ptr Hincliffe.J.
  L.14362.   Whlr Pring.e.E.
  L.11937.   Sadd Hall.J.
   143669.   " Heron.R.
    43572.   Gnr Anderson.F.
   174032.   " Arnold.J.T.
   139105.   " Gnr Bolster.A.G.
    48449.   " Berbridge.W.K.
  L.11972.   " Booth.J.
  L.11994.   " Barr.J.
  L.12036.   " Beach.J.
  L.11979.   " Brady.B.
  L.19465.   " Briggs.E.J.
    43577.   " Baker.J.

105511.	Dvr Blackhurst.H.	Posted from 32nd D.A.C. 12/9/17
123532.	" Bearman.A.	
L.11932.	" Clarke.E.W.	
L.28232.	" Chapman.J.	
114327.	" Cleaver.E.R.	
L.29291.	" Drake.G	
L.28107.	" Ellis.H.	
L.11969.	" Ewbank.J.H.	
L.12055.	" Farnery.T.	
L.19506.	" Fretwell.H.	
32242.	" Fitch.E.J.	
L.12037.	" Garfitt.J.T.	
L.19520.	" Garfoot.E.	
8397.	" Groutt.W.	Posted fro 32.D.A.C. 12.9/17.
L.11941.	" Hart.W.	
L.11967.	" Hancox.N.	
L.19510.	" Horsfall.E.	
L.19509.	" Hudson.J.	
L.11929.	" Kemp.R.	
L.19492.	" Lapish.J.	
L.19513.	" Lamb.M.	
L.28051.	" Lawton.H.	
L.29285.	" Lord.J.	
218502	" Leeves.A.E.	
L.14919.	" Marshall.S.	
L.12909.	" Mitchell.W.	
85571.	" O'Keefe.J.A.	
6074.	" Overland.H.	
75445.	" Pipe.E.	
L.27691.	" Poynton.G.W.	
2369.	" Price.W.	
L.19516.	" Priestly.B.	
L.28031.	" Parkin.H.	
L.25850.	" Pogson.H.	
40357.	" Powell.B.A.	
41796.	" Peckham.E.	
L.12011.	" Roberts.E.W.	
L.11965.	" Ross.C.A.	
826655.	" Schilling.B.M.	
177610.	" Scott.A	
132504.	" Studley.F.	
L.19467.	" Schofield.W.	
L.12033.	" Senior.E.K.	
120413.	" Shipman.H.	
L.29293	" Sutcliffe.W.	
L.28149.	" Scott.J.R.	
L.280448.	" Singleton.H.	
L.27993.	" Senior.J.W.	
186618.	" Stride.W.	
27747.	" Toothill.A.C.	
32459.	" Turner.H.	
L.26095.	" Turner.A.B.	
L.12008.	" Wales.A.	
L.12021.	" Walshaw.E.	
L.12006.	" Wrigglesworth.F.	
L.28169.	" Williams.J.	
L. 1344.	" Young.T.	
L.28124.	" Walton.R.	
L.29322.	" White.L	
51913.	" Wareham.B.	
145487.	" Wilson.W.J.	
2410.	" Wheeler.W.	
L.11978.	" Williams.H.	
211022.	" Woodward.	Posted from 32.d.D.A.C. 12(9/17.

2469.	Sgt Harding.W.	(A.V.C.)

6521.	Gnr	Braid.J.K.	
685266.	"	Brown.T.	
235293	"	Betteley.A.	
209056.	"	Bird.J.H.	Posted from 32nd D.A.C. 19/9/17.
L.23147.	"	Chapman.T.	
147114.	"	Creeper.H.	
196150.	"	Cook.F.	
830528.	"	Carter.G.H.	
L.25702.	"	Denton.F.	
217908.	"	Dykes.W.P.	Posted from 32nd.D.A.C. 19/9/17.
L.25411.	"	Ellis.V.	Wounded admitted to hospital 26/9/17. Evac'd
L.12017.	"	Farmery J.W.	
78330.	"	Frazer J.	
37084.	"	Gain.S.E.	
163921.	"	Gerrit.G.W.	
197894.	"	Grummitt.A.	
163727.	"	Goddard.W.E.	
88771.	"	Hall.N	
L.19490.	"	Horner C.	
34446.	"	Hutt.R.	
89444.	"	Holden.F.	
L.25751.	"	Higgins.H.	
110744.	"	Hugget.T.	
2933.	"	Hesford.H.	
32657.	"	Horder.W.	
L.12020.	"	Inman.H.	
305331.	"	Ineson.T.E.	
L 12011.	"	Jolley.W.	
19809.	"	James.T.	
L.19514.	"	Lynes.J.	Wounded and Evacuated 18/9/17.
L.11932.	"	Mulheir.J.	
L.12002.	"	Howell.E.F.	
L.11971.	"	Parkin.W	
184085.	"	Shephard.W.	
190804.	"	Shaw.N.	
L 19496.	"	Saberton.H.	
L.27339.	"	Spittle.T.A.	
13907.	"	Swim.J.	
1268.	"	Sellars.G.	
67727.	"	Smith.J.E.	
12965.	"	Smith.W.E.	
935803	"	Smith.W.A.	
32267.	"	Smith.A.	
123842	"	Sutton.E.T.	
13469.	"	Robinson.A.E.	
L.25715.	"	Taylor.J.T.	
229565.	"	Wall.A.	
L.19502.	"	Wales.W.	
L.12003.	"	Waldron.T.	
L.19717.	"	Wardell.G.H.	
208477.	"	Woodman.H.	
L.12022.	"		
219005.	"	Ward.L.T.	
46846.	"	Young.J.T.	

L.25711. Sergt Kirkham.T.   Returned from hospital previously reported Evac'd
20/9/17.

L.12022.	Dvr	Ainsworth.H.	
200790.	"	Bell.J.T.	
821420.	"	Beale.W.A.	
L.11919.	"	Backhouse G.H.	
L.11942.	"	Boullton.P.	
221666.	"	Brown.J.T.	
L.11980	"	Burnley.W.S.	
15220.	"	Bury.A.	

'D' Battery.   -:0:-   168th Brigade R.F.A.

NOMINAL ROLL OF ALL RANKS 1/10/17.

Officers:-. Major.J.C.POOLE.M.C.
             Lieut.R.DUNBAR.
             Lieut.G.C.WOOD.M.C.
             2/Lieut.E.P.PEEL.
             2/Lieut.C.A.BROWNE.
             2/Lieut.B.J.VALLANCE.

Other ranks.:-

    13705. B.S.M. Perigo.W.   T.P.H.& R.F.A.Base. 24/9/17.
   100360. Far Sgt Greenwood.W.
    11948. Sergt Allen.A.J.
    27580.   "   Briddock.   Wounded and Evacuated 11/9/17.
    35409.   "   Dinsdale.J.
    19965.   "   Hawkes.T.G.H.
    27577.   "   Hetherington.J. Wounded and Evacuated 9/9/17.
   950107.   "   Jeffery.S.A.
  L.25606.   "   Palframan.F.
    19914.   "   Wooffitt.F.E.
    27601. Cpl. Archer.S.T.
    27756. "   Bonner.S.
    26452. "   Bellamy.J.
    35389. "   Dobson.J.E.
   889565. "   Jackson.S.A.
    19919. "   Scholey.E.
    27590. Bdr Bradford.J.
   889522. "   Barker.W.
    35390. "   Beckett.E.
     2008. "   Croft J.
    35395. "   Hamilton.T.H.
     1986. "   Hempsall.T.
   889575. "   Last.S.
    14511. "   Male.F.J.
    35414. "   Padgett.J.E.
    26400. "   Smith.W.
    97676. "   Starkey.E.
    35665. a/Bdr Burke.E.   Posted to Battery 22/9/17.
  L.25688. "   Cain.J.E.
    27622. "   Dixon.L.
     8982. "   Flack.A.
   124923. "   Richardson.H.
    27520. "   Stacey.I.
    26411. "   Speight.A.
    24033. "   Tilston.R.
   221602. "   Percy.K.
   889535. s/a/Bdr Gutteridge.A.
    78512. Cpl s/s Emms.A.
    26450. "   Sadd Clawson.J.J.
       42. "   Whlr Derbyshire.W.
    27533. S/S Hellewell.A.
    27497. " Innocent.R.
    27759. " Popplewell.G.
    27612. " Smith.J.
    26447. " Varney.J.
    78446. Saddlr Batley.A.
    26676.   "   Schofield.J.
   146171. Ftr Collar.P.A.
   128068. Gnr Allen.C.
     2097. " Blythe.W.
    19896. " Badger.G.
    46330. " Brown.P.H.
    50035. " Ball.C.C.
   192042. " Bishop.H.H.
    26385. " Boler.H.E.   Evacuated.Sick. 13/9/17.

889581.	Dvr	Cocker.B.	
889534.	"	Chittock.A.	
L.32488.	"	Dutton.J.W.	
889546.	"	Dalton.E.	
13985.	"	Donleavy.W.	
27621.	"	Denby.F.	
889535.	"	Driver.R.	
27606.	"	Fisher.A.	Posted to Battery. 5/9/17.
31333.	"	Faulkner.A.	
35381.	"	Guest W.	
19943.	"	Green.J.	
19803.	"	Greenwood.J.	
889556.	"	Garner.G.E.	
889555.	"	Gray.S.E	
26422.	"	Havenhand H.	
19953.	"	Howson.W.	
19749.	"	Hughes.W.	
889563.	"	Honeywood.B.	
27610.	"	Jewitt.W.	
35411.	"	Jackson.F.	
88935.	"	Kernon.J.	
203238.	"	Keates.C.	
35380.	"	Lunn.G.	
92590.	"	Llewelyn.T.	
69627.	"	Lewis.D.J.	
889570.	"	Lay.G.	
78643.	"	Marshall.R.E.	Evacuated Sick. 17/9/17.
5079.	"	Mc Laughlin.L.	To Base Dental Ttreatment. 26/9/17.
8328.	"	Lindley.A.	Transferred to 161st Bde. 4/9/17.
20085.	"	Luxford.R.T.	-ditto-
35376.	"	Lowe G.	Posted from 32nd D.A.C. 4/9/17.
231942.	"	O'Hara.J.	-ditto-
219699.	"	Oldfield.W.	"
889587.	"	Piper.W.	
19787	"	Peacock.J.C.	
27222.	"	Phillips.F.	
27624.	"	Roebuck.V.	
25691.	"	Rigg.J.	
889596.	"	Read.A.	
889595.	"	Rayner.L.	Evacuated Sick. 4/9/17.
103962.	"	Smith.J.	
110494.	"	Seabrook.J.H.	
29405.	"	Stewart.A.	
36406.	"	Savage.W.	
819001.	"	Soupham.B.A.	
27505.	"	Shone.W.	
27609.	"	Smith J.	
27600.	"	Sykes.J.W.	
889601.	"	Sustins.E.	
202441.	"	Turner.A.	
19736.	"	Thomson.A.D.	
202430.	"	Townsend.A.	
71271.	"	Thompson.J.G.W.	
171541.	"	Twist.G.	
889616.	"	Theobald.W.	
83586.	"	Toms.R.	
40493.	"	Tandy P.	
889612.	"	Taylor E.F.	
12031.	"	Wilkinson.J.W.	
27498.	"	Wright.D.	
19794.	"	Whelan.J.	
889631.	"	Whitehead.J.	
25718.	"	Wilson J.	
038.	Sergt	Moore.W. (A.V.C.).	

27589.	Gnr	Blood.J.A.	
201448.	"	Board.A.	
15049.	"	Cavanagh.J.	Transferred to C'71st.B.F.A.12/9/17.
185893.	"	Clarke.J.S.	
889531.	"	Cook.G.M.	
27596.	"	Dixon.H.A.	
889542.	"	Dunnett.J.	Killed in action.19/9/17.
7772.	"	Edwards.J.H.	Posted from 32nd.D.A.C. 24/9/17.
77578.	"	Edwards.M.	-ditto-.
233258.	"	Emery.W.G.	
27537.	"	Elsom.G.H.	Posted from 32nd.D.A.C. 22/9/17.
27175.	"	Fowler.A.S.	-ditto-
232842.	"	Hill.M.H.	
179512.	"	Garnham.A.C.	
104591.	"	Howard.A.	
19343.	"	Hellewell.G.W.	
148368.	"	Keene.T.C.	
185690.	"	Pearson.J.W.M.	
197075.	"	Lancaster.J.	
212536.	"	New H.	
889584.	"	Podd.C.R.	
86332.	"	Powell.H.	Evacuated Sick. 19/9/17.
19796.	"	Parkinson.G.H.	
131526.	"	Philcox.A.J.	
35052.	"	Powley.F.A.	Wounded and Evacuated. 11/9/17.
1307.	"	Petchley.C.	Evacuated Sick. 5/9/17.
212552.	"	Robins.A.S.	
20270.	"	Robinson.J.	Killed in action. 11/9/17.
901599.	"	Richardson.C.H.	
209455.	"	Snewing.J.W.	
144699.	"	Spratt.J.	
138464.	"	Sagar.R.	
851331.	"	R.F.Stirratt.	
26125.	"	Simmons.E.G.	
103314.	"	Samuels.R.	
956164.	"	Slyfield.J.	
156473.	"	Sherwin L.	
297097.	"	Smith.S.J.	
889603.	"	Simmons.W.	
135253.	"	Sartin.H.	
889604.	"	Smith.F.J.	
199469.	"	Tomlin.T.W.	
26463.	"	Townsend.A.V.	
92601.	"	Tully.J.	
106866.	"	Scatchard.G.	Wounded and Evacuated 19/9/17.
20016.	"	Thompson.J.	
696070.	"	Thomas.J.	
955804.	"	Tarrant A.E.	
38810.	"	Tinsley.G.	
190085.	"	Taylor A.	
35404.	"	Williams.J.	
889632.	"	Woodward.F.	
889624.	"	Wain F.	
19763.	Dvr	Armitage.G.	
35402.	"	Bainbridge.J.C.	
27757.	"	Battin.W.	
26491.	"	Bell.A.	
26524.	"	Bellamy.F.	
12107.	"	Bond.P.	
305852.	"	Barnforth.P.	
28059.	"	Barker.W.	Evacuated Sick. 1/9/17.
200771.	"	Birch.G.	
20007.	"	Bradley.J.	
217097.	"	Bush.H.H.	
889511.	"	Bell.C.	
889521.	"	Burn.A.	
889509.	"	Brightwell.E.	

CONFIDENTIAL.

WAR DIARY

of the

168th. BRIGADE, R. F. A.
-:0:-:0:-:0:-

from 1st. October 1917 to 31st Octr 1917.

(Volume 22.)

Army Form C. 2118.

WAR DIARY
or
INTELLIGENCE SUMMARY.
(Erase heading not required.)

168th Brigade R.F.A.
Commanded by Lt-Col. R. FITZMAURICE, D.S.O.

Instructions regarding War Diaries and Intelligence Summaries are contained in F.S. Regs., Part II. and the Staff Manual respectively. Title pages will be prepared in manuscript.

Place	Date	Hour	Summary of Events and Information	Remarks and references to Appendices
	Oct. 1.		D/168.R.F.A. carried out Aeroplane shoots on enemy bridges in vicinity of NIEUWENDAMME FORT. Two bridges damaged. Weather continued excellent. Enemy's Artillery fairly active and carried out a number of registered shoots by Aeroplane. 2nd Manchester's relieved 5/6th Royal Scots night of 1/2nd.	OK
	" 2nd		Weather still excellent. Enemy's Artillery very active against trenches on ST GEORGE'S Sector, our Artillery replied. D/168. continued to carry out a number of shoots with Aeroplane observation against enemy bridges. Results very successful. B/168 put one gun into a single gun position.	OK
	" 3rd		Weather good. Day very quiet.	OK
	" 4th		15th H.L.I. relieved 1st Dorsets on night 3/4th. D/168.put one gun into alternative position. Weather bad most of the day. Considerable amount of rain.	OK
	" 5th		Weather showery and windy. Fair Intervals. 125th Infantry Bde relieved the 97th Infantry Bde in the LOMBARTZYDE Sector.	OK
	" 6th		Cold and wet day for the most part. 126th Infantry Brigade relieved the 14th Infantry Brigade in the ST GEORGE'S Sector.	OK
	" 7th		Cold and wet. Little Artillery activity on both sides. 42nd Division less Artillery took over from 32nd Division less Artillery.	OK
	" 8th		Cold and wet. Little Artillery activity on both sides.	OK
	" 9th		Very quiet day. Preparations for withdrawal from action.	OK
	" 10th	8.pm	Batteries are relieved by 210th Brigade. R.F.A. 42nd Division and withdraw from action to Wagon Lines at COXYDE.	OK
	" 11th		Brigade marched to GHYVELDE.	OK

Army Form C. 2118.

WAR DIARY
or
INTELLIGENCE SUMMARY.
(*Erase heading not required.*)

168th Brigade R.F.A.
Commanded by Lt-Col.R.FITZMAURICE.D.S.O.

Instructions regarding War Diaries and Intelligence Summaries are contained in F. S. Regs., Part II. and the Staff Manual respectively. Title pages will be prepared in manuscript.

Place	Date	Hour	Summary of Events and Information	Remarks and references to Appendices
	12/X/17		Brigade remains at GHYVELDE and spends the time in generally cleaning up and overhauling.	AL
	13/X/17.		Batteries remain at GHYVELDE. Weather glorious.	AL
	14/X/17.		Day spent in general cleaning up, and preparing for the march.	AL
	15/X/17.			AL
	16/X/17.	5.30.am	The Brigade marched from GHYVELDE to WORMHOUDT. Brigade and Battery Commanders went by bus to reconnoitre the positions of 256th Brigade R.F.A. north of ST JULIEN.	AL
	17/X/17.	8.am	Batteries marched from WORMHOUDT to temporary lines at A.28. (Sheet 28). Personnel of Batteries proceeded by bus and relieved the Batteries of the 256th Brigade R.F.A. in action north of ST JULIEN. Brigade H.Q. established on the bank of the Canal C.25.a.8.7 (Sheet.28).	AL
	18/X/17.		Batteries marched to Wagon Lines in B.26.b. (Sheet 28).and are attached to 'A' GROUP 18th Div Artillery. Brigade H.Q. remain out of action.	AL
	19/X/17.		Preparations carried out for forthcoming attack. Ammunition supply entirely by pack animals.	AL
	20/X/17.		Bombardments of enemy's positions carried out.	AL
	21/X/17.		Bombardments continued.	AL
	22/X/17.	5,30.am	Batteries took part in an attack made by the 18th Division on POELCAPPELLE, which was very successful. Number of rounds fired between 20/X/17 and 22/X/17 18-Pdrs 9000 rds 4.5" Hows. 2610 rounds.	AL

Army Form C. 2118.

WAR DIARY
or
INTELLIGENCE SUMMARY.

168th Brigade R.F.A.
Commanded by Lt-Col.R.FITZMAURICE.D.S.O.

(Erase heading not required.)

Instructions regarding War Diaries and Intelligence Summaries are contained in F. S. Regs., Part II. and the Staff Manual respectively. Title pages will be prepared in manuscript.

Place	Date	Hour	Summary of Events and Information	Remarks and references to Appendices
	23/X/17.		Enemy's bombing planes very active in this area.	OK
	24/X/17.	5.30.am.	Very wet. 48 hours bombardment commenced.	OK
	25/X/17.	10.am	58th Div: relieved the 18th Div: on the front covered by Batteries of the 168th Brigade R.F.A. Day very wild.	OK
	26/X/17.		Batteries took part in an attack made by the 58th Division east of POELCAPPELLE. The weather was very wet. Ammunition expended between 23/X/17 and 26/X/17, 18-Pdrs 9726 rds, 4.5" Hows 2880 rds.	OK
	27/X/17.		Quiet day.	OK
	28/X/17.		Bombardments of enemy's positions carried out.	OK
	29/X/17.			OK
	30/X/17.		Batteries took part in an attack made by the 58th Division east of POELCAPPELLE. Ammunition expended between 27/X/17 and 30/X/17-18-Pdrs 5934 rds, 4.5" Hows 1734 rds. 1 Howitzer of D/168.R.F.A. blown up by a Premature.	OK
	31/X/17.		Day very fine and quiet.	OK
			Total casualties during the month, 2 Officers & 71 Other ranks wounded. 10 " killed, & 1 Missing.	OK

Ashmaurice Lieut - Colonel.
Commanding 168th Brigade R. F. A.

Headquarters Staff.   -:O:-   168th Brigade R.F.A.

NOMINAL ROLL OF ALL RANKS FOR MONTH OF OCTOBER 1917.

Officers :- Lt - Colonel.R.FITZMAURICE.D.S.O
Captain ALAN LUMB.
Lieut HAROLD FISHER
Lieut HAROLD.L.JAMES
Capt.D.FERGUSON.(R.A.M.C.)

Other ranks:-

1362 R.S.M.McGowan.M.C.
L.25839.Cpl Lee.G.
L.25881.Bdr Gibson.H.
  29811. " Anderton.A.
  12245 a/Bdr Wright.J.
L.29430. " Sugden.E.
L.28042. " Eyre.F.
L.28206.Gnr Akroyd.H.
L.25910. " Bottomley.C.
  59688. " Clark.B.J.
L.29404. " Greenwood.C.
  56777. " Grindley W.
L.25626. " Slater.H.
L.29296. " Windle.A.T.
L.27581. " Postlethwaite.T.
L.25422.Dvr Armitage.J.
L.32440. " Baker.G.
L.32450. " Blake.F.
L. 5742. " Dickenson.J.
198817. " Foote.G.
  1573. " Gutteridge.A.
  35766. " Hirons.E.
L.5855. " Gowan.W.
L.32511. " Iredale.E.A.
L.25825. " Iredale.A.E.
L.28129. " Meller.A.
L.28132. " Martin.J.
  79511. " Mc Intyre.T.
L.29424. " Parker.J.
L.25853. " Radley.T.
L.29357. " Reddington.M.
L.29389. " Stansfield.P.
  6267. s/s Periera.A.T.
  1305 Sadd Williams.T.

A.O.C.Staff Sergt Barker.H. (Artificer).

'A' Battery.   -:0:-   168th Brigade R.F.A.

NOMINAL ROLL OF ALL RANKS. 1/11/17.

Officers:- Major R.EMMET.
          Capt.G.O.d'IVRY.
          Lieut.L.A.RAVALD.
          "   W.A.EBBELS.
          2/Lieut.J.WEEDON.
          "   F.J.CLARKE.

Other Ranks:-

Number	Rank	Name	Remarks
L.18467.	B.S.M.	Stephenson.C.	
L.28064.	BQMS.	Brearley.H.	
L.25426.	Sergt	Field.P.J.	
L.25679.	"	Roberts.J.T.	
43312.	"	McGowan.A.H.	
L.25425.	"	Firth.A.	Wounded and evacuated 20/10/17.
53261.	"	Smith.E.F.	-ditto-
L.32584.	"	Williams.W.	
L.25679.	Cpl	Rhodes L.	Wounded in action 30/X/17.
L.25561.	"	Povey.J.	Evacuated Wounded 12/9/17.
L.25619.	"	France W.	
L.29407.	"	Taylor.F.	Proceed to Base 8/10/17.
L.29312.	"	Armitage W.B.	
1985.	"	Harding.R.C.	
81562.	"	Jackson.R.	Posted from 32nd.D.A.C. 3/10/17. Wounded and evacuated 24/10/17.
41257.	"	Fitzpatrick.F.	Posted from 32nd Div Supply Park
1105.	"	Witney.T.	Posted to 42nd.D.A. 8/X/17.
86310.	"	Squires.A.E.	
L.28100.	Bdr	Bentley.J.	
L.32479.	"	Pitchforth A:	
L:25708.	"	Crawshaw.J.T.	
L.25574.	"	Whiteley.C.H.	
L.25414.	"	Wood.B.	Killed in action. 20/10/17.
L.25731.	"	Rhodes J.	
L.28188.	"	Padgett.S.	
L.25464.	"	Richardson.G.H.	Admitted to hos'l Shell Shock 20/X/17
83594.	"	Simpson.C.	
L.28034.	"	Beevers.M.	
169899.	a/Bdr	Halliday.R.	Wounded in action 24/10/17.
L.32539.	"	Fenton.E.	
54101.	"	Perkins.F.J.	
L.29297.	"	Noble.C.	Wounded in action 20/10/17.
L.32523.	"	Phillipson.R.	
L.28126.	"	Shaw.N	
L.28174.	"	Tetlow.H.	Wounded in action 23/10/17
L.28217.	"	Bower.E.	
167074.	"	McGeachie.J.	
W.2815.	"	Rice E.F.	Admitted to hos'l Shell shock 20/X/
L.25536.	s/a/Bdr	Mansfield.W.G.	Wounded in action 24/10/17.
167423.	"	Sweet.J	
L.32449.	Far Sgt	Andrews.R.	
L.25783.	Cpl.s/s	Town E.	
765.	" "	Parks.J.	Killed in action 28/10/17.
L.29282.	S/S	Nuttal.G.T.	
L.28175.	"	Waterhouse L.	
L.25690.	"	Kaye.J.T.	
173878.	"	Ackroyd.C.	
L.32485.	Sadd	Jackson.W.R.	
62728.	"	Oliver J.	

12
X

154173.	Sadd	Skipp.J.W.	
147472.	Ftr	Hellewell.A.	Posted to C/168.R.F.A. 24/10/17.
72465.	"	Bambrough.R.	Wounded and evacuated 24/10/17.
42821.	"	Norton.A.	Admitted to hospital now evac'd 18/X/17
121451.	Whlr	Weaver J.	
L.25790.	Bnr	Allet.C V.	
221345.	"	Alston.D.	
10574.	"	Alford.C.	
L.25575.	"	Billington.T.	
100556.	"	Beamish.R.	
100774.	"	Baird.S.	
L.29379.	"	Beaumont.L.	Wounded and evacuated 20/10/17.
L.25768.	"	Brooksbank.S.	
202446.	"	Birrel.W.	
92721.	"	Black.W.	
651912.	"	Bruten.A.G.	
222460.	"	Birks.F.	
115729.	"	Bell E.N.	Posted from 32.nd.D.A.C. 19/10/17.
L.32471.	"	Calvert.F.	
L.29345.	"	Craigie.F.	
132664.	"	Curd.W.A.	
5556.	"	Chappel.A.	
190397.	"	Cross.F.	
212321.	"	Crawford D.	
L.28178.	"	Dawson.W.	Wounded and evacuated 26/10/17.
12049.	"	Edwards.L.	
130451.	"	Edwards.W.H.	Wounded and evacuated 12/10/17.
86276.	"	Franklin.A.	
190415.	"	Foote.G.	
15256.	"	Fearn.H.	
L.25472.	"	Green.N.	
L 25823.	"	Hynes.W.H.	Wounded and evacuated.19/10/17.
226993.	"	Hancox.H.P.	
18757.	"	Hart.C.	
733.	"	Keighley.F.J.	
L.32512.	"	Lumb.W.	Admitted hos'l Shell Shock 20/X/17.
184485.	"	Lewis.E.J.	
L.28177.	"	Leatham.F.	
197866.	"	Mc Ewing.H.	Wounded in action. 25/10/17.
159371.	"	McCarthy E.	
168568.	"	Miller.W.	
197863.	"	McPherson.A.	Wounded and evacuated 24/10/17.
150416.	"	Mallet.H.	
L 28129.	"	Marshall.L.	
L.25392.	"	Milnes.H.	Transferred to C/168.R.F.A. 24/X/17.
L.25443.	"	Nuttal.P.	
44251.	"	Offen.F.	
192477.	"	Ormiston.A.	
L.29306.	"	Pearson.F.	Wounded in action Evac'd 19/10/17.
L.28186.	"	Perkins.J.E.	
L.25653.	"	Rushworth.A.	Wounded and evacuated 19/10/17.
211705.	"	Robinson.H.	
199083.	"	Roskilly.P.	
224342.	"	Rockett.B.	
66262.	"	Rhodes A.E.	
L.32491.	"	Roberts.J.	
L.25566.	"	Smith.A.	
L.28006.	"	Singleton.H.W.	
126034.	"	Spence R.	
81446.	"	Slack.H.	Wounded and evacuated 24/10/17.
L.25735.	"	Spencer H.	
221089.	"	Soloman.L.	Wounded and evacuated 12/10/17.
821657.	"	Swadling.A.	
22365.	"	Speed.A.	
150668.	"	Schaefer.A.	
38812.	"	Symonds.H.	Wounded and evacuated. 20/10/17.
156164.	"	Sargent.C.	
L.25771.	"	Thornton.J.	
30526.	"	Thorpe.W.J.	
L.29355.	"	Townend.J.	Admitted hospital Evac'd 3/10/17.
L.32535.	"	Thornber.W.H.	

L.28088. Gnr Wilkinson.T.		Killed in action 24/10/17.
L.29300. " Wood.F.		
L.32441. " Walker.A.		
L.29318. " Wood.R.		
L.25649. " Wood.C.E.		
L.25485. " Williams.G.		
133713. " Young.W.		
19805. " Yates.W.		
234892. " Woeff.F.L		

175251. Dvr Adams.F.		
L.25524. " Bamforth.H		
L.25525. " Bray.H.		
L.25436. " Brearley.A.		
L.25395. " Brook.G.L.		
L.25658. " Chapman.B.		
L.29323 " Crowther.J.G.		
109981. " Chapman.H.		
41489. " Crisp.E.	Wounded and evacuated 19/10/17.	
L.29409. " Dyson.W.		
L.28079. " Green.F.		
L.25820. " Ganley.J.		
L.29316. " Gledhill.J.R.		
L.25579. " Griffiths.T.C.		
L.28201. " Horsfall.E.		
L.25849. " Holmes.E.		
L.28153. " Harrison.F.		
L.29347. " Hardcastle.C.W.		
93514. " Hartley.A.		
L.32541. " Kershaw.C.		
L.25419. " Kerton.E.		
L.28161. " Lodge.A.		
L.28021. " Mallinson.A.		
L.25639. " Millard.H.		
826369. " Morse.L.		
L.35046. " Marshall.R.		
204732. " Malbon.H.		
101698 " O'Neill.J.		
147602. " Orris.H.		
L.32464. " Pogson.S.		
35864. " Quinn.D.		
L.28074. " Robertshaw.G.		
L.28075. " Roe.F.		
L.28013. " Sykes.W.		
99859. " Spencer.P.G.		
L.25632. " Shaw.E.		
L.25503. " Shaw.H.		
L.28224 " Shaw.C.A.		
L.25797. " Singleton.V.		
L.25450. " Smith.J.R.		
186514. " Smith.W.J.	To hospital Evacuated 20/10/17.	
217881. " Shotten.R.		
219990. " Tall.F.		
74290. " Tanner.A.		
L.28101. " Taylor.T.H.		
L.25483. " Varley.L.	Missing 19/10/17.	
L.25650. " Wood.A.		
10586. " Westgate.F.	Wounded and evacuated 19/10/17.	
L.29331. " Woodcock.W.		
L.28087. " Walters.H.		
L.25394. " Wortley,T.		
L.25541. " Woodhead.E.		
L.25819. " Whitehead.J.A.		
159419. " Weeden.W.		
21116. " Wainwright.W.C.		
L.28214. " Wood.W.N.		
SE.1514. Sgt Jolly.A.J.	Posted to No.2.Vet Hospital 21/10/17.	
SE14113. S/Sgt Sweet.W. attached.	Posted to A/168 from No.2.Vet Hospital 20/10/17.	

'B' Battery.   168th Brigade R.F.A.

NOMINAL ROLL OF ALL RANKS 1/11/17.
- - - - - - - - - - - - - - - -

Officers:- Major.F.FITZGIBBON.D.S.O.
            Captain.L.M.HASTINGS.MC.
            Lieut.W.P.ROBINSON.
            2/Lieut W.L.CHAMBERLIN
            2/Lieut.J.MITCHELHILL
            2/Lieut.C.P.BASNETT.   Suffering from Shell Gas
            2/Lieut.S.A.STOREY.   20/X/17.

Other Ranks:-

   58482. B.S.M.Stenning.T.
 L.32437. B.Q.M.S. Lane.A.C.
 L.32514. Far Sergt Sutcliffe.R.
 L.25548. Sergt Beaumont.F.
 L.25599.   "   Crooks.H.
 L.29344.   "   Gutherie.A.
 L.28210.   "   Greenwood M.R.
 L.25874.   "   Shaw.L.
   98737. Cpl s/s Brennan.J.
 L.28138. Corpl Bramley.S.M.
 L 25693.   "   Littlewood.K.
 L.28076.   "   Murray.A.
   24990.   "   Mayers.A.   Wounded in action 23/10/17.
 L.25491.   "   Sherwood.J.T.
 L.29826.   "   Temperton.H.K.
 L.12248.   "   Vincent.H.
 L.25871.   "   Walker S.
 L.25446. Bdr Bottomley.T.
 L.32480.   "   Bancroft L.
  125511.   "   Christie.H.
   79093.   "   Drewitt.W.C.   Admitted to hospital evac'd 20/10/17.
 L.25472.   "   Dyson.F.
 L.25746.   "   Hargreaves.A.
 L.25545.   "   Turner J.   To hos'l Gas Shell 30/X/17.
 L.25451.   "   Spendlove.T.
 L.25808. a/Bdr Broomhead.W.H.
   16381.   "   Cawthorne.J.
 L.32576.   "   Bentley.T.
  152375.   "   Holmes.N.
 L.29403.   "   Horrocks.H.
 L.25547.   "   Ibbotson.M.
   11578.   "   Gouldsmith.S.O.
  115275.   "   Leach.A.
 L.29382.   "   Riley.A.
 L.25463.   "   Scott.N
    5035. S/S Boswell.H.
 L.32549.   "   Berry.A.
 L.25552.   "   Hoyle.C.
 L.25510   "   Readyhough.G.W.
 L.25452.   "   Sidebottom.J.
 L.32552.   "   Wilson.J.W.
 L.25747. Sadd Brooksbank.G.
 L.25607.   "   Stansfield.F.
 L.25596. Whlr Yates F.
 L.32456. Ftr Hill.W.   To Hos'l Shell Gas 30/X/17.
  785047. Gnr Ball.T.H.
 L.25382.   "   Ainley.W.H.   Posted from R.H.& R.F.A. 16/10/17.

162912.	Gnr	Allen.T.W.	
223019.	"	Bell.S.	Posted from 32nd.D.A.C. 20/10/17. (To Hos'l Shell Gas 30/X/17.
229157.	"	Belfield.S.	To Hos'l Shell Gas 30/X/17.
156556.	"	Benton H.J.	
168329.	"	Bevan.J.G.	
L.25616	"	Billington.H.	
L.32483.	"	Binns.A.O.	
L.32521.	"	Bottoms.H.	
L.29265.	"	Broadley.J.T.	
18820.	"	Brown.F.	
8993.	"	Blake.A.	
211607.	"	Bone.E.W.	
211547.	"	Bush.A.J.	
211574.	"	Cartwright.H.J.	
211662.	"	Cheeseman.A.	
120237.	"	Charman.H.	
162927 205152.	"	Clarke.H.	
205152.	"	Cooke.W.	
182839.	"	Cousins.A.T.	
L.25671.	"	Cocker.F.	
2295.	"	Coward.T.	
L.29283.	"	Dewar.W.	To Hos'l Shell Gas 30/X/17.
68234.	"	Doggett.J.	
L.29263.	"	Fowler.B.	
93752.	"	Farmer.H.	
198809.	"	Gigg.B.	
L.29262.	"	Greenwood.L.A.	
L.29380.	"	Hansen.E.	
L.32454.	"	Hargreaves.D.	
L.25664.	"	Hartley.A.	Posted from R.H.&.R.F.A. 16/10/17.
11819.	"	Harris.G.	
L.28046.	"	Holdsworth.A.	
218427.	"	Irvine.L.	
L.25428.	"	Kiddle.F.	
L.32510.	"	Knight.S.	
L.25562.	"	Lawford.F.	
L.28220.	"	Laycock.A.	
L.25623.	"	Lee.F.	To hos'l Shell Gas 30/X/17.
160940.	"	Leng.J.	
L.25622.	"	Littlewood.H.	
197864.	"	Mc Pherson..D.	
L.28126.	"	Mallinson.F.	
164025.	"	Miller.L.	
L.29400.	"	Mitchell.D.	Wounded in action 20/10/17.
L.32544.	"	Mitchelhill.R.	
221036.	"	Mole.T.	
197395.	"	Mullard.G.H.	
188576.	"	Nash.J.T.	
156134.	"	Nightingale.D.	
L.25632.	"	Onyon.A.	To Hos'l Shell Gas 20/X/17
2358.	"	Platt.H	To Hos'l Gas Shell 28/X/17.
L.25827.	"	Riddlesden.A.	
46249.	"	Scott.F.J.	To Hos'l Gas Shell 30/X/17
159803.	"	Shaw.J.A.	To Hos'l Gas Shell 29/X/17
L.5824.	"	Spence.D.	To hos'l Shell Gas 20/X/17.
165748.	"	Stannage.J.W.	
L.32473.	"	Stafford.H.	
L.29372.	"	Tidswell.H.T.	
L.25683.	"	Thompson.J.T.	
67704.	"	Tunstall.A.	
L.25629.	"	Turner.H	
208386.	"	Rix.H.	
221070.	"	Rogers.S.R.	To Hos'l Shell Gas 30/X/17.
176283.	"	Ritchie.G.	
L.25727.	"	Winteringham.E.	
150477.	"	Woolf.C.H.	To hos'l Shell Gas 28/X/17.

L.29381.	Dvr Barraclough.H.	
L.29258.	" Barraclough.T.E.	
L.28213.	" Beaumont.H.	
L.28199.	" Berry.A.	
L.25837.	" Berry.S.	
L.32528.	" Barrissow.F.	
L.32566.	" Braithwaite J.F.	
L.25470.	" Brook.J.W.	
185735.	" Chesters.D.	
L.25878.	" Clear.A.	
L.28113.	" Crossley.J.	
L.32518.	" Crowther.H.	
L.25446.	" Davies.J.	
112102.	" Dennis.S.	
L.25442.	" Eastwood.G.	
L.25732.	" Firth.H.	
L.32538.	" Gray.D.	
L.29367.	" Greenwood.J.W.	
L.25728.	" Greenwood.C.	
1396.	" Green.R.	
L.25831.	" Hall.H.	
L.28204.	" Harrison.F.	
L.25479.	" Hattersley.F.	
L.25822.	" Hincliffe.A.	
L.25558.	" Hobson.A.	
L.32524.	" Horthornthwaite.T.	Evacuated 15/10/17.
L.32506.	" Holmes.W.	
L.32447.	" Jackson.P.	
L.28070.	" Jewett.J.H.	
L.29270.	" Ledgard.E.	
L.23748.	" Leckenby.J.	
79005.	" Lynch.P.	
217555.	" Mackie.J.	
L.28077.	" Martin.L.	
219114.	" Markham.C.	
930739.	" Mathis.M.C.	
81569.	" Mayers.F.	
L.28066.	" Medley.O.	
152302.	" Milner.J.	
47044.	" McCormick.A.	
L.29401.	" Moody.A.	
121959.	" Morley.A.T	
L.28127.	" Mellor.H.	Wounded in action 27/X/17.
L.25870.	" Murray.R.	
213085.	" Newns.A.	
L.25675.	" Nicholson.J.	
L.28194.	" North.M.	
73229.	" Parnaby.W.	
L.28071.	" Robinson.F.	
5116.	" Roberts.G.	
L.25861.	" Robinson.T.	
L.25512.	" Robinson.W.J.	
L.25730.	" Rushworth.E.	
20609.	" Ray.D.	Evacuated Posted to 298thA.F.Bde.X/X/17.
L.25625.	" Scott.J.J.	
L.28041.	" Scholefield.J.	
L.25624.	" Senior.G.	
203373.	" Sharples.J.E.	
L.32579.	" Shepherd N.	
L.25454.	" Snell.A.	
L.29397.	" Southwell.J.	
L.28090.	" Stanton.A.	
L.25644.	" Singleton.L.M.	Evacuated 4/10/17.
180180.	" Tooth.V.S.	
L 25569.	" Turner.J.	
2088.	" Turner.J.	
L.25866.	" Townsend.H.	
L.25598.	" Townsend.W.	
L.25499.	" Tallis.G.	

```
L.32515.   Dvr Wilkinson.L.
L.29257.    "  Wilkinson.L.F.
 185398.    "  Willat.W.
 164826.    "  Williams.E.
L.29269.    "  Wood.H.
 141214.    "  Worth.W.D.
L.28089.    "  Wright.F.


   8949. Vet Sgt White.F.A. attached.
```

'C' Battery.   —:0:—   168th Brigade R.F.A.

NOMINAL ROLL OF ALL RANKS 1/11/17.

Officers:— Major. HERBERT COTTEE. DSO.
Captain. B.T. GROVES.
2/Lt G.O.J. BARRICK.
2/Lt S.J. HINTON. MC.
2/Lt C.A. ANELAY.
2/Lt H R.M. RONALDSON.

Other Ranks:—

53473.	B.S.M.	Malone.M.J.	
L. 5688.	BQMS.	Tomlinson.H.	
L.12004.	Sergt	Turgoose.W.	
22239.	"	Fitzgerald.W.	
L.28195.	"	Garside.I.	
L.25711.	"	Kirkham.T.	
L.19481.	Corpl.	Ward.J.S.	
L.27727.	"	Ward.A.S.	Wounded and evacuated 27/10/17.
L.28121.	"	Palmer.R.	
L 19484.	"	Bailey.B.C.	
L.11993.	"	Holdroyd.T.	
L.25473.	"	Earnshaw.S.	
L.25812.	"	Terry.L.	
L.19479.	Bombr	Wardle.L.M.	
L.19478.	"	Todd.J.A.	
L.12016.	"	Maguire.T.F.J.	
19830.	"	Goldsbrough.L.	
L.27730.	"	Walton.H.	
L.29414.	"	Elliott.C.H.	
L.19519.	"	Milnthorpe.G.	
L.19487.	"	Carr.W.C.	
L.11962.	"	Wilcock.J.	
L.28010.	"	Steele.J.W.	
L.28200.	"	Brook.J.	
138424.	a/Bdr	Kirkham.	
L.11959.	"	Ellis.W.R.	
L.12035.	"	Wathy.A.	
935644.	"	Seymour.W.	
L. 2285.	"	Lewis.E.W.	
50143.	"	Smith.T.	
115097.	"	Muste.W.T	
48296.	Far Sgt	Key.J.	
L.25954.	Cpl s/s	Chappel.E.	
L.11926.	S/S	Fletcher.F.	
L.27751.	"	Bailey.H.	
L.11934.	"	Ismay.T.H.	
107905.	"	Copping.H.E.	
63915.	"	Irving.W.A.	
L.12041.	"	Kershaw.H.	
L.14862.	Whlr	Pringle.E.	
L.11937.	Sadd	Hall.T.	
143669.	"	Heron.R.	
45372.	Gnr	Anderson.F.	Slightly Wounded 21/10/17.
174032.	"	Arnold.J.T.	
129105.	"	Bolster.A.G.	
42449.	"	Berbridge.W.J.	
L.11973.	"	Booth.J.	
L.11994.	"	Barr.J.	
L.12026.	"	Beach.J.	
L.11979.	"	Brady.B.	
L.19485.	"	Briggs.E.J.	
45377.	"	Baker.J.	

6521.	Gnr	Braid.H.K.	Admitted to hospital Sick Evac'd 23/X/17.
685266.	"	Brown.T.	
235293.	"	Betteley.A.	
L.28147.	"	Chapman.T.	
147114.	"	Creeper.H.	
196150.	"	Cooke.F.	
830528.	"	Carter.G.H.	Killed in action 20/X/17.
L.25702.	"	Denton.F.	
217908.	"	Dykes.W.P.	Posted from 32nd D.A.C. 19/9/17.
209056.	"	Bird.J.H.	Posted from 32nd. D.A.C. "
L.12017.	"	Farmery.J.W.	Wounded and evacuated 20/X/17.
78830.	"	Fraser.J.	
37084.	"	Gale.S.E.	Wounded & evacuated 28/X/17.
163921.	"	Gerrett.G.W.	
197894.	"	Grummitt.A.	Wounded and evacuated 21/X/17.
163727.	"	Goddard.W.E.	
88771.	"	Hall.N.	Hospital Sick Evacuated 23/X/17.
L.19490.	"	Horner.C.	
34446.	"	Hutt.R.	Killed in action 20/X/17.
89444.	"	Holden.F.	
L.25751.	"	Higgins.H.	Wounded in action 28-X-17.
110744.	"	Huggett T.	-ditto-
2933.	"	Hesford.A.	
32657.	"	Horder.W.	Admitted hospital Evac'd 20/10/17.
L.12020.	"	Inman.H.	Wounded and evacuated 22/10/17.
205331.	"	Imeson.T.E.	
L.12011.	"	Jolley.W.	
L.19809.	"	James.T.	
L.11932.	"	Mulheir.J.W.	
L.12002.	"	Newell.E.M.	
206785.	"	Procter.H.	
L.11971.	"	Parkin.W.	
190804.	"	Shaw.N.	To hospital Sick Evacuated 23/10/17.
L:19496.	"	Saberton.H.	
L.27999.	"	Spittle.T.	
13907.	"	Swinn.J.	
1268.	"	Sellars.G.	
67727.	"	Smith.J.F.	
12965.	"	Smith.W.E.	
933803.	"	Smith.W.A.	
32267.	"	Smith.A.	Wounded and evac'd 28-X-17
123842.	"	Sutton.E.T.	
13469.	"	Robinson.A.E.	
217663.	"	Thompson.R.	Killed in action 28-X-17
L.25715.	"	Taylor.J.T.	
306519.	"	Turner.S.	Wounded and evac'd 28-X-17
229565.	"	Wall.A.	Killed in action 23/10/17.
L.19502.	"	Wales.A.T.	
L.12003.	"	Waldron.T.	
L.19717.	"	Wardle.G.H.	
208477.	"	Woodman.H.	
219005.	"	Ward.L.T.	
46846.	"	Young.J.T.	
L.12002.	Dvr	Ainsworth.H.	
200790.	"	Bell.J.T.	
821420.	"	Beall.W.A.	
L.11919.	"	Backhouse G.H.	
L 11942.	"	Boulton.P.	
221666.	"	Brown.J.T.	
L.11980.	"	Burnley.W.S.	
15220.	"	Bury.A.	
105511.	"	Blackhurst.H.	
123532.	"	Bearman.A.	
L.11982.	"	Clarke.E.W.	
L.28232.	"	Chapman.J.	
118327.	"	Cleaver E.R.	
L.29291.	"	Drake.G.	
L 28107.	"	Ellis.H.	
L.11969.	"	Ewbank.J.A.	
31531.	"	Easten.W.	
L.12055.	"	Farmery.T.	

L.19506.	Dvr	Fretwell.H.	
22242.	"	Fitch.E.J.	
211982.	"	Flint.S.	Posted from 32nd.D.A.C. 15/10/17.
L 12037.	"	Garfitt.J.T.	
L.19520.	"	Garfoot.E.	
L.11941.	"	Hart.W.	
L.11967.	"	Hancock.N.	
L.19510.	"	Horsfall.E.	
L.19509.	"	Hudson.J.	
L.11929.	"	Kemp.R.	
L.19492.	"	Lapish.J.	
L.19513.	"	Lamb.M.	
L.28051.	"	Lawton.H.	
L.29285.	"	Lord.J.	
218502.	"	Leeves A.E.	
L.11919.	"	Marshall.S.	
L.18909.	"	Mitchell W.	
85571.	"	O'keefe.J.A.	
6074.	"	Overland.H.	
75445.	"	Pipe.E.	
L.27691.	"	Poynton.G.W.	
2869.	"	Price.W.	
L.19516.	"	Priestley.B.	
L.28031.	"	Parkin.H.	
L.25850.	"	Pogson.H.	
40357.	"	Powell B.A.	
41796.	"	Peckham.L.	
L.12011.	"	Roberts.E.W.	
L 11965.	"	Ross.C.A.	
826655.	"	Schilling.R.M.	
177610.	"	Scott.H.	
132504.	"	Studley.F.	
L.19487.	"	Schoefield.W.	
L.12033.	"	Senior.F.K.	Wounded and evacuated 20/X/17.
120413.	"	Shipman.H.	
L.29293.	"	Sutcliffe.W.	
L.28149.	"	Scott.J.R.	
L.20448.	"	Singleton.N.	
L.27993.	"	Senior.J.W.	
186618.	"	Stride.W.	
L.27747.	"	Toothill.A.C.	
32459.	"	Turner.H.	
L.28095.	"	Turner.A.B.	
8397.	"	Troutt.W.	Evacuated 20/10/17.
L.12008.	"	Wales.A.	
L.12021.	"	Walshaw.E.	
L.12006.	"	Wrigglesworth.F.	
L.28169.	"	Williams.J.	
L 28124.	"	Walton.R.	
L.29322.	"	White.L.	
51913.	"	Wareham.E.	
145487.	"	Wilson.W:J.	
2410.	"	Wheeler.W.	
L.11978.	"	Williams.H.	
211022.	"	Woodward.C.S.	
2489.	AVC Sergt	Harding.W.	attached.

'D' Battery.   —:0:—   168th Brigade R.F.A.

NOMINAL ROLL OF ALL RANKS 1/11/17.

Officers:— Major.J.C.POOLE. M.C.
Lieut G.C.WOOD. M.C.
Capt.R.DUNBAR.   Wounded & evac'd 23/X/17.
2/Lt C.A.BROWNE.
2/Lt B.J.VALLANCE.

Other Ranks:—

21136.	B.S.M.	Leahy J.	Posted from R.H.& R.F.A. 18/10/17.
950107.	BQMS.	Jeffrey.S.A.	
100360.	Far Sgt	Greenwood.W.	
11948.	Sergt	Allen.A.J.	
35409.	"	Dinsdale.J.	
11965.	"	Hawkes.T.G.H.	
25606.	"	Palframan.F.	
19914.	"	Wooffitt.F.E.	
27601.	Cpl	Archer.S.T.	
27756.	"	Bonner.S.	
26452.	"	Bellamy.W.	
35389.	"	Dobson.J.E.	
889565.	"	Jackson.A.A	
889591.	"	Philpot.J.E.	Posted from 32nd.D.A.C. 2/10/17.
19919.	"	Scholey.E.	Wounded in action 30/X/17. Evac'd
27590.	Bdr	Bradford.J.	
889522.	"	Barker.W.	Wounded in action 30/X/17.
35390.	"	Beckett.E.	
20008.	"	Croft.J.	
35395.	"	Hamilton.T.H.	
1986.	"	Hempsall.T.	
889575.	"	Last.S.	
14511.	"	Male.F.G.	
35414.	"	Padgett.J.E.	
26400.	"	Smith.W.	
97676.	"	Starkey.E.	
35665.	a/Bdr	Burke.C.	Wounded in action 30/X/17.
L.25688.	"	Cain.J.E.	Killed in action 30/X/17.
27622.	"	Dixon.L.	
8982.	"	Flack.A.	
24083.	"	Tilston.R.	
124923.	"	Richardson.H.	
27520.	"	Stacey.I.	
221366.	"	Sugar.C.	
26411.	"	Speight.A.	
221602.	"	Percy.K.	
889535.	s/a/Bdr	Gutteridge.A.	
78512.	Cpl S/S	Emms.A.	
26450.	" Sadd	Clawson.J.J.	
42.	" Whlr	Derbyshire.W.	
27533.	S/S	Hellewell.A.	
27759.	"	Popplewell.G.	
27612.	"	Smith.J.	
26447.	"	Varney.J.	
78446.	Sadd	Batley.A.	
146171,	Ftr	Collar.P.A.	
128068.	Gnr	Allen.C.	
2097.	"	Blythe W.	Wounded in action 30/X/17.
19896.	"	Badger.G.	

	46330.	Gnr Brown.P.H.	
	50035.	" Ball.G.C.	Wounded in action 29-X-17
	192042.	" Bishop.H H.	
	112332.	" Burlingham.J.	Posted from 32nd.D.A.C. 7/10/17. Killed in action 30/X/17.
201448.	~~27582~~	" Board.A.	Wounded in action 29/X/17.
	27589.	" Blood.A.	Wounded in action 26/X/17. Evac'd
	206877.	" Corran.G.	Posted from 32nd.D.A.C. 7/10/17.
	185893.	" Clarke.J.S.	
	2486.	" Curtis.J.	Wounded in action 24/10/17.
	889531.	" Cook.G.M.	Wounded in action 28/X/17.
	27596.	" Dixon.H.A.	~~Wounded in action 28/X/17~~
	7772.	" Edwards.J.H.	
	77578.	" Edwards.J.M.	
	223258.	" Emery W.G.	
	27537.	" Elsom.G.H.	
	27175.	" Fowller.A.S.	
	179512.	" Garnham.A.E.	
	232842.	" Hill.M.H.	Wounded in action 21/10/17.
	104591.	" Howard.A.	Wounded in action 30/X/17.
	19848.	" Hellewell.G.W.	
	148368.	" Keene.G.W.	
	197075.	" Lancaster.J.	
	78643.	" Marshall.R.E.	Killed in action 30/X/17.
	185690.	" Pearson.J.W.M	
	212536.	" New H	Wounded in action 29/X/17.
	889584.	" Podd.C.R.	
	19796.	" Parkinson.G.H.	
	131526.	" Philcox.A.J.	
	212552.	" Robins.A.S.	
	901599.	" Richardson.C.H.	
	209455.	" Snewing.J.W.	Wounded in action 20/10/17.
	144699.	" Spratt.J.	
	138484.	" Sagar.R.	
	851331.	" Stirratt.R.F.	Wounded in action 30/X/17.
	26125.	" Symonds.E.G.	
	103314.	" Samuels.R.	Wounded in action 29/X/17.
	956164.	" Slyfield.J.	Wounded in action 29/X/17.
	156473.	" Sherwin.L.	
	297075.	" Smith.S.G.	Killed in action 29/X/17.
	889608.	" Simmons.W.	
	135253.	" Sartin.H.	
	889604.	" Smith.F.J.	
	199489.	" Tomlin.T.W.	Wounded in action 29/X/17.
	26463.	" Townend.S.V.	
	92601.	" Tully.J.	
	20016.	" Thompson.J.	
	696070.	" Thomas.J.	
	955804.	" Turrant.A.E.	
	190085.	" Taylor.A.	
	35404.	" Williams.J.	
	889632.	" Woodward.F.	
	889624.	" Wain.F.	
	19783.	Dvr Armitage.G.	
	35402.	" Bainbridge.J.G.	
	27757.	" Battin.W.	
	26401.	" Bell A.	
	26524.	" Bellamy.F.	
	12107.	" ?Bond.P.	
	805852.	" Bamforth.P.	
	200771.	" Birch.G.	
	20007.	" Bradley.J.	
	217097.	" Bush.H.H.	
	889511.	" Bell.C.	
	889521.	" Burn.A.	
	28059.	" Barker.W.	
	889509.	" Brightwell.E.	
	889581.	" Cocker.B.	
	889534.	" Chittock.A.	
	32488.	" Dutton.J.W.	

889546.	Dvr	Dalton.E.	
13985.	"	Donleavy.W.	
27621.	"	Denby.F.	
889535.	"	Driver.R.	
93655.	"	Edward.D.	Posted from 32nd.D.A.C. 14/10/17.
771977.	"	Elliott.H.	-ditto-
217592.	"	Forsyth.J.	"
31333.	"	F-aulkner.A.	
35381.	"	Guest.W.	
19943.	"	Green.J.	
19803.	"	Greenwood.J.	
889556.	"	Garner.J.E.	
889555.	"	Gray S.V.	
26422.	"	Havenhand.H.	
19953.	"	Howson.W.	
19749.	"	Hughes.H.	
889565.	"	Honeywood.B.	
27610.	"	Jewitt.W.	
35411.	"	Jackson.F.	
88935.	"	Kearnon:J.	
208238.	"	Keates.C	
35380.	"	Lunn.J.	
92590.	"	Lewellyn.J.	
696267.	"	Lewis.D.J	
889570.	"	Lay.G.	
35376.	"	Lowe.G.	
27222.	"	Phillips.F.	
231942.	"	O'Hara.J.	
219699.	"	Oldfield.W.	
19789.	"	Peacock.J.E.	
889587.	"	Piper.W.	
27624.	"	Roebuck.V.	
25691.	"	Rigg.J.	
889596.	"	Read.A.	
27505.	"	Stone.W.	
889595.	"	Seabrook.J.H.	
130962.	"	Smith.J.	
29405.	"	Stewart.A.	
27600.	"	Sykes.J.W.	
26406.	"	Savage.W.	
889601.	"	Sustins.E.	
219001.	"	Soupham.A.E.	
202441.	"	Turner.A.	
27609.	"	Smith.J.	
19736.	"	Thomson.A.D.	
202430.	"	Townsend A.	
71271.	"	Thomspon.J.G.N.	
171541.	"	Twist.G.	
889616.	"	Theobald.W.	
83586.	"	Toms.R.	
40493.	"	Tandy.P.	
889612.	"	Taylor.E.F.	
12031.	"	Wilkinson.J.W.	
27498.	"	Wright.D.	
19794.	"	Whelan.J.	
889631.	"	Whitehead.J.	
25718.	"	Wilson.J.	

8038. A.V.C.Sergt Moore.W. attached.

CONFIDENTIAL.

WAR DIARY

of

168th. Bde. RFA.

from 1st November 1917 to 30th November 1917.

(V O L U M E 24.)

Army Form C. 2118.

WAR DIARY
or
INTELLIGENCE SUMMARY.

(Erase heading not required.)

168th BRIGADE R.F.A.
COMMANDED BY Lt.Col.C.R.R.CARRINGTON.DSO.

Instructions regarding War Diaries and Intelligence Summaries are contained in F. S. Regs., Part II. and the Staff Manual respectively. Title pages will be prepared in manuscript.

Place	Date	Hour	Summary of Events and Information	Remarks and references to Appendices
	1/11/17.		Batteries remain attached to "A" GROUP 58th Divl Artillery. Brigade H.Q.still out of action. B/168 heavily shelled and had 5 guns put out of action.1 man Wounded.	
	2/11/17.	5.30.am	1 18-pdr Battery) per Brigade withdrawn from action to Wagon line and used to ½ 4.5" How ") reinforce the Batteries in action, with personnel and guns. B/168.R.F.A.withdraw to their wagon lines.	
	3/11/17.		Very dull day, front quiet.	
	4/11/17.			
	5/11/17.			
	6/11/17.		A.C.&.D.168.R.F.A.supported an attack made by the 1st Canadian Division on PASSCHENDAELE. All objectives were taken. Ammunition expended 18-pdrs. 1300 rds 4.5" Howitzers 190 rds.	
	7/11/17.			
	8/11/17.			
	9/11/17.			
	10/11/17.		A.B.& D/168 Supported an attack by the 1st Division along the Ridge of PASSCHENDAELE. All objectives were taken,but most of them lost later. Ammunition expended 18-pdrs 3240 rounds 4.5" Howitzers. 75.rounds.	
	11/11/17.		Very Wet.	
	12/11/17.		Fine day. Enemy Aircraft flew over back areas almost all the day.	
	13/11/17.			

Army Form C. 2118.

WAR DIARY
or
INTELLIGENCE SUMMARY.

(Erase heading not required.)

168th Brigade R.F.A. Commanded by
Lt.- Colonel.C.R.B.CARRINGTON.D.S.O.

Instructions regarding War Diaries and Intelligence Summaries are contained in F. S. Regs. Part II. and the Staff Manual respectively. Title pages will be prepared in manuscript.

Place	Date	Hour	Summary of Events and Information	Remarks and references to Appendices
	14/11/17.			
	15/11/17			
	16/11/17.	3.pm	Personnel of B/168 relieved personnel of A/168.RFA in action. A/168 withdrawn to Wagon Line for a rest.	
	17/11/17.		B.C.& D.Batteries 168th Brigade RFA relieved the 9th,17th and 47th Batteries in action N.E.of ST JULIEN. H.Q.168th Bde RFA relieved H.Q. of 41st Bde RFA. at CHEDDER VILLA C.17.c.5.0 (Sheet 28).	
		5.pm	Lt.-Colonel.FITZMAURICE.DSO. assumed command of No.2.GROUP.1st Divl Artillery, which consisted of B.C.& D.168.R.F.A., A.B.& C.161.R.P.A. Night firing on enemy communications carried out.	
	18/11/17.		Very dull day. Enemy quiet. Our Batteries carried out Registration.	
	19/11/17.			
	20/11/17.			
	21/11/17.	11.am	Lt.-Colonel.C.R.B.CARRINGTON.DSO. took over command of 168th Brigade R.F.A.from Lt.-Colonel.R.FITZMAURICE.DSO who proceeded to England.	
	22/11/17.		Batteries carried out firing through-out the night on enemy's communications.	
	23/11/17.		145111.a/Bdr Mole.F.G. 889535.a/Bdr Gutteridge, and 221602.a/Bdr Percy K. awarded the Military Medal.	
	24/11/17.		Quiet day. Our Batteries carried out concentrations on enemy communications.	
		10.am	32nd Divl Artillery H.Q. relieved 1st Divl Arty H.Q., 97th Inf Bde relieved 2nd Inf Bde in the Sector covered by No.2.Group.R.F.A.	

Army Form C. 2118.

WAR DIARY
or
INTELLIGENCE SUMMARY.
(Erase heading not required.)

168th Brigade R.F.A.
Commanded by Lt-Col.C.R.B.CARRINGTON,DSO

Instructions regarding War Diaries and Intelligence Summaries are contained in F.S. Regs, Part II. and the Staff Manual respectively. Title pages will be prepared in manuscript.

Place	Date	Hour	Summary of Events and Information	Remarks and references to Appendices
	25/11/17	7.45 pm	All Batteries fired in answer to S.O.S.Signal. Usual night firing on enemy's communications.	
	26/11/17		Quiet day.	
	27/11/17			
	28/11/17		Personnel of A/168.R.F.A. relieved personnel of B/161.R.F.A. in action near WINNIPEG.N.E.of ST JULIEN.	
	29/11/17		Harassing fire carried out Night and Day. D/168.R.F.A.carried out wire cutting with No.106.Fuze. Corps C.R.A. visited Battery Positions.	
	30/11/17	7.am.	Batteries fired in response to S.O.S.Signal.	

1st December 1917.

R Carrington
Lieut - Colonel.
Commanding 168th Brigade R. F. A.

Headquarters Staff.   168th Brigade R.F.A.

NOMINAL ROLL OF ALL RANKS 1/12/17.

Officers.   Lt-Colonel.R.FITZMAURICE.D.S.O.(transferred to
                                                England 21/11/17)
               Lt-Colonel.C.R.B.CARRINGTON.DSO.(Posted from 2nd
               Captain.A.LUMB.   Divn.21/11/17)
               Liwut H.L.JAMES.
               Lieut.H.FISHER.
               Capt.D.FERGUSON.

Other ranks:-

                1362. R.S.M.McGOWAN.R.H. (M.C)
         L.25839. Corpl Lee.G.
         L.25881. Bdr Gibson.H.
         L.29811. " Anderton.A.
         L.29430. a/Bdr Sugden.E.
           12245. " Wright.J.
         L.29430. " Sugden.E.
         L.28042. " Eyre.F.
         L.28206. Gnr Akroyd.H.
         L.25910. " Bottomley.C.
           59688. " Clark.R.
         L.29404. " Greenwood.C.
           56777. " Grindley.W.
         L.25626. " Slater.H.
         L.29296. " Windle.A.T.
         L.25781. " Postlethwaite.T.
         L.25422. Dvr Armitage.J.
         L.32440. " Baker.G.
         L.32450. " Blake.F.
         L.5342.   " Dickenson.J.
          198817. " Foote.G.
            1573. " Gutteridge.A.
           35766. " Hirons.E.   Transferred to 161 Bde
                                   H.Q. 24/11/17.
         L.5855.   " Gowan.W.
         L.32511. " Iredale.A.
         L.25825. " Iredale.E.
         L.28129. " Mellor.A.
         L.28132. " Martin.J.
           79511. " McIntyre.A.
         L.29424. " Parker.J.
         L.25853. " Radley.T.
         L.29357. " Reddington.M.
         L.29389. " Stansfield.P.
            6267. S/S Pereira.A.T.
            1305. Sadd Williams.T.
           17163. Dvr Field.G.   Posted from 2nd Divn 21/11/1
            6589. Gnr KNOWLES.J   -ditto-
             625. Staff Sergt Barker.H. (Artificer).

'A' Battery.   168th Brigade R.F.A.

NOMINAL ROLL OF ALL RANKS.   1/12/17.

Officers:- Major.R.EMMET.
Captain.G.O.d'IVRY.
Lieut W.A.EBBELS.
Lieut.L.A.RAVALD.
2/Lt.J.W.WEEDON. Wounded & Evacuated 6/11/17.
" F.J.CLARKE. Admitted to hospital
& Evacuated 14/11/17.
" F.THORNE. Posted by 32nd D.A. 22/11/17.
" R T WEAVER. Posted by 32nd DA 2/11/17

Other ranks.

L.18467.	B.S.M.Stephenson.C.		
L.28064.	BQMS. Brearley.H.		
L.25426.	Sergt Field P.J.		
L.25679.	" Roberts.J.F.		
43312.	" Mc Gowan.A.H.		
L.25425.	" Firth.A.		
L.32584.	" Williams.W.J.		
86310.	" Squires.A.E.		
1985.	" Harding.R.C.		
L.25697.	Cpl Rhodes.L.	Wounded and evacuated 31/10/17.	
L.29313.	" Armitage W.B.		
41257.	" Fitzpatrick.R.		
L.28100.	" Bentley.J.		
L.28188.	" Padgett.S.		
L.28034.	" Beevers.M.		
L.32479.	Bdr Pitchforth.A.		
L.25708.	" Crawshaw.J.I.		
L.25574.	" Whiteley.C.H.		
L.25781.	" Rhodes J.		
L.25464.	" Richardson.C.H.	Wounded and evacuated	
83594.	" Simpson.C.		
L.28217.	" Bower.E.		
167074.	" Mc Geachie.J.		
92721.	" Black.W.		
L.32539.	a/Bdr Fenton.E.		
54101.	" Perkins.F.J.		
L.32523.	" Phillipson.R.	Evacuated 1/11/17.	
L.28126.	" Shaw N.		
W.2810.	" Rice.E.F.	Wounded and evacuated	
L.32471.	" Calvert.F.		
L.28161.	" Lodge.A.		
L.25536.	s/a/Bdr Mansfield.W.G.		
167423.	" Sweet.J.		
L.32449.	Farr Sgt Town.E.		
L.25783.	Cpl S/S Andrews.R.		
L.29282.	S/S Nuttall.G.T.		
L.28175.	" Waterhouse L.		
L.25690.	" Kaye.J.		
173872.	" Ackroyd.A.		
695392.	" Harrington.J.	Posted from 32nd D.A.C. 18/11/17.	
L.32485.	Sadd Jackson.W.R.		
62728.	" Olliver J.		
154173.	" Skipp.J.W.	Evacuated sick 2/11/17.	
42821.	Ftr Norton.A.		
121451.	Whlr Weaver J.		
L.35990.	Gnr Allott C.V.		
160345.	" Alston.J.D.		
10574.	" Alford.C.		

No.		Name	Notes
L.25575.	Gnr	Billington.T.	
100556.	"	Beamish.R.	Wounded and evacuated 8/11/17.
100774.	"	Wounded and evacuated 8/11/17.	
L.25678.	"	Brooksbank.S.	
302446.	"	Birrel.W.	
651912.	"	Bruton.A.G.	
222460.	"	Birks.F.	
11973.	"	Booth.J.	Transferred to C/242 Bde R.F.A. 22/11/17. Transferred from C/168. 1/11/17.
115729.	"	Bell.E.N.	
L.29345.	"	Craigie.T.	
132664.	"	Curd.W.A.	
5556.	"	Chappel.A.	
190397.	"	Cross.F.	
212321.	"	Crawford.C.	
15582.	"	Collinson.W.L.	Posted from 32nd D.A.C. 1/11/17.
12049.	"	Edwards.L.	
86276.	"	Franklin.A.	
190415.	"	Foote.G.	
15256.	"	Fearn.H.	
L.25472.	"	Green.N.	
226903.	"	Hancox.H.	
18757.	"	Hart.C.	
220277.	"	Kyle.A.	Posted from 32nd.DAC. 3/11/17.
733.	"	Keighley.F.J.	Evacuated 1/11/17.
L.32512.	"	Lumb.W.	
3308.	"	Leech A.C.	Posted from 32nd.DAC. 25/11/17.
209688.	"	Lawrence W.G.	-ditto- 3/11/17.
184485.	"	Lewis.E.J.	Evacuated
L.28177.	"	Leatham.F.	
640551.	"	Mc Gandy F.	Posted from 32nd.D.A.C. 3/11/17.
220401.	"	Morris.J.	-ditto-
796892.	"	Measey.T.W.	"
56354.	"	McCrae J.	"
306422.	"	Martin.J.W.	"
127781.	"	Meir.S.	"
210739.	"	Newell.A.T.	"
5083.	"	Monger.A.	"
174170.	"	Morland.S.	"
159371.	"	McCarthy E.	Wounded & Evacuated 5/11/17.
168568.	"	Miller.W.	-ditto-
150416.	"	Mallett H.	
L.28129.	"	Marshall.E.	
L.25392.	"	Milnes.H.	Posted to C/168th Bde. 1/11/17.
L.25443.	"	Nuttall.P.	
46593.	"	Horfan.A.V.	Posted from 32nd.DAC 3/11/17.
44251.	"	Offen.F.	
750500.	"	Ord J.T.	Posted from 32nd.DAC. 8/11/17.
192477.	"	Ormiston.A.	
243993.	"	Oultram.A.	Posted from 32nd.DAC. 8/11/17.
L.28186.	"	Perkins.J.C.	
89584.	"	Piddleston.F.A.	Posted from 32nd.DAC. 8/11/17.
L.27683.	"	Price.F.	-ditto- " Evacuated
211861.	"	Pearl.J.	"
123979.	"	Parson.A.	
211705.	"	Robinson.H.	Wounded and evacuated 5/11/17.
199083.	"	Roskilly.B.	-ditto-
224342.	"	Rockett.B.	"
66362.	"	Rhodes.A.E.	Missing since 8/11/17.
L.32491.	"	Roberts.J.	
148166.	"	Smith.A.	
L.28006.	"	Singleton.H.W.	
L.25566.	"	Shaw.J.E.	
126034.	"	Spence R.	Wounded and evacuated 9/11/17.
81446.	"	Slack.H.	
L.25935.	"	Spencer H.	
821657.	"	Swadling.A.	Evacuated Sick
22365.	"	Speed.A.	

```
150668. Gnr Schaefer.A.E.
156164.  "  Sargent.C.
L.25771. "  Thornton.J.
 30526.  "  Thorpe.W.J.
L.32535. "  Thornber.W.H.
144975.  "  Thornhill.R.T.  Posted from 32nd.D.A.C. 1/11/17.
L.29300. "  Wood.F.
L.32441. "  Walker.A.
L.29318. "  Wood.R.
L.35649. "  Wood.C.E.
L.25485. "  Williams.G.
153713.  "  Young.W.
 19805.  "  Yates.W.
234892.  "  Wooff.F.L.


175251. Dvr Adams.F.
L.25524. "  Bamforth.H.
L.25525. "  Bray.H.
L.25436. "  Brearley.A.
L.25395  "  Brook.G.L.       Evacuated Sick 27/11/17.
L.25658. "  Chapman.R.
L.29323. "  Cartwright.P.
L.28590. "  Crowther.J.G.
109981.  "  Chapman.H.
L.29409. "  Dyson.W.
L.28079. "  Green.F.
L.25820. "  Ganley.J.
L.29316. "  Gledhill.J.R.
L.25579. "  Griffiths.F.C.
L.28201. "  Horsfall.E.      Evacuated Sick.
L.25849. "  Holmes.E.
L.28153. "  Harrison.F.
L.29347. "  Hardcastle.C.W.
 93514.  "  Hartley.A.
L.32541. "  Kershaw.C.
L.25419. "  Kerton.E.
L.28021. "  Mallinson.J.A.
L.25639. "  Millard.H.
826369.  "  Morse.L.    Wounded and evacuetd 6/11/17.
L.35046. "  Marshall.R.
204732.  "  Malbon.H.       Evacuated Sick
 17978.  "  McCavish.       Posted from 32nd.D.A.C. 1/11/17.
147602.  "  Orriss.H.
L.32464. "  Pogson.S.
 35864.  "  Quinn.D.
L.28074. "  Robertshaw.G.
L.28075. "  Roe.F.
 18172.  "  Rigby.F.        Posted from 32nd.DAC. 9/11/17.
 99859.  "  Spencer P.G.
L.25632. "  Shaw.E.
L.25503. "  Shaw.H.
L.28224. "  Shaw.C.A.
L.25797. "  Singleton.V.
L.25450. "  Smith.J.R.
198346.  "  Smith.F.J.      Posted from 32nd.DAC. 4/11/17.
231871.  "  Springthorpe.E.P.    -ditto-
217881.  "  Shotton.R.
219990.  "  Tall.F.              Wounded & Evacuated 18/11/17.
 74290.  "  Tanner.A.
L.28101. "  Taylor.T.H.
L.25650. "  Wood.A.         Evacuated 'Sick'
L.29331. "  Woodcock.W.
L.28087. "  Walters.H.
L.25394. "  Wortley.T.
L.25541. "  Woodhead.E.
L.25819. "  Whitehead.J.A.
159419.  "  Weedon.W.
 21116.  "  Wainwright.W.
L.28214. "  Wood.W.
SE14113 S/Sgt. Sweet.W. AVC. attached.
```

'B' Battery.   168th Brigade R.F.A.

NOMINAL ROLL OF ALL RANKS 1/12/17.

                Major. F. FITZGIBBON. D.S.O.
                Captain. L.M. HASTINGS. MC.
                Lieut W.P. ROBINSON.
                2/Lieut W.L. CHAMBERLIN.
                    "   J. MITCHELHILL.
                    "   S.A. STOREY.
                    "   C.P. BASNETT.   Evacuated 'Gas Shell' 4/11/17.
                    " J.R. WATSON   Posted from 32nd D.A. 28/11/17.

Other ranks:-

    58482. B.S.M. Stenning. T.
  L.32437. BQMS. Lane. A.C.
  L.32514. Far Sgt Sutcliffe. R.
  L.25548. Sergt Beaumont. F.
  L.28138.   "   Bramley. S.M.
  L.29344.   "   Gutheric. A.
  L.25599.   "   Crooks. H.   Evacuated Sick 6/11/17.
  L.28210.   "   Greenwood. M.R.
  L.25693.   "   Sergt Littlewood. K.
  L.25874.   "   Shaw. L.
    98737. Cpl S/S Brennan. J.
  L.25466.   "   Bottomley. T.
  L.28076.   "   Murray. A.
    24990.   "   Mayers. A.   Evacuated   6/11/17. 'Gassed'
  L.25491.   "   Sherwood. J.T.   Evacuated   4/11/17.   "
  L.29826.   "   Temperton. H.K.
  L.25463.   "   Scott. N.
  L.12248.   "   Vincent. H.
  L.25871.   "   Walker. S.   Evacuated   11/11/17. 'Gassed'
  L.32480. Bdr Bancroft L.
  L.35756.   "   Broomhead. H.   Posted from D.A.C. 19/11/17.
    79093.   "   Drewitt. W.C.   Evacuated   7/11/17.
   125511.   "   Christie. H.
  L.25472.   "   Dyson. F.
  L.25746.   "   Hargreaves A.
  L.29382.   "   Riley. A.
  L.25451.   "   Spendlove. T.
  L.25545.   "   Turner. J.F.   Evacuated Gas Shell. 6/11/17
    67704.   "   Tunstall. A.
  L.25808. a/Bdr Broomhead. W.H.
  L.32576.   "   Bentley. T.
    16381.   "   Cawthorne. J.
    11578.   "   Gouldsmith. S.
  L.29403.   "   Horrocks. H.   Evacuated Gas Shell. 1/11/17.
   152375.   "   Holmes. N.
  L.25547.   "   Ibbotson. M.
  L.32510.   "   Knight S
   115275.   "   Leach A.
   164826.   "   Williams. E.
     5035. S/S Boswell. H.
  L.32549.   "   Berry. A.
  L.25552.   "   Hoyle. C.
  L.25510.   "   Readyhough. G.W.
  L.25452.   "   Sidebottom. J.
  L.32552.   "   Wilson. J.
  L.25747. Sadd Brooksbank. G.
  L.25607.   "   Stansfield. F.
  L.25596. Whlr Yates. F.
  L.25382. Gnr Ainley. V.

152912. Gnr Allen.T.W.		
156556. " Benton.H.J.		
L.32483. " Binns.A.O.		
785047. " Ball.T.H.	Evacuated Gas Shell.	6/11/17.
223019. " Bell S.	Evacuated " "	6/11/17.
229157. " Bellfield.S.	" " "	6/11/17.
8993. " Blake.A.	" " "	6/11/17.
168329. " Bevan.G.	" " "	6/11/17.
L.32521. " Bottoms.H.		
L.29265. " Broadley.J.T.		
18820. " Brown.F.		
211547. " Bush A.J.		
211574. " Cartwright.H.J.		
120237. " Charman.H.		
182839. " Cousins.A.T.		
L.25674. " Cocker.F.		
46240. " Scott.F.J.	Evacuated Gas Shell.	6/11/17.
159803. " Shaw.J.A.	-ditto-	"
164927. " Clarke.H.	"	6/11/17.
221662. " Cheeseman.F.	"	"
205152. " Cooke.W.	"	7/11/17.
2295. " Coward.T.	"	6/11/17.
68234. " Doggett.J.	" 'Sick.	21/11/17.
L.29263. " Fowler B.		
93752. " Farmer.F.		
211607. " Bone.E.	Evacuated Gas Shell	11/11/17.
198807. " Gigg.B.		
L.29362. " Greenwood.L.A.		
L.29382. " Hanson.E.		
L.32454. " Hargreaves D.		
L.32456. Ftr Hill.W.	Evacuated Gas Shell	6/11/17.
111819. s/a/Bdr Harris.G.		
L 25554. Gnr Harrison.W.	Posted from 211 Bde	9/11/17.
L.28046. " Holdsworth.A.		
L.29399. " Hollas.J.	Posted from Base	9/11/17.
93564. " Hoskins.F.	Posted from D.A.C.	31/10/17
L.25664. " Hartley.A.	Evacuated Gas Shell.	5/11/17
L.29383. " Dewar.W.	-ditto-	6/11/17.
191072. " Ladbrook.J.R.	Posted from D.A.C.	14/11/17.
204140. " Lamb.G.	-ditto-	9/11/17.
200987. " Laverack.F.	"	9/11/17.
160940. " Leng.J.		
226480. " Luff.J.	Posted from 32nd.D.A.C.	9/11/17.
L.28220. " Laycock.A.	Evacuated Gas Shell	6/11/17.
L.25562. " Lawford.F.	" " "	6/11/17.
L.35622. " Littlewood.H.	" " "	6/11/17.
L.28126. s/a/Bdr Mallinson.F.		
L.29400. Gnr Mitchell.D.	Wounded & Evacuated	4/11/17.
17825. " Mapley.J.	Posted from 32nd.D.A.C.	9/11/17.
197864. " McPherson.D.		
227149. " Marsh.W.E.	Posted from 32nd.D.A.C.	9/11/17.
212137. " Martin.S.A.	-ditto-	"
164025. " Miller.L.		
771760. " Moore.R.	Posted from 32nd.D.A.C.	9/11/17.
735630. " Morrison.H.	-ditto-	"
197395. " Mullard.G.H.		
188576. " Nash.T.J.		
156134. " Nightingdale.D.		
219695. " Norris.J.	Posted from D.A.C.	14/11/17.
832124. " Riley.W.H.	-ditto-	"
L.29376. " Rhodes.A.	"	"
680601. " Roberts.R.	"	"
124305. " Rutherford.H.	"	"
308386. " Rix H.	Evacuated Gas Shell.	6/11/17.
176283. 221070. " Ritchie.	" " "	"
321070. " Rogers.S.R.	" " "	"
1505. " Shufflebottom.W.	Posted from 32nd.D.A.C.	14/11/17.
165748. " Stannage.H.		
L.32473. " Stafford.H.		
5824. " Spence C.	Evacuated Gas Shell.	7/11/17.
L.29372. s/a/Bdr Tidswell.H.T.		

L.25683 Gnr	Thompson.J.T.	
711697. "	Tompkins.G.	Posted from 32nd.D.A.V. 14/11/17.
L.25629. "	Turner.H.	
218427. "	Irwine.L.	Evacuated Gas Shell 6/11/17.
L.25623. "	Lee.F.	Evacuated " " 6/11/17.
2358. "	Platt.H.	" " " 4/11/17.
L.25458. "	Kiddle.F.	" " " 4/11/17.
L.25727. "	Winteringham.E.	
221036. "	Mole.T.	Evacuated Wounded 11/11/17.
185870. "	Womack.W.H.	Evacuated Transferred to A/161 20/11/17.
150477. "	Woolf.C.H.	" Gas Shell.6/11/17.
L.25827. "	Riddlesden.A.	Evacuated 25/11/17.
L.25632. "	Onyon.J.	" Gas Shell 6/11/17.
L.29381.Dvr	Barraclough.H.	
L.29258. "	Barraclough.T.E.	
L.28213. "	Beaumont.H.	
L.32528. "	Borrisow.F.	
L.32566. "	Braithwaite.J.F.	
L.25470. "	Brook.J.W.	
L.28199. "	Berry.A.	Transferred to England for mining 25/11/17.
L.25837. "	Berry.S.	-ditto- Authy D.A.G. 18/11/17.
"	Buckley.T.	Posted from Base 23/11/17.
185735. "	Chesters.D.	
L.25878. "	Clear.A.	
L.32443. "	Crossley.A.	Posted form Base 19/11/17.
L.28113. "	Crossley.J.	
L.25446. "	Crowther.J.	
L.25446. "	Davies.J.	
112102. "	Dennis.S.	
L.25442. "	Eastwood.G.	
L.25732. "	Firth.H.	
L.32538. "	Gray.D.	
L.29367. "	Greenwood.J.W.	
L.25728. "	Greenwood.C.	
1396. "	Green.R.	
L.25851. "	Hall.H.	
L.28204. "	Harrison.F.	
L.25479. "	Hattersley F.	
L.25822. "	Hincliffe.A.	
L.25558. "	Hobson.A.	
L.32506. "	Holmes.W.	
L.32447. "	Jackson.P.	
L.28070. "	Jowett.JH.	
L.29290. "	Ledgard.E.	
L.23743. "	Leckenby.J.	
79005. "	Lynch.P.	
L.28077.s/a/Bdr	Martin.L.	
L219114.Dvr	Markham.C.	
930739. "	Mathis.M.C.	
815569.s/a/Bdr	Mayers.F.	
217555.Dvr	Mackie.J.	Transferred to D/107.Bde.14/11/17.
L.28127. "	Mellor.H.	Evacuated Wounded 6/11/17.
L.28066. "	Medley.O.	
152302. "	Milner.J.	
47044. "	McCormick.A.	
L.29401. "	Moody.A.	
121959. "	Morley.A.T.	
L.25870. "	Murray.R.	
213085. "	Newns.A.	
L.25675. "	Nicholson.J.	
L.28194. "	North.M.	
73229. "	Parnaby.W.	
33422. "	Parker.H.V.	Evacuated 21/11/17.
L.28071. "	Robinson.F.	
5116. "	Roberts.C.	
L.25861. "	Robinson.T.	
L.25512. "	Robinson.W.J.	
L.25730. "	Rushworth.E.	

L.25655.	Dvr Scott.J.J.	
L.28041.	" Senior.G.	
203373.	" Sharples.J.E.	
L.32579.	" Shepherd.N.	
208351.	" Smithers.J.E.	Posted from 32nd.DAC.31/10/17.
L 25454.	" Snell.A.	
875702.	" Steward.P.	Posted from.32nd.D.A.C. 1/11/17.
180180.	" Tooth.V.S.	
L.29397.	" Southwell.J.	
L.28090.	" Stanton.A.	
L.25569.	" Turner.J.	
2088. L.25868.	" Turner.J.	
L.25866.	" Townsend.W.	
L.25499.	" Tallis.G.	
L.25598.	" Townend W.	
L.32515.	" Wilkinson.L.	
L 29257.	" Wilkinson.L.F.	
185398.	" Willatt W.	
L.29269.	" Wood.H.	
141214.	" Worth.W.D.	
L.28089.	" Wright.F.	

8949. Sergt White.A.V.C. (Attached).

'C' Battery.   168th Brigade R.F.A.

NOMINAL ROLL OF ALL RANKS 1/12/17.

Officers:- Major.H.COTTEE.D.S.O.
           Capt.R.T.GROVES.
           2/Lieut.G.O.J.BARRICK. Killed in action
              "   S.J.HINTON.M.C.   6/11/17.
              "   H.R.M.RONALDSON.
              "   C.A.ANELAY. Wounded in action 6/11/17
              "   MAC OLIVE. Posted from 32ndDA.9/11/17
              "   ~~P.THORE~~. Posted from 32ndDA.28/11/17
              "   S.A.BELSHAM.

Other ranks:-

   53473.B.S.M.Malone.M.J.
  L.5688.RQMS. Tomlinson.S.
 L.12004. Sergt Turgoose.W.
 L.25711.   "   Kirkham.T.
   22339.   "   Fitzgerald.W.
 L.28195.   "   Garside.I.
 L.19481.   "   Ward.T.S.
 L.11993.   "   Holdroyd.T.
 L.28121.   "   Palmer.R.
 L.27727. Cpl. ~~Palmer.R.~~   Wounded and Evacuated
                Ward.A.
 L.25475.   "   Earnshaw.S.   Killed in action.11/11/17.
 L.19484.   "   Bailey.B.C.
 L.25912.   "   Terry.L.   Evacuated Gas Shell 6/11/17.
 L.28200.   "   Brook.J.   Wounded & Evacuated 10/11/17.
   50143.   "   Smith.T.
 L.19478. Bdr   Todd.J.A.
 L.19479.   "   Wardle L.M.
 L.27730.   "   Mc Guire.E.F.J.
   19830.   "   Goldsborough H.L.
 L.29414.   "   Elliott.C.H.
 L.19519.   "   Milnthorpe.G.
 L.19487.   "   Carr W.C.
 L.28010.   "   Steele.J.W.
 L.12035.   "   Wathy.A.   Evacuated.Gas Shell. 5/11/17.
 L.11968.   "   Wilcock.G.   Reverted to Gunner at own request.
  935644.   "   Seymour.W.
 1150797.a/Bdr Musto.W.
  138424.   "   Kirkham.T.
   40357.   "   Powell.B.
 L.19520.   "   Garfoot.E.
 L.12006.   "   Wrigglesworth.F.
  L.2285.   "   Lewis.E.J.   Wounded Gas Shell. Evac'd 6/11/17.
 L.11959.   "   Ellis.W.R.   Wounded and evacuated. 2/11/17.
    8296. Far Sgt Key.J.
 L.25954. Cpl S/S Chappel.E.
 L.11926. S/S   Fleether.F.
 L.27751. "   Bailey.H.
 L.11934. "   Ismay.T.H.
  107905. "   Copping.H.E.
   63915. "   Irving.W.A.   Evacuated Gas Shell. 5/11/17.
 L.12041. "   Kershaw.H.
 L.14862.Whlr   Pringle.E.
  147472. Ftr. Hellewell.A.   Evacuated   8/11/17.
 L.11937. Sadd. Hall.T.
  143669.   "   Heron.A.
   45372. Gnr   Anderson.F.   Wounded and evacuated 24/10/17.

174032.	Gnr	Arnold.J.T.	
129105.	"	Bolster.A.G.	
42469.	"	Berbridge.W.J.	
L.11973.	"	Booth.J.	Posted to A/168.R.F.A.
L.11994.	"	Barr.H.	Evacuated 13/11/17.
L.12026.	"	Beach.J.	Wounded and evacuated 11/11/17.
L.11979.	"	Brady B.	
L.19485.	"	Briggs.E.J.	Evacuated. 30/10/17.
5377.	"	Baker.J.	" 23/10/17.
235293.	"	Betteley.A.	
209056.	"	Bird.J.H.	
	"	Banton.F.	Attached from DAC.
L.28167.	"	Chapman.T.	Evacuated 4/11/17.
147114.	"	Creeper.H.	
L.35702.	"	Denton.F.	
217908.	"	Dykes.W.P.	
L.12017.	"	Farmery.J.V.	Wounded & Evacuated. 20/10/17.
78830.	"	Fraser J.	" " 2/11/17.
37084.	"	Gale.S.E.	" " "
163921.	"	Gerritt.G.W.	
197894.	"	Brummitt.A.	Wounded & Evacuated 21/10/17.
163727.	"	Goddard.W.E.	
88771.	"	Hall.N.	
L.19490	"	Horner.C.	
34446.	"	Hutt.R.	Killed in action 20/10/17.
89444.	"	Holden.F.	Evacuated 9/11/17.
L.25751.	"	Higgins.H.	Wounded & Evacuated 28/10/17.
2933.	"	Hesford.A.	
205331.	"	Imeson T.E.	
206785.	"	Procter H.	
L.11971.	"	Parkin.W.	
L.19496.	"	Saberton.H.	
L.27999.	"	Spittle.T.A.	Wounded and evacuated 10/11/17.
13907.	"	Swinn.J.	
L 1268.	"	Sellars.G.	
67727.	"	Smith.J.	Appointed a/Bdr 22/7/17.
12965.	"	Smith.W.E.	
L.3244.	"	Smith.T.	Posted from 32nd.D.A.C. 5/11/17 Wounded and evacuated 10/11/17.
123842.	"	Sutton.E.T.	
13469.	"	Robinson.A.E.	
L.25715.	"	Taylor.J.T.	
L.19502.	"	Wales.W.	
L.12003.	"	Waldron.T.	
L.19717.	"	Wardell.G.H.	
219005.	"	Ward.L.T.	Evacuated 6/1 /17.
196150.	"	Cook.F.	" 5/11/17.
935803.	"	Smith.W.A.	
19809.	"	James.T.	Promoted a/Bdr.
L.25423.	"	Milnes.H.	Transferred from A/168 Bde.
51875.	"	Linton.F.	attached from DAC.Evac'd 15/11/17.
675516.	"	Halstead.B.	" " " " "
232968.	"	Metclafe.J.J	Posted from 32nd D.A.C. 9/11/17.
113859.	"	Metcalfe.T.	-ditto-
23956.	"	McDermott.	"
232693.	"	Kemp.A.C.	"
232920.	"	Pounder.C.	"
217799.	"	Mather.J.	"
231213.	"	Molldy.W.H.	"
200554.	"	Melville.A.	"
931576.	"	Wetherill.J.	" 14/11/17.
756123.	"	Stoker.H.	" "
38236.	"	Robbins.H.E.	" "
201339.	"	Withall.W.H.	" "
87972.	"	Marshall.S.	" "
240203.	"	Rumble.G.	" "
695727.	"	Turner F.	" "
113582.	"	Walters S.	" "
845724.	"	Loveridge.G.	

```
L.12002. Gnr Nowell.E.      Evacuated Gas Shell.  5/11/17.
L.25411.  "  Ellis.W.
  46846.  "  Young.F.J.
685266.  8521  "  Brown.T.
  20111.  "  Jolly.W.


L.12022, Dvr Ainsworth.H.
L.11919.  "  Backhouse G.
L.11942.  "  Boulton.P.
 221666.  "  Brown.G.T.
L.11980.  "  Burnley.W.S.
  15220.  "  Burry.A.
 105511.  "  Blackhurst.H.
 123532.  "  Bearman.A.
L.11982.  "  Clark.E.W.
L.28232.  "  Chapman.J.
 118327.  "  Cleaver E.R.
L.29291.  "  Drake.G.
L.28107.  "  Ellis.H.
L.11969.  "  Ewbank.J.A.
L.12055.  "  Farnery.T.
L.19506.  "  Fretwell.H.
  22242.  "  Fitch.E.J.
L.12037.  "  Garfitt.J.H.
L.11941.  "  Hart.J.
L.11967.  "  Hancock.N.
L.19509.  "  Hudson.J.
L.11929.  "  Kemp.R.
L.19492.  "  Lapish.J.
L.19513.  "  Lamb.M.
L.28051.  "  Lawton.H.
L.29285.  "  Lord.J.
 218502.  "  Leeves.A.E.
L.14919.  "  Marshall.S.
L.18909.  "  Mitchell.W.
  85571.  "  O'keefe.J.H.
   6074.  "  Overland.H.
  75445.  "  Pipe.E.
L.27691.  "  Poynton.C.W.
L.19516.  "  Priestley.B.
L.28031.  "  Parkin.H.
L.25850.  "  Pogson.H.
  41796.  "  Peckham.L.
L.12011.  "  Roberts.E.W.
L.11965.  "  Ross.C.A.
 121310.  "  Roake.J.
 177610.  "  Scott.H.
   2869.  "  Price.W.
 132504.  "  Studley.F.
L.19487.  "  Schofield.W.
L.12033.  "  Senior.E.K.    Wounded and evacuated.
 120413.  "  Shipman.H.
L.29293.  "  Sutcliffe.W.
L.28149.  "  Scott.J.R.
L.20448.  "  Singleton.N.
L.27993.  "  Senior.J.W.
 186618   "  Stride.W.
L.27747.  "  Toothill.A.C.
L.32459.  "  Turner.H.R.
L.28095.  "  Turner A.B.    Wounded and evacted 22/11/17.
   8397.  "  Troutt.W.
L.12008.  "  Wales.A.
L.12021.  "  Walshaw.E.
L.28169.  "  Williams.J.
L.28124.  "  Walton.R.      Evacuated 15/11/17.
L.29322.  "  White.L.
  51913.  "  Wareham.E.
```

```
145487. Dvr Wilson.W.J.
  2410.  "  Wheeler.W.
L.11978.  "  Williams.H.
211032.   "  Woodward.C.S.    Evacuated.
L.11920.  "  Thompson.R.
821420.   "  Beale.W.A.
200790.   "  Beel.T.
826655.   "  Schilling.R.M.
L.28122.  "  Mxxxxxx.
 54552.   "  O'Neill.W.I.     Posted from 32nd D.A.C. 25/11/17.

  2489. Sergt Harding.W. A.V.C.attached.
```

'D' Battery.   168th Brigade R.F.A.

NOMINAL ROLL OF ALL RANKS. 1/12/17.

Officers:-   Major. J.C. POOLE. M.C.
             Lieut. G.C. WOOD. M.C.
             2/Lt. E.P. PEEL.
             2/Lt. C.A. BROWNE.
             2/Lt. B.J. VALLANCE.
             "   G.B. PATTERSON. Posted by 32nd DA. 21/11/17

Other ranks:-

```
  21136. R.S.M. Leahy. J.
 950107. BQMS. Jeffrey S.A.
 100360. Far Sgt Greenwood. J.
  11948. Sergt Allen. A.J.
  35409.   "   Dinsdale. J.
  11968.   "   Hawkes. T.
L.25606.   "   Palframan. F.
  11914.   "   Wooffitt. T.E.
  27601. Cpl  Archer. S.T.
  27756.   "   Bonner. S.
  26452.   "   Bellamy. J.W.
  35389.   "   Dobson. J.E.
 889565.   "   Jackson. A.A.
 889591.   "   Philpot J.E.
  27590. Bdr  Bradford. J.
  35390.   "   Beckett. E.
  20008.   "   Croft. J.
  35395.   "   Hamilton. T.H.
   1986.   "   Hempsall. T.
 889575.   "   Last S.
  14511.   "   Male. F.G.
  35414.   "   Padgett. J.E.
  26400.   "   Smith. W.
  97676.   "   Starkey. E.
  27622.   "   Dixon. L.
   8982.   "   Flack. A.
 124923.   "   Richardson. H.
  27580.   "   Stacey. I.
 221366.   "   Sagar. C.
  86411.   "   Speight. A.
  24083. " "  Tilston. R.
 221603.   "   Percy. K.
 830209.   "   Lee. D.
 889535.   "   Gutteridge. A.
  78512. Cpl S/S Emms. A.
  26450.   "   Sadd Clawson. J.J.
     42.   "   Whlr Derbyshire. W.
  27533. S/S Hellewell A.
  27759.   "   Popplewell. G.
  27612.   "   Smith. J.
  26447.   "   Varney J.
  78446. Sadd Batley. A.
 146171. Ftr Collar. P.A.
 128068. Gnr Allen. C.
 181761.  "  Barker. F.      Posted from 32nd.D.A.C. 15/11/17.
   5040.  "  Beet. W.             -ditto-                "
```

19896.	Gnr	Badger.G.	Posted from 32.D.A.C.	15/11/17.
129611.	"	Bowker.C.	" " "	
46330.	"	Brown.P.H.		
212325.	"	Broomfield.H.H.	Posted from 32nd.DAC.	15/11/17.
192042.	"	Bishop.H.H.		
87589.	"	Blood.J.		
206887.	"	Corran.G.		
185893.	"	Clarke.J.S.		
27596.	"	Dixon.H.A.		
230589.	"	Davis.S.E.		
7772.	"	Edwards.J.H.		
77578.	"	Edwards.M.		
233458.	"	Emery.W.C.		
27175.	"	Fowler.A.S.		
179512.	"	Garnham.A.C.		
192073.	"	Greaves.W.G.		
104591.	"	Howard.A.		
59930.	"	Hackett.E.	Posted from 32nd.DAC.	15/11/17.
19848.	"	Hellewell.G.W.		
236763.	"	Lawson.R.J.	Posted from 32nd.DAC.	9/11/17.
148368.	"	Keene.T.C.		
218671.	"	Mann.	Posted from 32nd.DAC.	5/11/17.
197075.	"	Lancaster J.		
198279.	"	Nursey.H.	Posted from 32nd.D.A.C.	5/11/17.
153360.	"	Pickard.C.	-ditto-	"
185690.	"	Parsons.J W.M.		
35112.	"	Pocock.J.	"	
155874.	"	Perry.W.J.	"	
889584.	"	Podd.C.R.	"	
216244.	"	Palfrey.S.	"	
19796.	"	Parkinson.G.H.	"	
663278.	"	Pitchers.S.	Posted from 32nd.D.A.C.	5/11/17.
131526.	"	Philcox.A.J.		
12205 :	"	Ogden.F.W.		
212552.	"	Robins.A.S.		
901599.	"	Richardson.C.H.		
961430.	"	Steward.W.D.		
138484.	"	Sagar.R.		
26125.	"	Simmons.E.G.		
156473.	"	Sherwin.L.		
889608.	"	Simmons.H.		
26463.	"	Sartin.H.		
26465.	"	Townsend.A.V.		
92601.	"	Tully.J.		
20016.	"	Thompson.J.		
696070.	"	Thomas.J.		
955804.	"	Tarrunt.A.E.		
190085.	"	Taylor.A.		
35404.	"	Williams.J		
889632.	"	Woodward.F.		
889624.	"	Wain.F.		
25804.	"	Webb.F.		
19783.	Dvr	Armitage.G.		
35402. 27757.	"	Bainbridge.J.G.		
27757.	"	Battin.W.		
26401.	"	Bell.A.		
26524.	"	Bellamy.F.		
12107.	"	Bond.P.		
805852.	"	Bamforth.P.		
200771.	"	Birch.G.		
20007.	"	Bradly.J.		
217097.	"	Bush.H.H.		
889511.	"	Bell.C.		
889521.	"	Bunn.A.		
28059.	"	Barker.W.		
889509.	"	Brightwell.E.		
889531.	"	Cocker.B.		
889534.	"	Chittock.A.		

L.32488. Dvr Dutton.J.W.
889546. " Dalton.E.
 13985. " Donleavy.W.
 27621. " Denby F.
 92655. " Edwards D.
889535. " Driver R.
771977. " Elliott.H.
 37606. " Fisher A.
217592. " Forsyth.J.
 31333. " Faulkner A.
 35381. " Guesr.W.
 19943. " Green.J.
 19803. " Greenwood.J.
889556. " Garner.J.E.
889555. " Gray S.V.
 26422. " Havenhand.H.
 19953. " Howson.W.
 19749. " Hughes.H.
889563. " Honeywood.B.
 27610. " Jewitt.W.
 35411. " Jackson.F.
 88935. " Kearnon.J.
208238. " Keates.C.
 35380. " Lunn.G.
 92590. " Lewellyn.T.
696267. " Lewis.D.J.
889570. " Lay.G.
 35376. " Lowe G.
681306. " Mooney.H.
 27222. " Phillips.F.
231942. " O'Hara.J.
219699. " Oldfield.W.
 19789. " Peacock.J.E.
889587. " Piper.W.
 27624. " Roebuck V.
236698. " Rogers.J.
 25691. " Rigg J.
889596. " Read.A.
 27505. " Shone.W.
889595. " Rayner L.
 40494. " Seabrook.J.H.
130962. " Smith.J.
 29405. " Stewart.A.
 27600. " Sykes.J.
 26406. " Savage.W.
889601. " Sustins.E.
202441. " Turner.A.
 27609. " Smith.J.
 19736. " Thompson.A.D.
202430. " Townsend.A.
 71271. " Thompson.J.G.H.
171541. " Twist.G.
889616. " Theobald.W.
 40493. " Tandy P.
889612. " Taylor.E.F.
 38748. " Taylor.D.
 12031. " Wilkinson.T.W.
 27498. " Wright.D.
 19794. " Whelan.J.
889631. " Whitehead.J.
 25718. " Wilson.J.

  8038. Sergt Moor.W. A.V.C. attached.

CONFIDENTIAL.

WAR DIARY

of the

168th. Bde. R. F. A.

from 1st December 1917 to 31st Dec.1917.

VOLUME XXIV

Army Form C. 2118.

WAR DIARY
or
INTELLIGENCE SUMMARY.
(Erase heading not required.)

168th BRIGADE R.F.A.
Commanded by Lt-Col. C.R.B. CARRINGTON. DSO.

Instructions regarding War Diaries and Intelligence Summaries are contained in F.S. Regs., Part II. and the Staff Manual respectively. Title pages will be prepared in manuscript.

Place	Date	Hour	Summary of Events and Information	Remarks and references to Appendices
	1/12/17		Harassing fire carried out all day.	O.K.
	2/12/17		No. 2. GROUP supported an attack by the 97th Infantry Brigade. All objectives were taken, but enemy Counter-attacks drove our troops back to their original line.	O.K.
	3/12/17		14th Infantry Brigade relieved the 97th Infantry Brigade in the Sector covered by No. 2. GROUP.	O.K.
	4/12/17		Batteries carried out day and night shooting on enemy roads and communications.	O.K.
	5/12/17		Trench Warfare.	O.K.
	9/12/17.		96th Infantry Brigade relieved the 14th Infantry Brigade in the Sector covered by No. 2. GROUP.	O.K.
	10/12/17.	10.am	Divisional Artillery re-grouped, No. 2. GROUP now consists of A.B.C.&D. Batteries 168th Brigade R.F.A.	O.K.
	11/12/17.		Trench Warfare.	O.K.
	17/12/17.		97th Infantry Brigade relieved the 96th Infantry Brigade in the line.	O.K.
	18/12/17.		C/168.R.F.A. heavily shelled with 8" Howitzers, two guns damaged.	O.K.
	19/12/17.		An Infantry Officer attached to the Brigade for a 3 days course.	O.K.
	20/12/17.		Thick fog all day, front extremely quiet.	O.K.
	22/12/17.		C/168.R.F.A. moved to a new position at D.7.A.5.5. (Sheet 23).	O.K.
	23/12/17.		14th Infantry Brigade relieved the 97th Inf Brigade in the line.	O.K.

Army Form C. 2118.

WAR DIARY
or
INTELLIGENCE SUMMARY.
(Erase heading not required.)

168th Brigade R.F.A.
Commanded by Lt-Col.C.R.B.CARRINGTON,D.S.O

Instructions regarding War Diaries and Intelligence Summaries are contained in F. S. Regs., Part II. and the Staff Manual respectively. Title pages will be prepared in manuscript.

Place	Date	Hour	Summary of Events and Information	Remarks and references to Appendices
	26/12/17	7.45.pm	All Batteries fired in response to S.O.S.Signal, no enemy attack took place.	OL
	27/12/17		Day remarkably quiet.	OL
	28/12/17	7.30.am	B/168.R.F.A.Wagon Line Bombed. 1 man killed and 2 Wounded American General visited Battery Positions.	OL
	29/12/17		B/168.R.F.A.heavily shelled, 2 Gunners killed, 3 wounded and 1 Gun damaged.	OL
	30/12/17		18-Pounder Gun of A/168.R.F.A.placed in the STROOMBEEK VALLEY for Sniping purposes. 117th Infantry Brigade relieved the 14th Infantry Brigade in the line.	OL
			Casualties during month 3 O.R's Killed. 10 O.R's wounded. 1 Officer wounded Ammunition Expended during month :- 27,375 rds 18 Pdr Shrapnel. 14,552 rds H.E. 535 rds Smoke 7,692 rds R.X. 45"Hz	(OL)

1st January 1918.

R.Barry
Lt-Colonel.
Commanding 168th Brigade R.F.A.

A/168 R.F.A

DIARY.

G.  R.

ARMY BOOK 136.

From records of
166th Bde R.F.A.
war

S.O. 1218. 140,000 Bks. 5/17.—McC. & Co., Ltd.

1917

Jany 1 — On rest at ST OUEN
An advance party left for gun position
2 — Left ST OUEN for action
3 — Arrived at AMPLIERS
4 — Arrived at wagon line LOUVENCOURT same place as before.
Right Section went in open action at AUCHONVILLERS
5 — Centre & left Sections went into action
During the time the Battery was in action the 7th Div took MUNICH TRENCH
17 — Came out of action & went to COLINS CAMP to gun pits. wagon line moved to BUS in Stables

Feby 2 — Gas Shells on the position at 9.30 p.
5 men slightly gassed & removed to Hospital.
18 — Came out of action & went to the wagon line for 2 days
20 — Marched on the road to WARGNIES stayed there 2 days
22 — Marched to ARQUIEVES
23 — Marched to DOMART & stayed there

		2 days
Feby	25	Marched to LE QUESNIL to the wagon Line, in Stables. We took over the Stables from the French & were in a lousy condition. The same night all the guns came into action near ROUVROY & relieved the French
	28	We took over from the French & became settled down in good dug outs & gunpits.
March	17	Germans have evacuated FOUQUES-COURT. We advanced to a position (open action) close to the R.A. behind LA CHAVATTE O.P.
	18	Crossed "No Mans Land" & arrived at HATTENCOURT The guns went into action for the night about 1000 yards from the wagon Line
	19	Arrived at NESLE Guns went into action for the night in a valley which to my opinion was used by the Huns as an Aerodrome
	20	Arrived at —— The guns are in a Field

	about 1000 yds from the Billet. The wagon line is E of NESLE - HAM Road NE of HOMBLEUX. Billeted in barn & house on N. H. Rd about 200 yds away from the Battery Position. We stayed here 2 days & then got to know we had to move about 1 mile further forward. We arrived at that position & got the guns in action when we got orders to come back to the old position again.
23	80 men & 130 horses went back to WARVILLERS to get the lines up to strength. About 27 men & 20 horses were left behind & are now with the guns.
23 to 27	Stayed at the barn for 5 days then went to take up a position in the valley at VAUX. A working party under Lt Miller went 2 days ahead of the Battery to prepare the position
29	About 7 PM. the "Boche" sent over about 70 77 mm & 4.2 The continued until 8.15 PM
30	About 5.30 PM we had a "Strafe" & the

Infantry gained their object in front of ETREILLERS taking SAVVY. Later in the day we advanced to a valley near ROUPY & fired about 60 rds the Infantry taking SAVVY WOOD. At night we went to another valley on the left just to the right of SAVVY where we remained 6 days.

April 2 Battery & Wagon Line heavily shelled. The Wagon Line was in the same valley previously occupied by Battery on the 30th ult. The Wagon Line had to move to the other side of the valley & at 8 P.M. the same night they were shelled out & had to move to DOUCHY. One driver was slightly wounded also one gunner. Since leaving VAUX we had only five guns in action

Apl 4 We came out of action from the Valley Position & proceeded to HOLNON WOOD & remained there 10 days. We came through ETREILLIERS. Half of the teams "gibbed" at the first craters near ETREILLIERS. We left the valley position at 3.30 P.M. & arrived at the Battery Position at

2 AM (3 miles Route) The position was at
E. edge of wood N of ATILLY - HOLNON Road
N° 1. gun got into action first & it took
18 horses to get it into action. The next
gun was N° 5, this gun got into action
with 6 horses only & then N° 4 gun
was the last to be in action. All guns
were reported in action at 7 AM the
following morning. Two guns remained
in a position in orchard S of ATILLY -
HOLNON Road to the right of the wood
under the charge of Lt. d'Ivry.

Apl 9th The "Boche" started sweeping the wood
at 5.30 P.M. for about ¾ hr. We evacuated
the position & went to the top of the
wood. 2/Lt. Finnie got wounded at the O.P. &
is now in England.

14 We had an early morning strafe which
lasted 2 hrs & the rate of fire was mostly
3½ secs. — Infantry taking FAYET —.
Infantry took high ground beyond FAYET in the
afternoon with artillery barrage. At 5.30 P.M. we
took up a position in the valley in front of

HOLNON VILLAGE.

Apl 15. The Major went to the wagon Line, near VILLEVEQUE, sick & Capt. Brown came to the guns to take charge. Night firing started at this position.

22. We moved to a forward position about 1000 yards in front. We have 3 guns in each flank M 33 d 17 (1/20000) between HOLNON & FRESNOY

26. Capt Brown attached to 60 Pdr. Battery & Major Emmet returned to guns; L'd d'Ivry to wagon lines

27. N°4 gun had a premature which burst in the bore & broke about 4 ft of piece into splinters. Luckily no one was hurt.

May 1. Left Section went out of action to the wagon Line

2. Centre & Right Sections went out of action to the wagon Line where we remained for a rest for 7 days.

3. Capt W.R. Brown promoted to B.C. & sent to 15 Div

5. FSMO by B.C.

7. Maj. General Schute inspected the Brigade A Bty complimented as best in Brigade

8. Left Section came into action in previous park

9. Right & Centre Section came into action We

		relieved the same Battery who relieved us A/306 Bgde R.F.A
May	10	We had a short 'strafe' for about 20 minutes & during this time Enemy Baloons were up & they must have spotted us as on the 11th we were shelled out of the Position
	12	The "Boche" started a bombardment at 10AM & went on until 10PM. He sent about 200 shells on the position Calibre 4.2. N°1 gun was Knocked out of action No casualties
	17	A section of the Battery went out of action & was relieved by a section of a French battery
	18	The remainder of the Battery came out of action & was relieved by the French Battery
	19	The Brigade started off at 7am for LANGUE VOISIN where the Battery remained one night
	20	The Battery marched off for BOUCHOIR
	21	The Battery marched to IGNACOURT. We remained here 2 days & entrained at
	23	GUILLAUCOURT 11AM. & arrived at our destination — BAILLEUL — at 1PM.
	24	We arrived at the wagon Lines about 4AM (about 1½ miles out of BAILLEUL)

May 25	B.C's' report at 8.30 A.M. to reconnoitre positions
26	A working party under 2 sergeants were sent to make gun-pits & dug-outs in front of WYTSCHAETE
29	N°2 gun came into action
30	N°3 gun came into action
31	N°s 4 & 5 guns came into action. Registrating Zero Line.
June 1	N°s 1 & 6 guns came into action
2	Battle of MESSINES RIDGE bombardment started. L28079 D⁺ Green F. & 147602 D⁺ Orriss H. taking rations to new position were caught in a severe barrage with other transport; at first opportunity retired returning under shell fire & delivering rations; showed conspicuous bravery & each awarded M.M.
7	At 3.0am the strafe started & we opened fire. Six mines went up & machine gun fire was very active. During the strafe we fired 4398 rounds. At 9.37 pm S.O.S. went up & we opened fire at 9.38 pm. We carried out a night task
9	Six guns out of action to wagon Line.

June 11	Marched to EECKE
13	Battery horses redistributed by colour. "A" sub – "black", "B" sub – "Brown", "C" sub – Dark Bays, "D" sub – "Bays", "E" sub "Bays" & "F" sub "Chestnuts"
14	Marched to WORMHOUDT. B.C's reconnoitred new Battery positions Capt d Ivry stayed with French at position M21d 52 near Zouave Rd
16	Marched to CAPPELLE
17	Marched to LEFFRINCKOOCKE. At 6pm the Right Section marched on to the Battery Position between OOST DUNKERKE & NIEUPORT & relieved a French section. The Centre & Left Sections remained at LEFFRINCKOOCKE for the night & marched next morning to a Company wagon line near COXYDE
18	Centre Section came into action. "D" sub took over a French 75mm gun at REDAN NIEUPORT (NORTH) relieving the French. "C" sub took over a position – M 35 a 85 – called the "RAGEUSE GUN" E.N.E of NIEUPORT & was working under the 161 Bgde RFA.
19	Left Section joined Right Section in action.

June 19	2/Lt Ebbels went on leave. The Wagon Line moved to outside COXYDE X14a3560
20	A working party was sent to make new Position at S.E. edge of NIEUPORT by canal M 34 c 8073
28	Right Section guns went to NIEUPORT position
29	New position shelled with 4.2 heavily during our registration; stopped when we stopped & opened when we began registering again. Position cleared, no damage, shooting very close. "C" sub section gun returned from the "RAGEUSE" to NIEUPORT under rifle & machine gun fire by 5 Bridges. 2/Lt Ebbels returned from leave
July 1	Battery supported raid by KRUISDIJK, very high wind dangerous shooting but very satisfactory. Enemy trench found empty. 2/Lt Weedon posted to the Battery.
2	"E" sub. sec. gun went to NIEUPORT position & "D" sub. sec. gun to RAGEUSE. Capt d'Ivory relieved
5	Major Emmet to Wagon Line.
6	Major Emmet proceeded on leave
7	2/Lt Bell admitted to hospital. Notification BSM Ratchets commission, ordered to report to 39th Div after leave

July 9	About 1.30 pm shelling of position & dug outs with 30" whizz-bangs wounding Bdrs. Boutty & Watts. The former lost part of his foot & the latter died in Hospital. Both evacuated.
10	Early bombardment of NIEUPORT kept up all day. Very few heavies retaliating. Bombardment continued throughout day & night. About midnight becoming very intense & included many gas shells. 4 dug outs were blown in & one gas shell penetrated the cellar occupied by the Cooks severely wounding Gnr Sykes J. in the face. This was unknown to Dty Officers. Capt Wood & L⁴ T.M Officer, & L⁰ Gillies H·L·I & Gnr Bolton N heard of it & rescued Sykes. Sykes however died in D.S. & is buried in NIEUPORT. Bolton awarded M.M. B+ Richardson also slightly wounded in the head. About 4 AM bombardment slackened at one point but B.C. & D Batteries received attention. Our dug outs evacuated, all ranks in covered trench. In the left sector during the attack enemy captured 2 lines of trenches, badly cutting up 2 battalions.

July 13	Wire cutting
14	B.S.M. Ratchet proceeded to the 39th How. Wire-cutting
15	Wire cutting. The 9th Battery, 3rd Brigade A.F.A (Aus) came into action in front of us, Officers messing with us, men using the covered trench.
17	A shell fell in F sub. Harness Hut at the wagon Line in COXYDE damaging a lot of harness.
20	Major Emmet returned from leave. N° 5 gun returned from I.O.M. Battery heavily shelled with 150 cm from 10 AM until 12.30 PM. N°s 1, 3 & 4 guns put out of action. N° 2 gun was at Ordnance undergoing repairs. About 800 rds of ammunition was damaged by shell & fire. N°s 1, 3, & 4 guns went to I.O.M. N° 2 gun returned from IOM
22	N° 5 gun went to IOM (piston head trouble) N° 2 gun carried out its night task & 2 SOS calls
25	The "RAGEUSE GUN" detachment relieved by 7th Australian Bty & went into action at New Position

July	26	near POOLS FARM 53c8.9 N°5 gun returned from I.O.M. & went into action at New Position. 2/Lt Ebbels slightly wounded in NIEUPORT going to O.P. on the breastbone but returned to duty from Dressing Station; he was sent to Coxyde for rest. Sig. Weldrake, who was accompanying Lt Ebbels, was also wounded in the neck. Evacuated. Moved to New Position between MAISON CAIREE & POOLS FARM with 5 guns in action
	27	Gun N° 1186 sent to I.O.M. for condemnation
	31	Gun N° 2094 returned from I.O.M.
Aug.	1	Position flooded after week of bad storms. 2/Lt A.C. Miller appointed Adjt to the 29th Bde (1 Div) 2/Lt Craft & 13 men attached to us from an Australian Battery. "B" & "C" detachments sent to the Coxyde for a rest. Lt de Juille relieved 2/Lt Craft
	5	"B" & "C" detachments returned from Coxyde & "E" & "F" went for a rest
	6	Successful raid. Captured 5 prisoners & 1 Machine gun. Fired about 100 rds per gun. 2/Lt ——— relieved Lt de Juille

Aug	7	Attached men from the Australian B'ty relieved
	8	Six men attached to us from the 158 Bde RFA. 4 guns only to be kept in action.
	9	"E" & "F" detachments returned from W/Line
	10	2/Lt Ebbels reported back for duty. 2/Lt Weedon sent to W/Line for a rest
	11	2/Lt Weedon sent to Hospital near BRAY DUNES
	12	About 12.39 P.M. one 4.2 shell dropped in D sub section sheds at W/Line killing & wounding 17 horses. Men luckily at dinner
	16	Battery returned to W/Line for 10 days rest; guard left over ammunition & contents at position
	17	Capt d'Ivry went on leave. Today horses moved to lines in a field during day.
	18	5 guns calibrated at COXYDE-BAINS by fall of shell out at sea & cross observation called Sound Ranging. Also fired through electrical wire screens. Results not at all corresponding to I.O.M. measurements in registration. 2/Lt Hinton from C/168 attached to us
	20	2/Lt Weedon returned from Hospital. 2/Lt Ebbels & 2 NCOs sent on a Gas Course at LA PANNE for 3 days.

Aug 21	Sports were held to-day at the W/Line. Relay; "Tug of war;" "100 yds" Pillow Fight" "Potato" 4 Legged Race. In the evening a very good concert was held in one of the huts. Lt Ravald in the chair.
22	O.C. 2/Lt Weedon, 6 Nos 1 & 6 J. Gunners went to Ordnance for instructions in the No 106 fuze. 2/Lt Hinton returned to C/168.
23	Lt Ravald went on leave.
25	Battery came into action five guns. C gun calibrated by sound ranging. Battery attached "D" Group under Lt Col Wickham
27	C Gun came into action
Sept 4	Battery position shelled by 4.2 from about 11 am to 2 pm. 2 gun pits ignited guns slightly scorched by heat & some 300 rounds ammunition damaged. J/Bdr Mansfield went back to position under heavy fire & recovered some 4000 fcs., money for pay, left in a dug-out though he was in no way responsible for the money.
5	Started work on an alternative position at M 33 c 8890 near BOIS TRIANGULAIRE.

Sept 5	Lt Ravald returned from leave. 2/Lt Clarke posted to us
6	2 Officers chargers transferred to 15th Batt. Lancs. Fusiliers
7	All shooting stopped by order except S.O.S.
14	2/Lt Clarke F.J. attached to B/168 for 10 days
15	The Battery Signallers were passed first of all units in Division at test in all branches of signalling at COXYDE when Division were at rest in August.
16	Capt d'Ivry to guns vice 2/Lt Weedon to wagon line
18	General Schute (Divisional Commander) inspected all Battery positions & pronounced this Battery the best he had seen. His inspection included Corps & Army R.A. as well as 32nd Divl Arty.
21	C.R.A. Brig. General Tyler 32nd Divl Chief visited the wagon lines. He wrote a most complimentary letter to B.C. on improvement of B'ty in fighting qualities & all interior economy.
22	About 7.15 PM neighbourhood bombed by aero

	planes, wounded C/pl Povey T/yBt. Peace; 10th evacuated.
Sept 23	2/Lt Weedon proceeded on leave. Capt d'Ivory returned to the wagon Lines
Oct 7	2/Lt Weedon returned from leave. "E" sub. gun was sent to Sound Ranging Section for calibration
8	Lt Ebbits proceeded on leave.
10	Gnr Soloman & Edwards W.H. wounded
11	Came out of action. Withdrew to W/ Line at COXYDE at 4 A.M. Remained at Wagon Line the day, marched at dusk to GHYVELDE where the Battery slept in tents
16	Marched to WORMHOUDT. B.Cs went by motors to the New Position
17	Marched to camp just outside POPERINGHE (temporary wagon Lines) 2/Lt Weedon, 2 Nos.1, 12 men & 2 Signallers went in lorries to Battery Position
18	Handed over 4 guns to relieved Battery A/256 Bgde taking over 4 guns in action at C6C 7080. Marched to wagon line near & N of VLAMERTINGHE B26 b80

Oct 17	Taking up ammunition by packs, D. Westgate F & D. Crisp E wounded. D. Varley L reported missing; 3 horses killed in the road & 1 missing. Varley found to have been killed
20	Guns in action behind POLECAPELLE on S.T JOLIEN – LANGEMARKE R.D The under-mentioned casualties occurred

   Bdr Wood B. – Killed
   Gnr Beaumont L – wounded
    " Hynes W.H – "
   Sgt Firth A – "
    " Smith E.T – "
   Bdr Noble C – "
   Gnr Pearson T – "
    " Symonds H – "
    " Rushworth A – "

Gnr Lewis, Bdr Richardson & ⅌/Bdr Rice Shell Shock

23	First attack. Advanced our line.
24	Started the second bombardment at 5 AM The undermentioned casualties occurred

   Gnr Wilkinson T.   Killed
    " M.c Pherson A.   Wounded

	Gnr Slack H —	wounded
	9/Bdr Tetlow H —	do
	Fitter Bambrough —	do
	9/Bdr Halliday R —	do
	" Mansfield W.G. —	do
Oct 25	Cpl. Jackson wounded	
26	Gnr McEwing A. wounded. Second attack	
27	Gnr Dawson W. wounded. Mjr Emmet to the wagon line; Capt d'Ivory relieving at the guns. 2/Lt Clarke to hospital, rheumatism	
28	Cpl S.S. Parks killed bringing up ammunition. Cpl Rhodes L. wounded at Battery Position	
30	Third Attack	
Nov. 3	Major Emmet to guns relieving Capt d'Ivory to W Lines.	
5	Gnr McCarthy C wounded	
	" Miller W.	"
	" Robinson H	"
	" Roskilly P.	"
	" Rockett B.	"

Nov 5	Sgt McGowan admitted to Hospital. Gnr Roskilly died of wounds
6	Fourth attack with 1st Div & Canadians. 2/Lt Weedon J.W. wounded & 2/Lt Barrick attached from C/168 Killed. 2/Lt Chamberlain & 2/Lt Storey attached from B/168. 2/ Morse J wounded
8	Gnr Baird S wounded
9	" Spence R "
	2/Lt Weaver R.I. attached
12	Fifth attack with 1st Div & Canadians
13	Major Emmet to W/Line; Capt d'Ivry to guns
16	Battery personell relieved by B/168, personell proceeded to Wagon Line
17	Dr Tall F wounded
24	Capt d'Ivry detailed for Liaison. 2/Lt Thorne F posted.

1918
Jany 29 Moved to new w/ lines at
         Canal Bank.
     31 Right Section action Relieved
         113 Bat: (1st Div) in position near
         Laurier & Boods. Officers Mess at
         Larain Farm 120x behind Bat:
         Position.
Feb   1 Centre & Left Section relieved
      4 A.L.1 Infantry Officer attached
         for Instructional purposes.
         2/Lt White T.M. Gunner
      5 Lt Ebbets Returned from Leave
         of Instruction.

1918

July 6 | L28188 Sergt Padgett S.
L263 Gnr Jackson J
Awarded Military Medal.

July 13 | L28188 Sergt Padgett S
L263 Gnr Jackson J
Presentation by the General

July 17 | Came out of action
" 18 | Marched to Humbercourt
20 | Entrained at Doullens.
21 | Arrived
22 |
23 |
24 |
25 |
26 |
27 |

1918
Aug 11   Battery Photographed

CONFIDENTIAL.

WAR DIARY

of the

168th Brigade R. F. A.

From 1st January 1918 to 31st January 1918.

(Volume XXV)

Army Form C. 2118.

WAR DIARY
or
INTELLIGENCE SUMMARY.
(Erase heading not required.)

168th Brigade R.F.A.
Commanded by Lt-Col.C.R.B.CARRINGTON.D.S.O.

Place	Date	Hour	Summary of Events and Information	Remarks and references to Appendices
	1/1/18		The 168th Brigade continued to be in action N.E.of ST JULIEN, erecting of Gun Pits etc commenced. Front abnormally quiet.	
	2/1/18			
	3/1/18		B/168 Wagon Lines Bombed by enemy aircraft. 3 men wounded. Trench Warfare.	
	4/1/18			
	7/1/18	7.am	1 Section per Battery 168th Brigade relieved by 1 Section per battery of the 174th Brigade R.F.A.	
	8/1/18	7.am	Relief of 168th Brigade by 174th Brigade completed. Batteries of 168th Brigade withdraw to Wagon Lines in the vicinity of BRIELEN.	
		11.am	H.Q.moved to A.28.b.1.1 (Sheet 28).	
	9/1/18		The Brigade is in Support of the 58th Division. The day spent in general cleaning up and overhauling.	
	20/1/18		3 Guns per Battery placed in action under a guard South of LAGEMARCK, Corps Line of Defence. From the 10th to 30th, the Brigade remained at rest in the Wagon Lines. Strict training was carried out.	
	31/1/18		One Section per Battery of 168th Brigade relieved one Section of Batteries of 1st D.A. in action S.E.of BIXSCHOOTE as follows:- A/168 relieved 113th Battery. B/168. " 54th " C/168 " 46th " D/168. " 40th " (How). Ammunition expended during month 2637 A. 1700 A.X. 994 B.X. 4 A.S. Casualties during month. 1 Gunner & 5 Drivers Wounded.	

31st Jany 1918.

Lieut-Colonel.
Commanding 168th Brigade R.F.A.

CONFIDENTIAL

WAR - DIARY.

of
the

168th BRIGADE R.F.A.

From 1st FEBRUARY 1918 to 28th FEBRUARY 1918.

VOLUME XXVI.

Army Form C. 2118.

WAR DIARY
or
INTELLIGENCE SUMMARY.

(Erase heading not required.)

168th BRIGADE R.F.A.
COMMANDED BY Lt-Col.C.R.R.CARRINGTON DSO

Instructions regarding War Diaries and Intelligence Summaries are contained in F. S. Regs., Part II. and the Staff Manual respectively. Title pages will be prepared in manuscript.

Place	Date	Hour	Summary of Events and Information	Remarks and references to Appendices
	1-2-18.	11.am	Relief of the Batteries of the 1st D.A.completed. Command of the Left Group 32nd D.A. passes to Lt-Col.CARRINGTON.D.S.O. Left Group consists of:- A/168 Battery. B/168. " C/168. " D/168. " A/28th " 124th " 14th Infantry Brigade is in the Sector covered by the Left Group R.F.A.	
	2-2-18.		Front very quiet.	
	3-2-18.		Trench Warfare.	
	4-2-18.		97th Brigade relieve the 96th Infantry Brigade in the Sector covered by Left Group.	
	5-2-18.		Front very quiet.	
	6-2-18.		Front very quiet.	
	7-2-18.		Front very quiet. 17th H.L.I. relieved the 11th Border Regt in the line. The 96th Infantry Brigade relieved the 14th and 97th on the Centre Brigade Front. The Divisional Front was thus divided into 3 Brigade Sectors with 1 Batt'n each in the line, one in Support and the third in Reserve.	
	8-2-18.		Front very quiet.	
	9-2-18.		Front very quiet.	
	10-2-18. night 10/11.		B/168 shelled by 15 c.m.Hows and 10.5.c.m.Hows at intervals during the day. The 35th Division extended its left, the 104th Infantry Brigade relieving the 14th Infantry Bde. The Front was thus held by 3 Brigades each with 1 Batt'n in the line.	

Army Form C. 2118.

WAR DIARY
or
INTELLIGENCE SUMMARY.

(Erase heading not required.)

168th Brigade R.F.A. Commanded by Lt.Col.S.R.R.CARRINGTON, DSO.

Instructions regarding War Diaries and Intelligence Summaries are contained in F.S. Regs., Part II. and the Staff Manual respectively. Title pages will be prepared in manuscript.

Place	Date	Hour	Summary of Events and Information	Remarks and references to Appendices
	11-2-18		Re-adjustment of Artillery Groups from 10.a.m. also front covered. The 168th Brigade R.F.A. consists of :- A/168.R.F.A. B/168.R.F.A. (2 Forward Guns). C/168.R.F.A. D/168.R.F.A. 124th Battery.	
	12-2-18		Front very quiet.	
	13-2-18		Brigade H.Q.moved to GREEK HOUSE. Front very quiet.	
	14-2-18		2nd K.O.Y.L.I. relieved the 16th H.L.I.in the line on the left Sector.	
	15-2-18	3.15.am	Belgian Division on left raided by Germans. Thirteen Killed and 2 prisoners. D/168 and 124th Battery fired Belge Barrage for 5 minutes. K.O.Y.L.I. raided Bosche lines on right of Divl Sector in the evening. Very successful. 1 Officer and 10 O.R's prisoners. Three s casualties suffered.	
	16-2-18		Trench Warfare. 11th A.F.A.came into position for purpose of supporting a prosposed raid for night 18/19th.	
	17-2-18		Front very quiet.	
	18-2-18		Very clear day. Aeroplanes activity above normal. One F.A.Brought down in enemy lines, another badly damaged.	
		11.pm to 11-45pm	Raids carried out by the 97th and 96th Infantry Brigades. The 2nd K.O.Y.L.I.and the 13th Border Regt carried out the one on the left. Both raids very sucessful and little enemy fire encountered. 97th Infantry Brigade took 8.prisoners and 1 Machine Gun. The 96th too 21 prisoners.	

Army Form C. 2118.

WAR DIARY
or
INTELLIGENCE SUMMARY.

(Erase heading not required.)

168th BRIGADE R. F. A.
Commanded by Lt.-Col.C.R.P.CARRINGTON.DSO.

Instructions regarding War Diaries and Intelligence Summaries are contained in F. S. Regs., Part II. and the Staff Manual respectively. Title pages will be prepared in manuscript.

Place	Date	Hour	Summary of Events and Information	Remarks and references to Appendices
	19-2-18.		14th Infantry Brigade relieved the 97th Infantry Brigade in the line on the left of the Divisional Front. The 5/6th Royal Scots relieving the 2nd K.O.Y.L.I. in the line.	
	20-2-18.		Front very quiet.	
	21.	5.a.m.	Enemy attempted to raid BELGIAN POST on the left Divn Front but did not succed in getting to the post. B & D/168 fired on Barrage B (a protective Barrage) for nearly ½ hour. Neighbourhood of C/168 R.F.A.shelled at intervals during the day with 77 m.m.shrapnel.	
	22 to 25th		Front very quiet.	
	26-2-18.		A/168.R.F.A. carried out wire-cutting.	
	27-2-18.	7-50pm	The 168th Brigade covered a Raid made by the 14th Infantry Brigade on the German Pill-Boxes in HOULTHUST FOREST. 4 Prisoners and 1 Machine Gun were captured and many Germans killed.	
	28-2-18.	8.pm	In connection with a Raid made by the 35th Division A.R. & D.168 fired a Standing Barrage.	

1st March 1918.

M Cotte
Major.
Commanding 168th Brigade RFA.

32nd Divisional Arty.

168th BRIGADE

ROYAL FIELD ARTILLERY

MARCH 1 9 1 8

Confidential

War Diary

of the

168th Brigade R.F.A.

from 1st March 1918 to 31st March 1918

Volume XXVII.

Army Form C. 2118.

WAR DIARY
or
INTELLIGENCE SUMMARY.

(Erase heading not required)

168th Brigade R.F.A.
Commanded by Lt-Col.C.R.B.CARRINGTON
D.S.O.

Instructions regarding War Diaries and Intelligence Summaries are contained in F. S. Regs., Part II. and the Staff Manual respectively. Title pages will be prepared in manuscript.

Place	Date	Hour	Summary of Events and Information	Remarks and references to Appendices
	1/3/18.		At 7.30.p.m.enemy attempted a raid on the Belgian Posts on our Right Inf., but was repulsed. Our Batteries fired in support of the Belgians. Our Batteries sniped enemy movement during the day.	
	2/3/18.		Front very quiet. Our Batteries carried out sniping on enemy movement.	
	3/3/18.		Front very quiet. During the night enemy fired gas shells in vicinity of our Battery Positions.	
	4/3/18.		Front very quiet. Sniping was again carried out by our Batteries.	
	5/3/18.		Front very quiet. Sniping was again carried out by our Batteries.	
	6/3/18.		B/168,D/168 and Brigade H.Q. was subjected to an area shoot by the enemy from 5.45.a.m. to 6.35 a.m. (500 rds 77 m.m,10.5.m.m. including some gas,and again from 4.15.p.m. (300 rds) Front system quiet.	
	7/3/18.		At 4.a.m. enemy under cover of artillery fire raided our posts on the left of the Right Brigade Sector. Our Batteries fired on S.O.S.Lines and in support of a counter attack carried (A)by our infantry at 9.30.a.m. All posts were re-taken by us.	
	8/3/18.		Front quiet. Our Artillery carried out sniping on enemy movement.	
	9/3/18.		-do-	
	10/3/18.		Front quiet. A post on the Right Bde sector was rushed by the enemy under cover of M.G. fire. Sniping was again carried out by our Batteries. Enemy's H.V.Guns were active on back areas.	

Army Form C. 2118.

WAR DIARY
or
INTELLIGENCE SUMMARY.

168th Brigade R.F.A.
Commanded by Lt-Col.C.R.R.CARRINGTON,DSO.

(Erase heading not required.)

Instructions regarding War Diaries and Intelligence Summaries are contained in F.S. Regs., Part II. and the Staff Manual respectively. Title pages will be prepared in manuscript.

Place	Date	Hour	Summary of Events and Information	Remarks and references to Appendices
	11/3/18.		Very quiet day. Unusually clear day and aircraft fairly active on both sides.	CRR.
	12/3/18.		Trench Warfare.	CRR.
	13/3/18. 7.35.pm		96th Bde relieved the 14th Infantry Bde on the left. Enemy put a heavy barrage down and machine raided COLOMBO POST on the right Brigade front. The raid was unsuccessful and the enemy was kept out. A/168 & D/168 fired on the HELP AJAX barrage, A/161 & B/168 fired on their S.O.S.Lines for a short time. Nothing developed on the left Brigade front. DSO	CRR.
	14/3/18.		Very quiet day. Lt-Col.F.R.SYKES took over command of the 168th Brigade R.F.A. while Lt-Col.CARRINGTON D.S.O. was away.	CRR.
	15/3/18. 8.56pm		S.O.S. rocket went up on the right of the right Battalion front. Right Brigade fired on S.O.S.Lines and "Help Ajax" was given. Apparently no Infantry action developed.	CRR.
	16/3/18.		Very quiet all day. Usual standing warfare.	CRR.
	17/3/18. 4.35 to 6.a.m.		Enemy subjected valley of BROEMBEEK and the 161st Batteries to a fairly heavy Gas bombardment our Heavy Artillery retaliated with effect. Our aeroplanes very active patrolling enemy's lines all day.	CRR.
	18/3/18. 2.25 to 3.10.am 4.10.am 5.45.am		Enemy repeated his gas bombardment on the same areas as on the morning of the 17th Enemy fire almost ceased on retaliation by our heavies. S.O.S. went up on right Divisional Front. S.O.S. went up at 5.47.a.m. Right Belgian Division heavily shelled. Our Batteries retaliated for heavy shelling of Belgian Front. Our aeroplanes again very busy patrolling lines as weather was exceedingly favourable.	CRR.
	19/3/18.		Usual standing warfare.	CRR.

WAR DIARY
or
INTELLIGENCE SUMMARY.

Army Form C. 2118.

168th Brigade R.F.A.
Commanded by Lt-Col.C.R.B.CARRINGTON.D.S.O.

(Erase heading not required.)

Instructions regarding War Diaries and Intelligence Summaries are contained in F. S. Regs., Part II. and the Staff Manual respectively. Title pages will be prepared in manuscript.

Place	Date	Hour	Summary of Events and Information	Remarks and references to Appendices
	20/3/18.	11.pm	A Raid was carried out on the Left Brigade Front by 2 coys of Lancs Fusiliers. They were held up by wire on the front of the raid not prove very successful. One prisoner of the 544th I.R. 36th Division was taken. 2/Lt PATTERSON D/168 went over with the Infantry as F.O.O.	£RR
	21/3/18.	5.a.m.	Enemy shelled Left Brigade front fairly heavily, gas & H.E. Our Batteries retaliated No infantry action developed.	ERR
	22/3/18.	2.am	Fairly lively day. Enemy heavily shelled back areas. Counter preparation was fired on during the day.	ERR
	23/3/18.	2.am.	15th Lancs Fusiliers raided enemy on the left front. Raid quite successful. Four Prisoners taken. Our casualties only two. Prisoners were of the 36th Division. Enemy heavily shelled our left front and right of Belgian front with H.E.& Gas as retaliation after the raid. Fairly quiet rest of the day.	ERR
	24/3/18.		Very quiet day. Ordinary standing warfare. Lt-Col.CARRINGTON.D.S.O. arrived back from leave and took over command of the Brigade again from Lt-Col.F.R.SYKES.DSO. Enemy attempted a raid on the left front against Belgians but was repulsed. We fired to help the Belgians also on the left part of our front.	ERR
	25/3/18.		Fairly quiet day. Enemy bombarded on left front with T.M.'s fairly heavily at 11.pm.	ERR
	26/3/18.		Trench Warfare.	ERR
	27/3/18.		Trench Warfare.	ERR
	28/3/18.		Our infantry relieved by infantry of 4th Belgian Division.	ERR
	29/3/18.		Enemy raided trenches in Sector covered by the Brigade and captured one Belgian.	ERR

Army Form C. 2118.

WAR DIARY
or
INTELLIGENCE SUMMARY.

Lt-Col.C.R.B.CARRINGTON.D.S.O.
Commanding 168th Brigade R.F.A.

(Erase heading not required.)

Place	Date	Hour	Summary of Events and Information	Remarks and references to Appendices
	30/3/18.		Batteries relieved by Batteries of 4th Belgian Infantry Division.	I21
	31/3/18.		Brigade entrained PESELHOEK and after an uneventful journey detrained TINQUES. Night of 31st spent at LATTRE ST QUENTIN. Ammunition fired during month 18-Pdr A. 12018 rds A.X. 15115 rds BX 4.5" Hows. BX. 6044 rds Gas 179 rds.	I22

R Carrington
Lieut - Colonel.
Commanding 168th Brigade R.F.A.

32nd Div.
VI.Corps.

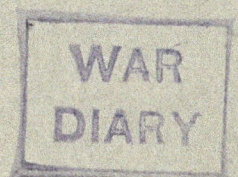

Headquarters,

168th BRIGADE, R.F.A.

A P R I L

1 9 1 8

C O N F I D E N T I A L

WAR   DIARY

of

the

168th BRIGADE R. F. A.

From 1st April 1918 to 30th April 1918.

VOLUME XXVIII

Army Form C. 2118.

WAR DIARY
or
INTELLIGENCE SUMMARY.
(Erase heading not required.)

168th Brigade R.F.A. Commanded by Lt. Col C.R.B. CARRINGTON, DSO.

Instructions regarding War Diaries and Intelligence Summaries are contained in F. S. Regs., Part II. and the Staff Manual respectively. Title pages will be prepared in manuscript.

Place	Date	Hour	Summary of Events and Information	Remarks and references to Appendices
	1/4/18.		Brigade remained at LATTRE ST QUENTIN. Reconnoitring parties proceeded by Bus to forward area and visited Batteries which are to be relieved.	R
	2/4/18.		Brigade marched to HUMBERCAMP. 1 Section per Battery relieved 1 Section per Battery of the 160th Brigade in action North of ADINFER.	
	3/4/18.		Relief of 160th Brigade completed without incident.	
		5.p.m.	168th Brigade H.Q. take over Command	
	4/4/18.		14th Infantry Brigade in the line East of AYETTE covered by 168th Brigade R.F.A.	
	5/4/18.		Anti Tank Gun of C/168 placed in action in ADINFER WOOD.	
	6/4/18.		Harassing fire carried out night and day by our Batteries.	
	7/4/18.		Very wet and stormy, day very quiet.	
	8/4/18.		Trench Warfare.	
	9/4/18.			
	10/4/18.			
	11/4/18.		Enemy Gas Shelled ADINFER WOOD very heavily.	
	12/4/18.		Forward Wagon Lines at RANSART Shelled 1 O.R. killed and 1 O.R. wounded. 24 horses are killed and 10 wounded.	
	13/4/18.		Very noticeable decrease in enemy Artillery fire.	

Army Form C. 2118.

WAR DIARY or INTELLIGENCE SUMMARY.

(Erase heading not required.)

168th Brigade R.F.A.
Commanded by Lt Col.C.R.R.CARRINGTON,DSO.

Place	Date	Hour	Summary of Events and Information	Remarks and references to Appendices
	14/4/18.		Synchronised Bombardments carried out on enemy positions.	
	15/4/18.			
	16/4/18.	9.p.m.	Outskirts of MOYENVILLE bombarded with Gas Shell.	
	17/4/18.		Weather bright and fine, after three days dull and windy.	
	18/4/18.		Trench Warfare.	
	19/4/18.			
	20/4/18.		Trench Warfare.	
	21/4/18.			
	22/4/18.		1 Section of D/168 moved to a forward position East of ADINFER in order to be available for C.B.work.	
	23/4/18.			
	24/4/18.		1st Guards Brigade relieved 14th Infantry Brigade in the Sector covered by the 168th Brigade R.F.A.	
	25/4/18.			
	26/4/18.	10.am	C.R.A. Guards Division took over Command from C.R.A. 32nd Division.	
	27/4/18.		1 Section per Battery 168th Brigade relieved 1 Section per Battery 75th Brigade R.F.A. in action N.E. of HENDECOURT. 10½z - RANSART.	
	28/4/18.	9.pm	Relief of 75th Brigade completed.	

Army Form C. 2118.

WAR DIARY
or
INTELLIGENCE SUMMARY.
(Erase heading not required.)

168th Brigade R.F.A. Commanded by Lt Col C.R.B.CARRINGTON.DSO

Place	Date	Hour	Summary of Events and Information	Remarks and references to Appendices
	29/4/18	11.30.am	168th Brigade H.Q. moved to BLAIRVILLE and formed a Sub-Group under 161st Brigade R.F.A. covering 6th Infantry Brigade.	
	30/4/18		Wet and dull — day quiet.	

30th April 1918.

R Carrington
Lieut Colonel.
Commanding 168th Brigade R. F. A.

CONFIDENTIAL.

WAR DIARY

OF THE

168th BRIGADE R.F.A.

From 1st May 1918 to 31st May 1918.

VOLUME XXIX

WAR DIARY
or
INTELLIGENCE SUMMARY.

(Erase heading not required.)

Army Form C. 2118.

168th Brigade R.F.A.
Commanded by Lt. Col. C.P.B. CARRINGTON. DSO.

Place	Date	Hour	Summary of Events and Information	Remarks and references to Appendices
	1/5/18.		Front quiet. Trench warfare.	///
	2/5/18.		No. 311600. Sapper RAMSDEN.A. awarded the Italian Bronze Medal for Military Valour. B/168 ran up a single gun to Boyou-Mut and carried out a shoot on house in BOYELLES which was reported to contain Snipers and Machine Guns. After the shoot the gun was withdrawn again.	///
	3/5/18.	2.30.am.	In connection with a Raid by the 2nd Canadian Division, our Batteries carried out a 'Feint' Creeping Barrage. The Raid was very successful, 7 Prisoners and 5 machine guns being captured.	///
	4/5/18.		Appreciable increase in enemy Artillery Fire. A.&.D.Batteries were both shelled by 8" Hows, but no damage done.	///
	6/5/18.		G.O.C. 2nd Division and C.R.A. 40th Division visited Battery Positions. S.O.S. reported on 5th Infantry Brigade Front, our Batteries fired on S.O.S. lines.	///
	7/5/18.		Trench Warfare.	///
	8/5/18.		Brigade H.Q. moved from the village of BLAIREVILLE, into dug-outs in a trench 100 yds South of the village. 'B' Battery withdrawn from action and goes into Mobile reserve. Its role is to be prepared to go into action on any part of the Divisional front, to engage Tanks etc.	///

Army Form C. 2118.

WAR DIARY
or
INTELLIGENCE SUMMARY.
(Erase heading not required.)

168th Brigade R.F.A.
Commanded by Lt Col.C.R.B.CARRINGTON,DSO.

Instructions regarding War Diaries and Intelligence Summaries are contained in F. S. Regs., Part II. and the Staff Manual respectively. Title pages will be prepared in manuscript.

Place	Date	Hour	Summary of Events and Information	Remarks and references to Appendices
	9/5/18.		Trench Warfare.	OK
	10/5/18.		D/168 carried out a Shoot with incendiary shell on R.E. Dump in BOYELLES, a large fire was caused.	OK
	11/5/18.	5.pm	The enemy commenced shelling A/168 with gas shell and continued for 16 hours, causing a large number of casualties.	OK
	12/5/18.	9.pm	D/168 placed a Howitzer in action west of MERCATEL, in order to get infilade fire on a sunken road in BOYELLES which is reported to contain several enemy Trench Mortars. 16th Lancashire Fusiliers relieved 17th Royal Fusiliers in Sector covered by 168th Bde.	OK
	13/5/18.	7.am 10.30 am.	The enemy again shelled A/168. All ranks were moved to a Plank in order to escape the gas. D/168, commenced a shoot by aeroplane observation on an enemy Battery, but after firing one round, the shoot was discontinued owing to rain.	OK
	14/5/18.		Trench Warfare.	OK
	15/5/18.		Trench Warfare.	OK
	16/5/18.		In order to deceive the enemy as to number of Batteries on our front, each Battery has a silent section, which is detached from the main Battery Position and does not fire except in case of S.O.S.	OK
	17/5/18.		Trench Warfare.	OK

Army Form C. 2118.

WAR DIARY
or
INTELLIGENCE SUMMARY.

(Erase heading not required.)

168th Brigade R.F.A.
Commanded by Lt Colonel. C.R.CARRINGTON.DSO.

Place	Date	Hour	Summary of Events and Information	Remarks and references to Appendices
	18/5/18.		C.R.A. 32nd Division assumed command of the Artillery covering the 32nd Division.	CC
	19/5/18.		Trench Warfare.	CC
	20/5/18.	7.30.p.m.	Stray enemy shell hit C/168 Officer's Mess, killing 1 Officer. Other Officers severely shaken.	CC
	21/5/18.	3.am	Batteries fired in conjunction with a raid by the 1st Dorsets on enemy trenches opposite HAMELINCOURT. 5 Prisoners were taken.	CC
	22/5/18.		D/168 shot at an enemy gun which was observed in the open, good shooting was done and several O.K's were obtained.	CC
	23/5/18.	2.30. to 4.30. pm.	A/168 shelled by a 10.5.c.m gun with 200 rounds. 1 gun was damaged, no other damage or casualties caused.	CC
	24/5/18.		C/168 put a Sniping gun in position North East of BOIRY ST MARTIN range to our front line 2,600.	CC
	26/5/18.		Increased activity of the enemy's artillery, heavy concentrations on selected area, being the order of the day.	CC
	27/5/18.		A/168 heavily shelled, no damage done beyond blowing up a small dump of ammunition. Enemy started a heavy gas and H.E. bombardment of Battery areas which last until 6.30.am. No damage was done to our Batteries.	CC

WAR DIARY
or
INTELLIGENCE SUMMARY.
(Erase heading not required.)

Army Form C. 2118.

168th Brigade R.F.A.
Commanded by
Lt.Colonel.C.R.B.CARRINGTON.DSO.

Place	Date	Hour	Summary of Events and Information	Remarks and references to Appendices
	28/5/18.		Trench Warfare.	
	29/5/18.		D/168 shelled by 15.c.m.How: 1 gun damaged, no casualties.	
	30/5/18.	1.pm	C/168 Shelled: direct hit obtained on their officers mess; no casualties.	
		9.pm	Lt-Col.CARRINGTON.DSO assumed Command of the Centre Group 32nd Div Arty, covering the 14th Infantry Brigade. The Group is composed of A.C.&D.168 and A/186.	
			Front covered is N.E.of HAMELINCOURT.	
	31/5/18.		Trench Warfare.	
			Casualties during month 5 Officers Wounded 40 Other Ranks Wounded.	
			1 Officer Killed.	
			Ammunition Expended during month. 11608 rds A. 5000 rds A.X. 6028.B.X. 1751.Gas	
			100 rds Incendiary Shell.	

[signature]
Lt Colonel.
Commanding 168th Brigade r.F.A.

1st June 1918.

WAR DIARY

OF THE

168th BRIGADE R. F. A.

From 1st June 1918 to 30th June 1918.

VOLUMNE XXX.

WAR DIARY
or
INTELLIGENCE SUMMARY.
(Erase heading not required.)

Army Form C. 2118.

168th Brigade R.F.A.

Place	Date	Hour	Summary of Events and Information	Remarks and references to Appendices
June 1918	1/6/18		The month commenced with the weather cool but fine. There is to change in the General situation since last month, except a marked decrease in the activity of the enemy artillery.	
	2/6/18	10.30am	Our Batteries took part in a concentration on enemy trench mortars in MOYENVILLE	O.R.
	3/6/18		D/168 carried out a successful shoot with aeroplane observation on enemy battery.	O.R.
	4/6/18	12.10am	S.O.S. reported on 19th Infantry Brigade Front, our batteries fired until 12.50 am when the situation was cleared. No enemy action took place.	O.R.
	5/6/18	6 am	Batteries Group R.F.A. is reorganised and now consists of the following batteries A.B.C. & D/168 & D/156, covering the front of the 19th Infantry Brigade opposite HAMELINCOURT.	O.R.
	6/6/18		Brigade HQ shelled for three hours with 10 cm & 7.7 cm guns, material damage slight, casualties 4 O.R. Wounded.	O.R.
	7/6/18		Wagon Lines at BRETENCOURT shelled. Several casualties amongst the horses.	O.R.
	8/6/18		Trench Warfare. Front very quiet	O.R.
	9/6/18		" " " " "	O.R.

WAR DIARY
or
INTELLIGENCE SUMMARY.
(Erase heading not required.)

Army Form C. 2118.

Instructions regarding War Diaries and Intelligence Summaries are contained in F. S. Regs., Part II, and the Staff Manual respectively. Title pages will be prepared in manuscript.

Place	Date	Hour	Summary of Events and Information	Remarks and references to Appendices
	10/6/18		Gas projected into HAMELINCOURT, our batteries co-operated by firing bursts of shrapnel over the village	OK.
	11/6/18		The 91st Infantry Brigade on our left, carried out a raid. In order to create a diversion, our batteries bombarded the enemy's lines N.E. of HAMELINCOURT. The 19th Infantry Brigade sent out patrols under cover of this, capturing one Boche and killing two.	OK.
	12/6/18		Trench Warfare - The enemy has been very harassing, replying feebly to our fire	OK.
	13/6/18 to 17/6/18		Nothing of note has happened during this period. The front has been remarkably quiet.	OK.
	18/6/18		D/165 shelled for 2 hours by a 5.9 How. the gun pits were damaged and ammunition affected, to other damage or casualties caused	OK.
			C/165 forward section which is in the COJEUL VALLEY - N.E. of BOIRY - St- MARTIN shelled by a 10.5 Cm How, one gun damaged	OK.
	19/6/18		Trench Warfare	
	20/6/18 1 am		Small Raid carried out on Enemy posts N. of HAMELINCOURT. This was supported by batteries of Centre Group. The enemy had apparently fled, as none were found	OK.

Army Form C. 2118.

WAR DIARY
or
INTELLIGENCE SUMMARY.
(Erase heading not required.)

Instructions regarding War Diaries and Intelligence Summaries are contained in F. S. Regs. Part II. and the Staff Manual respectively. Title pages will be prepared in manuscript.

Place	Date	Hour	Summary of Events and Information	Remarks and references to Appendices
	21/6/18	1am	D/165 - D/186. Gas shelled enemy trench mortar Emplacements in the COJEUL VALLEY (Sm.K)	O.L.
	22/6/18	1am	West of HAMELINCOURT. D/186 withdrawn from Action	O.L.
	23/6/18		D/175 relieved D/156 in the battle Group	O.L.
	24/6/18	2am	Single Raid carried out on Enemy Posts N. of HAMELINCOURT, supported by Batteries of batte Group. All objectives were reached, but the enemy had fled. No prisoners were taken.	O.L.
	25/6/18		Usual warfare. Have abnormally quiet	O.L.
	26/6/18		Forward section in the COJEUL VALLEY moved back to their battery positions and Four guns for Battery posts. In accordance with new scheme of defence.	O.L. O.L.
	27/6/18		Usual Warfare. No unusual incident has happened during the month.	O.L.
	30/6/18		It has been the quietest Appearance for some time. Ammunition fired during the Month 15Pdrs 15,056 rounds. 4.5How 5750 HE 1000 Gas.	O.L.
			Casualties 1 Officer & 6 OR wounded. Lt Col. Carnegie D.S.O. - Bomb F.F. Col. - Lieut. J.M.G.O. d'Arcy M/165 - M.C. Honours No L/55548 Sgt F Beaumont B/165 - D.C.M. - No 8949 Sgt F.A. White R.V.C. alt B/165 - M.S.M. No 935642 Sgt W. Seymour C/165 - M.M.	O.L. O.L.

Rowan Thos
Lt. Col
Cmdg 165th Brigade R.F.A.

32 Div-

WAR DIARY

OF THE

168th BRIGADE R.F.A.

From 1st July 1918 to 31st July 1918

VOLUME XXXI:

Army Form C. 2118.

WAR DIARY
or
INTELLIGENCE SUMMARY.

(Erase heading not required.)

168th Brigade R.F.A,
Commanded by Lt Col C.R.H.CARRINGTON DSO

Instructions regarding War Diaries and Intelligence Summaries are contained in F.S. Regs., Part II. and the Staff Manual respectively. Title pages will be prepared in manuscript.

Place	Date	Hour	Summary of Events and Information	Remarks and references to Appendices
	1/7/18		A/168 Forward Section in BOIRY - ST -RICTRUDE shelled by a 10,c,m,H,V,Gun;	
			1 Gun damaged, and 1 man wounded:	OK
	2/7/18		Trench Warfare, front quiet:	OK
	3/7/18	1,am	The 96th Brigade on our left and the 97th Brigade on our Right carried out raids:	OK
			Batteries of the CENTRE GROUP co-operated; 1 Machine Gun and 8 Prisoners were captured,	
			and a large number of the enemy w.r. killed:	OK
	4/7/18		Trench Warfare, Front quiet:	OK
	5/7/18		1st GUARDS Brigade relieved 14th Inf:Bde in the Sector covered by the 168th Bde RFA	OK
			and D/178,Bde RFA:	
	6/7/18			
	7/7/18	10,am	HQ 32nd Divl Arty relieved by HQ GUARDS Divl Arty:	OK
	8/7/18		Trench warfare:	OK
	10/7/18			
	11/7/18		Gas projected into BOYELLES: Our Batteries co-operated by sweeping the Area Gassed,	OK
			with H,E, and Shrapnel:	

Army Form C. 2118.

WAR DIARY
or
INTELLIGENCE SUMMARY.

168th Brigade R.F.A.
Commanded by Lt Col.C.R.B.CARRINGTON DSO:

(Erase heading not required.)

Instructions regarding War Diaries and Intelligence Summaries are contained in F. S. Regs., Part II. and the Staff Manual respectively. Title pages will be prepared in manuscript.

Place	Date	Hour	Summary of Events and Information	Remarks and references to Appendices
	15/7/18		Front remarkably quiet, nothing of note happened	CK
	16/7/18,			CK
	17/7/18,	5pm	72nd Army Field Brigade R.F.A. take over the Defence of the Front covered by this Brigade: Batteries of the 168th Brigade withdrew to their Wagon lines after dark: Brigade H.Q. marched to COULLEMONT:	CK
	18/7/18,	7am	Batteries marched to COULLEMONT:	CK
	19/7/18		Brigade entrained as follows:-	CK
			H.Q. BOUQUEMAISON, A/168 DOULLENS, B/168, MONDICOURT, C/168 DOULLENS, D/168. MONDICOURT,	
	20/7/18,		Except for an unsuccessful attack by an enemy aeroplane on the H.Q. train the journey was uneventful and the Brigade detrained as follows:-	CK
			HQ. 10. am PROVEN, A.&D/168 HERZEELE, B.&.C/168, WINNEZEELE, Afterwards marching to Wagon lines situated about 1½ miles due north of WATOU: One Section per Battery placed in action to cover the EAST POPERINGHE LINE:	
	21/7/18,		Brigade and Battery Commanders reconnoitred the positions & O.P's for the EAST POPERINGHE LINE:	CK

Army Form C. 2118.

WAR DIARY
or
INTELLIGENCE SUMMARY.
(Erase heading not required.)

168th Brigade R.F.A.
Commanded by Lt Col. C. R. B. CARRINGTON DSO.

Instructions regarding War Diaries and Intelligence Summaries are contained in F. S. Regs., Part II. and the Staff Manual respectively. Title pages will be prepared in manuscript.

Place	Date	Hour	Summary of Events and Information	Remarks and references to Appendices
	22/7/18		Training carried out:	A.
	23/7/18			
	24/7/18		Brigade and Battery Commanders proceed to XIX Corps Area to reconnoitre positions:	A.
	25/7/18		Major General R.A. 2nd Army inspected Wagon lines:	A.
			1 Officer and 30 Other Ranks per Battery proceeded to XIX Corps Area to work on positions reconnoitred on 24th:	
	26/7/18		Weather very unsettled: Strict training carried out during the period:	A.
	27/7/18			
	28/7/18			
	29/7/18			
	30/7/18		Brigade Sports were held and were a great success, the weather was glorious:	A.
	31/7/18			

1st August 1918

R Carrington.
Lt Colonel
Commanding 168th Brigade R.F.A.

CONFIDENTIAL

WAR DIARY

of the

168th BRIGADE R.F.A.

From 1st Aug: 1918 to 1st Sept 1918:

VOLUME XXXIII

Army Form C. 2118.

WAR DIARY
or
INTELLIGENCE SUMMARY.

(Erase heading not required.)

168th Brigade R.F.A.
Commanded by Lt. Col. C.R.E. CARRINGTON DSO:

Place	Date	Hour	Summary of Events and Information	Remarks, and references to Appendices
	1/8/18 to 5/8/18		The Brigade remained in Corps Reserve near HOUTKERQUE:	
	6/8/18:		C/168 marched past His Majesty the King near WATOU:	
	7/8/18:		Preparations for entraining carried out:	
	8/8/18:		The Brigade entrained as follows:- HQ. at PROVEN - 12-10, am 'A' Battery - 5-10, am 'B' Battery - 6-10, am 'C' Battery - 8-0, pm HQ detrained at LONGPRE, but were then ordered to march to MIENS where they bivouaced for the night: Batteries detrained as follows:- A,B,& C., LONGEAU) and bivouaced for the night near D. SALEUX,) the station:	
	9/8/18 12 Noon		Brigade concentrated at CAMLY, and at 4-30, pm marched to FOURGES: Owing to the enormous amount of traffic on the roads, this march took about 5 hours: A halt was made for the night in a field:	
	10/8/18 3, am		Brigade moved off again and marched to LE QUESNEL where a halt was made: Reconnoitring parties went forward and at 11, am the Brigade went into action East of P RVILLERS: 12-10, pm the 168th Brigade supported the 96th Infantry Brigade in an attack on PARVILLERS:	
	11/8/18:9-30,am		The 168th Brigade supported the 96th Infantry Brigade in a further attack on PARVILLERS, and at 5-30, pm supported the French in an attack on the BOIS de DAMERY:	
	12/8/18:		3rd Canadian Division relieved the 32nd Division less Artillery: The 168th Brigade covered the 116th Canadian Battalion:	

Army Form C. 2118.

WAR DIARY
or
INTELLIGENCE SUMMARY.
(Erase heading not required.)

168th Brigade R.F.A.
Commanded by Lt. Col C.R.R. CARRINGTON
DSO

Place	Date	Hour	Summary of Events and Information	Remarks and references to Appendices
	13/8/18	pm	Batteries fired in conjunction with a small operation by the 116th Battalion: Good progress was made round the South of PARVILLERS:	
	14/8/18:		1 Section per battery placed in action South of LE QUESNEL:	
	15/8/18:		PARVILLERS captured: 58th Canadian Battalion made good progress and advanced to the Western outskirts of DAMERY:	
	16/8/18	9.pm	A, & C, Batteries moved forward to old "No Man's Land" 500 yds South of the LE QUESNOY - PARVILLERS Road;	
	17/8/18	6.pm	Batteries of the 168th Brigade fired on BOIS de CROISETTE to assist the French: Batteries withdrew from action to their Wagon Lines on the outskirts of BOUCHOIR:	
	18/8/18:		1 Section per Battery of the 168th Brigade relieved one Section per Battery of the 5th Australian Brigade in action near FRAMERVILLE:	
	19/8/18:	10.am	Remainder of Brigade marched to Wagon Lines of the 5th Australian Brigade near the Railway S.W. of HARBONNIERS:	
		4.pm	Relief of 5th Australian Brigade cancelled, Sections which had been placed in action yesterday were withdrawn to Wagon Lines:	
		10.pm	O.C. 168th Brigade took over command of the Artillery covering the 97th Infantry Brigade which consists of The 14th (Army) Brigade RFA " 5th Australian Brigade RFA Front is particularly quiet:	
	20/8/18:		Trench warfare:	
	21/8/18:		Trench warfare:	

Army Form C. 2118.

WAR DIARY
or
INTELLIGENCE SUMMARY.
(Erase heading not required.)

168th Brigade R.F.A.,
Commanded by Lt Col. C.R.B. CARRINGTON DSO

Instructions regarding War Diaries and Intelligence Summaries are contained in F.S. Regs., Part II and the Staff Manual respectively. Title pages will be prepared in manuscript.

Place	Date	Hour	Summary of Events and Information	Remarks and references to Appendices
	22/8/18	5 am	Batteries moved into action in forward positions west of FRAMERVILLE:	
	23/8/18	4.45 am	The 168th Brigade supported the 97th Infantry Brigade in an attack on HERLEVILLE, the attack was very successful, all objectives being taken with about 400 Prisoners, 2 Guns and 4 Trench Mortars and a large number of Machine Guns. Ammunition expended by 168th Brigade 18-pdrs 3014 rds 4.5" Hows 963 rds: Casualties 1 O.R. killed:	
	24/8/18		Trench Warfare:	
	25/8/18		Trench Warfare:	
	26/8/18	10 am	14th Infantry Brigade relieved the 97th Infantry Brigade in the Sector covered by the 168th Brigade RFA: The Brigade is Commanded by Major REEVES DSO in the absence of Lt Col CARRINGTON DSO who is acting C.R.A.	
	27/8/18		Batteries moved forward a Section into the valley S.E. of FRAMEVILLE.	
	28/8/18	5 am	The Infantry moved forward and with but opposition entered SOYECOURT, and by night were East of HERBY: Our Batteries followed in close support of the Infantry and took up positions for the night near DEUNICOURT:	
	29/8/18		The Infantry moved forward and gained the left bank of the SOMME, without opposition: Our Batteries took up positions north of MISERY at 11 am and throughout the day carried out observed fire onto the enemy who were holding the right bank: "C" Battery had bad luck and enemy shells fell into the Cook House killing four men and wounding nine: The enemy's artillery now commenced to make its presence felt and harassed roads and valleys continuously:	

Army Form C. 2118.

WAR DIARY
or
INTELLIGENCE SUMMARY.
(Erase heading not required.)

168th Brigade R.F.A.
Commanded by Lt. Col. C.S.R.E. CARRINGTON DSO.

Place	Date	Hour	Summary of Events and Information	Remarks and references to Appendices
	30/8/18	6 pm	The 32nd Division relieved the 5th Australian Division as far north as a line due East and West through the North of BARLEUX: The 168th Brigade moved to positions a mile due East of Bellay-en-Santerre in order to cover this new front:	
	31/8/18		Trench warfare: Our Batteries carried out sniping and Harassing fire: AMMUNITION EXPENDED DURING MONTH 18-Pdrs 14,887 4.5" Hows 3,729 Casualties during month 1 Officer & 36 O.R's wounded 7 OR killed	
	1st September 1918:			

[signature]
Major,
Commanding 168th Brigade R.F.A.

WAR DIARY
or
INTELLIGENCE SUMMARY.
(Erase heading not required.)

Army Form C. 2118.

168 Bde R.F.A.

SEPTEMBER 1918.

Place	Date	Hour	Summary of Events and Information	Remarks and references to Appendices
	1/9/18		Pursuit of the enemy continued. Batteries loaned the enemy and fired at all movement	
	3/9/18		Patrols crossed the SOMME at BRIE, but had to retire owing to strong resistance	
	5/9/18	7am	Our Infantry crossed the SOMME and after stiff fighting advanced to the New Road west of PRUSSE, where the enemy resistance was overcome and our troops occupied MONS-en-CHAUSSÉE	
		9am	Batteries advanced to positions North of BRIE, West of the SOMME	
	6/9/18	4am	Batteries crossed the SOMME by Brie Bridge and took up positions North of ATHIES WOODS	
			One Section per Battery moved forward in close Support of the Infantry	
		11am	Batteries moved to Positions South East of MONS-en-CHAUSSÉE where they stayed the night	
			Our Infantry moved forward without opposition and occupied VRAIGNES	
	7/9/18	9am	168th Brigade R.F.A. withdrawn from action into Divisional Reserve, and moved to MONTECOURT	
	8/9/18 9/9/18 10/9/18		The Brigade remained at MONTECOURT, general overhauling carried out	
	11/9/18		Batteries moved into action N.E. of CAULINCOURT in order to fire a Barrage on the morning of 12th but owing the Infantry advancing during the night, the Barrage was cancelled	
	12/9/18		3rd Infantry Brigade relieved the 9th Infantry Brigade in the Sector covered by the 168th Bde R.F.A.	
		2pm	Batteries moved to positions EAST of VILLEVÊQUE	
	13/9/18	1pm	Brigade moved here to Wagon Lines at TREFCON and MONCHY LAGACHE on being relieved by the 298th Army Brigade R.F.A.	

WAR DIARY
or
INTELLIGENCE SUMMARY.
(Erase heading not required.)

Army Form C. 2118.

Instructions regarding War Diaries and Intelligence Summaries are contained in F. S. Regs., Part II. and the Staff Manual respectively. Title pages will be prepared in manuscript.

Place	Date	Hour	Summary of Events and Information	Remarks and references to Appendices
	14/9/18	12 Noon	The Brigade came under the orders of 1st Div. Artillery. Reconnaissance of Positions carried out East of MARTEVILLE.	QL
	15/9/18		Batteries commenced dumping Ammunition at the positions reconnoitred y/day.	QL QL
	16/9/18	5pm	1 Section per Battery moved into action just North of the VERMAND — St QUENTIN WOOD Road.	QL QL
	17/9/18		Remainder of guns moved into action.	QL
	18/9/18	5.20am	Right Group 1st Div Artillery composed of 16th Bde. R.F.A. — 25th Bde R.F.A. + 160th Bde R.F.A. — commanded by Lt.Col. Carrington D.S.O., Supported the 1st Infantry Brigade in an attack on the Enemy Trenches North of GRICOURT. The attack went well on the Left, but our troops were held up at FRESNOY. Several hundred prisoners were captured. Ammunition expended by the 16th Bde R.F.A. — 15Pdr. 5231 Rds. — 4.5"How 868 Rounds	QL QL QL QL
	19/9/18 20/9/18		TRENCH Warfare.	QL
	20/9/18		Artillery of 1st DIVISION Re-grouped. Right group now consists of 5th +16th Brigades R.H.A. and 16th Bde R.F.A. covering the 3rd Infantry Brigade in the Line West of FRESNOY.	QL QL
	23/9/18		Vigorous Harassing Fire and Wire Cutting carried out, all Batteries expended 1000 Rounds.	QL
	24/9/18	5am	3rd Infantry Brigade supported by the Right Group R.F.A. attacked FRESNOY + GRICOURT and the Trenches East of Same. The attack was very successful all objectives taken and nearly 1000 prisoners. Several counter attacks were repulsed.	QL

Army Form C. 2118.

WAR DIARY
or
INTELLIGENCE SUMMARY.
(Erase heading not required.)

Instructions regarding War Diaries and Intelligence Summaries are contained in F. S. Regs., Part II. and the Staff Manual respectively. Title pages will be prepared in manuscript.

Place	Date	Hour	Summary of Events and Information	Remarks and references to Appendices
	25/9/18	7 pm	Bde. was withdrawn from action to wagon lines at TREFCON	AL
	24/9/18		Brigade came under orders of 46th Div Artillery and moved into action East of LE VERGUIER	AL
			ASCENSION FARM. 18 Pdr Batteries fired Gas Shell for the first time	
			1200 Rounds being expended	
	27/9/18		Vapours firing for wire-cutting carried out.	AL
	29/9/18	5.50 am	Supported 46th Division in their attack on the Hindenburg Line at BELLENGLISE. The	AL
			attack was a great success, and several thousands of prisoners were captured	AL
		11 am	Batteries advanced to West of the Canal at BELLENGLISE	AL
		4 pm	137th Infantry Brigade supported by 186th Bde R.F.A. leap-frogged the 46th Division and	
			captured LE TRONQUOY, and LEVERGIES.	AL
			Dhks did great work by knocking out an enemy Battery which was observed	AL
			firing on our Infantry	
	30/9/18	7 am	Batteries moved to positions N.W. of LEHAUCOURT	
		4 pm	The 169th Bde supported the 1/4th of Brigade in an attack on SEQUEHART. The village was	
			captured without opposition, but an enemy Counter attack at 7.30 pm drove	
			our troops out again	AL

R. Cannon Lt. Col.
Comdg. 169th Brigade R.F.A.

(6339) Wt. W160/M3016 1,500,000 10/17 McA & W Ltd (E 1898) Forms W3091.   Army Form W.3091.

Cover for Documents.

Nature of Enclosures.

168th Brigade R.F.A., (32nd D.A.)

WAR DIARY for the month of OCTOBER 1918.

Notes, or Letters written.

166 Brigade R.F.A. WAR DIARY or INTELLIGENCE SUMMARY

Army Form C. 2118.

Instructions regarding War Diaries and Intelligence Summaries are contained in F. S. Regs., Part II. and the Staff Manual respectively. Title pages will be prepared in manuscript.

(Erase heading not required.)

Place	Date	Hour	Summary of Events and Information	Remarks and references to Appendices
	1/10/18	4pm	19th Infantry Brigade supported by the 166th Bde R.F.A. attacked and captured SEQUEHART without opposition, but an enemy counter attack at 8:30, drove our troops out again	
	2/10/18	6am	SEQUEHART again attacked and captured, but an enemy counter attack at 8.30 am again drove us out.	
	3/10/18	6.30am	SEQUEHART again attacked, and after stiff fighting the village was captured, and a strong counter attack was beaten off with heavy loss to the enemy. B/166 did good work, firing over open sights at the enemy in the open.	
	4/10/18		Quiet day.	
	5/10/18		14th Inf. Brigade relieved by the 139th Inf Brigade in the Sector covered by 166th Bde RFA	
	6/10/18	6am	166th Brigade came under the orders of the 6th Divisional Artillery. Right Group consists of 14th, 161st & 166th Brigades R.F.A. commanded by Lt Col Laurie.& A.S.O.	
	7/10/18	5pm	Batteries moved to forward positions in the valley just North of LEVERGIES.	
	8/10/18	5.10am	Right Group supported the 139th Inf Brigade in an attack on FRESNOY-LE-GRAND, at the commencement the attack was held up on the right, but later enemy resistance was overcome and by night all objectives were captured with several hundred prisoners.	

WAR DIARY
or
INTELLIGENCE SUMMARY.
(Erase heading not required.)

Army Form C. 2118.

Instructions regarding War Diaries and Intelligence Summaries are contained in F. S. Regs., Part II. and the Staff Manual respectively. Title pages will be prepared in manuscript.

Place	Date	Hour	Summary of Events and Information	Remarks and references to Appendices
			The capture of MANNEQUIN HILL at the commencement of the attack gave our O.P. Officers perfect observation, which they took full advantage of, by engaging enemy movements extensively.	
	9/10/18	5pm	Batteries withdrawn to Wagon lines for a rest.	
	10/10/18		General cleaning up & Overhauling carried out.	
	11/10/18	10.30am	The Divisional Commander addressed the Officers N.C.O's of the Brigade.	
	12/10/18 13/10/18		Resting at Wagon lines.	
	14/10/18		Batteries Headquarters moves to BRANCOURT.	
	15/10/18		Remained at BRANCOURT.	
	16/10/18		Batteries marched & took action near BUSIGNY, Hqrs at BUSIGNY.	
	17/10/18	05.20	Batteries fired Barrage in support of 6th Division Infantry attacking LA VALLEE MULATRE. The advanced to positions about BOIS ST PIERRE and fired another barrage for 1st Division who attacked WASSIGNY. Infantry was late to attack was no good. Batteries advanced very well & opened fire to time.	
	18/10/18	11.30	Batteries fired various days barrages for attack on WASSIGNY by 1st Division who gained their objectives. Reconnoitred new positions with new occupation East of VALLEE MULATRE.	

WAR DIARY
or
INTELLIGENCE SUMMARY.

(Erase heading not required.)

Army Form C. 2118.

Place	Date	Hour	Summary of Events and Information	Remarks and references to Appendices
	19/10/18		Battery occupied new position East of LA VALLEE MULATRE by 10 a.m. Our Infantry had advanced during the night & Battery found themselves out of range. New positions were then reconnoitred while Battery proceed to occupy about 3000x N.E. of WASSIGNY. Wagon lines still in WASSIGNY.	
	20/10/18		No change. Battery moved position a short distance covering its front towards CATILLON in enfilade. Battery carried out harassing fire during the night.	
	24/10/18		Battery checks registration & carried out harassing fire during the night.	
	22/10/18		Lt. Col. R. CARRINGTON D.S.O. proceeded to England on leave. Command of Brigade taken over temporarily by Major J.C. POOLE M.C. Battery all moved then reqd. new but biv/nette of LA VALLEE MULATRE.	
	23/10/18	0120	Battery fired Barrage to cover attack by 6th Division who with object of gaining enemy river SAMBRE canal. Our objection taken practically without opposition. Enemy Arty fire very heavy - Battery was still in a forward Gun pos during the night.	
	24/10/18		Divisional Arty remained which front during following day. 1st Inf Brigade with 2 Batteries in line relieved by 25th Brigade R.F.A. on the Right.	

Army Form C. 2118.

WAR DIARY
or
INTELLIGENCE SUMMARY.
(Erase heading not required.)

Instructions regarding War Diaries and Intelligence Summaries are contained in F. S. Regs., Part II. and the Staff Manual respectively. Title pages will be prepared in manuscript.

Place	Date	Hour	Summary of Events and Information	Remarks and references to Appendices
			29th Brigade R.F.A. with left & 168th Brigade R.F.A. available to fire over the whole front. Batteries remained in same position. General policy on	
	25/3/18		this particular front for a few days was on the defensive. Batteries carried out harassing fire during the night	
	26/3/18		Battery shelled heavily during afternoon, especially B/168 - D moved back about 1000x in the evening to position in front of WASSIGNY COPSE. Battery carried out harassing fire during the night.	
	27/3/18		"B" moved to North side of WASSIGNY COPSE. Batteries carried out harassing fire during the night	
	28/3/18		B & D were harassed a good deal during the night. Batteries carried out usual harassing fire at night	
	29/3/18		Usual harassing fire	
	30/3/18		2 small barrage fired to support attempt by 1st Div to retake of CATILLON - Not much success. Usual harassing fire	
	31/3/18	12.00	Barrage fired upon enemy troops attacking CATILLON. Attack was most successful. Batteries ordered to withdraw during the	

WAR DIARY
or
INTELLIGENCE SUMMARY.
(Erase heading not required.)

Army Form C. 2118.

Place	Date	Hour	Summary of Events and Information	Remarks and references to Appendices
	26/6/18		Night firing relieved but Btn in Same position by 298th Brigade R.F.A. The Brigade ceased to function at 1800 hrs 'D' withdrew this evening to Wagon lines A.B.C. waited until next morning Batteries have had a hard 10 days in their last position. Being well formed to enfilade the canal they have been subjected to harrying fire every night and we have much first class casualties having this month been seen as follows:-	
			Officers — Other Ranks	
			Killed — nil — 9	
			Died of Wounds — nil — 1	
			Wounded — 1 — 45	

[signature]

COMMDG. 168th BRIGADE R.F.A.

Vol 34

160th Brigade R.F.A.

War Diary

November 1918.

Army Form C. 2118.

WAR DIARY
or
INTELLIGENCE SUMMARY

(*Erase heading not required.*)

168th Brigade Royal Field Artillery Commanded by Lieutenant Colonel C.R.B. CARRINGTON D.S.O.

Instructions regarding War Diaries and Intelligence Summaries are contained in F.S. Regs., Part II. and the Staff Manual respectively. Title pages will be prepared in manuscript.

Place	Date	Hour	Summary of Events and Information	Remarks and references to Appendices
	1/11/18		Batteries pulled out of action on early morning, withdrawing to Wagon Lines at VALLEE MULATRE. Battle positions for attacks on SAMBRE CANAL were reconnoitred East of BAZUEL and the dumping of ammunition was commenced.	
	2/11/18		The Brigade marched to new Wagon Lines between ST. BENIN and LE CATEAU.	
	3/11/18		The Brigade went into action in positions reconnoitred on the 1st inst., but Batteries did not register.	
	4/11/18		32nd Division attacked the SAMBRE CANAL at 05.45 hours. Right Artillery Group under the command of Major J.C.POOLE MC and consisting of the 168th and 14th Brigades R.F.A covered the 14th Infantry Brigade. The attack was a complete success on this Brigade Front. The 1st DORSETS crossed the CANAL just South of ORS Bridge followed by the 5/6th Royal Scots on their Right, the 15th Highland Light Infantry being in reserve. The 96th Infantry Brigade on the Left failed to cross the CANAL and had to cross eventually behind the DORSETS and work North. They were held up for some time but all Objectives were eventually taken on the Divisional Front. A/168th and D/168th R.F.A. moved forward at mid-day to positions just West of the CANAL South of ORS to support the DORSETS but had little opportunity of shooting. One gun of A/168th Brigade R.F.A. went into action East of the CANAL. In the evening B/168th Brigade R.F.A. advanced to the Canal, C/168th Brigade R.F.A. remaining in it's Battle position, from which the S.O.S., could just be covered.	
	5/11/18		The advance was continued by the 97th Infantry Brigade and the 20th Hussars, supported by the 161st Brigade R.F.A. The 168th Brigade R.F.A. remained at the Canal bank in reserve.	
	7/11/18		The Brigade marched from ORS to billets at GRANDE FAYT.	
	11/11/18		Hostilities ceased at 11.00 hours, the Brigade being at GRAND FAYT in reserve.	
	12/11/18		The Brigade marched from GRAND FAYT to billets at AVESNES.	
	15/11/18		Major H.COTTEE DSO returned from leave and took over command of the Brigade from Major J.C.POOLE MC	
	16/11/18		Establishment of Batteries was reduced from 6 Guns to 4 Guns, one Section per Battery being despatched to IXth Corps R.A., Depot and struck off the strength of the Brigade.	
	19/11/18		The Brigade, forming part of the 14th Infantry Brigade Group for the march to the RHINE, marched from AVESNES to billets at SAUTAIN near SIVRY, Belgium.	
	20/11/18		The Brigade marched from SAUTAIN to FROID CHAPELLE.	
	23/11/18		Lieutenant-Colonel C.R.B.CARRINGTON DSO returned from leave and took over command of the Brigade from Major H.COTTEE DSO.	
	24/11/18		The Brigade marched from FROID CHAPELLE to SENEFFLLE.	
	25th to 30th 11/18		Preparations for Recreational Training.	

Carrington, Lieutenant Colonel,
Commanding 168th Brigade R.F.A.

W A R   D I A R Y.
****

168th BRIGADE R. F. A.
****

DECEMBER 1918.
****

Army Form C. 2118.

WAR DIARY
or
INTELLIGENCE SUMMARY.

(Erase heading not required.)

E.683

Instructions regarding War Diaries and Intelligence Summaries are contained in F. S. Regs., Part II. and the Staff Manual respectively. Title pages will be prepared in manuscript.

Place	Date	Hour	Summary of Events and Information	Remarks and references to Appendices
168th Brigade Royal Field Artillery.	December 1st - 11th.		At SENZEILLE. Educational and Recreational Training.	
	12/12/18.		Brigade marched from SENZEILLE to ST GERARD.	
	13/12/18.		Rested at ST. GERARD.	
	14/12/18.		Brigade marched to NAMUR AREA. - Headquarters to Chateau de Noisuil on the MEUSE 5 miles East of NAMUR - A/168 R.F.A. to LOYERS - B/168 R.F.A. to ANDOY - C/168 R.F.A. to Lock on the MEUSE 4½ miles East of NAMUR - D/168 R.F.A. to MOZET.	
	15 to 31st		Much work done to render billets and stabling as comfortable as possible. Educational and Recreational Training continued.	

Lieutenant-Colonel,
Commanding 168th Brigade Royal Field Artillery

LANCASHIRE DIVISION
(LATE 32ND DIVN)

168TH BDE R.F.A.
JAN - OCT 1919

War Diary.
168 Bry ade R.F.A.

January 1st - 31st 1919

Army Form C. 2118.

WAR DIARY
or
INTELLIGENCE SUMMARY.

(Erase heading not required.)

Instructions regarding War Diaries and Intelligence Summaries are contained in F. S. Regs., Part II. and the Staff Manual respectively. Title pages will be prepared in manuscript.

Place	Date	Hour	Summary of Events and Information	Remarks and references to Appendices
168 Bde. Royal Field Artillery	January 1st - 31st.		Brigade remained in Billets S.E. of NAMUR the whole month, during which period Recreational and Educational Training was carried out.	
			Advantage was taken of Trips arranged to the Battlefield of WATERLOO.	
			The strength of the Brigade was considerably depleted during the month by the despatch of men for demobilization. The increased amount of work which ensued was faced most cheerfully by all ranks. A considerable factor in the upkeep of the cheerful spirit of the troops was the numerous Whist Drives and Dances arranged by each Battery.	

[signature]
Lieutenant-Colonel,
Commanding, 168th Brigade, Royal Field Artillery.

Army Form C. 2118.

WAR DIARY
or
INTELLIGENCE SUMMARY.
(Erase heading not required.)

Appx 38

Place	Date	Hour	Summary of Events and Information	Remarks and references to Appendices
Germany	Mar. 1st to 31st.		The month was spent in General and Recreational Training. A number of interesting football matches were played between the Batteries and neighbouring Infantry Companies.	
			Throughout the month frequent changing of Animals took place. "Z" Class Animals being exchanged for "X" Class Animals.	
			Some 60 reinforcements arrived from other Armies and 12 officers and men were demobilized.	

Walter Myers Lt.
for Lieutenant-Colonel:
Commanding 168th Brigade Royal Field Artillery.

Army Form C. 2118.

WAR DIARY
or
INTELLIGENCE SUMMARY.
(Erase heading not required.)

Instructions regarding War Diaries and Intelligence Summaries are contained in F. S. Regs., Part II. and the Staff Manual respectively. Title pages will be prepared in manuscript.

Place	Date	Hour	Summary of Events and Information	Remarks and references to Appendices
S.E.BONN GERMANY	April 1st to May 1st. 1919		The month was spent in General and Recreational Training. During the month the whole of the men eligible for Demobilisation were sent to the Concentration Camp COLOGNE en route for ENGLAND for dispersal. This resulted in many changes throughout the Brigade both in Officers and in Other Ranks.	
	April 14th.		Lt-Col.H.Howden arrived on this day and took over Command of the Brigade, Lt-Colonel, C.R.B.Carrington D.S.O. having proceeded to England for Duty with the Home Forces.	

H. Howden   Lt-Col.
Commanding 168 Brigade Royal Field Artillery.

Army Form C. 2118.

WAR DIARY
or
INTELLIGENCE SUMMARY.
(Erase heading not required.)

Instructions regarding War Diaries and Intelligence Summaries are contained in F. S. Regs., Part II. and the Staff Manual respectively. Title pages will be prepared in manuscript.

Place	Date	Hour	Summary of Events and Information	Remarks and references to Appendices
S.E.BONN.	May 5th.		Inspection of Batteries by B.G.R.A. Xth Corps.	
GERMANY.	May 13th.		Inspection by Commander-in-Chief, British Army of the Rhine at HANGELAR.	
	May 13th to May 24th.		Each Battery in turn bivouacked for two days in the Flying Ground at HANGELAR to undergo training.	
			The remainder of the month was spent in general training.	
			All available men were demobilised by the end of the month and a number of reinforcements, both Officers and men, arrived.	

F. Wentworth Bowden   Lieut Colonel. R.A.

Commanding 168th Brigade, R.F.A.

4th June, 1919.

WAR DIARY
or
INTELLIGENCE SUMMARY

Army Form C. 2118

Place	Date	Hour	Summary of Events and Information	Remarks and references to Appendices
S.E. Bonn. GERMANY.	June 1st to June 16th.		This period was occupied in training for Practice Camp.	
	June 17th.		Divisional Artillery wired that to-day was "J" minus 3 day. Instructions re preparations for advance were carried out.	
	June 18th.		J-2 day. Brigade came under orders of 2nd Infantry Brigade.	
	June 19th.		J-1 day. Orders were received to stand fast.	
	June 20th to June 22nd.		In readiness to move at a moments notice.	
	June 23rd.		2nd Infantry Brigade wired that Germans had signified their intention to sign.	
	June 24th to June 27th.		Training but still ready to move at short notice.	
	June 28th.		Divisional Artillery wired that Peace Treaty was signed at 16.00 hours.	
	June 29th and June 30th.		Normal training resumed.	

4th July, 1919.

Mayne Myer
Lieut.Colonel, R.A.
Commanding 268th Brigade, R.F.A.

Army Form C. 2118

WAR DIARY
or
INTELLIGENCE SUMMARY
(Erase heading not required.)

Place	Date	Hour	Summary of Events and Information	Remarks and references to Appendices
S.E.BONN GERMANY	July 1st to July 31st		The whole month was occupied in general, educational and recreational training. Sports of all descriptions were organised. July 19th was observed as a general Holiday.	
	31/7/19			

Herbert Bowden Lieut-Colonel
Commanding 168 Brigade R.F.A.

Army Form C. 2118.

WAR DIARY
or
INTELLIGENCE SUMMARY.
(Erase heading not required.)

Instructions regarding War Diaries and Intelligence Summaries are contained in F.S. Regs., Part II. and the Staff Manual respectively. Title pages will be prepared in manuscript.

Place	Date	Hour	Summary of Events and Information	Remarks and references to Appendices
S.E.BONN GERMANY.	August 1st to August 31st.		The whole month was occupied in general educational and recreational training. Sports of all descriptions were organised. During the month numerous Horse Shows were held in the Army of the Rhine. The Divisional Horse Show being held at Seigburg on the 25th and 26th. The Brigade Sports were also held on the 4th, a very successful meeting.	
	1st Sept. 1919.		*[signature]* Lieut.Colonel.RA. Commanding 168th Brigade, R.F.A.	

Army Form C. 2118.

WAR DIARY
or
INTELLIGENCE SUMMARY.

Month Ending 31st. October. 1919.

(Erase heading not required.)

Summary of Events and Information

UNIT. 168 BRIGADE. ROYAL FIELD ARTILLERY.

LANCASHIRE DIVISION.

Place	Date	Hour	Summary of Events and Information	Remarks and references to Appendices
RAMERSDORF. GERMANY.				
	Oct.1st To 25th.		(Daily). Usual Training.	
"	19th.		Orders For Disbandoning Of Brigade Received.	
"	29th.		Postings of Personnel To 50th. 51st & 187 Brigades. R.F.A.	
"	30th.		Guns, Transport, Ammunition & Equipment, Returned To Dumps.	
"	"		Postings of Officers. Reg;- { A/Major. R.R.Hoare.M.C. To........ 50th. Brigade. }	
			{ do H. Cottee.D.S.O. .... 50th. do }	
			{ Lieut. G.W.Shilcock. .... 50th. do }	
			{ A/Major. C.E.Wauhope.M.C........... 51st. do }	
			{ Capt. G.L.Wisely. M.C.......... 51st. do }	
"	30th.		Officers To Consentration Camp, For Demobilization:-	
			2/Lt. Stuart. A.R. To Consent.	
			" Coleman.J.St.J. do do	
			" Lieut. Davis. G.I. do do	
			" " MorrisonC.M. do do	
			" " Wood. D.S. do do	
			Capt. Robinson. W. do do	
"	31st.		Brigade Finally Disbanded.	

Herbert Howden LT.COL.
COMMDG. 168th BRIGADE R.F.A.

www.ingramcontent.com/pod-product-compliance
Lightning Source LLC
Chambersburg PA
CBHW080802010526
44113CB00013B/2313